Cleveland Clinic

Healthy Heart

Lifestyle Guide and Cookbook

ALSO BY BONNIE SANDERS POLIN AND FRANCES TOWNER GIEDT:

The Joslin Diabetes Great Chefs Cook Healthy Cookbook
The Joslin Diabetes Healthy Carbohydrate Cookbook
The Joslin Diabetes Quick and Easy Cookbook
The Joslin Diabetes Gourmet Cookbook

Cleveland Clinic

Healthy Heart

Lifestyle Guide and Cookbook

Cleveland Clinic
Bonnie Sanders Polin, Ph.D., and Frances Towner Giedt

Foreword by Steven E. Nissen, M.D.
Chairman, Department of Cardiovascular Medicine

BROADWAY BOOKS
New York

PUBLISHED BY BROADWAY BOOKS

Published in the United States by Broadway Books, an imprint of
The Doubleday Broadway Publishing Group, a division of
Random House, Inc., New York.
www.broadwaybooks.com

BROADWAY BOOKS and its logo, a letter B bisected on the diagonal,
are trademarks of Random House, Inc.

This title may be purchased for business or promotional use or for
special sales. For information, please write to: Special Markets
Department, Random House, Inc., 1745 Broadway, MD 6-3,
New York, NY 10019, or specialmarkets@randomhouse.com.

LIBRARY OF CONGRESS CATALOGING-IN-PUBLICATION DATA
Polin, Bonnie Sanders, 1941–
Cleveland clinic healthy heart lifestyle guide and cookbook / Bonnie Sanders Polin
and Frances Towner Giedt with the Cleveland Clinic Medical and Nutritional staff ;
foreword by Steven Nissen.
p.   cm.
Includes bibliographical references and index.
1. Heart—Diseases—Diet therapy. 2. Low-fat diet—Recipes. 3. Salt-free diet—Recipes.
I. Giedt, Frances Towner. II. Title.

RC684. D5C554 2007
641.5'6311—dc22
2006022809

ISBN-13: 978-0-7679-2168-8

PRINTED IN THE UNITED STATES OF AMERICA

1 3 5 7 9 10 8 6 4 2

FIRST EDITION

This book is dedicated to the readers,

who have the courage, dedication, and commitment

to alter their habits and improve their lives.

Contents

PART 1 Lifestyle Guide

PART 2 The Cookbook

Foreword

Every day I meet people who ask my advice on a heart-healthy diet and lifestyle. This is strange. A great deal of information is already available. The Internet is full of it. Books about diet and exercise regularly climb the bestseller lists. What are people looking for that they're not getting from the lifestyle guides already out there? I'll tell you: authority. They want advice that rings true, from experts who not only talk the talk but also walk the walk. If this is what you're looking for, you've come to the right place. The *Cleveland Clinic Healthy Heart Lifestyle Guide and Cookbook* is the most authoritative guide to heart-healthy living you'll ever experience.

This book is based on the knowledge, research, and expertise of America's number one heart center—the heart experts to whom other heart experts go for the latest breakthroughs and advice. It distills the knowledge derived from seeing millions of patients, analyzing mountains of data, and performing groundbreaking research on every aspect of the heart and its care. The result is here, in a form that you'll find easy and fun to understand and use.

What will you get from these pages? You'll find the right foods to eat, the body weight that's best for you, and the exercise program you need to live a long and happy life. You'll see how stress reduction works, learn what smoking is doing to you (and how to quit), and get straight talk on alcohol—is it good for your heart or not?

How did we arrive at this priceless information? We looked for evidence. Not anecdotes. We laid out the hard facts that have been established by large-scale randomized trials. We looked at epidemiologic studies of whole populations. We combined that evidence with everything we know about the basic science of the heart and vascular disease models.

Some of what you'll read here is common knowledge. Some of it is the emerging wisdom of our medical specialty. Some of it is so new it will astound you.

Look at what we've learned about body fat. We all know it puts you at increased risk for coronary disease. But did you know that how much fat you carry may be less important than *where* you carry it? For instance, people who carry excess fat on the abdomen are at greater risk of developing heart disease than people who carry excess fat mainly on their hips and buttocks. The *Cleveland Clinic Healthy Heart Lifestyle Guide and Cookbook* gives you strategies to not only combat overall body weight but specifically target the danger belt between hips and ribs.

Then there's fiber. It has no nutritional value, vitamins, or minerals, and your body can't digest it to use for energy. Yet, if every American doubled his or her fiber intake, it would have a dramatic effect on heart disease and diabetes. A diet rich in certain forms of fiber can reduce bad cholesterol, lower your body weight, help control your blood sugar, and increase your intake of vitamins and minerals. Dietary fiber and the foods that contain it appear to be one of our strongest allies in the fight against heart disease.

The *Cleveland Clinic Healthy Heart Lifestyle Guide and Cookbook* advises you to eat whole fruits, vegetables, grains, and legumes rich in plant fiber and complementary nutrients that protect your heart. These foods are at the heart of the Mediterranean diet—the only nutritional plan that's been proven to protect the heart, promote longevity, and lower the risk of debilitating disease. The *Cleveland Clinic Healthy Heart Lifestyle Guide and Cookbook* weaves these mouthwatering foods into delicious recipes, snack tips, and easy-to-follow guidelines that you can incorporate into your lifestyle *now,* without traveling to Greece or southern Italy.

Lifestyle is the key here. A lifestyle that combines a Mediterranean diet, fiber, fruits, vegetables and whole grains, weight loss, relaxation, exercise, and tobacco avoidance can lower blood pressure, bad cholesterol, blood sugar, and insulin. These, in turn, affect what we now know is the underlying cause of coronary artery disease: inflammation.

Why is inflammation important? It has to do with some other big news not everyone has gotten. Our knowledge of coronary artery disease has undergone a revolution in recent years. Back in the 1990s, I had the privilege of helping to develop a new cardiac-imaging modality called *intravascular ultrasound,* or IVUS. What we saw using IVUS startled us. We saw pockets of fatty cholesterol built up inside the walls of the coronary arteries. These pockets of fat—or plaques—were hidden away from conventional imaging. We learned that these hidden plaques could become inflamed, and when inflamed, they could burst. And when they burst, they attracted blood clots that could plug the coronary artery. We learned that these sudden events—transpiring over the course of only a few seconds—were what caused most heart attacks, not the gradual narrowing of the coronary arteries taking place over the course of weeks or months, as was previously believed.

That's why inflammation is dangerous, and why anything that reduces inflammation is good. So what causes inflammation in the coronary arteries? Smoking. High blood pressure. Diabetes. Obesity. Genetic factors. Fortunately, all of these factors (except the last) are largely under our control. This book will show you how to control them, and how to get your heart pumping and your life moving!

Let me introduce you to the incredible team of Cleveland Clinic experts who will be your guides in the chapters to come. Melissa Ohlson, M.S., R.D., L.D., is the coordinator of the Preventive Cardiology and Rehabilitation Program at America's number one heart center. Her passion for cardiac health is only matched by her love of good food, and her deep understanding of the practical realities of the kitchen. Our exercise advisor Gordon Blackburn, Ph.D., is an expert in not only the physiology of exercise but the psychology of exercise. He knows how to motivate you! My outstanding colleague in Cardiovascular Medicine, Michael Lauer, M.D., is the complete expert on heart disease risk factors and a leading researcher in the field. When it comes to stress reduction and smoking cessation, few experts can match the experience of George Tesar, M.D., Michael McKee, Ph.D., and Amy Windover, Ph.D., all from Cleveland Clinic's Department of Psychiatry and Psychology.

But this book would be nothing without its unbelievably delicious recipes. Frances Giedt and Bonnie Sanders Polin will totally erase any negative ideas you might have had about heart-healthy eating. If your local restaurant served these dishes, it would have a four-star rating, the chef would have his own TV show, and there'd be lines of people stretching around the block waiting to get in. The food is *that* good.

These recipes have been tested—over 150 of them. For months, Cleveland Clinic's fussiest eaters have been evaluating them for taste, texture, eye appeal, and nutritional value. They have eliminated all but the tastiest and most delightful dishes. You and your family will love them.

As you can probably tell, I'm thrilled to be able to introduce this great book. But there's a serious reason for my enthusiasm. As cardiologists, my colleagues and I have a privileged view of heart disease in America today. And what we are seeing is not pretty. Obesity is changing our society. Fast food is trashing our diets, and video has riveted us to the couch. Heart-related diseases like diabetes and coronary artery disease have become epidemic. These factors, combined with our rapidly aging demographic, are building into a wave of heart disease that is bearing down on us like a tsunami.

This book is geared to the adult reader. But heart disease prevention cannot begin too young. Some years ago, my colleague, Murat Tuzcu, M.D., and I used intravascular ultrasound to examine the hearts of young heart transplant donors who died from trauma. We were shocked by what we found. Coronary disease is ubiquitous, and prevalent at a young age. One in six for those under 20, and one in three for those between 20 and 29.

What does this tell us? Prevention should begin earlier. Young people need to be aware of toxic dietary fats. They need to become aware of the dangers of a poor diet, before fast food becomes the habit of a shortened lifetime.

It is painful for those of us who treat heart disease to see its devastating effects and to know how easily it can be prevented. Excellent medications are available to control cholesterol. But a sound diet and healthy lifestyle will always be the bedrock of cardiovascular health. The diet and lifestyle tips in this book are the best you will ever hear. They are based on medical evidence and peer-reviewed studies. This is not fad data. The principles we set forth will still stand 10, 20, and 30 years from now. The basic facts about human metabolism (e.g., you have to burn more calories than you take in) will never change.

If every American followed the dietary and lifestyle guidelines in the book, some marvelous things would happen. Heart disease would be reduced dramatically. Diabetes would diminish to manageable proportions. People would live longer and need less medical care. Whole wings of our hospitals would have to be shut down. I, and most of my colleagues, could be thrown out onto the streets, unemployed. It would be the happiest day of my life.

Steven E. Nissen, M.D.
Chairman, Department of Cardiovascular Medicine

Acknowledgments from Cleveland Clinic

Cleveland Clinic would like to take this opportunity to thank and acknowledge some of the many people that contributed their time, expertise, and positive energy to this project. Gordon Blackburn, Ph.D., shared his insights on exercise and made a convincing case for the ease of beginning a daily fitness routine. Michael Lauer, M.D., gave us a thorough review of cardiovascular risk factors. Michael McKee, Ph.D., and George Tesar, M.D., shared their recipes for reducing and managing stress. Melissa Ohlson, M.S., R.D., L.D., contributed her dietary expertise to the nutritional guidelines, authored the chapters on good eating, and devoted countless hours to the nutritional analysis of recipes and menu planning. Amy Windover, Ph.D., shared her advocacy of smoking cessation. Melissa Mason provided the coordination, commitment, and common sense that made it possible for us to successfully complete this project with a minimum of fuss and tension.

Bonnie Sanders Polin, Ph.D., and Frances Giedt provided delectable recipes, combining the science of nutrition with the pleasures of good dining. Donna Bressan, Kathy Gambino, Melissa Mason, Nancy Melis, Melissa Ohlson, and Cindy Stevenson tested, tasted, and evaluated every recipe in this book. Donna Bressan provided medical editorial review.

Donna Hann created beautiful and tasteful food presentations for Cleveland Clinic Physicians. Betsy Stovsky, R.N., was an informational resource on Cleveland Clinic achievements in cardiac care. Char Surace provided expert graphic design. Finally, Lynn Novelli knit this great mass of information into a single editorial voice.

This project could not have been undertaken without the support and encouragement of James Blazar and Carl Aquila. It could not have been brought to successful completion without the expert guidance and friendship of our agent,

Loretta Fidel, and the passionate attention to detail of our editor, Jennifer Josephy, and her editorial staff at Random House, including editorial assistant Kristen Green. Finally, we would like to thank Eric Topol, M.D., former chair of Cardiovascular Medicine at Cleveland Clinic, for his endorsement, encouragement, and hard work on behalf of this project.

Thanks all!
Cleveland Clinic

From Bonnie Sanders Polin and Frances Towner Giedt

For at least 15 years we have researched and studied the best ways to protect our hearts. As type 1 and type 2 diabetics, we have developed recipes and menus as well as articles for our readers to ensure that they are informed consumers, and that they become people who protect their hearts, or the hearts of family, friends, or clients with heart disease. There is no way that we can thank all of the medical professionals who have guided us during these years. Our "heart felt" thanks go out to you as well as to nutritionists, chefs, friends, and family members who shared their ideas and expertise. Our goal in this book was to present readers with recipes that run the gamut from quick and easy to gourmet so that the entire family and their friends can dine together on healthy, varied, and delicious food, providing all with better heart health.

We send our thanks to colleagues at Cleveland Clinic. In order of our meeting, we thank Dr. James Loop, ex–Chief Executive Officer, who met with Dr. Polin and suggested a partnership for books; James Blazar, Chief Marketing Officer for Cleveland Clinic, who after several meetings helped to decide on this book with the Heart Institute; Melissa Mason, Program Manager for the Heart and Vascular Institute, who kept the book on target; Melissa Ohlson, M.S., R.D., L.D., Nutrition Project Coordinator, Preventive Cardiology and Rehabilitation, with whom we spoke weekly if not more often, and who did the nutritional analyses for the recipes. She is not only responsible for much of Part 1 of the book, but she coordinated the writing of sections that demanded specific expertise. She made our lives easy and educated us about heart health while becoming a valued friend. Steven E. Nissen, M.D., Chairman of the Cleveland Clinic Department of Cardiovascular Medicine, wrote the invaluable foreword to this book, and we thank him for his erudite and impassioned words. He and the current Chief Executive Officer, "Toby" Cosgrove, M.D., have shared their support for this project with staff. Our experience with Cleveland Clinic has been nothing if not exciting, educational, and satisfying.

Our thanks go to our editor, Jennifer Josephy, who has from the outset been a capable, knowledgeable, and flexible leader; to her assistant, Kristen Green; as well as to the entire production staff at Broadway Books, including the production editor, Ada Yonenaka; the designer, Pei Koay; the production manager, Luisa Francavilla; the copy editor, Sarah Weaver; and the proofreader, Maureen Clark. Thanks also to our cover designer, Eric Baker of Design Associates, Inc.

To our agent Loretta Fidel, whose wealth of advice and encouragement from the beginning has brought this book from concept to publication: we are honored to be your colleague and friend and admire your intelligence, fortitude, and creativity. Having you in our corner made this book a reality. Thank you.

To our families: Gerald M. Polin, M.D., and David Giedt were our honest critics as we developed the concept for this book and, later, the recipes. They were the cheerleaders of our lives as we cooked many recipes per day, supporting us with smiles and quick trips to the market. With your pride and exuberance for each of us, you gave us time and space to complete this project.

Finally, to our readers: we thank you for your confidence in us and desire to learn how to modify cooking styles. This book comes to you with our best wishes for the good health of your families and guests.

Bonnie Sanders Polin, Ph.D., and Frances Towner Giedt

History of the Cleveland Clinic Heart and Vascular Institute

Cleveland Clinic, located in Cleveland, Ohio, is among the nation's largest and busiest hospitals. A multidisciplinary medical center with a medical staff of more than 1,800 physicians, Cleveland Clinic is a national referral center and an international health resource dedicated to providing patients with excellence in all aspects of their health care.

This commitment is reflected in the Cleveland Clinic Heart and Vascular Institute's number one ranking in the *U.S. News & World Report*'s annual "Best Hospitals" survey every year since 1995. Our doctors are leaders in cardiovascular medicine and surgery, cardiothoracic anesthesia, and heart-related research. No heart program has more experience, more knowledge, or more expertise with the latest technology.

Cardiovascular Medicine at Cleveland Clinic

1921—Four Cleveland physicians, Frank E. Bunts, M.D., George W. Crile, M.D., William E. Lower, M.D., and John Phillips, M.D., establish Cleveland Clinic as a not-for-profit group practice.

1940s—Researcher Irvine H. Page, M.D., and colleagues isolate angiotensin and serotonin, which play key roles in hypertension (high blood pressure).

1950s—Scientists discover dietary cholesterol's role in heart disease and Helen Brown, Ph.D., a key investigator in the National Diet Heart Study, creates one of the first diets to reduce blood cholesterol levels.

1956—Surgeons Donald B. Effler, M.D., and Laurence Groves, M.D., perform the first "stopped-heart" operation on a 17-month-old boy, using the heart-lung machine developed by Cleveland Clinic surgeon Willem J. Kolff, M.D., Ph.D.

1958—Cardiologist F. Mason Sones, M.D., develops coronary angiography, a method for viewing the heart and its vessels on moving X-ray. His invention opens the door to the modern era of cardiology.

1967—Cardiac surgeon René Favaloro, M.D., pioneers coronary artery bypass graft surgery using a leg vein graft to shunt blood around a diseased coronary artery.

1968—Cleveland Clinic cardiovascular and transplant surgeons perform Ohio's first heart transplant.

1971—Surgeon Floyd D. Loop, M.D., demonstrates better results for bypass surgery by using the internal mammary artery instead of a leg vein for the procedure.

1972—Cardiovascular specialists William L. Proudfitt, M.D., William C. Sheldon, M.D., and Floyd D. Loop, M.D., establish the world's first computerized registry of data on cardiac diagnosis and treatment, a powerful tool for studying heart disease.

1973—Section of Electrophysiology and Pacing established to treat irregular heart rhythms.

1976—Cleveland Clinic establishes the first Department of Cardiothoracic Anesthesiology in the United States.

1980s—Cardiothoracic surgeon Delos M. Cosgrove, M.D., develops a device to improve heart valve surgery, a better system for recirculating blood during open-heart surgery, an autotransfusion system that transfuses patients with their own blood during heart surgery, and a computerized postoperative drug delivery system.

1990s—Cleveland Clinic creates the Heart and Vascular Institute, combining the departments of Cardiology, Thoracic and Cardiovascular Surgery, and Cardiothoracic Anesthesiology. Surgeons perform the world's first minimally invasive heart valve repair. Researchers and surgeons collaborate to develop artificial hearts and mechanical heart-assist devices for patients awaiting heart transplant, new surgical treatments for heart failure, heart valve repair techniques, and an array of new cardiac-imaging technologies.

1993—Cardiologists participate in a worldwide study that reveals that deaths from heart attack can be reduced 15 percent through treatment with the blood-thinning drug t-PA. Researchers identify genetic mutations related to inherited risk for early heart disease.

1994—Heart and Vascular Institute surgeons perform Cleveland Clinic's 300th heart transplant.

Late 1990s—Cleveland Clinic heart surgeons perform the world's first combined mitral valve repair and treatment for too-rapid heartbeat. Heart surgeons implant more HeartMate left-ventricular-assist devices than any other hospital in the world.

The Twenty-First Century and Beyond

Cleveland Clinic Heart and Vascular Institute continues to blaze new trails in the diagnosis and treatment of heart disease, pioneering new technology, treatments, and techniques. Here are a few of the institute's latest innovations:

Emboli-prevention devices for safer stenting: Combined with potent drug therapy, these devices help avoid complications during angioplasty and stenting of the carotid arteries (the arteries in the neck that transport blood to the brain).

Heart attack gene: Cleveland Clinic researchers have identified the first gene that is confirmed to cause coronary heart disease in humans.

Synthetic HDL to reverse atherosclerosis: Infusions of synthetic HDL cholesterol (the good kind) can clear significant amounts of plaque from coronary arteries.

Off-pump coronary artery bypass surgery: Open-heart surgery without a heart-lung bypass pump is made possible by special instruments that stabilize portions of the beating heart.

Surgical treatment for aortic endocarditis: An infected heart valve and aorta can be rebuilt using heart tissue from a donor heart.

New treatments for rapid heart rate: Ablating or isolating the posterior veins and sections of the heart's left atrium can restore normal heart rhythm.

Calcium score screening: High-speed computed tomography (CT) can diagnose atherosclerosis by detecting areas of calcium buildup in the coronary arteries.

Radiation for restenosis: Giving minuscule amounts of radiation helps keep coronary arteries open after placement of a stent (a tiny coil inserted into an artery to prop it open).

Pulmonary vein ablation: Certain heart rhythm disorders can be treated by applying energy to the pulmonary vein.

Coated stents decrease restenosis: Coating stents with a special agent may prevent the artery from closing again and reduce the need for bypass by 50 percent.

1

Lifestyle Guide

Whether you have a personal history or a strong family history of heart disease or just want to improve your health and the health of your loved ones, this lifestyle guide and cookbook is essential to your success. We've combined the brainpower and experience of the nation's leading heart and vascular center with solid scientific findings on the powerful role a healthy lifestyle plays in reducing risk factors for heart disease—the leading killer of men and women in the United States today.

Our goal is to put the power of "cardioprotection," which is protection from heart and vascular disease, into your hands. This essential guide and cookbook translates the science of healthy eating into practical, everyday strategies you can apply at home, in the office, and on the go. We then take you the next step along the path to healthy eating with more than 150 mouthwatering dishes, plus quick tips and dietitian's notes. A food diary, cooking strategies, and menu plans are also included—providing you with an entire healthy lifestyle guide, all in one volume!

It is our mission for you to make the changes espoused in this book and experience the profound sense of well-being, heightened energy, and vigor that a cardioprotective eating pattern and lifestyle can provide. So, let's get you started on a fun and delicious journey to a healthy heart.

Know Your Risks

CHAPTER 1

We live our lives knowing that risks are all around us. Simply put, risk is the probability that something adverse may happen. There is a risk that our home may be struck by lightning. A shark could attack us while swimming. A drunk driver might strike us down. The plane we are about to board may crash. The risk that any of these events could happen today is small but real.

Risk Factors

Risk also can be applied to an individual's chances of having a heart attack, stroke, or other cardiovascular problem. By assessing your age, height, weight, family history, health status, and lifestyle, a doctor can determine if your risk of a cardiac event is low, intermediate, or high.

A risk factor is a personal characteristic that signifies a higher probability of developing disease. Your personal risk for heart disease is determined by looking at a combination of classic and newly identified risk factors. The classic risk factors are age, male gender, smoking, diabetes, elevated cholesterol, and hypertension (high blood pressure). To this, some also add family history of early heart disease.

Age: This is the strongest risk factor for coronary heart disease, but it is not a simple one. While a 40-year-old person may be at increased risk compared to a 30-year-old person, the degree of increased risk will be different from, say, that of an 80-year-old compared to a 70-year-old. In general, as age rises beyond 50, 60, and 70 years, the rate of increase in risk increases dramatically.

Gender: For almost any given age, men are at higher risk for developing heart disease than women. For women the risk of coronary disease is very low prior to menopause, except in those who smoke, have a genetic problem, or have diabetes. After menopause, however, the risk of heart disease climbs steeply until it equals that of men.

Smoking: Cigarette smokers have approximately one and a half to two times the risk of developing heart disease that nonsmokers do. Unlike age or gender, smoking is a risk factor that is potentially modifiable. We cannot change our age (Botox injections notwithstanding), but we can quit smoking. There is good evidence that stopping smoking can reduce the risk of heart disease, perhaps as early as one to two years after quitting.

Diabetes: Diabetes is a condition in which the level of sugar in the blood is increased. There are two different forms of the disease, type 1 and type 2, which have different underlying causes.

All diabetics, whether type 1 or type 2, are at substantially increased risk for coronary heart disease. Some data suggests that having diabetes elevates the risk of a future heart attack as high as for someone who has already had a heart attack. In fact, many doctors consider diabetes to be a "coronary heart disease equivalent." The risks of premature death from subsequent heart attack are so high in diabetes that doctors consider diabetics the same as heart disease patients and treat them accordingly.

Cholesterol: Cholesterol is the classic, best-known risk factor for coronary heart disease. Cholesterol is a substance that is made in the liver and is absolutely necessary to maintain the integrity of the membranes, or walls, of our body cells, and is thus necessary for life. The problem is that too much cholesterol damages the artery walls, ultimately leading to an increased risk of heart attack and stroke.

There are different types of cholesterol. LDL, or low-density-lipoprotein cholesterol, and HDL, or high-density-lipoprotein cholesterol, are the two most often discussed. High LDL cholesterol levels increase the risk of coronary heart disease. Higher HDL levels are associated with decreased risk.

Total cholesterol is the sum of LDL cholesterol, HDL cholesterol, and other types of cholesterol. A number of investigations have shown that the ratio of total cholesterol to HDL cholesterol is a powerful predictor of heart disease risk.

Hypertension: Hypertension means an increase in blood pressure. Many years ago, physicians focused primarily on diastolic blood pressure (the bottom number). More recently, it has become apparent that systolic blood pressure (the top number) is the more important predictor of risk. People who have elevated blood pressures are at substantially increased risk for stroke, heart disease, and kidney disease. A number of large-scale studies have shown that lowering blood pressure reduces the risk of stroke and may reduce the risk of heart disease.

Despite all the incredible work that has been done in discovering the classic risk factors of age, gender, smoking, diabetes, cholesterol, and hypertension, we are still puzzled by the fact that many people who develop heart disease have no apparent risk factors. Some cases may have genetic causes that are only now beginning to be discovered. Other researchers have focused on new risk factors such as inflammation, blood clotting, homocysteine, and physical fitness that may help explain risks over and above the classic risk factors.

Inflammation: Inflammation involves activation of white blood cells, which accumulate in a particular area and secrete a variety of chemicals, leading to numerous local damaging effects. Although inflammation is good for fighting off infection, misplaced inflammation leads to tissue damage. Research now indicates that heart disease is an inflammatory disease characterized by inflamed, hardened arteries where tissue damage is occurring. Measuring the level of C-reactive protein, a substance in the blood that is a marker for inflammation, may predict the risk of coronary heart disease over and above the classic risk factors.

Fibrinogen: Fibrinogen is a substance related to blood clotting, and people with high levels of fibrinogen are more likely to form blood clots. There is some evidence that individuals with elevated fibrinogen levels are at increased risk for heart disease, and research about its additive effect to other risk factors is continuing.

Homocysteine: Homocysteine is an amino acid related to the metabolism of some B vitamins. Although some research indicates that elevated homocysteine levels increase the risk of heart disease, more recent work suggests that the link is relatively weak.

Fitness: There is overwhelming evidence that poor physical fitness predicts a substantially higher risk of death and premature heart disease. Some studies also have shown that people who have slow increases in their heart rate during exercise or a slow decrease after exercise are at increased risk. More research is needed to explain the link between physical fitness and heart disease risk.

Putting It All Together

Researchers have inundated us with information about how various risk factors can predict heart disease risk. The most helpful information for you personally is to know your own risk. An easy and commonly used risk calculation, based on the famous Framingham Heart Study, is shown on page 7. Simply select the categories that apply to you, sum up your points, and translate the total into your ten-year risk. If your score indicates that you are at low risk (less than 10 percent), you probably do not require any intervention. If your score is anything greater than 10 percent, you should discuss this information with your doctor.

Your best approach is to know your risk factors and work with your doctor and dietitian to take the needed steps to lower your risk as much as possible. The strategies outlined in this book can help you make changes that can impact some of the most significant risk factors for heart disease—weight, cholesterol, blood pressure, and type 2 diabetes. Let's get started!

The Framingham Risk Score for calculating risk of death or premature heart disease death within ten years.

(This scoring system is designed for people without diabetes.)

Estimate of 10-Year Risk for Men

Age	Points
20-34	-9
35-39	-4
40-44	0
45-49	3
50-54	6
55-59	8
60-64	10
65-69	11
70-74	12
75-79	13

Total Cholesterol	Points				
	Age 20–39	Age 40–49	Age 50–59	Age 60–69	Age 70–79
<160	0	0	0	0	0
160-199	4	3	2	1	0
200-239	7	5	3	1	0
240-279	9	6	4	2	1
≥280	11	8	5	3	1

	Points				
	Age 20–39	Age 40–49	Age 50–59	Age 60–69	Age 70–79
Nonsmoker	0	0	0	0	0
Smoker	8	5	3	1	1

HDL (mg/dL)	Points
≥60	-1
50-59	0
40-49	1
<40	2

Systolic BP (mmHg)	If Untreated	If Treated
<120	0	0
120-129	0	1
130-139	1	2
140-159	1	2
≥160	2	3

Point Total	10-Year Risk %
< 0	< 1
0	1
1	1
2	1
3	1
4	1
5	2
6	2
7	3
8	4
9	5
10	6
11	8
12	10
13	12
14	16
15	20
16	25
≥ 17	≥30

10-Year Risk _____ %

Estimate of 10-Year Risk for Women

Age	Points
20-34	-7
35-39	-3
40-44	0
45-49	3
50-54	6
55-59	8
60-64	10
65-69	12
70-74	14
75-79	16

Total Cholesterol	Points				
	Age 20–39	Age 40–49	Age 50–59	Age 60–69	Age 70–79
<160	0	0	0	0	0
160-199	4	3	2	1	1
200-239	8	6	4	2	1
240-279	11	8	5	3	2
≥280	13	10	7	4	2

	Points				
	Age 20–39	Age 40–49	Age 50–59	Age 60–69	Age 70–79
Nonsmoker	0	0	0	0	0
Smoker	9	7	4	2	1

HDL (mg/dL)	Points
≥60	-1
50-59	0
40-49	1
<40	2

Systolic BP (mmHg)	If Untreated	If Treated
<120	0	0
120-129	1	3
130-139	2	4
140-159	3	5
≥160	4	6

Point Total	10-Year Risk %
< 9	< 1
9	1
10	1
11	1
12	1
13	2
14	2
15	3
16	4
17	5
18	6
19	8
20	11
21	14
22	17
23	22
24	27
≥25	≥30

10-Year Risk _____ %

U.S. DEPARTMENT OF HEALTH AND HUMAN SERVICES
Public Health Service

National Institutes of Health
National Heart, Lung, and Blood Institute

NIH Publication No. 01-3305
May 2001

Healthy Body Weight

CHAPTER 2

Your body weight is one of the most influential and modifiable risk factors for the development of heart disease. Statistics generated by the United States Department of Health and Human Services indicate that poor diet and inactivity, the root of our obesity problem, will soon surpass smoking as the leading preventable causes of death.

Overweight and obesity is no longer a "middle-aged" problem. Our nation is experiencing epidemic-like obesity across all age groups, races, and sexes. Sadly, the number of children who are obese is one of the fastest-rising statistics. With more than two-thirds of Americans considered overweight and one-third obese, something needs to be done. If we do not reverse this staggering health problem, which is spreading around the globe, we can rest assured that heart disease will continue to prevail as the world's leading cause of death, regardless of how extensive are our treatments, medications, and interventions. The good news is that we can eliminate this obesity crisis through simple, everyday lifestyle changes that you can put into practice starting today.

We know that each person holds the power to change his or her life. If you are tired of quick fixes and weight-loss gimmicks that lure you into diet plans requiring special trips to health food stores, unappetizing recipes, or calculations that leave your head spinning, you are reading the right book. What you will find on every page of this book is a straightforward approach to a healthier heart and improved body weight. We'll show you everyday strategies that will help you make appropriate food and lifestyle choices for the long term, not until the next diet craze. And we'll do it in a manner that makes eating healthy fun. Our focus is on enhancing your eating patterns, not depriving you of foods you love.

Being "overweight" means you carry too much body weight in relation to your height. "Obesity" is defined as having an excessively high amount of body fat in relation to your body's lean mass (muscle mass). While these definitions may seem simple enough, your risk for heart disease is not determined solely by your weight on the scale. Other aspects of your body weight, such as how much of your weight is carried in your abdominal region, its relation to your height, and how much weight you've gained since your early twenties, strongly predict your risk of having a heart attack or stroke. Other cardiovascular risks associated with being overweight include high blood pressure, high levels of LDL ("bad") cholesterol, low levels of HDL ("good") cholesterol, elevated blood triglycerides, and diabetes. And that's not all: a host of still other health conditions are related to being overweight and obese, such as certain types of prostate and breast cancer, sleep apnea, infertility, arthritis, and gallstones.

Your Waistline

You may be surprised to learn that where your body fat is distributed is a stronger predictor of heart disease risk than how much total fat you have. People who tend to store most of their weight around their hips and buttocks have roughly "pear-shaped" figures, while people who tend to store weight in their abdominal region have more of an "apple" shape. Those with an "apple" shape, who hold excess fat around their internal organs, are at an increased risk of developing high blood pressure, high blood cholesterol, diabetes, and heart disease. Although there is nothing you can do to change your overall body type—that's something you inherited—you can take special steps to keep your weight at a healthy level and reduce the risk posed by your "apple" shape.

Research shows that women whose waist measures more than 35 inches and men more than 40 inches are at a greater risk for developing heart disease. What's more, the ratio of this waist measurement relative to your hip measurement appears to be one of the strongest predictors of the chances of having a heart attack. In a recent study of more than 27,000 people from around the globe, the waist-to-hip ratio was the strongest predictor of heart attack risk; the higher the ratio, the higher the risk. In fact, the waist-to-hip ratio was three times better at predicting risk than were measures of body mass index (BMI, explained in detail in the next section). The conclusion is that a larger waist size (which reflects excess abdominal fat) is harmful, whereas a larger hip size (which could indicate large lower-body musculature) may actually be protective.

To determine your waist-to-hip ratio, check out our calculation on page 10.

Body Mass Index

Another important approach to assessing your risk is the calculation of your Body Mass Index, or BMI. BMI is a ratio of weight to height. The research on BMI is pretty solid: the higher the BMI, the greater the risk of developing heart disease and the other debilitating diseases. In fact, the correlation is so high that risk continues to rise as an individual's obesity increases. For adults age 20 and older, those with a BMI of 25 or more are considered at increased risk of premature death and disability.

The BMI is another valuable measurement clinicians use to assess a person's level of fatness, but the calculation does have limitations. Two people of the same height and weight can have the same BMI but very different levels of body fat. For example, an active athlete with a high level of muscle mass and a low level of body fat may have the same high BMI as an inactive person with a high level of body fat and little muscle. Despite the high BMI, odds are that the active athlete has a much lower risk of developing heart disease than the inactive person. For this reason, we always assess an individual's waist-to-hip ratio as well as his or her BMI.

Calculating Your BMI

What you need:
1. Your weight in pounds (e.g., 182 pounds)
2. Your height in inches (e.g., 5'5" = 65 inches)

What to do:
1. Divide your weight by your height (e.g., 182/65 = 2.8)
2. Divide that number by your height again (e.g., 2.8/65 = 0.043)
3. Multiply this number by 703 (e.g., 0.043 × 703 = 30.28)
4. Find this number on the following weight status table (e.g., a BMI of 30.28 = obese)

Weight Status Based on BMI

BMI	Weight Status
Below 18.5	Underweight
18.5–24.9	Normal weight
25.0–29.9	Overweight
30.0 and above	Obese

Weight Gain After Age 20

So, you've put on a few pounds since high school—it's no big deal. Or is it? Researchers who have followed middle-aged men and women for decades have linked weight gain after age 20 to the development of heart disease, diabetes, and high blood pressure. How much does it take? Eleven to 20 pounds in, say, 20 years can triple your risk of developing these diseases. Even if you are still in a healthy BMI range after gaining 20 pounds since your early twenties, your risk is still increased.

An active person can have a high BMI and still be at low risk of developing coronary disease, but don't assume that a thin person in a healthy BMI range is always healthy or "fit." Every decade after age 30, we lose a small amount of muscle mass. Even if we do not gain weight, we will lose this metabolically active lean tissue if we do not engage in regular physical activity. This results in accumulation of excess body fat that can still put us at risk of developing heart disease. As you consider the weight loss strategies in this chapter, keep in mind that regular, sustained physical activity is a key component in maintaining lean body mass, losing excess body fat, and reducing your overall risk of heart disease.

Studies show that even a modest weight loss of 5 to 10 percent of your starting weight (for example, a 10- to 20-pound weight loss for someone 200 pounds) can have significant health benefits. One study, the Diabetes Prevention Program, showed that this degree of weight loss, achieved through modest diet and lifestyle changes, reduced a person's risk of developing diabetes nearly 60 percent. We are certain that the lifestyle strategies in this book, the result of thousands of hours spent counseling and working with patients, will lead you in the right direction. Here are our "secrets" to successful weight loss.

Understand That Calories Count

We have become a nation fixated on blaming specific nutrients like carbohydrates, protein, or fat for our obesity epidemic. Let's set the record straight: the blame for our nation's rise in obesity rests solely on calories. We consume too many. A calorie is simply the energy derived from the foods we consume. Our bodies use calories for normal daily metabolic processes like breathing, circulating blood, and muscle movement and for physical activities like jogging or walking.

Part of the reason we consume too many calories is that food surrounds us everywhere we go. The American mind-set when it comes to food is "more is better." Couple this with the fact that most people get little exercise, drive instead of walk, spend increasing hours in front of the television or computer, and have sedentary jobs, and you've got a recipe for major caloric excess.

Weight management can be broken down to simple mathematics. If the amount of calories you consume from food equals the number your body metabolizes or "burns off" from activity, you will maintain your weight. If you consume fewer calories than your body needs for metabolism and activity, you will lose weight. And, in most cases, if you consume more calories than your body needs for these metabolic processes, you will gain weight. Any excess of calories—whether they're derived from carbohydrates, protein, or fat—will result in weight gain. It really is that simple.

The prospect of having to lose weight, whether it's 5, 50, or 150 pounds, can be daunting. No wonder we run toward quick-fix diet schemes that promise rapid weight loss with minimal effort. Many of these fad weight-loss plans exclude one or more major food groups. This tends to distort one's view of what it takes to lose weight, as if excluding a single food like bread will result in significant long-term weight loss. Not only is this thinking false, it often results in our failure to lose weight and keep it off.

This is not to say fad diets won't work in the short run. It is possible to lose some weight by following a diet book's advice. This weight loss, however, doesn't result from eliminating a specific food or nutrient but from becoming more conscious of what we put in our mouths, which leads to eating fewer calories. In fact, most popular diet plans do not exceed 1,500 calories a day, much less than what the average person consumes. But the initial weight loss usually lasts no longer than six months, and most people then experience rapid weight gain, sometimes adding back more pounds than they lost in the first place.

It is our philosophy that weight loss can be achieved only when we shift the mind-set from being "on a diet" to being on an eating plan for life. With this approach, counting calories is not necessary to lose weight and keep it off.

We should approach weight loss in a manner that changes our entire eating behavior patterns, with a focus on what foods we eat and how much. With this approach, all foods—even the occasional doughnut, French fries, or milkshake—can fit into a heart-healthy way of life. Overall, 90 to 95 percent of the time you should be eating a variety of delicious vegetables, fruits, whole grains, and legumes, sprinkled with healthy fats and moderate, lean protein sources. The other 5 to 10 percent of what you eat can be left for some of your favorite foods that may not necessarily promote a healthy heart. This mind-set reduces frustration, leaves you satisfied and replete with disease-fighting plant nutrients, and results in successful, long-term weight management.

Remove "But . . ." from Your Vocabulary

This applies to you, whether you are reading this book to reduce your risk of developing heart disease, prevent another heart attack, or lose weight in a healthful way. We have counseled thousands of patients on positive dietary and lifestyle strategies, and the most common word that comes out of a person's mouth when we try to initiate change is *but*. As in, "But my family won't eat that," "but I don't know how to cook vegetables," "but I don't have time."

Be open to change and give it an honest try; if you feel certain strategies absolutely won't fit into your lifestyle, work on others that will. And in reference to "but my family won't eat it," just try our recipes. You'll never hear "but eating healthy doesn't taste good" again.

Don't Forget Breakfast

Are you too busy for breakfast? Not hungry in the morning? These are excuses we hear from patients on a daily basis. They may sound legitimate to you, but we can't stress enough how important breakfast is to optimizing your heart health and achieving your weight-loss goals. Your body needs energy in the form of calories to wake it up and jump-start your metabolism. Consider this: how far can a car go without gas? Think about your body as that car and breakfast as the gas. You will get much more mileage on a full tank, or full stomach, than an empty one. And you'll get more mileage out of a breakfast that includes whole wheat products and fresh fruit versus one made up of highly processed foods.

Studies show that adults and children who eat breakfast are generally leaner than those who don't, probably because breakfast eaters tend to eat fewer calories later in the day. Breakfast eaters also have been shown to think more clearly and be more efficient in their daily work tasks. Children who eat breakfast have improved memory; do better on math, reading, and other standardized tests; behave better; and visit the school nurse less often.

Eat During Daylight Hours

How often we eat during the day can also impact our weight. For many people, eating three meals—breakfast, lunch, and dinner—will be all it takes to control weight and consume essential nutrients for optimal heart health. For others, spacing out calories by eating small, frequent meals and snacks seems to do the trick. But one thing is for sure—meal timing and consistency are keys to success.

At one time in human history, people whose bodies were able to store calories from food efficiently enjoyed a survival advantage during times of famine. Unfortunately for some of us today, excess calories still result in storage of fat—fat that our bodies are programmed to think we'll need during famine. Except that in our society, we don't experience famine; our weight just goes up.

We can't combat this inherent way of storing calories, but we can avoid consuming too many calories. Eating consistently throughout the day prevents large fluctuations in blood sugar and energy levels and gives the body time to burn off the calories consumed. We call it "daylight-hour" eating. If you eat your meals between the hours of 7 A.M. and 7 P.M., for example, you are likely to metabolize the calories you've consumed during times when you are most active and avoid storing them as fat.

In contrast, most people skip breakfast, eat little to no lunch, and end the day with a hefty dinner followed by snacking or grazing before bedtime. Before they know it they've consumed over a thousand calories after dinner. This is practically a guaranteed recipe for weight gain because most people aren't as active at night and don't use the excess calories for energy. Instead, calories end up as fat stores in the body. Spreading calories among a hearty breakfast, sizable lunch, small midday snack, and moderate dinner makes a person less apt to consume excessive calories at night. The end result: weight loss.

Keep in mind that depriving yourself of food will not help you lose weight. When you skip meals for long periods, your body perceives this as starvation. When you do eat, the body holds on to these calories in the form of fat so it has a reserve to survive the next famine.

Eating is your way to successful weight loss—but success lies in portion control.

Use Your Plate for Portion Control

Understanding appropriate serving sizes can be useful when trying to lose weight. But there are times when just one serving won't satisfy you, you don't have measuring utensils, or you are just tired of measuring your food. That's okay, because when it comes to portion control, we've done the hard work for you. You can put the Cleveland Clinic Healthy Eating Guidelines provided throughout this text into practice by knowing how to portion specific foods on your plate.

Where you place foods on your plate can be a useful way to control portions and cut calories. This method is based on our fists and palms as good indicators of our portion needs, considering that women usually have smaller fists and palms than men.

For breakfast, consider plating meals this way, using a standard 10½-inch plate (or your fists/hands if using a bowl):

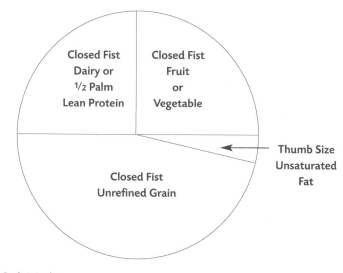

- One-quarter (25 percent) of the plate should contain either a closed-fist-size serving of nonfat/low-fat dairy or dairy alternative (such as soymilk or almond milk) or half of a palm-size serving of lean protein (such as an egg substitute omelet, vegetarian sausage patty, or light turkey sausage). These portions range from 1 cup for women to 1 1/2 cups for men. The amount of lean protein is approximately 2 to 3 ounces for women and 3 to 4 ounces for men.
- One-quarter (25 percent) of the plate should contain a closed-fist-size serving of vegetables (such as spinach and tomatoes to fill an omelet) or fruit (such as blueberries to top oatmeal). This is equivalent to about 1 1/2 cups for men and 1 cup for women.
- One-half (50 percent) of the plate should contain about one closed fist of un-refined grain, such as oatmeal, whole-grain cereal, or whole-grain toast. This would equal about 1 1/2 cups of cereal or two slices of toast for men and 1 cup of cereal or one to two slices of toast for women.
- Add a thumb-size portion (1 to 2 tablespoons) of healthy unsaturated fats, like ground flax seed, crushed raw walnuts, or slivered almonds, or the tip of the thumb (1 to 2 teaspoons) of liquid or tub *trans*free margarine such as Smart Balance.

For lunch and dinner, consider plating meals this way, using a standard 10 1/2-inch dinner plate:

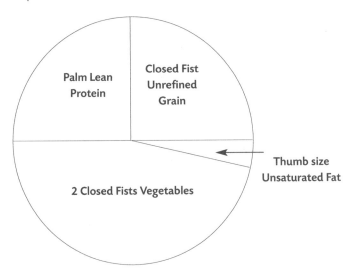

- One-quarter (25 percent) of the plate, or about the size of your closed fist, should come from a high-fiber, unrefined grain, such as brown rice, whole-grain pasta, whole wheat bread, or whole-grain crackers (such as Wasa or Triscuit).
- One-quarter (25 percent) of the plate, or about the size of your palm, should be a lean protein source, such as skinless chicken or turkey; fish; seafood; lean beef; cottage cheese; or even a meatless protein source such as beans, lentils, tofu, or tempeh. Everyone's palm is a different size, so portion accordingly. In most cases this will average 3 to 5 ounces.
- One-half (50 percent) of the plate or approximately 2 cups should be filled with vegetables. This would be a little over a closed-fist for a man and two closed fists for a woman. Choose from a variety of colorful dark green, red, yellow, purple, and orange sources to maximize your intake of disease-fighting nutrients.

Add to this meal:

- *A tip-of-your-thumb portion of unsaturated fat.* For example, 1 teaspoon of olive oil drizzled on vegetables. You can have a slightly larger portion if you choose nuts or avocado. For example, a golf-ball-size portion of nuts sprinkled over your vegetables, or two to three small avocado slices. Each is a perfect example of adding some healthy fat to your meal without going overboard.
- *A fist-size portion of fruit.* Enjoy fresh, seasonal fruits as dessert, such as a bowl of berries rich in vitamin C and antioxidants, topped with fresh chopped nuts and a dab of light yogurt. Or end your meal with a crispy, cool apple. Use this serving of fruit as a substitute for high-fat desserts and sweets on most days of the week.
- At lunch or dinner, feel free to add a closed-fist-size serving of nonfat or low-fat dairy or dairy alternative such as skim milk, calcium-fortified soymilk, or yogurt.

Read Food Labels

You will find a Nutrition Facts panel on the label on most packaged foods. Use it to your advantage. This panel contains a lot of important information, but the first thing you should do is look at the serving size. "Serving Size" is listed first, followed by "Servings per Container." You may find that the serving size you usually eat is much larger than what is suggested on the label. If a serving size is pretty small but the calories high, you may want to consider skipping that food. Do not estimate a serving size; instead, read for yourself and double-check.

Choose Bulking Foods First

Another way to get a handle on your portions is to begin a meal with foods that tend to have a lot of bulk, or volume, but few calories. Vegetables, broth-based vegetable soups, and even fruits are good examples. If you begin a meal with a low-fat tossed salad or a broth-based soup (both of which provide a lot of volume), you can reduce the number of calories you consume at the main course by 12 to 13 percent. Research suggests this is because fiber and fluid from these foods take up more space in your stomach and add to a premature feeling of fullness.

This is a great way to get your recommended servings of vegetables with the added bonus of portion control. In addition to making you feel full, vegetables provide an array of heart-disease-fighting phytonutrients (plant nutrients that protect us from disease), vitamins, minerals, and dietary fiber. We call these foods "nutrient-dense" because they provide lots of nutrients in few calories.

Avoid Liquid Calories

You not only want to choose more nutrient-dense foods but also want to eliminate foods that are "calorie-dense," those that offer few nutrients but lots of calories. Liquid calories from regular soda are a prime example. Research shows that consuming a calorie-dense beverage such as regular soda with a meal does not cause you to eat less. These liquid calories do not provide a feeling of fullness, so you continue to eat what you normally do, and over time you will gain weight.

Prepare and Plan

Like a lot of things in life, planning is part of the secret to effective weight control. When you prepare your meals, whether breakfast at home or a packed lunch for work or school, you have control over what you are eating. You know the ingredients of each item, and you control the portion sizes. When you don't leave your meal choices to chance, or to the menu at the local lunch spot, you are far more likely to control the portions, calories, and nutritional value of what you are eating.

This is not to say that eating out or choosing foods from vending machines can't fit into a healthy, weight-conscious eating plan, but we recommend our patients consume no more than one meal per week at restaurants and highly encourage the use of preportioned, planned snacks.

There are a variety of snack options; just choose wisely and watch your portion sizes. (See pages 20–21 for lots of good ideas.) Many snack foods come prepackaged and contain a Nutrition Facts panel. Check the label to determine how many servings that food contains and how many calories are provided per serving size. You don't need to count all your day's calories, but when snacking, keeping track of how many calories you take in will help you be successful in losing weight. Calories should not exceed 200 per snack for most active people and 150 for those who are not active.

Tips for Preparing Meals in Advance

Although meal planning seems like a huge time commitment, you'll be amazed at how much time, money, and heartache you will save each week by not having to worry about what you are going to make (or buy) for dinner. Here's how to make meal planning work for you.

1. Set aside some time on the weekend or a convenient weeknight to plan a week's worth of meals, including lunch ideas for work and school, healthy snacks, and dinners. Make a list of some heart-healthy favorite recipes and challenge yourself to try at least one new recipe each week (we have more than 150 recipes for you to choose from!). Incorporate leftovers into meals, and repeat certain items like fruits, veggies, yogurt, or pudding to go with lunches.

    Now, make a list of the breakfast foods you commonly consume. For example, oatmeal, oat bran cereal, or high-fiber, low-sugar cold cereals. Prefer toast? You might list whole-grain breads, bagels, or English muffins—and make sure you have natural peanut butter (e.g., Smucker's Natural Peanut Butter), or other nut butter such as almond butter, on hand to top your toast. Other breakfast staples include skim milk or soymilk, low-fat yogurt, egg substitutes, egg whites, and low-fat cottage cheese.

2. After you create your list of ingredients, think about what snacks you will have around the house to take to work or school. Plan healthy snacks like fresh fruits and vegetables, low-fat cheese with whole-grain crackers, low-fat yogurt, or nonfat pudding. Keep the list simple and avoid high-fat or high-sugar foods like candy bars, chips, ice cream, cookies, and pastry.

3. Based on your meal ideas, create a shopping list. Don't forget to include any herbs, spices, or condiments you may need. Follow with a run-through of the kitchen, listing items that you don't have but will need to make your meals complete.

    Although this may seem like a lot of work, 30 minutes of planning can save you hours of time spent trying to figure out what you will feed your family throughout the week. Plus, you'll feel more organized and in control of your food choices.

4. After you've made your list, organize it by food categories, preferably following the aisle-by-aisle layout of the grocery store. List these categories in the same order you walk through the store. One tip: never, under any circumstances, go to the grocery store hungry. You are more likely to indulge in expensive, impulse purchases.

5. When you return home, place the week's menu on your refrigerator. Remember, we've allotted one meal away from home each week, so mark one FREE night on the calendar. This posted list serves an important purpose: it helps remind you to defrost certain ingredients in the refrigerator ahead of time. Plus, it's a great way for the family to see what meals are planned for the week.

You still may want to set aside a few hours on the weekend to prepare some dinners ahead of time. By cooking and freezing whole meals or single servings in advance, you don't have to worry about what's for dinner as you drive home late at night—it's all ready for you! This strategy has worked well for many of our patients and fellow employees who have children with after-school activities. To help get you started, we've put together a week's worth of menus (see the Meal Plans section at the back of the book).

We recommend that you plan all your meals in advance, not just your snacks. We've provided detailed suggestions for planning quick, easy, and inexpensive meals and snacks. Remember that a large part of your success in weight loss depends on planning meals to avoid temptations or situations where healthful eating is difficult.

Snack Wisely

Snacks Under 200 Calories

6–8 ounces nonfat fruited or plain yogurt (choose yogurt with 150 calories or less per 6–8 ounces)

8 ounces nonfat yogurt with 1 tablespoon slivered almonds, ground flax seed, or wheat germ

---

4 ounces nonfat or 1% cottage cheese with $1/2$ cup canned fruit in its juice

1 ounce soy cheese and 3–5 whole-grain crackers

6 ounces skim milk or soymilk and 2 whole wheat graham crackers

8 ounces skim milk or soymilk and 1 small piece of fruit

8 ounces reduced-sodium V8 juice and 3–6 whole wheat crackers

1–2 cups raw vegetables (carrots, celery, cherry tomatoes, cucumbers, peppers)

1 cup raw vegetables dipped in 2 tablespoons reduced-fat salad dressing

1 tablespoon natural peanut butter on a medium apple or 2 celery stalks, topped with 2 tablespoons raisins

1 cup cooked vegetable with 1 ounce melted 2% cheese

1 tennis-ball-size serving of most fruits or $1/2$ cup fruit canned in its juice

6 ounces skim milk, $3/4$ cup diced strawberry and banana, 1 tablespoon chocolate syrup, and 1 cup ice, blended to make a smoothie

1 ounce whole wheat or oat bran pretzels, lightly salted

3 cups air-popped or *trans*free microwave popcorn

Read food labels and come up with your own nutritious snack ideas— we've provided a variety of healthy snack recipes in this book!

What Are You Craving?

Many times when we snack, we are craving a characteristic of a particular food rather than a specific food. For example, if you crave something sweet, try unsweetened canned fruit, low-fat yogurt, or fresh fruit instead of a candy bar. Looking for crunch? Go for crisp fresh fruit, cut-up vegetables, low-fat ginger snaps, or whole-grain cereal instead of cookies or chips. Like something hot? Instead of a sugar- and fat-filled coffee drink, opt for low-fat, *trans*free, low-sugar hot chocolate, a cup of tea, or a low-sodium broth. Craving cold? Try frozen banana slices or grapes, 100 percent fruit bars, or a low-calorie pudding pop. Just feel like snacking? It may be that you're actually thirsty, so have a tall glass of water before you reach for anything to eat. It might just hit the spot, and it won't end up on your waistline.

Keep Tempting Foods Out of Sight

If you have trouble controlling your intake of certain foods, get them out of the house and away from your workspace. Cookies, chips, nachos, soda, desserts, sweets, candy bars, and frozen treats should be consumed on an infrequent basis (remember the 90 percent/10 percent approach). Your children or grandchildren don't need these foods either. Save your treat for a night out with family or friends, and share a single serving with everyone. Indulge in the company of others, not the food itself.

What About Dessert?

Let's be realistic: there will be times when you crave a "forbidden" dessert, holiday parties you will indulge in, and that extra slice of cake you just couldn't stop eating! This is okay—you are only human and you are allowed to indulge occasionally. In fact, our experience with many patients has been that if they completely deny themselves foods they love, like a favorite dessert or entrée, they often end up retaliating and overindulging in these foods the first chance they get. But if they know they can enjoy this food once a week or month, they don't view it as deprivation and they'll limit themselves to moderate amounts. We want you to realize that you can enjoy small "treats" on occasion without wreaking havoc on your heart-health endeavors.

A common strategy many of our patients find helpful is to set aside one day per week when they will allow themselves a small indulgence. For example, some will choose their one weekly dinner night out to splurge a little. By "little" we mean they may order their favorite slice of pie and share the dessert with a friend. The key is to enjoy the flavors of this food in a small package and not go overboard.

Dine Consciously

Dining out can be one of the biggest challenges when trying to watch your weight. We have a few strategies that should help.

1. Avoid eating fast food or limit it to no more than once a week. Research indicates that those who eat fast food just twice a week weigh an average of 10 pounds more than those who don't.
2. Limit sit-down restaurant dining to once a week. Dining out can fit into your weight-loss plans—just not every day.
3. When you dine out, share a meal with a friend and cut your calories in half.

4. Take half of your meal home. Ask for the to-go container when the meal is served to avoid temptation.

5. If you are going to a familiar restaurant, prepare yourself ahead of time and think of healthy items available on the menu. Plan in advance what you are going to order and stick with the decision. If you keep looking at the menu and wait until others order, you are more likely to change your choice.

6. If low-fat items are not indicated on the menu, ask your server if any heart-healthy or "dieter friendly" meals are available. Don't fall prey to the items labeled "low-carb." These tend to be very high in total fat, saturated fat, and calories.

7. Start your meal with a salad—but forget the creamy dressing, cheese, bacon bits, or croutons. Choose light or nonfat dressing served on the side. If neither is available, choose an oil-based dressing. Dip your fork into the dressing and then take a bite of salad—the last thing on your lips will be the taste of the dressing.

8. Avoid menu items that refer to a dish as fried, sautéed, breaded, creamy, or cheesy. These tend to be high in fat and calories.

9. Limit most appetizers. Very few restaurants offer low-fat, calorie-controlled appetizers. Save these for special occasions such as birthdays or special events and share, share, share.

10. If a healthy appetizer is available, such as a green salad, grilled shrimp, or vegetable platter, consider choosing it as your entrée. Most appetizer portions are smaller than dinner portions.

11. Ask if vegetables, potatoes, and meat, chicken, or fish are prepared with extra oil or butter. If so, request that it be eliminated from your dish.

12. Ask the server not to place rolls, crackers, or other starchy food on your table. No one needs the extra empty calories.

13. Check the restaurant's Web site before dining out. Many restaurants now offer the nutritional analysis of menu items online so you can make your food choice before leaving your home or office.

14. If you're heading to a restaurant that offers few healthy options, consider having a light snack before leaving to help curb your appetite and cut down on the amount you eat.

15. Consider staying home instead of dining out! Instead, use the time to try some new time-efficient, tasty, and economical recipes, like the ones provided in this book.

Keep a Food Diary

We've been telling patients for decades to keep a diary of what they eat. And those who have kept an eye on their intake have been successful with long-term weight loss. Often, we realize our eating patterns only after we write down what we eat. By keeping track of the foods you eat, how much, when, and how you feel when you eat, you can begin to notice certain behaviors. Taking note of unhealthy behaviors, such as gobbling a big bowl of ice cream at bedtime, is an effective way to break the habit.

See page 346 for a blank food diary that you can copy and use on your own.

How to Inventory Your Eating Patterns

Before you make any dietary change, it's important to understand where you are right now. Taking inventory of what you eat and how frequently you dine out can really be an eye-opener.

- *Write it down.* For three to five days (including at least one weekend day), keep a diary of everything that goes into your mouth. Keep track of the timing of your meals, the quantity you've eaten, fats or condiments added, and beverages consumed. Include how you felt before and after you ate; for example, were you bored, hungry, or angry?
- *Take stock of eating out.* Do you eat most meals at home or on the go? How often do you stop at fast-food chains or restaurants? What are you ordering? Are you snacking from vending machines? Think back over the past month and inventory how often you dined or snacked away from home.

After you complete your food diary and inventory, assess the patterns and find healthier alternatives.

- *Assess your food diary.* Reviewing your food diary can reveal a lot about your eating patterns. Now all you have to do is find healthier solutions. For example, if you have little time to eat in the mornings, keep healthy breakfast foods at work instead. Stock up on breakfast essentials each week and store them in the office refrigerator; your supplies might include rolled oats, skim milk, and fresh fruit; or whole-grain bread, yogurt, and natural peanut butter. Before you start your workday, take a few minutes to enjoy a healthful meal. If lunch is always on the fly, find some ways to avoid last-minute choices, such as bringing your lunch to work instead of resorting to fast foods. Pack your lunch the evening before, perhaps when you're cleaning up the dinner dishes. Put it in the refrigerator, and the next day all you have to do is grab it on your way out the door. And if you find you're eating the bulk of your calories late at night, decide whether you're eating out of habit or boredom, or because you haven't eaten enough calories during daylight hours.

- *Do a fast-food inventory.* How often are you dining out? If it's more than once a week, try to find ways you can cut back, such as bringing your lunch to work, meeting friends for a movie instead of dinner, or scheduling one night a week to eat out and planning the rest of your meals at home. Take a look at what you are eating when you dine out, and notice items that are high in calories and fat. Decide if there are healthful substitutes to choose from. If not, it's really not worth your time (or the calories) to dine at that restaurant. Refer back to our dining out tips.

Get Moving, Consistently

Weight loss, that intricate balance between calories in and calories out, is more likely to be achieved and maintained when a regular exercise regimen is followed. Exercise alone won't drop your weight overnight, but it will provide you with a host of additional benefits, including these:

- *Increased energy.* Regular exercise revs up your body temperature and gives you an energy boost.
- *Better night's sleep.* No daytime behavior is more closely associated with better sleep than exercise. New research also finds a link between lack of sleep and obesity, giving us more reason to use exercise as a means to get some zzz's.
- *Greater sense of accomplishment.* Regardless of the kind of day you are having, you can always feel a sense of accomplishment after completing your daily exercise routine. Nobody can take that away from you!
- *Enhanced well-being.* During exercise you can get away from the stresses of the day and focus on you alone. We all need to give ourselves some time each day to nourish our bodies and souls with renewed energy. You deserve it.

These are just a few of the extensive health benefits you'll find in Chapter 3, "Exercise Is Essential." This chapter, dedicated solely to exercise, will provide tips and tools on how to incorporate exercise into your daily life, how to do so safely if you've never exercised before, and ways to keep it interesting.

Reward Yourself

We all feel good when someone else compliments us, or when we've accomplished a big task. So for each positive nutritional strategy or behavior you implement—big or small—reward yourself!

Separate a sheet of paper into two columns. In one column, list nutrition and exercise goals and a time frame for accomplishing them, such as one or two weeks. In the second column, list nonfood rewards that you will give yourself once you reach each goal. Here are some examples:

Goals	Rewards
Bring lunch to work each day this week.	Meet best friend for a movie.
Eat a healthy breakfast at home for two weeks.	Buy that favorite book I've been meaning to get.
Keep a food diary for one month.	Treat myself to a manicure.

Remember, rewards should not be centered on food. That habit will only sabotage you in the long run.

Avoiding negative self-talk is also an important strategy for weight-loss success. You are human, and humans do make mistakes. Don't write yourself off just because you had a piece of cake, skipped your workout, or had lunch out twice in a week. Take things one day at a time and always pick up where you left off. If you have a doughnut for breakfast, don't write off the rest of the day as a "food fest" and gobble down all the foods you know you shouldn't eat. When you allow this behavior, you are more likely to use the same excuse day after day until you are sabotaging your efforts. Pick yourself up after a pitfall and vow that the rest of your meal choices and portions will be healthful ones. This will help you feel in control of your choices and motivate you to continue with positive behaviors.

Your body weight is one powerful risk factor for heart disease that is in your control. After assessing your weight status, the next step is to do something about it. Use the tools provided in this chapter to change your eating behaviors and patterns to obtain a healthy body weight.

Keep in mind that healthy weight loss does not happen fast. You didn't gain the weight in a week, and you won't lose it in a week. Losing one to two pounds a week will result in safe, long-term weight loss.

Start with the healthy basics: eating breakfast, watching portions, reading food labels, planning your meals, limiting fast foods and unhealthy snacks, keeping track of your food intake, staying active, and being kind to yourself. No one piece of the puzzle can fit without the others. Approaching your weight loss or maintenance with an open mind, positive attitude, and the right tools is the best way to start.

Exercise Is Essential

CHAPTER

As you consider the strategies we discussed in Chapter 2 for shedding excess body weight and improving your heart health, you'll be happy to discover that a lifestyle featuring regular exercise not only enhances these goals but also provides additional health benefits: improved energy levels, reduced risk of developing diabetes, lower blood pressure, reduced risk of bone mineral loss, increased self-confidence, and stress management. Now that's just what the doctor ordered!

When it comes to improving the health of your heart, the benefits of regular exercise have been demonstrated consistently for more than half a century in the scientific literature. Regular activity can cut your risk of developing heart disease in half. Even if you already have heart disease, or have had a heart attack or bypass surgery, moderate regular exercise can decrease your risk of death by 25 to 30 percent compared with inactive individuals.

In fact, any level of increased activity offers modest health gains. Regular activity can offer significant and progressive health and fitness benefits equivalent to the benefits of cholesterol reduction, smoking cessation, and improved blood pressure control. And the great news is that these benefits are available to almost everyone, regardless of your age, gender, or current health status.

Reading this chapter will give you the basic knowledge, skills, and strategies you need to begin your own personal activity plan geared toward a healthier, more energetic, and more self-confident you!

Selecting an Exercise Program That Meets Your Personal Needs and Goals

Although the specifics of your exercise program must be adjusted to meet your individual needs, interests, and goals, all exercise programs should include three essential components: a warm-up, the conditioning phase, and a cool-down.

The warm-up and cool-down are essential transitions in any exercise program, allowing the body to adjust from rest to more vigorous exercise (warm-up) or from vigorous exercise back to a resting state (cool-down). The activities in these phases reduce the stress on the body, minimize the risk of injury, and allow the body to function more effectively during the conditioning phase.

The conditioning phase is the key component of the exercise program, the period in which you gain the personal and health benefits you are striving for. So let's focus on this phase first.

Conditioning Phase

The conditioning phase of your exercise program is based on four key elements that can be represented by the acronym FITT:

Frequency—how often you exercise
Intensity—how vigorously you exercise
Time—how long you exercise
Type—which specific exercise(s)/activity(ies) you participate in

Every element of FITT should be matched to your personal abilities, interests, and goals.

Frequency

To gain health and fitness benefits from exercise, you should participate in your exercise program at least three days a week and ideally five to six days a week. Three days per week appears to be a threshold for improving fitness levels, but most people will gain additional benefits by increasing the frequency to five or six times per week.

Remember, these are targets and recommended goals. If you currently are not doing any regular activity, setting an initial goal of two days per week and progressing to three days a week next month and four days each week the month after is an excellent strategy.

If weight loss is a primary goal for you, the more days you can exercise, the greater the impact on your calories out. Moreover, regular exercise complements and reinforces the eating strategies provided in this book.

Intensity

Intensity is perhaps the most complicated element of the conditioning phase to discuss, but it can be summed up in just one word: moderate. The vast research conducted on exercise and general health benefits indicates that to gain health benefits, exercise intensity need only be moderate. However, *moderate* is a relative term that must be tailored to your current and evolving physical ability.

Using the exercise heart rate is one of the more accurate techniques to identify what moderate is for you and determine appropriate exercise intensity. Your goal is to engage in activity at a level that requires you to function at 40 to 60 percent of your capacity, or between 50 and 70 percent of your peak heart rate.

Estimate your peak heart rate using the formula 220 minus your age. For example, a 40-year-old's age-predicted peak heart rate is $220 - 40 = 180$ beats per minute (bpm).

To establish your target heart rate range (THRR), use 50 and 70 percent of your peak heart rate to set the lower and upper limits of your THRR. Using the example of a 40-year-old with a peak heart rate of 180, the lower target heart rate is 90 bpm (180 $\times$ 0.5). The upper target heart rate is 126 bpm (180 $\times$ 0.7).

MEASURING YOUR EXERCISE HEART RATE

Heart rate can be determined by feeling your pulse at your wrist or neck. Every time your heart beats, it generates a surge of blood (pulse) within the arteries.

Take your pulse by placing the tips of your index, second, and third fingers on the palm side of your opposite wrist, just below the base of your thumb, or on the middle of your neck, on either side of your windpipe. Press lightly with your fingers until you feel the blood pulsing beneath your fingers. If you can't feel your pulse, try moving your fingers slightly up or down, or back and forth, until you locate it. If you check your pulse at your neck, avoid pressing on both sides of the neck simultaneously as this can significantly reduce your heart rate. Once you have located your pulse, use a watch with a sweep second hand or a digital count of seconds and count the number of beats you feel in a ten-second period. Multiply this number by six to get your heart rate (pulse) per minute. This is your pulse rate.

During exercise, check your pulse after at least five minutes of exercise and two to three more times throughout the exercise session. For greatest accuracy, stop the activity briefly, quickly locate your pulse at the neck or wrist, and determine your exercise heart rate. If your heart rate falls within your THRR and you are tolerating the activity without difficulty, continue at the current pace. If your heart rate is below the lower end of your THRR, pick up the intensity slightly and recheck your pulse three to five minutes later, repeating this as necessary until you fall within your THRR.

If your exercise heart rate exceeds the upper level of your THRR and your goal for exercise is general health benefits, you should reduce the exercise intensity. If you are just starting your activity program, you should stay within the 50 to 70 percent THRR for greatest safety and benefit.

Note that peak heart rate can be affected by some medications and/or medical conditions. If you are taking medications or have a medical condition such as heart disease, high blood pressure, diabetes, pulmonary disease, or persistent arrhythmia or have a pacemaker, ask your physician or health care provider if these factors could significantly alter your maximal heart rate. In this case, you cannot use the age-predicted peak heart rate equation. Discuss appropriate optional strategies to assess your exercise intensity with your physician.

Always contact your personal physician before beginning any regular activity program if you have been inactive; are a male over 45 or a female over 55; have known cardiovascular, pulmonary, or metabolic disease; or have any of the following symptoms:

- Discomfort, pressure, tightness, or pain in the chest, neck, jaw, or arms that comes on with exertion, emotional upset, or exposure to the cold
- Shortness of breath at rest or with mild exertion
- Dizziness or light-headedness at rest or with exercise
- Difficulty breathing when lying down or during sleep
- Ankle swelling
- Feelings of the heart fluttering, racing, or suddenly pounding
- Leg muscle discomfort, pain, or cramping that comes on with exercise and resolves with rest
- Extreme or unusual exhaustion, fatigue, or shortness of breath with daily activities
- Known heart murmur

(Adapted from the American College of Sports Medicine Guidelines for Exercise Testing and Prescription, 6th ed., 2000)

HEART RATE MONITORS

To simplify your heart rate monitoring during exercise, you may want to consider purchasing a heart rate monitor. Relatively inexpensive and accurate heart rate monitors can be purchased at most fitness stores, with a basic monitor selling for $50 to $60. The most accurate models include a chest strap that you wear against your skin, under your T-shirt. The strap has built-in electrodes and a microprocessor/transmitter that measures the heart rate and sends it to a wristwatch monitor. You can read your heart rate continuously and easily from the wristwatch face.

RATING OF PERCEIVED EXERTION

Heart rate levels can help you adjust your exercise intensity, but how you feel during activity is also important. The Rating of Perceived Exertion (RPE) Scale is a well-documented tool that can help you assess and adjust your exercise intensity according to how you feel. The scale is also referred to as the Borg RPE scale, named after G. Borg, who developed it.

The RPE scale runs from 0 to 10. The numbers correspond to phrases that describe how easy or difficult an activity is for you. For example, 0 (Nothing at all) corresponds to how most people feel when sitting relaxed in a chair. Ten (Maximum) typically describes how a person feels just before exhaustion occurs—as if unable to go one step further.

Rating of Perceived Exertion Scale

Rating	Definition—How does the activity feel?
0	Nothing at all
0.5	Just noticeable
1	Extremely light
2	Light
3	Moderate
4	Somewhat hard
5 to 6	Hard
7 to 8	Very hard
9	Extremely hard
10	Maximum

WHAT LEVEL IS RIGHT FOR ME?

Before starting any exercise program, it's important to consult with your doctor or health care provider. Your health care provider can offer advice about the exercise intensity that's right for you, based on your current health and presence of any medical conditions.

During your activity, remember to take into consideration shortness of breath, muscle fatigue, and general discomfort when you determine your current RPE rating.

If you are just beginning an exercise program, start at the light intensity level (2) and gradually progress to a moderate intensity (3) level during the next 4 to 6 weeks. After this time, your health care provider may recommend that you increase your intensity further to the upper range of moderate intensity (4 to 5).

If you are already participating in an exercise program (under your doctor's supervision), your exercise should be at a level that feels 3 (Moderate) to 4 (Somewhat hard).

If you are within your recommended RPE zone during your activity, continue at the same intensity. If you are lower than your recommended RPE zone, work a little harder. If you are higher than your recommended zone, slow down. You will reduce the risk of injury and enjoy your exercise more if you do not try to overdo it.

TALK TEST

One other easy, inexpensive way to assess your exercise intensity is the talk test. In general, the more vigorous the activity, the more you need to work at breathing, leaving less capacity for conversation. If you are unable to complete one sentence out loud without gasping for breath, you probably are working too hard for general health and fitness benefits, and you should decrease the intensity.

Time

Time refers to the amount of time you exercise each day as well as each week. To gain the health benefits of exercise, you should exercise for at least 30 minutes each session, although 45 to 60 minutes is desirable. For exercise to play a key role in weight management, more than 60 minutes of exercise each day may be required, especially if your fitness level is low.

One great thing about exercise time is that there is no one time of day that's best to exercise. Whenever you can exercise is the best time. If you cannot do all your exercise in a single session, you can gain similar health and calorie-burning benefits by exercising for multiple 15- to 20-minute periods throughout the day.

Intensity also influences time. As your fitness level improves and you can engage in more vigorous activities, still staying in the 50 to 70 percent range, you burn calories more efficiently. For example, if you start your exercise program weighing 165 pounds and walking at a pace of 2 miles per hour (determined to be 50 percent intensity), you would need to walk for approximately 64 minutes to burn 200 calories. After three months of regular exercise, you realistically might have a 30 percent improvement in functional capacity and a 15-pound weight loss. Still exercising at 50 percent intensity, your new walking pace would be 3 miles per hour, and now you would need to walk just 53 minutes to burn 200 calories. Or you could stay at 64 minutes per session and increase your calories burned to 240.

Type of Exercise

In your quest to achieve fitness, don't be stymied by the question, What is the best type of exercise?—the final T in our FITT acronym. The answer is that there is no one correct answer! As long as the activity is repetitive and rhythmic, uses large muscle groups of the body, is performed at the appropriate intensity, and is one that you engage in routinely—it's the best activity for you. If the activity satisfies the appropriate intensity requirement (50 to 70 percent of predicted peak heart rate), is performed for at least 20 minutes per session, is part of a program that reaches or exceeds 30 minutes of total time per exercise day, and is performed at least three times a week, it is likely a good exercise.

RECOMMENDED WARM-UP EXERCISES

Just as allowing a cold car engine to warm up prevents damage to the motor, the warm-up phase of exercise lessens the stress placed on the heart and the muscles at the start of activity. The warm-up activity usually is a lower intensity of the conditioning phase activity, although any aerobic exercise that uses the same large muscle groups is acceptable. The warm-up activity should feel very easy to perform. The primary goal is to gradually increase the heart rate from the resting state toward the intensity associated with your conditioning level. Perform the warm-up exercises for five to ten minutes to make the transition easiest.

SUGGESTIONS FOR THE COOL-DOWN PHASE

A cool-down allows the body to return gradually to a resting level. To accomplish this, simply decrease the intensity of the conditioning activity to a comfortable level and continue for three to ten minutes.

The cool-down allows the dilated arteries to slowly return to their resting state. This helps avoid pooling of blood in the extremities, which can lead to light-headedness and arrhythmias. The active cool-down also helps prevent the stiffness and muscle soreness that may occur one to two days after an exercise session.

THE ROLE OF STRETCHING

Stretching exercises correctly performed can improve flexibility and help to decrease muscle soreness after exercise. You can gain the same benefits from stretching whether you do it as part of your warm-up, the cool-down, or both. Without definitive data to support stretching at one specific time, we recommend that you include stretches whenever you prefer, as long as you perform them gently and focus on the feeling in the muscles during stretching.

Technique is the key focus of stretching. Proper stretching exercises should emphasize all major muscle groups used in the conditioning activities, muscle groups that are used or stressed routinely throughout the day, and any muscle groups that feel tight or cause discomfort. To do it properly, stretch the muscle slowly until you feel a gentle pulling sensation in the target muscle. Hold the stretch position for 20 to 30 seconds, without bouncing or lunging, maintaining a gentle pulling sensation for the entire period. If the stretch causes pain, it is a sign that you are stretching too aggressively, and you should back off. Remember to breathe as you stretch.

Progression

Progression—advancing from a starting level to a more efficient or advanced activity program—should take place gradually, with changes made about every two to three weeks. The body adapts to exercise gradually, with the most rapid changes occurring over the first three to six months of a new program. Once you have been regularly active for more than a year, your body's progression will slow, and your focus will shift to maintenance rather than steady improvement.

Increase your exercise time (duration) in 10 to 20 percent increments per workout. For example, if you started at 20 minutes per session, after two to three weeks of regular exercise, you could consider increasing the time by 2 to 4 minutes per session for a total exercise time of 22 to 24 minutes. If this is well tolerated over the next two to three weeks, increase by another 10 to 20 percent, to 24 to 29 minutes per session.

Increase exercise frequency in stages of one extra session per week every three to four weeks. If you start at a basic level of three times a week, it should take approximately three months or longer before you progress to six times a week.

Keep in mind that as your functional capacity increases and weight decreases, the absolute exercise settings (e.g., the speed of walking, the pace of the tennis match, the cadence of your swimming stroke) required to achieve the necessary intensity will increase. If you are using your THRR to guide your exercise intensity, use it to help you determine when to pick up the pace. If your heart rate falls below your lower THRR for two to three consecutive days, you probably would benefit from increasing the pace of the activity.

One other guiding principle for safe progression is to advance only one or at most two elements—frequency, intensity, or time—together.

Making Your Exercise Program a Success

The first step in making any lifestyle program successful is to get reliable information about what changes you need to make, how to make them, and what the benefits will be. After reading this book you should have the basic knowledge to begin developing an appropriate heart-healthy exercise program.

Next, set some personal goals that are realistic, specific, and measurable and a clear time frame for reaching them. Take time establishing your goals and be as specific as possible: for example, "Start a walking and dietary program August 1 to help me lose 15 pounds by the end of October." This is a specific goal, is realistic, has a clearly defined target, and a specific start and stop period.

A detailed plan that describes the specific steps you'll take to reach your goal helps promote compliance and success. Your overall strategy should include both long- and short-term plans. A long-term plan usually describes the specific actions you will take over the next year, and short-term plans outline the detailed steps you will take over the next two weeks.

The next steps are to commit to your plan and accept responsibility. This is your lifestyle program; nobody else can exercise for you, and it is you who stands to gain by following the plan. But don't get too upset if you stray from the program, or need to modify the goals. Don't expect perfection—if that were the case we wouldn't be writing this book, because everyone would already be totally compliant with our cardioprotective recommendations. Most important, don't forget to build specific and realistic rewards into your plans to recognize your success and progress.

Find an Activity That Fits into Your Schedule

Pick a time of day that you feel is the best for you to exercise, then write it down in your calendar and treat it like you would other appointments. Scheduled group activity classes can help with compliance, if they mesh with your schedule. But if you find you're missing more than one class per week because you sleep in or other commitments prevent you from arriving on time, no matter how much you like the class, you should look for another exercise time or a more convenient location.

Plan Ahead

Identify schedule changes or other barriers that may disrupt your activity routine and work around them to ensure you can get your planned exercise. For example, if your job requires you to travel, call the hotel you'll be staying in before you leave town and find out what exercise equipment their fitness facility has and what hours the facility is open. Or substitute a walk or jog for your usual activity when out of town.

If you prefer outdoor activities, develop a back-up plan for rainy or snowy days, or purchase appropriate exercise apparel that will allow you to exercise outdoors even in inclement weather.

Keep an Exercise Record

Recordkeeping can be a great way to track your compliance and progress with any lifestyle-change program. These records can be very simple, such as writing your exercise time on a calendar every day you perform an activity.

Pedometers

Pedometers are another popular and easy method to document your activity. These small, inexpensive devices can be clipped on your belt or waistband to count the number of steps walked each day. The more steps you take, the greater the distance walked, and the more calories burned.

The most publicized goal for pedometer programs is to achieve 10,000 steps a day. However, this goal may not be achievable for all, does not address issues of intensity (necessary to achieve improvement in fitness), and focuses on only one type of activity. Pedometers do not accurately record steps during activities such as cycling, swimming, or exercising on an elliptical trainer, but tracking the steps you walk in a day is a great way to identify your current activity level, help you set goals for improvement, and track your progress.

If you choose to use a pedometer, follow these guidelines:

1. Establish your baseline activity level by wearing the pedometer daily for two weeks while you go about your usual routine. At the end of each day, record the number of steps you took that day and reset the pedometer. At the end of two weeks, calculate your daily average.
2. Set a goal to increase your daily steps by 10 to 30 percent a day. For

example, if you are averaging 4,000 steps a day during the baseline period, set a goal of 4,400 steps per day (a 10 percent increase), up to 5,200 steps per day (a 30 percent increase).

3. When you reach that goal and maintain it for two weeks, set a new goal. Each step up should be a 10 to 30 percent increase as you progress toward your long-term goal.

Once you reach your pedometer program goal, consider walking 4,000 to 6,000 of those steps at a pace that is of moderate intensity for you. This can satisfy the intensity part of the program and result in improved fitness, as well as increase the efficiency with which you burn your calories.

Make Exercise Fun

To increase your enjoyment of whatever exercise activity you choose, consider listening to your favorite music or watching television to help pass the time. Social support and interaction can also reinforce your activity commitment. Knowing that friends are expecting you to show up for the fitness class at the club or go for a walk may be just the incentive you need to get you out the door and stick with your activity program.

Exercise can be a common thread that pulls a family together. Instead of each family member sitting down to watch TV after dinner, take a family walk or bike ride around the neighborhood one or two evenings a week. You may also find it helpful to track your general mood when you exercise. If you feel good about your activity program, you are more likely to keep it up. A positive emotional change can be a significant reward of regular activity. But persistent feelings of sadness, loneliness, anger, anxiety, or stress can act as barriers to any activity and may indicate that you should explore additional lifestyle strategies to optimize your overall health.

Focus on Fiber

CHAPTER

The basis of a heart-healthy lifestyle is choosing foods that supply your body with the greatest nutritional bang for your buck—foods that pack an abundance of disease-fighting nutrients in a small package, or in a few calories. One of the primary nutrients essential for optimal health and reduction of heart disease is carbohydrate. But not just any type of carbohydrate will do—we're talking whole grains.

Carbohydrates make up more than 50 percent of the calories in most eating plans, and, contrary to popular fad diets, this is the level most of us should be eating. But the revival of low-carbohydrate diet schemes has prompted many people to question the relevance of carbohydrates to good health. Add to this mix the confusion over the purported "ratio" of carbohydrates to protein some diet books say is necessary for weight loss, and you've got a lot of people confused over what's right and wrong with carbohydrates.

To help ease your frustration on this issue, we'll explore the cardioprotective nature of carbohydrate-containing foods. By the end of this chapter, we're confident you'll approach carbohydrates in a whole different light.

Carbohydrates 101

Carbohydrates are a broad category that includes sugars, starches, fibers, cellulose, and other compounds. Foods that contain carbohydrate include fruits, vegetables, milk, breads, beans, and table sugar. When chosen sensibly, carbohydrates provide our bodies with powerful nutrients, aid in weight loss, and help prevent heart disease.

During digestion, carbohydrate-containing foods are converted into glucose, what we commonly refer to as sugar. This sugar is essential for our survival. The body relies on it to provide energy to our brain, organs, and skeletal muscles and fuel for normal metabolic processes such as digestion and breathing, as well as exercise. Without carbohydrates, basic bodily functions would not work efficiently.

After carbohydrates are digested, the sugar that results is sent into the bloodstream. To use this sugar for energy, the body must get assistance from insulin, a hormone secreted from the pancreas with the primary role of regulating blood sugar levels. With the help of insulin, sugar enters cells, where it can be used as an immediate energy source or stored for future use. The rate at which this metabolic system works depends heavily on what type of carbohydrate food you consume.

Good and Bad Carbohydrates— Fact or Fiction?

Carbohydrates have generated considerable controversy and discussion in the medical field. The debate, which has surfaced and resurfaced in the diet industry for decades, has tried to categorize carbohydrates in a number of different ways.

- *"Good" or "bad" carbohydrates.* Some people believe that labeling a carbohydrate-containing food as either "bad" or "good" will enable us to make healthier choices. We believe labeling foods as such creates a negative approach to eating healthfully and should be avoided. Instead, think of putting carbohydrates into categories such as to be eaten "rarely," "sometimes," or "all of the time."
- *High or low glycemic index.* Some researchers believe it's useful to categorize carbohydrate-containing foods by how rapidly they are converted to sugar in the body when compared to a standard dose of glucose or white bread. Foods labeled "low" (those that are metabolized more slowly) are believed to have a favorable effect on our health. Numerous tables and charts ranking various foods' glycemic indexes are available. However, this system has not been standardized. Plus, the rate at which a food is converted to glucose in the body depends on a food's ripeness, how long it has been cooked, and what other foods are eaten with it. Because of this variability, we currently do not recommend looking up the glycemic index of individual foods as a practical means to reduce weight and improve your heart health. Since most, but not all, low-glycemic-index foods are generally whole, unprocessed, high-fiber foods, we feel our carbohydrate guidelines are a more practical way to determine what type of carbohydrate to consume to lose weight and improve your heart health.
- *High or low glycemic load.* To confuse the glycemic index matter further, some

people believe determining the glycemic load of a food—a food's glycemic index multiplied by the total amount of carbohydrate in the food—is the ideal predictor of a food's impact on health. We do not support this current system of carbohydrate labeling.

- *Food labeling lingo.* Food manufacturers have gotten on the carbohydrate bandwagon, too. You may have seen a number of foods labeled "low carbohydrate," "low sugar," or "low net impact carbs" in your grocery store. Does labeling a food "low-carb" mean it will improve your health? Not necessarily. In many cases, manufacturers just shrink the serving size of the food to cut the carbohydrates. Or fats, sugar alcohols, proteins, or other ingredients are substituted for carbohydrate, resulting in a food just as high in calories as what it's replacing. Right now, there are no definitions sanctioned by the U.S. Food and Drug Administration (FDA) for labeling carbohydrates, which means there is no consistency in the way the food industry is using these terms.

Have these terms started your head spinning yet? This jargon has confused us, and that is why we've gone back to basics. We feel that focusing on three carbohydrate categories—refined, simple sugars, or unrefined—will allow you to reap the cardioprotective benefits of carbohydrate-containing foods without wasting time doing calculations, looking up values in tables, or avoiding whole foods altogether. These three categories enable you to identify why certain foods provide our bodies with more heart protection than others.

Refined Carbohydrates

When you think refined, think "white." Most refined carbohydrates are found in the form of white flour—such as white breads, crackers, and pasta. The first ingredient in these foods is a highly processed or refined grain. In fact, most of the foods found in our markets are made with refined flour, what we often call "enriched flour." Why does this matter? It all has to do with what is removed from the grain during the refinement process.

During refining, the germ and bran of the whole grain are removed and all that is left is the endosperm. Because most, if not all, of the important B vitamins and trace minerals are removed from refined grains, manufacturers often "enrich" the foods with niacin, riboflavin, thiamin, folic acid, and the mineral iron. The problem is, even when a food is enriched, the fiber component is never added back. This has significant consequences on how our bodies digest carbohydrates and, in turn, can affect our risk of gaining weight and developing heart disease.

Refined carbohydrate foods include white breads, crackers, white rice, corn-flake cereals, puffed rice cereals, regular pasta, and most baked goods. Refined carbohydrates have been stripped of their natural dietary fiber, so they are rapidly digested and converted to sugar in the body. The result is a blood sugar "spike." In response to this surge of sugar, the pancreas must release more insulin than usual. This rush of insulin drives any excess sugar into the liver and muscles, where it is stored in a form called glycogen. This glycogen can be converted to sugar later when the body calls upon it for energy. But if the glycogen stores are filled to their capacity, any excess sugar we consume is stored as fat, known as triglyceride.

Feeling tired? Gaining weight? It could be due to your choice of carbohydrate—and the impact it has on triglycerides. Since refined carbohydrates produce a rapid rise in blood glucose, the pancreas secretes a hefty dose of insulin to get blood sugars back to normal. This large secretion of insulin causes our blood sugar levels to drop quite low, often lower than they were before we ate the refined grain. As a result, we often experience rebound hunger, and sometimes headaches, dizziness, low energy, or fatigue. Most of us are uncomfortable feeling this way, so we reach for a quick "pick me up"—refined carbohydrates—the same foods that gave us the problem in the first place. And so the vicious cycle of increased energy, decreased energy (or increased/decreased blood sugars) continues. If we don't stop this cycle, we end up throwing this normal metabolic process off track and causing continuous abnormally high blood sugar and insulin. Over time, this disrupts the liver's production and clearance of triglyceride, which can have significant heart-health consequences:

- *Weight gain.* Excess triglyceride (read: fat) fills our body's cells, causing weight gain, often in the abdominal region, which can put us at greater risk for developing heart disease.
- *Elevated blood triglycerides.* Triglycerides also build up in the bloodstream, leading to hypertriglyceridemia, or high blood triglycerides. High blood triglyceride levels are independently linked to an increased risk of developing heart disease.
- *Less HDL, more artery-clogging LDL.* The presence of high triglycerides drives down heart-protective HDL cholesterol, the cholesterol that actually cleans up the "bad" LDL cholesterol particles. To make matters worse, as HDL is being lowered, triglycerides alter the structure of the "bad" LDL cholesterol to a small, dense size. This allows LDL particles to build up in the lining of the arteries, which over time can lead to a heart attack or a stroke.
- *Insulin resistance.* As a result of the constant roller-coaster ride of blood sugar and insulin, our cells eventually become resistant to insulin's ability to let sugar

in. This can severely damage our cells and greatly increase our risk of developing type 2 diabetes.

So how do we combat this vicious cycle? By choosing whole grains, of course. But first, let's discuss another triglyceride and blood sugar booster—simple sugars.

Simple Sugars

Simple sugar foods are just that, sugars. Simple sugars consist of the basic sugar molecule, referred to as a monosaccharide (such as glucose, fructose, maltose, and lactose), or the branching of two sugar molecules, referred to as a disaccharide (for example, the glucose-fructose combination makes up table sugar). Simple sugars come from two main dietary sources. Some occur naturally in fruits, vegetables, and dairy. Others are added to foods via table sugar, honey, brown sugar, and other sweeteners.

The simple sugars naturally present in fresh whole fruits, vegetables, and dairy are a necessary part of your eating plan because these foods contain a host of heart-protective vitamins, minerals, and dietary fiber. These simple sugars should not be avoided. On the other hand, added simple sugars offer zero nutritional value. These "empty-calorie" foods lack any vitamin, mineral, or fiber value. In addition, consumption of added simple sugars causes a rapid rise in blood sugar, resulting in the same fluctuations in blood sugar and insulin that occur when your eat/ingest refined grains. Because they lack any value in our diets, we should all make a conscious effort to limit added simple sugars in our eating plans.

Sugar by Any Other Name ... *Is* Just as Sweet

If you look only for the word *sugar* in the ingredients list on a food label, you may be eating more sugar than you think. Sugar sneaks its way into countless foods using many aliases. Be on the lookout for other key words, such as those in the following list, and try to cut back on your intake of foods that contain these added sugars.

Brown rice syrup	Fruit juice concentrate
Brown sugar	High-fructose corn syrup (HFCS)
Cane sugar	Honey
Confectioners' sugar	Invert sugar
Corn sweetener	Malt
Corn syrup	Maple syrup
Crystallized cane sugar	Molasses
Dextrose	Raw sugar
Evaporated cane juice	Turbinado sugar

SUGAR Q&A

Q: I thought brown sugar was supposed to be healthier than table sugar. What's the story?

A: Many people believe that brown sugar has more nutritional value than table sugar. Unfortunately, that couldn't be further from the truth. Brown sugar is simply sugar crystals combined with molasses. Ounce for ounce, brown sugar has the same number of calories as table sugar. One tablespoon of each is approximately 50 calories and 12.5 grams of carbohydrate—all of which come from sugar.

Q: What about honey? My grandmother always told me it was healthier than table sugar.

A: This is a common misperception. While some research has indicated that the darker the honey's hue, the more antioxidants it contains (although small), all in all, honey is sugar to the body. And we don't have to consume honey to get our antioxidants. In fact, ounce for ounce, honey is sweeter than sugar, and because honey is also denser, a tablespoon of honey has a few more calories (64 calories) and carbohydrates (17.5 grams) than a tablespoon of granulated sugar (50 calories, 12.5 grams).

Q: What does the term "added sugar" mean? Isn't the total amount of sugar listed on the food label just added sugars?

A: "Added sugars" are sugars and syrups added to foods during manufacture or preparation. They include white sugar, brown sugar, and high-fructose corn syrup, and are primarily found in soft drinks, cakes, cookies, pies, fruit drinks, dairy desserts, and candy. It can be difficult to determine just how much added sugar is in a food because all sugars, naturally occurring and added, are listed under "Sugars" on the Nutrition Facts panel of a food label. Look for foods labeled "no sugar added," "sugar free," or "reduced sugar" to help cut some of the added sugar in your favorite foods. Here's what they mean:

- "No sugar added." No additional sugar was added during the processing or preparation of a food, but it may contain sugar naturally present in other ingredients.
- "Sugar free." Contains less than 0.5 gram of sugar per stated serving size.
- "Reduced sugar." Contains 25 percent less sugar than the regular food product it is replacing.

Remember that not all of these foods are low calorie.

Q: How much added sugar can I have each day?

A: The average American consumes more than 20 teaspoons of sugar each day, much more than what is recommended by the USDA's *Dietary Guidelines for Americans*. The extra calories that come from sugar could otherwise come from whole, unprocessed, high-nutrient foods like fresh fruits, vegetables, whole grains, and nonfat dairy. That's why we recommend you consume no more than 8 to 10 percent of your total daily calories from sugar. While we know it is not practical for most people to count their grams of added sugar each day, make a conscious effort to limit the total amount of added sugar you consume by reading food labels.

Q: If I should be watching how many added sugars I consume, what can I use as an appropriate substitute? I thought aspartame, sucralose, and other low-calorie sweeteners were bad for me.

A: Use of low-calorie sweeteners (also called artificial sweeteners, nonnutritive sweeteners, or sugar substitutes) can help reduce the total carbohydrate or added sugar content in many of your favorite foods, while maintaining the flavor and texture you are accustomed to. These sugar substitutes contain few to no calories or carbohydrate and do not raise blood sugar or insulin levels, which can be very useful for people who have diabetes or desire to lose weight. The FDA currently allows four sugar substitutes to be used as additives in foods. All have undergone extensive safety evaluation and approval by the FDA. They are acesul-fame potassium (acesulfame K), aspartame, saccharin, and sucralose.

Contrary to what you may have read about sugar substitutes, scientific data has shown no link to adverse health effects. Although they are a great way to cut added sugars in your diet, this is no excuse to eat unlimited quantities.

Stevia is another sugar substitute on the market. It is calorie free and hun-dreds of times sweeter than table sugar. Although used in food products in many countries, unresolved health concerns concerning stevia have prompted the FDA to deny its use as a food additive. Stevia can be found in the supplement section of health food stores for home use; however, until more research indicates it is safe to consume, we recommend avoiding it.

Q: What are sugar alcohols? Are they safe to consume?
A: Sugar alcohols are used as a substitute for sugar in a variety of foods like hard candy, ice cream, chewing gum, and soft drinks labeled "low sugar" or "sugar free." Found under the alias mannitol, sorbitol, or xylitol, these fruit and berry ex-tracts provide fewer calories (average 2.6 calories per gram) than regular sugar (4 calories per gram), and don't require insulin for uptake and metabolism. In ad-dition to sweetness, sugar alcohols provide texture, retain moisture, and prevent browning when a food is heated. Eaten in excess, sugar alcohols can also provide you with some unwanted side effects such as gastrointestinal distress, bloating, gas, or diarrhea. But these side effects need not occur if you watch your portion size, which is important since foods containing sugar alcohols are not necessarily low calorie.

Q: Do you allow sugar in your recipes? If not, can I use sugar substitutes?
A: As long as sugar is consumed moderately (no more than 8 to 10 percent of calories), it can be part of your heart-healthy eating plan. Although sugar doesn't provide any heart protection, it does offer more than sweetness to many foods. For example, sugar balances acidity in sauces and dressings; is energy for yeast; and provides baked goods with bulk, even browning, and air stabilization and re-tention. When sugar is necessary in a recipe, we use as little as possible without compromising flavor or texture. If and when you do choose sugar sources, we recommend you limit the use of white sugar and high-fructose corn syrup and opt for unrefined versions of sugar such as honey, molasses, pure maple syrup, pure cane sugar, or agave nectar. All of these are excellent sources of sweetness that undergo less processing than granulated sugar or high-fructose corn syrup. Where sugar substitutes can be used, such as aspartame or sucralose, we use those instead. Reduced-sugar blends, which use half sugar and half sugar substi-

tute, also are available at your local grocery stores and are used in some of our recipes.

Q: You recommend avoiding foods and beverages with high-fructose corn syrup. Why?

A: Fructose is a naturally occurring sweetener found in a variety of fruits and honey and is widely used as a sweetener in juices, soft drinks, and other nonbeverage foods (e.g., breads, crackers, cereal bars, and cereals). In soft drinks, fructose is usually found in the form high-fructose corn syrup (HFCS), which is a little over 50 percent fructose. In the 1970s, soft drink manufacturers started using HFCS as a replacement for sucrose in their beverages. Between 1970 and 1990, Americans increased their intake of HFCS by 1,000 percent. Yes, you are reading that right—1,000 percent! Now consider that obesity has doubled in our country since the 1960s. Coincidence? Many scientists think not. Researchers estimate that the average American consumes 200 to 300 more calories per day than they did in the 1960s, of which one-third is derived from soft drinks. In fact, it has been estimated that roughly 130 calories each day come from HFCS in the average American diet (up to 200 calories for some). While we cannot blame HFCS alone for our obesity epidemic, preliminary research indicates fructose may alter the body's metabolism in a way that promotes storage of body fat. Most of the controversy surrounding fructose and weight gain points to soft drinks and beverages. However, eliminating HFCS added to foods like breads and cereals is also recommended as a prudent means to avoid weight gain.

Unrefined Carbohydrates

A primary source of unrefined carbohydrates is whole grains, in which the bran, endosperm, and germ from the grain are intact.

A whole grain is the entire edible part of any grain, be it wheat, oat, rice, or corn. Whole grains (and foods made from them) consist of the entire grain seed. The whole grain is important to a growing plant because it supplies nourishment and is the seed from which other plants develop. Just as this seed is important to the health of the plant, it also provides important nutrients to our bodies—in the form of B vitamins, iron, magnesium, selenium, dietary fiber, and other disease-fighting components.

- The bran makes up the outer layer of the grain and supplies large amounts of B vitamins, trace minerals, and dietary fiber.

- The endosperm, the inner part of the grain, contains most of the protein and carbohydrates and trace amounts of vitamins and minerals.
- The germ, a small but important part of the grain because it generates or "sprouts" to form a new plant, also contains B vitamins, trace minerals, and some protein.

These unadulterated grains maintain levels of naturally present iron, B vitamins, dietary fiber, magnesium, and a host of additional heart-protective substances called phytonutrients (described in Chapter 7). What's more, because of their dietary fiber component, whole grains help you avoid high and low blood sugar fluctuations and between-meal hunger pangs and give you longer-term energy.

Unrefined grains include whole wheat, oats, barley, and brown rice. However, we consume a number of other unrefined carbohydrate foods, such as whole fruit, vegetables, and legumes (beans, lentils, split peas). These powerful carbohydrate-containing foods will be discussed at greater length in Chapter 7.

Is It Really Whole Grain?

Never judge a grain by its color. Just because bread is brown by no means indicates it is made from a whole grain. In fact, decades ago savvy manufacturers realized that if they added caramel food coloring, molasses, or brown sugar to refined grains, a bread or cracker would look "whole grain." Even if bread is named after a grain, such as rye or wheat bread, or lists that it is "natural" or "contains no preservatives," this does not mean that it is made from whole grain. Don't be fooled by appearance or titles—instead, use these guidelines to help you choose your grains.

Look for "whole grain" on the label—but be skeptical. The FDA has established that a food can be labeled "whole grain" as long as 51 percent of the ingredient weight comes from a whole grain. But buyer beware: a number of foods in our marketplace, specifically cereals and cereal bars, are promoted as "whole grain." Unfortunately, these foods often contain fiber-added derivatives and a lot of sugar—virtually voiding the benefit of the food coming from a whole grain in the first place. Read on to become a better whole-grain investigator.

Look at ingredients. Read the ingredient list on the product first. It should always say "whole grain" or "whole wheat." Other key words are "100% whole wheat" (or other grain) or "stone-ground whole wheat." Don't be fooled by deceptive terminology such as "wheat flour," "unbleached wheat flour," "stoned wheat," or even "made with oatmeal." This does not tell you how much whole wheat, whole grain, or even oatmeal is in the product. It may be way down the list of ingredients. Ingredients are listed by weight, so if enriched flour is the first ingredient, that means there is more white flour than any other flour in the product. Whole grain must be listed first.

Look for fiber on the label. An equally important strategy when determining if a grain is really a whole grain is to read the Nutrition Facts panel on the food label. The amount of dietary fiber in a given food will be listed as Dietary Fiber, found directly under Total Carbohydrate. Look for grams of total dietary fiber, not percentages. The percentages are for someone following a 2,000-calorie eating plan, a calorie level that is not representative of everyone.

Here are some quick and easy fiber guidelines to follow when purchasing foods.

- *Breads, pita, flatbreads, and crackers:* These should contain 3 grams or more dietary fiber per slice or serving. Since English muffins and most store-bought bagels are really two servings, they should contain a minimum of 6 grams of fiber for the whole muffin or bagel. Note that some foods in this category are sweetened with sugars like high-fructose corn syrup. Avoid those that list sugar or high-fructose corn syrup as one of the first few ingredients.

- *Cold cereal:* This should contain 5 or more grams of dietary fiber per serving. Since many cereals are also high in added simple sugars, you should also choose cereals that contain no greater than 8 to 10 grams of sugar per serving. Excellent examples are Fiber One, Kashi Go Lean, and Complete Wheat or Oat Bran Flakes.
- *Hot cereal:* Most hot cereals should contain at least 4 grams of dietary fiber per 1-cup cooked serving (such as oatmeal) but no added sugar. Good examples are oat bran, or oatmeal listed as Irish, steel-cut, or old-fashioned.
- *Pasta, rice, and other grains:* Look for 3 grams or more dietary fiber per serving. And don't be fooled by tricolored pasta and other grains—whole grains still need to be listed first.
- *Starchy snack foods:* You should limit foods like pretzels, baked chips, and whole wheat graham crackers, but when you do buy such snacks, make sure they are made primarily from a whole-grain flour. Choose those that contain at least 2 grams or more dietary fiber and the least amount of added sugar per serving.

Look for the Whole Grain Stamp

A new tool is available for consumers searching for whole grains in grocery stores—the Whole Grain Stamp, created by the nonprofit Whole Grains Council. The stamp features a sheaf of grain on a golden-yellow background with a black border. Two stamps indicate the level of whole grain in a food: a food stamped "Whole Grain" has a half serving of whole grain, and a "100% Whole Grain" stamp is a full serving of whole grain, and all the grain in the food is from whole grain. An increasing number of food manufacturers have participated in this whole-grain initiative, so be on the lookout.

Fiber Facts

As opposed to the single and double sugar bonds that constitute simple sugars, refined and unrefined grains are made up of multiple sugar molecule linkages called polysaccharides. Unrefined whole grains have a different effect on blood sugars than refined grains do. It's all due to a key ingredient the average American sorely underconsumes—dietary fiber. Dietary fiber provides no calories and is not digested or absorbed by the body. Instead of being used for energy, fiber is excreted through our stool. This non-nutrient, however, has a host of disease-fighting benefits.

- *Fewer blood sugar fluctuations and more energy.* The fibers in whole grains cause foods to take longer to digest. This slow digestion of carbohydrate releases sugar into the bloodstream at a steady pace, which curtails the surge of insulin that occurs when you eat refined grains. As a result, you experience a feeling of fullness for an extended period of time, encounter fewer high and low blood sugar fluctuations, and are less prone to snack between meals.

- *Weight control.* The link between whole grains and weight management is also likely the result of fiber. In addition to long-lasting fullness, whole grains take longer to chew. The process of chewing and the effort this takes help curb the appetite, resulting in early-onset fullness and fewer calories consumed.
- *Reduced inflammatory markers.* In a survey of more than 4,900 adults in the United States, those who consumed the highest amount of dietary fiber (more than 19.5 grams a day) had a 46 percent lower risk of having elevated levels of C-reactive protein (CRP), an inflammatory marker associated with increased risk of heart disease.
- *Lower cholesterol.* Extensive research has established a definitive link between high LDL or "bad" cholesterol and the risk of developing or dying from heart disease. Soluble fiber, one of two forms of fiber, reduces this bad cholesterol and our chance of developing heart disease.

Soluble (viscous) fiber dissolves in water. Instead of giving foods a coarse texture, soluble fiber, such as that in oat bran or oatmeal, dissolves and forms a gel (picture a bowl of cooked oatmeal). As soluble fiber passes through our intestines, this gel binds with certain digestive enzymes (called bile acids) made in the liver, promoting their excretion as waste. Because the liver uses cholesterol from the body to manufacture these bile acids, it must draw additional cholesterol from the blood to make more. The net result is a reduction in cholesterol absorption by the body and a decrease in total and LDL cholesterol in the blood.

Research has indicated that a 5 percent or greater decrease in total and LDL cholesterol can be achieved by eating between 5 and 10 grams of soluble fiber each day. This may not seem like much, but when you factor in all of the other health benefits from fiber (e.g., blood sugar control and weight loss) with the fact that every 1-point drop in cholesterol reduces your risk of heart disease 2 to 3 percent, this can have a big impact on your overall risk of developing heart disease.

Good sources of soluble fiber include oats, oat bran, barley, legumes (e.g., dried beans, lentils, and split peas), psyllium, flax seeds, hemp seeds, apples, pears, citrus fruits, and a variety of vegetables.

Just how much soluble fiber is needed to lower cholesterol? According to the National Heart, Lung, and Blood Institute's National Cholesterol Education Program (NCEP) Expert Panel, consuming 10 to 25 grams of soluble fiber will maximize LDL cholesterol reduction. How easy is it to get this much soluble fiber in your diet? Refer to the following table for grams of soluble fiber in specific foods.

Selected Sources of Soluble Fiber

Food Source or Supplement	Serving	Soluble Fiber (in grams)	Total Fiber (in grams)
Old-fashioned oats, dry	1/2 cup	1.9	3.7
Oat bran, dry	1/3 cup	2.0	4.8
Brown rice, cooked	1/2 cup	0.1	1.8
Whole barley, cooked	1/2 cup	1.4	6.8
Flax seed, ground/milled	2 tablespoons	1.1	4.5
Benefiber powder	1 tablespoon	3.0	3.0
Metamucil powder	1 tablespoon	2.4	3.0
Citrucel powder	1 tablespoon	10.2	10.2
Apple, with peel	1 medium	1.0	3.7
Pear, whole	1 medium	2.4	4.4
Orange	1 medium	2.1	3.1
Grapefruit	1/2 medium	1.4	1.8
Dried plums/prunes	6 medium	3.1	5.7
Kidney beans	1/2 cup	2.7	6.6
Pinto beans	1/2 cup	2.1	5.5
Black beans	1/2 cup	2.0	7.5
Broccoli, raw	1 cup	2.0	3.7
Brussels sprouts, cooked	1 cup	1.9	4.1
Carrots, raw	1 cup	1.5	3.6
Eggplant, with skin, cooked	1 cup	1.0	2.4

Nutrition data derived from Food Processor for Windows, version 8.6.0, ESHA Research, Salem, Oregon.

Following the Cleveland Clinic Healthy Eating Guidelines will ensure that you consume the minimum required amount of soluble fiber on a given day.

To get the most out of soluble fiber's cholesterol-lowering benefit:

- Eat at least three 1/2-cup portions of soluble-fiber-rich legumes each week. Enjoy vegetarian chili, bean-based soups, bean and rice mixtures, pureed bean dips, black bean burgers, and even beans in your favorite pasta dish for an additional fiber boost. Try some of our tasty high-fiber bean dishes like Black-eyed Pea Relish (page 134), Great Northern Beans with Tomatoes and Herbs (page 281), and Spicy Black Bean Cakes (page 276).
- Incorporate oats, one of the greatest sources of the soluble fiber called beta-glucan, into your daily regimen. Enjoy a hearty bowl of hot oat bran or oatmeal for breakfast, or try some of the many oat bran–based cold cereals on the market.
- Oats or barley can replace rice as side dishes; can be added to soups, stews, and pilafs; sprinkled over your favorite yogurt; or added to a granola. Try barley cooked in a reduced-sodium chicken broth (instead of plain water) for a flavor-infused side dish. Or enjoy our Mexican Barley Risotto (page 278).
- Follow our Cleveland Clinic Healthy Eating Guidelines and include a minimum of three fists of fruit and four or more fists of vegetables each day.
- Flax seeds, a source of healthy omega-3 fat, are also a great source of fiber. Enjoy 1 to 2 tablespoons of ground or milled flax seeds daily in oatmeal or cold cereals, to top yogurt or cottage cheese, or mixed in a smoothie.

Insoluble fiber is generally referred to as "roughage." Unlike soluble fiber, insoluble fiber gives carbohydrate-containing foods their coarse texture. Insoluble fiber promotes regularity and helps prevent constipation and diverticulosis by adding bulk and softness to stools and decreasing the time food spends in our intestines. While it has not been shown to help lower cholesterol, foods rich in insoluble fiber still provide our bodies with a host of cardioprotective B vitamins, essential fats, antioxidants, and phytochemicals. Good sources of insoluble fiber include wheat bran, whole wheat and other whole-grain cereals and breads, nuts, and vegetables.

How Much Fiber Should I Be Eating?

Apparently more people should be asking this question. That's because the Continuing Survey of Food Intakes by Individuals (CSFII) indicates the average American consumes no more than 15 grams of dietary fiber each day. This is way below national recommended guidelines, restricts our ability to enjoy the health benefits of this very important non-nutrient, and is a sign that we still consume too many of our carbohydrates in the refined form. The Institute of Medicine (IOM), the leading board for nutrition recommendations, advocates the following daily fiber goals:

Men less than 50 years old:	38 grams
Men over 50 years old:	30 grams
Women less than 50 years old:	25 grams
Women over 50 years old:	21 grams

Children aren't excluded from these fiber recommendations either. Until age 18, children should consume their age plus 5 grams of dietary fiber each day. For example, a six-year-old should consume 11 grams of dietary fiber daily (6 years plus 5 grams = 11 grams). From our perspective, these levels are just the starting point for obtaining optimal health; if possible, we prefer you aim for higher amounts.

Go for Variety

All fiber-containing foods have a mixture of both insoluble and soluble fiber. Therefore, we encourage you to choose a wide variety of fiber-rich foods each day, instead of tediously counting grams of soluble and insoluble fiber from every food you eat. If you have high cholesterol, however, it is especially important that you incorporate foods high in soluble fiber into your daily eating plan. For sample daily menus for 1,600, 2,000, and 2,400 calories a day, check out page 340. We'll give you one week's worth of menus for each calorie level.

The following table is a quick reference comparing refined versus unrefined grains in the typical American eating plan.

Fiber Comparisons: Refined Versus Unrefined

Food Source	Serving Size	Total Dietary Fiber (in grams)
Instant white rice	1/2 cup cooked	<1
Instant brown rice	1/2 cup cooked	1.5
Long-grain brown rice	1/2 cup cooked	2.0
Wild rice	1/2 cup cooked	1.5
Enriched spaghetti	2 ounces cooked	<1
Whole wheat spaghetti	2 ounces cooked	2.6
Instant oatmeal	1 cup cooked	3.75
Old-fashioned oatmeal	1 cup cooked	3.75
Irish oat "groats"	1 cup cooked	8.0
Oat bran	1 cup cooked	5.7
Corn grits	1 cup cooked	<1
Cream of Wheat	1 cup cooked	1
Pearled barley	1/2 cup cooked	3.0
Whole barley	1/2 cup cooked	6.8
Couscous	1/3 cup dry	4.3
Whole wheat couscous	1/3 cup dry	7.0
White bread	1 ounce	<1
Whole wheat bread	1 ounce	2.0
Pumpernickel bread	1 ounce	1.8
Rye bread	1 ounce	1.6
Whole rye bread	1 ounce	2.0
French bread	1 ounce	<1
Bran flakes cereal	1 cup	7.0

Food Source	Serving Size	Total Dietary Fiber (in grams)
Kashi Go Lean cereal	1 cup	10.0
Fiber One cereal	1/2 cup	14.0
Post 100% Bran	1/3 cup	9.0
Optimum Slim cereal	1 cup	11.0
Shredded wheat cereal	1 cup	6.0
Grape-nuts	1/2 cup	6.0
Cheerios	1 cup	3.5
Rice crisp cereal	1 cup	<1
Potato with skin	3 ounces	2.5

Is there such a thing as eating too many whole grains? Overeating any food could potentially hamper your heart-health goals. Any excess of calories can result in weight gain. Excess carbohydrates, especially refined ones, can raise blood triglycerides. Before cutting back, consider where the majority of your carbohydrate calories are coming from. For example, if you have oatmeal for breakfast, a sandwich made of whole-grain bread for lunch, and dinner rolls and white rice with your dinner, don't cut back on your high-fiber foods (i.e., oatmeal and whole-grain bread); cut out the white roll or reduce your white rice portions first. When you can, substitute brown rice for white and keep your portion size to about the size of your fist. None of us needs the extra calories or carbohydrates from rolls or dinner breads, especially if they're highly refined, so save these for special occasions.

Remember our guidelines from Chapter 2 on estimating serving sizes for carbohydrates. Fifty percent of your breakfast plate should contain whole grains, and 25 percent of your plate at lunch and dinner. Throw in a snack or two (a half-fist portion) and you'll be one step closer to achieving your daily fiber goal.

Choosing and Using the Right Fats

CHAPTER

Fats are just as confusing as carbohydrates. For decades the nutrition pendulum has swung from recommending very low fat diets to allowing unrestricted amounts of fat, as long as it's the "healthy" kind. If you are confused by these flip-flop messages, you are not alone. While research on fats continues to evolve, we will explain what long-term, sound scientific evidence, as well as years of treating millions of patients, has revealed.

Fats to Avoid

"What fats should I avoid?" Patients who want to know what fats they should eliminate from their diet often begin with this question. At Cleveland Clinic, we avoid labeling foods as "bad" or "good" because the reality is that sometimes you will be in situations where a healthy food choice is not available. This doesn't mean that you should write off your heart-health goals if you occasionally eat a less-than-healthy food.

With that in mind, let's first discuss fats that promote heart disease—fats you should limit most of the time. We will follow with fats that promote a healthy heart—fats you should consider putting *back* into your diet if you've left them out.

Fats That Promote Heart Disease

Saturated fats and trans fats are the two main groups of fats to avoid. You may wonder where cholesterol—for many years considered the primary villain among the various causes of heart disease—fits into the picture. Scientists long believed that the amount of cholesterol in the body was related directly to the amount of cholesterol we consume in the diet. But research over the last 50 years has shown that dietary cholesterol plays an important but minor role in regulating blood cholesterol levels. The current hypothesis is that dietary fats are far more important in the development of high cholesterol and heart disease.

Saturated Fats

This "diet-heart" hypothesis is based on research that linked people's eating habits to heart disease progression. A landmark trial involving more than 11,000 men from seven different countries over 25 years added support to this hypothesis. The Seven Countries Study was the first major research to link a diet high in saturated fat to elevations in total and LDL cholesterol, two important indicators of heart disease risk.

This study found a direct relationship between saturated fat consumption and death from coronary heart disease. In regions where heart disease was very low, such as Japan, Greece, and southern Italy, people ate low levels of saturated fat. And in regions where saturated fat intakes were high, like Finland and the United States, rates of disease were much higher.

These additional facts further strengthen the link between saturated fat and coronary heart disease:

- When people move from Japan—a country with a low overall risk of heart disease—to the United States and start eating a diet rich in animal fats and processed foods, their rate of heart disease increases rapidly.
- In the China Study, researchers found that Chinese who ate a traditional diet rich in low–saturated fat plant foods and low in animal products had rates of obesity, cancer, and heart disease that were among the lowest in the world. In areas of China where people changed their diet to include high intakes of animal protein, rates of obesity, cancer, and heart disease were much higher.
- Overall, dietary studies indicate that every 1 percent increase in calories from saturated fat pushes LDL cholesterol levels up by 2 percent.
- Looking at the impact of high–saturated fat foods on blood flow, researchers found that a single meal containing foods high in saturated fat significantly reduced blood flow in a major artery. It is frightening, then, to note that this study was conducted on healthy young men with no apparent risk for disease. Consider the impact a high–saturated fat meal, or a lifetime of such meals, could have on someone with existing coronary disease!

These research findings provide insight on the powerful impact foods have on your risk for disease. Even when genetics, age, sex, weight, physical activity, and a host of other lifestyle factors are accounted for, saturated fats still clearly increase your risk. Read on to learn how you can reduce the odds of letting this dangerous fat impact your health.

HOW TO SPOT A SATURATED FAT

It's easy to identify saturated fats because they remain solid or waxy at room temperature. This solid state of a saturated fat results from its molecular structure—all of the carbon atoms on the fatty acid bond are linked, or "saturated," with hydrogen.

Once you learn some saturated fat basics, you'll be surprised at how savvy you'll become at identifying them in foods. Saturated fats are found in high-fat cuts of animal meat and dairy. Interestingly, as you can see from the following list of foods high in saturated fat, some plant-derived foods also contain saturated fat.

- Beef, pork, lamb, veal, and the skin of poultry
- Hot dogs and high-fat luncheon meats (e.g., salami, bologna)
- Regular cheese (aged or processed)
- High-fat dairy products (e.g., whole milk, 2% milk, 4% cottage cheese)
- Butter and lard
- Sauces and gravies made from animal fat
- Bacon fat
- Tropical oils—palm, palm kernel, and coconut
- Desserts and sweets made with lard, butter, or tropical oils

Ideally, we would eliminate these foods from our diets, but that is not reasonable or practical for most people. That's why we've come up with these strategies for cutting saturated fat.

Instead of . . .	Choose . . .
Butter	Light or diet *trans*free margarine
Regular cheese	Low-fat or nonfat cheese
Creamer or half-and-half	Nonfat creamer or nonfat half-and-half
Whole or 2% milk	1% or nonfat (skim) milk
Regular ice cream	Nonfat frozen yogurt or sorbet
2%–4% cottage cheese	1% or nonfat cottage cheese
Alfredo or other cream sauces	Marinara, primavera, or light olive oil–based sauces

Mayonnaise	Light or nonfat mayonnaise
Prime grades of beef	Choice or Select grades of beef
Spareribs	Tenderloin
Chicken with skin	Chicken without skin
Whole eggs	Egg whites or egg substitutes

Besides being aware of animal-derived foods high in saturated fat, you also must be alert to this artery-clogging fat in processed or "convenience" foods. Candy bars, snacks, cookies, chips, frozen entrées, and the like are everywhere in our workplaces, stores, gas stations, homes, and schools. The best way to curb your saturated fat intake from these foods is to eliminate them altogether. But if you find that difficult, follow these guidelines.

Read food labels first. Food labels must list the amount of saturated fat in a food on the Nutrition Facts panel. Use this information to your advantage.

- *Saturated fat free:* The food contains less than 0.5 gram of saturated fat per serving and less than 0.5 gram of trans fat (described in the section "Trans Fatty Acids") per serving. Choose these foods most often.
- *Low in saturated fat:* A food must contain no more than 1 gram of saturated fat per serving. Main entrées should have no more than 1 gram of saturated fat for every 100 grams. These foods are your next best choice.
- If all else fails, at least keep your saturated fat level to 2 grams or less per serving.

Keep in mind that if you eat more than the serving size, you'll also increase the amount of saturated fat.

Read the ingredients. Ingredients in a food are listed by weight. If palm kernel oil is the second ingredient in your favorite brand of cookie, for example, the saturated fat content will likely be higher than 1 or 2 grams. If palm kernel oil is among the last of a long list of ingredients, the saturated fat content may not be as high.

Be wary of cholesterol-free or trans-free foods. Just because a bag of chips claims to be cholesterol free doesn't mean they weren't fried in tropical oil. On the other hand, just because a food claims to be trans free doesn't mean it's healthy, either. Many manufacturers have eliminated artery-clogging trans fats from their food products, but in the process they have added back palm kernel and other tropical oils. Read those labels—or simply eliminate these empty-calorie "junk" foods in the first place and you won't have to worry about the fine print.

SATURATED FAT GUIDELINES

The National Cholesterol Education Program (NCEP) guidelines recommend that no more than 7 percent of your calories come from saturated fat. We suggest cutting your saturated fat even further, to no more than 5 percent of your total daily calories. If you follow our eating guidelines, you don't need to calculate your grams of saturated fat—we've done the math for you!

How many grams of saturated fat do these guidelines translate to? Your daily limit of 5 to 7 percent of calories from saturated fat of course varies with the number of calories you consume. The following table lists the range of saturated fat in grams by calorie level.

Daily Calories	Daily Saturated Fat Limit (grams)
1,200	6.5–9
1,400	7.5–11
1,600	9–12
1,800	10–14
2,000	11–15.5
2,200	12–17
2,400	13–18.5

Now you can look at the foods you commonly consume and see how many grams of saturated fat you are taking in. If you are eating too much, consider the simple food substitutions provided on the next page. You'll be amazed at how many grams of saturated fat you can shave off with minimal effort.

Saturated Fat Substitutions and Savings

Food	Sat Fat (grams)	Substitute	Sat Fat (grams)	Sat-Fat Savings (grams)
Rib-eye steak (3 ounces)	4.86	Filet (3 ounces)	1.13	3.73
Ground round (3 ounces)	5.92	Ground sirloin (3 ounces)	1.5	4.42
Spareribs (3 ounces)	9.46	Beef tenderloin (3 ounces)	3.31	6.15
Pork hot dog	6.63	Light turkey hot dog	2.96	3.67
Chicken breast with skin (3 ounces)	1.86	Chicken breast without skin (3 ounces)	0.86	1.0
Salami (3 ounces)	7.18	Turkey breast (3 ounces)	0.41	6.77
Breakfast sausage patty (2 ounces)	7.0	Meatless "sausage" patty (2.68 ounces)	1.02	5.98
Cheddar cheese (1½ ounces)	8.97	Reduced-fat Cheddar (1½ ounces)	4.5	4.47
Whole milk (8 ounces)	4.55	Skim milk (8 ounces)	0.40	4.15
Ice cream (1 cup)	15.29	50%-less-fat ice cream (1 cup)	3.86	11.43
Whole egg	1.55	2 egg whites	0	1.55
Mayonnaise (2 tablespoons)	3.28	Fat-free mayonnaise (2 tablespoons)	0	3.28
Half-and-half (2 ounces)	4.06	Fat-free half-and-half (2 ounces)	0.48	3.58

Nutrition data derived from Food Processor for Windows, version 8.6.0, ESHA Research, Salem, Oregon.

Trans Fatty Acids

It wasn't so long ago that vegetable shortening was considered a superb substitute for butter in making pie crusts, cookies, and other baked goods. Everyone knew butter was taboo for spreading on toast, but margarine, which contained no cholesterol and less saturated fat than butter, was believed to be a healthier option for our cholesterol levels. It's only recently that scientists discovered that hydrogenation, the method of making shortening and margarine, isn't so good for our health after all.

Hydrogenation is a chemical process that adds hydrogen to a liquid vegetable oil. The end result is a fat, now also solid at room temperature, called trans fat. These were believed to be neutral to our health, and so trans fats grew in popularity for home cookery as a perfect solid fat substitute for saturated fat–rich butter or lard. Food manufacturers also found them useful because they were cheaper, provided the same "mouthfeel" and texture that customers were used to, and extended a product's shelf life. Fast-food restaurants chose trans fat–rich oils over beef tallow because they could be used longer in deep fryers without having to be changed.

Naturally occurring trans fat can be found in small amounts in some plant foods and makes up about 5 percent of dairy and beef fat. Although we are not as concerned with the small amounts of trans fat present in these foods, "small" is no longer the case if you down a 16-ounce prime rib, which contains over 7 grams.

Scientific research has shown that trans fat is associated with significant heart disease risk. Among its effects:

- *Increases LDL cholesterol.* Just like saturated fats, trans fats raise artery-clogging LDL cholesterol. In a prospective study (in which participants or groups are identified and then followed over time) conducted on more than 85,000 women, those who had the highest trans fat intake had a 50 percent higher risk of heart disease. Women who ate at least 4 teaspoons of trans-laden margarine each day had a 66 percent higher risk for heart disease than women who consumed margarine less than once a month.
- *Increases lipoprotein a.* Commonly referred to as Lp(a) or "Lp little a," this lipoprotein is similar in structure to LDL and is associated with an increased risk of developing atherosclerosis.
- *Decreases HDL cholesterol.* All other fats in our diet raise HDL cholesterol to some degree. Trans fat actually reduces it, which can result in a higher ratio of total cholesterol to HDL cholesterol, another important indicator of heart disease risk.

Cleveland Clinic Healthy Heart Lifestyle Guide and Cookbook

- *Increases blood triglycerides.* Trans fats also increase triglycerides, which opens up a host of additional risk factors.
- *Worsens insulin resistance.* Research has linked a high trans diet to an increased rate of insulin resistance and risk of developing type 2 diabetes.
- *Increases likelihood of blood clots and reduces arterial blood flow.* Trans fats make our blood platelets "stickier," which can lead to more fat and cholesterol deposits in the arteries. In addition, like saturated fats, trans fats can cause arteries to stay restricted for longer periods and relax less quickly, thus reducing blood flow.
- *Overall increase in heart disease risk.* Many studies link a high intake of trans fat to increases in the development of and death from heart disease.
- *Increased risk for certain cancers.* A high intake of trans fat is linked to an increased risk for breast and other cancers.

HOW TO SPOT A TRANS FAT

As long as you choose lean meats and nonfat dairy products, the small amount of trans fat naturally present in these foods is not a concern. The trans fat that comes from partially hydrogenated oil and shortening is another story. These should be eliminated or reduced to the best of your ability. Here are a few quick tips on finding trans fat in foods.

- *Read food labels first.* An FDA ruling established January 1, 2006, as the final date that all manufacturers must comply with listing trans fat on their food labels. The FDA has estimated that adding this information to labels will save this country $900 million to $1.8 billion per year in medical costs, lost productivity, and pain and suffering.

    The rule requires that the amount of trans fat in a serving be listed on a separate line under saturated fat on the Nutrition Facts panel. Trans fat does not have to be listed if the total fat in a food is less than 0.5 gram per serving. If it is not listed, a footnote will be added stating that the food is "not a significant source of trans fat." Choosing foods that are "trans fat free" or "0 grams trans fat" is a great way to cut back on this deadly fat. Remember that if a food is labeled "saturated fat free" it also must be trans free. This is a very helpful food labeling rule.

- *Read the ingredients.* Any food that contains shortening or partially hydrogenated vegetable oil will contain some level of trans fat and should be limited. Foods containing partially hydrogenated oil as one of the first few ingredients will have more trans fat than foods listing it as one of the last ingredients.

    Trans-free tub margarines can still contain hydrogenated or partially hydrogenated fats. Remember that the definition for "trans free" means a food can contain 0.5 gram or less trans fat per serving. If you exceed the serving, that food is no longer "free" of trans fat.

To successfully cut the trans fat from your eating plan, it's important that you know its main sources. Here is a quick list of common foods laden with trans fat and tips on cutting back.

- *Shortening.* Traditional shortening (such as Crisco) contains 4.2 grams of trans fat and 3.4 grams of saturated fat per tablespoon. *Trans*-free versions are now available (Crisco also makes a *trans*-free version), but some of them substitute saturated fat–laden palm kernel oil for partially hydrogenated oils. Overall, keep your intake of these foods to a minimum as they offer zero nutritional value.
- *Stick margarine.* Stick margarine has 2.8 grams of trans fat and 2.1 grams of saturated fat per tablespoon. What makes stick margarine a "stick" is partially hydrogenated oil. Eliminate stick margarine from your diet and use liquid or tub *trans*free margarine instead.
- *Tub margarine.* Unless the tub margarine label states it's trans free, do not buy it! Although typical tub margarine contains only 0.6 gram of trans fat per tablespoon (and 1.2 grams saturated fat), it's still more than you need. Read labels and choose margarines that contain the least amount of saturated fat and zero trans fat. The first ingredient in these foods should be water or liquid vegetable oil. If margarine is listed as trans free but still lists partially hydrogenated or fully hydrogenated oils in the ingredients, be very careful not to exceed the serving size.
- *Liquid or spray margarine.* Liquid margarines should contain no trans fat and should be your preferred margarine source. Just don't get "trigger happy" with the spray margarines, please.
- *Fast food.* An order of fries with fried chicken strips contains about 15 grams of trans fat. And that's without the trans-laden pie for dessert. There isn't much good to say when it comes to fast foods, because just about everything is fried in partially hydrogenated oil. Some chains have started using *trans*free liquid frying oil; however, if they purchase prefried (in trans fat) French fries, they have defeated their own efforts to cut the trans.
- *Chips and crackers.* Just a small bag of potato chips can contain more than 3 grams of trans fat per serving. That "buttery" taste of your favorite cracker? Trans fat. A number of manufacturers have switched to liquid vegetable oils for these products, but that still doesn't mean you can eat unlimited quantities of

these calorie-dense foods. Most of them are laden with sodium, few contain whole grains, and they offer zilch in terms of heart-protective nutrients. Your best choice is whole-grain crackers made with no fat or liquid vegetable oils. If you really must have chips, choose tortilla chips or potato chips baked in non-hydrogenated oils, and eat them sparingly.

- *Baked goods.* Virtually *every* store-bought cookie, cake, pastry, or pie contains shortening or partially hydrogenated oil, unless of course it's totally fat free (then it's loaded with sugar). Top it with trans-laden icing and you've got two days' worth of trans in a few bites. The baked goods industry has been trying to cut out shortening and add *trans*free ingredients in everything from toaster pastries to cookies, but they often use palm, palm kernel, or coconut oil instead. Pass these up. Whether a dessert is fat free, trans free, or saturated fat free, it's still not a healthy food, so keep your intake of such sweets to a minimum and save them for a special occasion.
- *Candy and energy bars.* Next time you reach for that caramel-nougat, rich chocolate bar or that purported "low-sugar" energy bar, consider reading the food label first. You may be surprised at how much saturated and trans fat are in it. Look for crunchy granola bars, trail mix bars, or uncoated, high-fiber energy bars made with liquid vegetable oil instead.
- *Coffee creamers.* You'll be surprised to find out that most nondairy creamers are made with hydrogenated oils. Choose nonfat half-and-half, *trans*-free creamers, or skim milk, or drink your java black.
- *Dips and other toppings.* Be on the lookout for cheese dips, salad dressings, whipped toppings, sauces, and gravies containing partially hydrogenated oil. Try making your own using the phenomenal recipes we have in this book.
- *Cereals and breads.* Many cereals and breads contain hydrogenated oils and high-fructose corn syrup. Read the labels.
- Kids' treats and other packaged foods. Fortunately, many traditional children's treats such as crackers and cereals have been modified to reduce or eliminate the trans fat. Always read the label to see how many grams of saturated and trans fat a food contains before you buy it.

TRANS FAT GUIDELINES

No national standard has been established as to how much trans fat a person can safely consume each day. The consensus, however, among the NCEP, American Heart Association (AHA), and National Academy of Sciences is to keep trans intake as low as possible. We recommend you try your best to eliminate all trans fat from your food selections and implement the trans fat–cutting strategies we've provided.

Q: I recently looked at the ingredients on *trans*free vegetable shortening and noticed that one of the ingredients was fully hydrogenated oil? What gives? I thought hydrogenated oils meant trans fat?

A: This issue can be confusing. Here's the straight and skinny—fully hydrogenated oils do not contain trans fat. Food manufacturers don't often use fully hydrogenated oils because these fats are so hard they're impossible to cook with. That's why you'll usually find some liquid vegetable oil also in the ingredients list—it's usually there to make the fully hydrogenated oil spreadable.

Although *trans*free vegetable shortening is free of partially hydrogenated oil, it is by no means a healthy food and should be consumed sparingly. To show how you can cook with these foods in small quantities, we've used *trans*free vegetable shortening in our pie crust recipes.

Dietary Cholesterol—Why You Still Should Cut Back

Although saturated and trans fatty acids tend to raise your cholesterol and heart disease risk more than dietary cholesterol, you should still keep your cholesterol intake in check. Some people are more sensitive to dietary cholesterol than others so that the more they consume, the more their blood cholesterol levels go up. Since most of us don't know our individual sensitivity to dietary cholesterol, we should all consider keeping our intake low. How low? If you have high cholesterol or a history of heart disease or diabetes, limit your daily intake to 200 milligrams. If your cholesterol is within the normal range, you should not exceed 300 milligrams each day. Keep in mind that any food that is derived from an animal contains cholesterol.

Here's the good news about reducing the cholesterol in your diet: cholesterol-rich foods are generally high in saturated fat, too. This means that if you follow basic saturated fat–lowering techniques, you'll also be cutting back on dietary cholesterol. Of course, you can always read labels to see if the food is "cholesterol free." Keep in mind, however, that a cholesterol-free food is not always saturated or trans fat free.

CHOLESTEROL Q & A

Q: How many eggs can I eat each week?

A: Although dietary cholesterol may not raise blood cholesterol as much as saturated and trans fats, it is still important to monitor your weekly egg consumption. Just one large egg yolk contains more than 200 milligrams. If you have elevated cholesterol, this already sets you over your daily limit (not counting the bacon, sausage, and cheese many people eat with eggs), which means your remaining meals that day should not contain any additional cholesterol (read: animal foods). Current AHA guidelines recommend eating no more than three whole eggs per week. If you have a hankering for scrambled eggs or omelets, try using egg whites (two egg whites are equivalent to one egg) or a cholesterol-free egg substitute ($^1/_4$ cup is equivalent to one egg).

Additional Cholesterol-Lowering Strategies: Sterols and Stanols

Adding phytosterols (called sterols and stanols) to your diet is another effective cholesterol-lowering strategy. These compounds block cholesterol absorption in the body. They occur naturally in fruits, vegetables, nuts, seeds, and legumes, but in such small quantities that you'd have to eat an impractical amount of these foods to see significant cholesterol reduction. As a result, manufacturers have isolated these compounds and added them to margarine spreads, juices, yogurts, candy chews, other foods, and supplements. When eaten in recommended quantities, these sterol-enhanced foods have been shown to lower total cholesterol up to 10 percent and LDL or "bad" cholesterol 14 to 17 percent. The following products contain sterols or stanols, and can be incorporated into your heart-healthy eating plan as an additional cholesterol-lowering strategy:

• Benecol or Benecol Light spread
• Take Control or Take Control Light spread
• Minute Maid Heart Wise orange juice
• Rice Dream Heart Wise rice milk
• Nature Valley Healthy Heart chewy trail mix bars
• Cocoa Via snack bars or chocolate bars

These products were available in most major markets at the time of publication.

Fats to Add

Reducing fats that promote heart disease is clearly important, but it's not the only strategy that will lead to enhanced heart health. In fact, *adding* certain fats to your diet can offer more cardioprotection than lowering the total amount you consume. Research over the past several decades has unquestionably linked unsaturated fats, called mono- and polyunsaturates, to preventing heart disease. This benefit applies to individuals who have never had heart disease and want to prevent it from occurring, as well as to those who have a history of heart disease such as a heart attack, stroke, or bypass surgery and are trying to prevent disease from reoccurring.

Fats That Help Prevent Heart Disease

You may recall back in the 1980s and 1990s it was widely believed that reducing the amount of total fat in the diet was the most effective way to lower cholesterol and heart disease. However, more clinical research has been conducted, and new findings have emerged: substituting unsaturated fats for saturated fats has more impact on reducing cholesterol and the risk of heart disease than does cutting total fat. What's more, consuming unsaturated fats has a greater cholesterol-lowering effect than does substituting carbohydrates for saturated fats.

Monounsaturated Fats
Monounsaturated fats (their fat molecules have only one double bond) appear to confer significant cardioprotection.

- When substituted for saturated or trans fat in the diet, monounsaturated fats lower both total and LDL cholesterol up to 10 percent.
- When compared to carbohydrates as a substitute for saturated or trans fat, monounsaturated fats more effectively lower total and LDL cholesterol, and they prevent the increase in triglycerides and drop in HDL normally seen when saturated fats are replaced by carbohydrates alone.
- In a large, prospective study conducted on more than 80,000 women, substituting monounsaturated fats for just 5 percent of saturated fat calories cut the risk of heart disease by 19 percent.
- Nuts, such as peanuts, almonds, and macadamia nuts, are excellent sources of monounsaturated fat. Substituting these nuts for saturated fats in the diet can result in greater reduction of total and LDL cholesterol and weight loss than following a traditional low-fat diet. For more information on the health benefits of nuts, see page 74.

HOW TO SPOT A MONOUNSATURATED FAT

Monounsaturated fats are liquid at room temperature. Put them in the refrigerator, and they will coagulate a bit. This does not alter the health benefits of the monounsaturated fat (refrigeration will extend its shelf life); just let it sit at room temperature, and it will liquefy again. While all fats contain a mixture of monounsaturated, polyunsaturated, and even saturated fats, those that are primarily rich in monounsaturated fat (about 50 percent of calories) include

- Olive oil
- Olives
- Canola (rapeseed) oil
- Soybean oil
- Peanut oil
- Avocados
- Peanuts (a legume) and most tree nuts (excluding walnuts) and their nut butters

Although not required by the FDA to be on the Nutrition Facts panel, you can spot a monounsaturated fat by reading the ingredients list and looking for the preceding food sources.

MONOUNSATURATED FAT GUIDELINES

The NCEP recommends that monounsaturated fats not exceed 20 percent of your total calories. Use our Healthy Eating Guidelines, plating suggestions and fabulous recipes to help you effortlessly reap the benefits of this powerful fat.

Polyunsaturated Fats

Polyunsaturated fats (their fat molecules contain two or more double bonds) also provide a host of heart-health benefits:

- When substituted for saturated and trans fats in the diet, polyunsaturated fats can lower total and LDL cholesterol up to 10 percent.
- When compared to carbohydrates as a substitute for saturated fats, polyunsaturated fats more effectively lower total and LDL cholesterol and prevent the increase in triglycerides normally experienced with high-carbohydrate diets.
- Certain forms of essential polyunsaturated fats, called omega-3s, are known for their triglyceride-lowering potential.
- Extensive research has also linked diets rich in polyunsaturated fat to a reduced risk for heart disease. In fact, substituting 5 percent of saturated fat calories

with polyunsaturated fats (as opposed to carbohydrates) lowered the risk of developing heart disease in more than 80,000 women by 38 percent!

HOW TO SPOT A POLYUNSATURATED FAT

Polyunsaturated fats stay liquid at room and refrigerator temperatures. Good sources of polyunsaturated fats include

- Corn oil
- Safflower oil
- Sunflower oil
- Sesame oil
- Grapeseed oil

Omega-3 fatty acids are one of two essential polyunsaturated fatty acids (*essential* meaning our bodies cannot make these fats; they must be consumed in the diet) our bodies depend on for a host of metabolic processes. The two types of omega-3s that play an important role in our bodies are eicosapentaenoic acid (EPA) and docosahexaenoic acid (DHA). The heart-health benefits of consuming adequate omega-3 fatty acids in the diet are nothing short of astounding. Observational, epidemiological, and clinical trials have generally revealed that omega-3 fats:

- Lower triglycerides (immediately following a meal and fasting levels)
- Reduce irregular heartbeats
- Promote relaxation of arterial lining (vasodilation)
- Reduce blood clotting, "thin" the blood
- Have an anti-inflammatory effect, which helps slow the growth of atherosclerotic plaque
- May reduce mortality from heart disease and all causes of death
- May lower blood pressure and stroke risk
- Reduce the risk of coronary heart disease in women who consume two or more servings of omega-3-rich fish (about 6 ounces) weekly
- Reduce overall risk of death in men who have already had a heart attack

The following foods are good sources of omega-3 polyunsaturated fats:

- Fatty fish such as mackerel, salmon, sardines, and herring (see the table on page 72)
- Ground flax seeds and flaxseed oil
- Hulled hemp seeds

- Walnuts
- Soy foods and soybean oil (also a good source of monounsaturated fat)
- Canola oil (also a good source of monounsaturated fat)

The largest randomized, controlled trial examining the benefits of fish oil supplements offers dramatic evidence of the benefits of omega-3. In this study, more than 11,000 individuals who had experienced a heart attack were divided into four different dietary groups: placebo (inactive sugar pill), 1 gram EPA and DHA fish oil supplements alone, 300 milligrams vitamin E alone, or 1 gram fish oil plus the vitamin E. The group that took the fish oil supplement had a 35 to 45 percent reduction in sudden cardiac death over three and a half years and a 20 percent reduction in cardiac death, nonfatal heart attack, and nonfatal stroke. These are quite amazing findings!

Omega-3 fats aren't only found in fish. As you can see from the preceding list, flax seeds, flaxseed oil, hemp seeds, walnuts, canola oil, soy foods, and soybean oil are rich in the plant form of omega-3, called alpha-linolenic acid (ALA). This form is more slowly converted to EPA and DHA in the body, but ALA does play an important role in heart disease prevention.

The most notable demonstration of ALA's cardioprotective effect is the landmark Lyon Diet Heart Study. In this trial, more than 600 participants with a history of heart attack ate either a typical low-fat, heart-healthy diet or an ALA-enriched diet (known as the "traditional Mediterranean diet" because it was also rich in monounsaturated fat, fruits, legumes, whole grains, and vegetables) for 46 months. The group following the ALA-rich Mediterranean diet showed an amazing 68 percent reduction in cardiac death and nonfatal heart attack. No other study in history has shown such a phenomenal impact of foods on people with known heart disease.

Amount of Omega-3 Fatty Acids in Selected Fish and Seafood

Foods	Serving Size	Amount of Omega-3 Fat (grams)
Atlantic salmon or herring	3 ounces cooked	1.9
Bluefin tuna	3 ounces cooked	1.5
Sardines, canned	3 ounces in tomato sauce	1.5
Anchovies, canned	2 ounces drained	1.2
Atlantic mackerel	3 ounces cooked	1.15
Salmon, canned	3 ounces drained	1.0
Swordfish	3 ounces cooked	0.90
Sea bass (mixed species)	3 ounces cooked	0.65
Tuna, white meat, canned	3 ounces drained	0.5
Sole, flounder, mussels	3 ounces cooked	0.4
Wild catfish, crabmeat, clams	3 ounces cooked/steamed	0.3
Prawns (jumbo shrimp)	6 pieces	0.15
Atlantic cod, lobster	3 ounces cooked/steamed	0.15
Trout, orange roughy	3 ounces cooked	< 0.1

Nutritional data derived from Food Processor for Windows, version 8.6.0, ESHA Research, Salem, Oregon.

POLYUNSATURATED FAT GUIDELINES

There are a few cautions about consuming too much polyunsaturated fat. Due to their molecular structure, polyunsaturated fats are thought to be more susceptible to free radical damage and have a greater tendency to oxidize LDL, which can lead to plaque formation. Monounsaturated fats do not pose such a risk. When eaten in excess, polyunsaturated fats may also lower heart-protective HDL cholesterol. Although it is not known just how much polyunsaturated fat you'd need to eat to have this effect, the NCEP advises we limit our total daily calories from polyunsaturated fat sources to 10 percent or less. We recommend that you focus on consuming a variety of ALA and omega-3 fatty fish sources to unleash the powerful health benefits of polyunsaturated fats, rather than increasing its other sources (e.g., safflower or sunflower oil). Instead, use olive and canola oils as your principal form of unsaturated cooking and baking fats.

OMEGA-3 Q&A

Q: I've been told that taking fish oil capsules can give me the same health benefits as eating fish. Can't I just take a pill instead?

A: Most of the research conducted on omega-3 fats has included the consumption of fish, not fish oil capsules. It appears that consuming fish and plant forms of omega-3 fat is your best defense against heart disease. However, there are instances when supplementation may be necessary. Always check with your physician before taking a fish oil capsule as it may interact with other medications you are taking.

How much is enough? The AHA makes the following recommendations for incorporating omega-3s in your diet:

- If you have no known heart disease, consume oily fish twice a week and include plant sources of omega-3 (ALA) in your daily eating plan.
- If you have a history of heart disease but normal triglycerides, you should consume 1,000 milligrams (1 gram) of combined EPA and DHA, preferably from oily fish, each day. If you can't incorporate this level of omega-3s in your daily diet, talk to your physician about taking omega-3 supplements. Supplementation of omega-3 fats in this case is something to consider only with the consent of your physician.
- If you have high triglycerides, you need 2 to 4 grams of EPA + DHA, but take supplements only under your physician's care. Consuming fish and plant sources rich in omega-3s is still important for overall cardioprotection.

If you and your physician decide that supplementation is right for you, note that the amount of EPA and DHA varies from one brand of fish oil to the next. To reap the benefits of this essential fat, the EPA plus DHA must add up to the recommended levels. For example, just because a fish oil capsule says 1,000 milligrams does not mean that you are getting 1,000 milligrams of EPA and DHA. Fish oil capsules contain other oils that are not known to be of heart-health benefit. Therefore, add only the total amount of EPA and DHA to reach your daily goals. Read the back of the label to see how many milligrams of each are available per capsule. To avoid having to take up to ten pills a day, purchase those that give you the most EPA plus DHA per capsule.

Q: If I don't like fish or have an allergy, can I take flaxseed oil capsules to reach my daily omega-3 goals?

A: Because ALA, a precursor to EPA and DHA, is not converted as effectively to these essential fats in the body, we do not recommend supplementing with flaxseed oil capsules. Your best bet is to take fish oil capsules or consume oily fish. If you are vegetarian or allergic to fish, incorporating a variety of ALA-rich foods is of utmost importance in your diet. In addition, taking flaxseed oil capsules may be an option that you should address with your physician.

UNSATURATED POWERHOUSES

Nut-ritional Fat

In case you haven't heard lately—nuts are a hot topic when it comes to heart health. Substituting monounsaturated fat–rich nuts such as peanuts or almonds for saturated fats yields greater improvements in lowering LDL cholesterol than a low-fat diet, while maintaining or raising heart-protective HDL cholesterol. In addition, research shows that adding just 1/4 cup (small palm size) or 1 ounce of nuts five times a week is associated with a significant drop in the risk of developing or dying from coronary heart disease.

The Scoop on Flax

Have you had your scoop of flax today? If not, you may want to consider adding this tiny seed into your daily eating plan. Flax seed is the richest plant source of alpha-linolenic acid (ALA), a precursor to omega-3 fats. Flax is a powerful food. In addition to its value as a source of omega-3 fat, it is also a good source of cholesterol-lowering soluble fiber, cancer-fighting lignans, high-quality protein, and potassium.

• Flax seeds can be found at some grocers, most natural health food stores, direct through a manufacturer, or from the Internet. Flax seeds can be purchased in whole, ground, or milled form. Because the body is unable to fully digest whole seeds, you'll need to grind them first (or purchase them already ground or milled). Store flax seed in the refrigerator;

---

it can go rancid quickly. Known for their nutty flavor, these reddish-brown or golden-yellow seeds taste great added to oatmeal, bread and muffin recipes, yogurt, soups, salads, or shakes.
- Flaxseed oil is a great source of ALA but lacks the fiber, lignans, and protein found in the seed. For the benefits of ALA, add small amounts (1 to 2 teaspoons) of flaxseed oil to a marinade, smoothie, shake, or salad dressing.
- Although flaxseed oil can be purchased in a pill form, we do not recommend using it to lower triglycerides. Fish oil is the preferred source.
- Flax can also be found added to a variety of foods like ready-to-eat cereals, hot cereals, breads, crackers, granola bars, frozen pancakes and waffles, and snacks.

No specific serving sizes have been established for flax seed. To maximize cardioprotection, we recommend you consume 2 to 3 tablespoons of ground or milled flax on most days of the week.

Total Fat: Choosing Wisely

Now that you've got the skinny on fats, you need to be able to put this information into practical, everyday strategies that you and your family can follow for life. To determine how much total fat you should consume per day, we are not asking you to count grams, calculate percentages, or even do a lot of measuring. Instead, we recommend a diet that includes a variety of foods rich in mono- and polyunsaturated fats, with between one-fourth and one-third (25 to 35 percent) of your calories from these types of fat.

Some of you may worry that this range of fat is excessive. Let's face it, gram for gram, fats have double the calories of carbohydrates or proteins. But when added carefully to a heart-healthy eating plan, fats can help you feel full and satisfied, which may prevent overeating. Fats also provide a certain mouthfeel and palatability to meals that carbohydrates or proteins cannot. In addition, studies have shown that when fat is reduced too low, carbohydrate intake soars—and not usually in the form of whole grains. Finally, when patients know they can add a bit of healthy fat to meals and snacks, it is our experience that they feel less deprived and restricted, which results in long-term compliance.

Q: I've recently had bypass surgery, but have been told that some of my other coronary arteries show blockage. A friend told me that a very low fat diet was shown to reverse blockage. Is this true? If so, what is your opinion of these diets?

A: This is a very good question our patients often ask. Some data suggest that a plant-based, very low fat diet (about 10 percent total fat) is linked to reversal of coronary disease when incorporated with stress management, physical activity, and behavioral counseling. However, from our experience over thousands of patient-hours, we've found the plant-based guidelines described in this book to be the most successful and sustainable. We too place an emphasis on whole, un-refined plant foods and discourage the use of animal fats shown to promote heart disease. But we do not advocate severe restriction of all fat as a means to optimize cardiovascular health, especially if this risks an increase in triglycerides, drop in HDL, or essential fatty acid deficiency. Before you consider initiating a very low fat diet, talk with your physician and a registered dietitian.

Guidelines

We've covered a lot of ground regarding fats in this chapter. Following are some suggestions on incorporating our guidelines effortlessly into your daily lives.

1. Limit or eliminate your trans fat intake:
- Choose only foods labeled "trans free."
- Eliminate foods containing partially hydrogenated oil.
- Cut down on processed "junk" foods that are high in trans: fast foods (partic-ularly fried ones); cookies, pastries, and other baked goods; candy bars; and chocolate- or yogurt-coated treats.

2. Limit your saturated fat (and cholesterol) and substitute healthier options:
- Reduce your portions of high-fat cuts of meat, processed meats (e.g., hot dogs and sausage), and poultry skin and eat these foods less often.
- Substitute meatless meals, fish, seafood, or skinless poultry for fatty cuts of meat.
- Cut out butter, stick margarine, and lard. Replace with *trans*-free margarine, olive oil, or canola oil. Purchase only 1% or nonfat dairy foods. This includes milk, buttermilk, chocolate milk, half-and-half, ricotta cheese, sour cream, cot-tage cheese, processed and aged cheeses, and ice cream.
- Try egg whites and egg substitutes. They make excellent omelets. Use as a re-placement for whole eggs in most recipes.

- Limit foods, particularly snack foods, containing palm, palm kernel, or coconut oils.
- Select snack foods and frozen meals that contain no more than 2 grams of saturated fat per serving.

3. Add monounsaturated and polyunsaturated fats to your meals:
- Use canola or olive oil in cooking.
- Mix raw nuts or seeds into your favorite cereal, yogurt, salad, or stir-fry.
- Add a slice or two of fresh avocado to sandwiches.
- Mediterranean-ize a salad with a dash of olive oil and a good shake of vinegar and fresh herbs.
- Toss a few olives into a salad or use to garnish your plate.
- Stir ground flax seed into your morning oatmeal for a nutty-tasting treat.
- Make your own midday trail mix snack of a handful of mixed dried fruit and raw nuts.
- Enjoy two palm-sized portions of fish each week.
- Eat up to 5 ounces of nuts each week (1 ounce = $1/4$ cup of most nuts).

Adding a small amount of healthy fats can add flavor, zest, and satisfaction to your meals, but remember to be conscious of serving sizes. Take a look at the following list of recommended portion sizes and then refer to the plating guidelines in Chapter 2 to get an idea of where fat should fit on your plate.

Suggested Serving Sizes for Fats

Men can consume up to two servings, and women up to one serving of fat per meal. Snacks should include no more than one serving.

- Size of the tip of your thumb (1 teaspoon): olive oil, grapeseed oil, flaxseed oil, sesame oil, canola oil, peanut oil, soybean oil, regular mayonnaise
- Size of two thumb tips (2 teaspoons): regular *trans*-free margarine, tahini (sesame seed butter), peanut butter or other nut butter, creamy salad dressings
- Size of your whole thumb (1 tablespoon): light *trans*-free margarine; most nuts ($1/4$ to $1/2$ ounce)—almonds, walnuts, pecans, pistachios, peanuts, and macadamia nuts; ground or milled flax seed; most seeds ($1/2$ ounce)—sesame, pumpkin, and sunflower; oil-based salad dressing (made with olive or canola oil); nonfat or light mayonnaise (choose soy or canola based); light cream cheese; most olives (approximately 10 green olives, 6 black olives)

- Size of a golf ball (2 tablespoons): nonfat or light salad dressing; nonfat or light sour cream; nonfat or light whipped cream cheese; approximately 1/8 avocado

When you choose fats wisely, you can reap the health benefits and control your weight. Enjoy the additional flavor, texture, and fullness that fats have to offer as part of an overall heart-healthy eating plan. In the next chapter we'll discuss what protein foods to choose to stave off hunger, control your weight, and optimize your heart health.

The Right Mix of Protein

CHAPTER 6

Now that you understand which fats and carbohydrates can help prevent heart disease, let's explore how protein contributes to cardioprotection. Despite the commonly held belief that we don't get enough protein in our diets, the average healthy American is far from deficient. The problem is that most of us get too much of our protein from animal foods high in saturated and trans fats and not nearly enough from plant sources.

We've already explained that diets rich in saturated and trans fats promote high cholesterol and heart disease. Research indicates replacing high-fat animal foods with foods lower in saturated fat, like fish and poultry, can reduce blood cholesterol and the risk of heart disease. Replacing these fatty animal sources with plant protein foods can reduce the risk of developing heart disease even further.

It is hypothesized that the low–saturated fat and trans fat–free properties of plant foods, combined with their high dietary fiber, vitamins, minerals, and phytonutrients, provide the body with much-needed cardioprotection. People in regions of the world that enjoy low rates of heart disease don't consume the quantities of high-fat protein foods that Americans do. In fact, when people in these regions have adopted more affluent or Westernized dietary practices, the rates of obesity and heart disease have soared. This solidifies our resolve to cut back on high-fat animal foods and consume more whole, unprocessed plant foods.

Throughout this chapter we will challenge you to take a good look at how frequently you consume animal foods, specifically those high in saturated and trans fats. We'll also encourage you to modify the quantity of these foods that you consume at meals. Simply limiting how often you eat animal protein and how much can have positive effects on both your heart and your waistline. Combine these changes with adding more plant protein foods to your diet and the potential to protect your heart (and lose weight) is astounding.

What Protein Sources Are Best for My Heart?

The impact of proteins in heart disease progression has not been studied as extensively as that of fats or carbohydrates. We base our dietary guidelines on evidence from a number of novel studies conducted over the past few decades. The China Study, mentioned on page 57, indicates that protein derived from animals is directly linked to increases in blood cholesterol, heart disease, obesity, cancer, and other ailments. In addition to following a lower-fat diet than Americans, the Chinese in the study consumed just 10 percent of the amount of animal protein that Americans consume. Average cholesterol values in rural China were significantly lower than in the United States, while mortality from heart disease was more than 16 times greater for U.S. men and almost six times greater for U.S. women compared to their Chinese counterparts. Even after accounting for other diet and lifestyle factors, the authors concluded that animal protein was a significant contributor to these differences.

Studies have shown that substituting some plant protein for animal protein has cardiovascular merit. In a prospective trial conducted on postmenopausal women, those who consumed more red meat and dairy had a 40 percent higher risk of heart disease. When some vegetable protein (e.g., soy, legumes, greens, variety of vegetables) was substituted for animal sources, the risk of heart disease was reduced 30 percent.

PROTEIN Q & A

Q: What foods are the primary sources of protein?

A: The main source of protein in most Americans' diets is of animal origin. This includes beef, pork, lamb, chicken, duck, and turkey, as well as fish and shellfish. Animal protein sources also include milk, yogurt, cheese, and other dairy. The plant kingdom provides us with a host of flavorful protein sources, such as dried beans (black, kidney, garbanzo, navy), lentils, split peas, nuts, seeds, soy (which includes soymilk, soybeans, soy "nuts," soy cheese, textured soy protein, tempeh, and tofu), and wheat gluten (seitan). Vegetables and whole grains also contain protein, but to a smaller degree.

A healthy eating plan should be based on an abundance of nutrient-rich plant foods, particularly those derived from legumes, whole grains, fruits, leafy greens, and other colorful vegetables. This is not to say that chicken, fish, and beef have no role in a heart-healthy way of life. On the contrary, these foods do fit, just in a different proportion than we are used to.

Animal foods and plant foods differ in the types and proportions of amino acids that they contain. Amino acids are the biochemical building blocks of proteins, and it is speculated that some of the disease protection conferred by plant foods is due to their amino acid content.

Plant and animal foods differ not only in the number of calories they contain but also in their levels of saturated fat, cholesterol, fiber, and omega-3 fat. For example, skinless poultry and fish have fewer calories and saturated fat than some cuts of red meat and skin-on poultry. In addition, although fish isn't void of fat, it contains much larger proportions of heart-protective omega-3 fats than do red meat and poultry.

Foods derived from plants are nearly saturated fat free, chock-full of dietary fiber, and cholesterol free. In addition, soy, nuts, seeds, and beans provide heart-protective nutrients like magnesium, potassium, and folic acid, which will be discussed at greater length in Chapter 7, "Fruits, Vegetables, and Other Nutrients That Support a Healthy Heart." Now that you know the main differences among these protein foods, let's discuss how often each should be eaten to protect your heart.

How Often Should I Eat Red Meat and Other Proteins?

It's nice to be aware that certain plant foods and fish are healthier protein sources, but putting this knowledge into practice is another story. We've got the tools for putting your smarts into action with ten simple strategies. (The following guidelines assume that you will eat 21 meals—three meals a day—in a typical week.)

- *Work your way up.* Start by substituting a meatless meal using heart-protective beans, grains, legumes, nuts, seeds, or soy for one meal of red meat or chicken. Ideally, two-thirds of your weekly meals—14 in all—should come from plant foods. Use a high-fiber whole-grain breakfast as a way to bump up your plant protein, and try eating more meatless lunches during the workweek. Then slowly add more meatless dinners to your family's menu. To help you, we've included more than 21 meatless recipes!
- *Savor the flavors of a* minimum *of two meatless dinners each week.* You can choose more, but just make sure breakfast and lunch aren't your only meatless meals in a given week. Dinner is often the only time we commune with our families.

By making at least two family dinners meatless, you will encourage your children and significant other to try new foods, tastes, and textures as well as to eat foods that contain cardioprotective nutrients.

- *Bump up your omega-3s by enjoying two or more meals containing fatty fish each week.* No trimming of the fat necessary—with fish, if you trim the fat you'll lose those heart-healthy omega-3s. Enjoy a variety of 3- to 4-ounce portions of fish such as mackerel, salmon, tuna steaks, anchovies, herring, or sardines. Because of safety concerns regarding mercury in farmed fish, we highly recommend buying wild fish varieties when possible. In addition, if you are pregnant, lactating, very young, very old, or have a weakened immune system, you should limit species with potentially high mercury levels: king mackerel, shark, swordfish, and tilefish.

- *Enjoy two to three skinless poultry (white meat) meals each week.* Monday through Friday meals shouldn't read "chicken, chicken, chicken." Too often in our attempts to improve our heart health, we rely on chicken for every meal. Enjoy the variety of dishes to which you can add chicken, but don't go overboard. Use it, like other animal foods, as an accompaniment to the wonderful flavors and textures of vegetables and whole grains.

- *Substitute poultry, fish, or plant foods for red meat,* aiming for no more than one meal containing red meat in a week. If you currently eat red meat seven meals a week, cut down to five for a while, slowly weaning yourself. Cutting down on red meat is another great way to trim calories.

- *Look for lean.* When it comes to meats, poultry, seafood, and game, choosing lean isn't as tough as you might think, thanks to the specific definitions of *lean* set by the Food and Drug Administration (FDA).

  Lean: Less than 10 grams of total fat, less than 4.5 grams saturated fat, and less than 95 milligrams of cholesterol per 3.5-ounce serving.

  Extra lean: Less than 5 grams of total fat, less than 2 grams saturated fat, and less than 95 milligrams of cholesterol per 3.5-ounce serving. Most loin cuts (sirloin, tenderloin) from pork or beef are generally leaner than others. Eye of round, bottom round, flank, and filets are also leaner cuts.

  95% lean: This means that 5 percent of the weight is from fat. Avoid 80% and 85% lean—too high for heart-healthy eating.

- *Don't assume all turkey (or chicken) products, like turkey bacon, sausage, hot dogs, or ground turkey, are lean.* In fact, many ground turkey and turkey bacon products are just as high in fat as beef or pork varieties. Make sure you compare the saturated fat content of these foods when shopping and choose the leanest.

- *Remove the skin from poultry and trim visible fat.* Don't forget to watch that portion size. A serving size is the size of your palm. This equals 3 to 4 ounces for most people, all you need at one meal.

- *Choose nonfat (skim) or 1% dairy.* Trim excess calories and saturated fat by choosing nonfat (skim) or 1% milk or chocolate milk, plain or fruited yogurt, and cottage cheese.
- *Say cheese infrequently.* There are a variety of nonfat cheese products on the market that taste good and melt better than their fat-free predecessors. If fat-free cheese isn't appealing to you, choose 2%, reduced-fat, or low-fat versions. Limit full-fat cheese to one meal a week. Instead of adding more saturated fat to a meat meal, enjoy cheese when you go meatless, such as sprinkling 2% shredded Cheddar cheese on meatless chili. If you want to totally cut the saturated fat and cholesterol from cheese, try using soy or rice cheeses instead. Some are excellent alternatives to dairy.

Confused over what a meatless meal looks like? Here are a few suggestions.

- Try a meatless chili by adding more beans or substituting vegetable (soy) crumbles (available in the frozen food section of grocery stores) for ground meat.
- Make a vegetarian lasagna filled with colorful vegetables like spinach, broccoli, carrots, yellow squash, and mushrooms. You can even crumble tofu in place of the ricotta cheese for a twist on the old favorite.
- Enjoy split pea soup without the ham.
- Top your favorite salad with rinsed and drained canned beans like garbanzo (chickpeas), black, kidney, or navy.
- In the mood for a burger? You can eat one guilt free when you try one of the many meatless bean, soy, veggie, or grain-based burgers available in the frozen food and produce sections of your grocer. Top with lettuce, tomatoes, onions, pickles, and some zesty mustard for a flavor-filled treat.
- Love tacos and burritos? Fill your favorite with lettuce, tomato, cilantro-infused brown rice, salsa, reduced-fat cheese, and a dollop of fat-free refried beans for a tasty meat alternative.
- Stir crazy? Try a stir-fry loaded with fresh, crisp vegetables and tossed with some crunchy peanuts for a meatless masterpiece.

Where Does Soy Protein Fit In?

Another benefit of adding more meatless meals to your weekly eating plan: soy foods. What is so great about soy? In addition to being low in saturated fat and cholesterol free, soy appears to have cholesterol-lowering properties. Although researchers haven't agreed if it's the protein in soy or other nutrients that confer heart protection, they've found that, when added to a diet low in saturated fat and cholesterol, soy can help lower cholesterol by an additional 3 percent on average.

Soy foods like tofu, soy nuts (roasted soybeans), edamame, and textured soy protein come from the soybean, a legume that offers high-quality protein second in value only to the protein we get from animal foods. Like other legumes, soy is also a good source of the fiber and B vitamins essential to a healthy heart. What's more, many soy foods are fortified with additional vitamins and minerals, such as calcium and vitamins D and B_{12}, an advantage if you're not getting adequate amounts in your diet.

Just how much soy do you need to eat to reduce cholesterol? Research indicates that four servings of at least 6.25 grams of soy protein (for a total of 25 grams) must be eaten each day to lower cholesterol. The following table shows the protein found in many common soy foods.

Soy Food	Serving Size	Soy Protein (grams)
Water-packed tofu	3 ounces	8.5
Silken firm tofu	3 ounces	6.0
Plain soymilk	8 ounces	8.0
Vanilla soymilk	8 ounces	6.0
Soy nuts, dry roasted	1/4 cup (1 ounce)	12.0
Soy nut butter	2 tablespoons	8.0
Soy crumbles	1/2 cup (2 ounces)	9.0
Soy burger	1	10.0
Soy breakfast sausage	2 links or 1 patty	6.5
Tempeh	1/2 cup (4 ounces)	16.0
Cooked or canned soybeans	1/2 cup	13.0
Green soybeans (edamame)	1/2 cup	7.0
Black soybeans	1/2 cup	9.0
Textured soy protein	1/4 cup	8.0

Since we've already challenged you to cut some of the excess animal protein from your eating plan, why not try soy? Here are some simple tips:

- Pour calcium-fortified soymilk over cereal for breakfast.
- Sip a cup of warmed chocolate soymilk for a hot chocolate treat.
- Toss firm tofu into your favorite stir-fry.
- Try soy yogurt or soy puddings for a healthy snack.
- Mix together ice cubes, soymilk, and fresh fruit for a tasty smoothie treat.
- Make a healthy trail mix of roasted soy nuts and dried fruit.
- Spread some soy nut butter on whole-grain toast instead of peanut butter.
- Use textured soy protein (also called vegetable crumbles) instead of ground beef in dishes like chili or spaghetti sauce.
- Replace ricotta cheese with silken tofu in stuffed shells or lasagna.
- Substitute soy-based sausage for high-fat pork or beef sausage at breakfast.
- Enjoy edamame (green soybeans in the pods) as a refreshing appetizer like the Japanese do—and try our yummy Edamame Hummus on page 132.
- Try a soy-based burger instead of a hamburger—top it with your favorite veggies and condiments and you won't miss the meat.

Check out our vegetarian recipes starting on page 179 and try some of the tasty dishes where we incorporate various forms of soy. You'll be pleasantly surprised.

SOY Q & A

Q: Should everyone add soy to his or her diet? What about soy supplements?

A: In addition to soy's cholesterol-lowering potential, it's also an excellent source of biologically active components collectively called phytoestrogens. Phytoestrogens act like weak estrogens in the body and have been studied for their potential to relieve hot flashes in perimenopausal women. The impact of soy phytoestrogens on breast cancer prevention also has been studied. Soy has been linked to protection against breast cancer in some women. If you have a personal or family history of breast cancer, we advise that you speak with your physician first before adding large quantities of soy to your eating plan.

We discourage the use of soy supplements and powders as part of a heart-healthy diet. Isolating protein or other attributes of the soybean (e.g., isoflavones) has been studied, but efficacy and safety have not been confirmed. You'll derive greater health benefits by eating whole, less-processed soy foods (such as soybeans, soy nuts, edamame, tofu, soymilk). The sum of the soybean's nutritional parts (dietary fiber, phytoestrogens, vitamins, minerals, and protein) appear to confer greater health benefits than individual components.

As you can see, there are unlimited ways to enjoy protein in your diet—and it doesn't all have to come from chicken or beef! Overall, we encourage you to cut down on the frequency of high-fat meat and dairy and reduce your portion size when you do eat these foods. These changes may be easier to implement if you consider placing your protein foods into "anytime," "sometimes," and "rarely" categories:

- "Anytime" protein foods are plant sources like vegetables, legumes, beans, nuts, seeds, and soy. (However, soy may not be recommended as an anytime food for everyone; check with your physician first if you have a history of breast cancer.)
- "Sometimes" protein foods include fish, skinless poultry, and low-fat or nonfat dairy foods. A few servings of each per week is a great heart-healthy strategy.
- "Rarely" foods include meat, full-fat dairy, and regular cheese. These foods can be consumed once a week.

Building a heart-healthy foundation does not mean you have to eliminate animal foods altogether; just balance their intake with more plant foods. Gradually add these plant protein sources at your own pace. Even if substituting one meatless meal a week is all you can do right now, your heart can still benefit. You'll soon realize that cutting down on meat really isn't a chore. In fact, based on our experience with patients, most people tend to prefer it, perhaps because they begin to feel healthier.

Fruits, Vegetables, and Other Nutrients That Support a Healthy Heart

CHAPTER 7

You're probably thinking, "What else could I possibly learn about fruits and vegetables that I don't already know? Mom always told me that a colorful meal was a healthy meal." Although most people know this to be true, they still aren't following Mom's advice. Overall, less than a quarter of Americans meet the minimum five servings of fruits and vegetables previously recommended by nutrition and health experts.

In fact, the link between consumption of fruits and vegetables and a reduced risk for heart disease, cancer, and other ailments is so strong that it prompted a revision to the 2005 Dietary Guidelines for Americans (the U.S. Departments of Agriculture and Health and Human Services), which now recommend between 5 and 13 servings a day. For the average person, this would mean 4 1/2 cups a day. If you don't count potatoes—which are considered in our "unrefined carbohydrate" category—the average American consumes a daily total of only three servings of fruits and vegetables, or 1 1/2 cups. When you see just how powerful these foods can be, you'll realize that three daily servings won't get you very far if you want to improve your heart health or lose weight.

Throughout this chapter we'll unveil the powerful protective nature of whole foods—specifically fruits, vegetables, and legumes. We'll go a step further by including vitamins, minerals, and phytonutrients—and why they are absolutely vital to heart protection.

Fruits, Veggies, and Your Heart

Over the past three to four decades, researchers have unleashed a lot of information on the health benefits of fruits and vegetables. Where your heart is concerned, these advantages became clear:

- *Lower risk of developing heart disease.* Results from two studies that followed more than 110,000 healthy men and women for 14 years indicate that those who consumed the most fruits and vegetables had the lowest chance of developing cardiovascular disease. Compared to those who consumed the fewest fruits and vegetables (less than 1.5 servings a day), those who averaged eight or more servings a day were 30 percent less likely to have a heart attack or stroke. In fact, increasing fruit and vegetable intake by as little as one serving a day can reduce the risk of heart disease by 4 percent. A large part of the protection was attributed to dark leafy green vegetables like kale, spinach, collard greens, Brussels sprouts, broccoli, and bok choy, as well as vitamin C–rich citrus fruits such as limes, lemons, oranges, and grapefruit.
- *Greater reduction in risk for those with diabetes.* In this same study, among those with diabetes, every additional serving of fruit or vegetable resulted in a 10 percent (men) and 7 percent (women) lower relative risk of heart disease.
- *Lower risk of dying from heart disease.* A large Finnish study reported similar findings on the benefits of eating more fruits and vegetables. Subjects who consumed the most vegetables had a 44 percent lower risk of dying from heart disease than those who ate few vegetables. Higher fruit consumption produced similar results: a risk reduction of 44 percent in women and 33 percent in men.
- *Reduced risk of stroke.* In a study following more than 800 middle-aged healthy men for 20 years, every increment of three daily servings of fruits and vegetables equated to a 22 percent reduction in risk of stroke.
- *Lower blood pressure.* The DASH (Dietary Approaches to Stop Hypertension) study measured blood pressure responses to a diet low in saturated fat and rich in fruits, vegetables, and low-fat dairy products. People with high blood pressure who followed this diet reduced their systolic blood pressure (the top number of a blood pressure reading) by about 11 mmHg and their diastolic blood pressure (the lower number) by almost 6 mmHg. Blood pressure was previously lowered to this degree only with medication—highlighting the powerful protective benefit of a diet rich in fruits and vegetables.
- *Lower cholesterol.* The DASH study also highlighted the cholesterol-lowering property of a high fruit and vegetable intake. A study conducted by the National Heart, Lung, and Blood Institute on more than 4,400 people found that when compared to those who consumed few fruits and vegetables, men and women who consumed the highest amount (around 4 servings a day) had the lowest cholesterol. Just imagine the potential cholesterol-lowering impact the actual recommended servings (5 to 13) could have!
- *Improved nutritional profile.* A recent study compared the effects of a typical "low-fat" diet that included more processed convenience foods to a diet similar in fat that included no convenience foods but more whole, unprocessed

fruits and vegetables. As was suspected, a greater cholesterol-lowering response was seen in the group that included more unrefined foods. Not only did the participants experience lower cholesterol, their overall dietary intake of nutrients like fiber, beta-carotene, vitamin C, vitamin E, and folate was much greater than that of the "low-fat" dieters. What's more, the whole-foods group consumed five times more vegetables, one and a half times more fruit, four times more legumes, half as much red meat, and three and a half times more whole grains than the convenience-foods group—all key cardioprotective strategies we've been espousing throughout this book.

The research on the value of a diet rich in fruits and vegetables to manage weight is vast. Here's why and how fruits and vegetables help with weight control:

- *High nutrient density, low energy density.* Fruits and vegetables are low calorie and nutrient packed. Gram for gram, no other foods on the planet provide so many nutrients in so few calories. A serving of fruit contains 60 calories, while a vegetable serving has only 25.
- *High water content.* Research shows that around 15 percent fewer calories are consumed at a meal following a vegetable-rich salad starter. Beginning a meal or enjoying a snack with these water-filled wonders will help curb your hunger and control your cravings.
- *Fiber boost.* In addition to helping you feel satisfied and free of hunger, fruits and vegetables are a great source of dietary fiber, which has been shown repeatedly to aid in weight control.
- *Protein for hunger control.* A small amount of protein at meals and snacks can also help in the battle of the bulge. Soy foods and starchy vegetables like legumes are excellent sources of plant protein and a great way to boost your overall nutrients. Although legumes and soy fit more into the lean protein category of our plating guidelines (because they often substitute for meat in a meatless meal), they still are a great way to cut calories and enjoy the health benefits of the bounty of vitamins, minerals, and phytonutrients found in vegetables.

How Much Is Enough?

To answer that question, we recommend the following servings of fruits and vegetables each day:

- *Women:* Caloric needs vary based on age, activity level, and current weight. With that in mind, most women should consume a minimum of three closed-fist portions of fruit, half of a closed-fist portion of legumes, and at least four closed-fist portions of vegetables daily. This equates to approximately 7 to 8 cups of fruits and vegetables each day.

- **Men:** Keeping in mind that caloric needs vary, most men should consume a minimum of three closed-fist portions of fruit, half of a closed-fist portion of legumes, and at least three closed-fist portions of vegetables each day. This equates to approximately 8 to 9 cups of fruits and vegetables each day.

Like unrefined whole grains, fruits and vegetables are a good source of dietary fiber. Therefore, make sure you drink adequate fluids to facilitate proper digestion and avoid constipation, which can occur if you increase your fiber without increasing your fluids.

Vitamins and Minerals That Support a Healthy Heart

The health benefits of a diet rich in fruits and vegetables don't stop at dietary fiber. In fact, research shows that fiber coming from whole grains offers the greatest benefits. When it comes to fruits and vegetables, fiber still counts, but the most significant health benefits come from their high vitamin, mineral, and phytonutrient (also called phytochemical) content.

To understand the role vitamins and minerals play in heart health, it's first important to define what they are. Vitamins are complex chemical substances found in foods that are essential to the proper functioning of the body. They help regulate metabolism, support the conversion of fat and carbohydrates into energy, and assist in bone and tissue formation.

Minerals are another important class of micronutrients occurring abundantly in nature. Minerals help regulate a number of processes in the body, such as muscle contractions, fluid balance, and nerve impulses.

The following list highlights vitamins and minerals that are key players in the fight against heart disease. (Note: *DRI* stands for daily Dietary Reference Intakes for most healthy people.)

Vitamins

FOLATE (FOLIC ACID)

Why it's important: A water-soluble B vitamin, folate occurs naturally in a variety of foods (folic acid is the synthetic form). Folate has been shown to lower homocysteine, an amino acid that is linked to increased cardiovascular disease. Folate appears to offer the greatest protection against heart disease early in life, in adolescence, when the development of atherosclerosis first begins.

Although it was once believed that the homocysteine-lowering effect of folate, along with vitamins B_6 and B_{12}, would improve outcomes in patients with coronary disease, this has not been borne out in recent research. If you have undergone stent placement or angioplasty, it is important to individualize your folate needs with your physician and dietitian.

DRI: Men and women, 400 micrograms a day; the upper limit is set at 1,000 micrograms (or 1 milligram) daily. For those with high homocysteine, 800 to 1,000 micrograms of folic acid is generally recommended. Since adequate folate is so important in preventing neural tube defects in infants, all women of childbearing age should ensure that they receive at least the minimum DRI for folate.

Good food sources: Dark leafy green vegetables (spinach, kale, broccoli), asparagus, citrus fruit, bananas, melons, legumes, mushrooms, and fortified whole grains. (But be aware: If you take blood thinners such as Coumadin, you'll need to limit your intake of vitamin K–rich foods like dark leafy greens. Consult with your physician or dietitian.)

Take-home message: Choose whole foods first. If your doctor prescribes a folic acid supplement for lowering homocysteine, still include good food sources because these contain other heart-protective nutrients.

VITAMIN B_6 (PYRIDOXINE)

Why it's important: Vitamin B_6 often is used in conjunction with folate and vitamin B_{12} to lower blood homocysteine. Low pyridoxine levels have also been associated with increased C-reactive protein (CRP), an inflammatory marker linked to increased risk of heart disease.

DRI: Men, 1.3 milligrams (19–50 years), 1.7 milligrams (50+ years); women, 1.3 milligrams (19–50 years), 1.5 milligrams (50+ years).

Good food sources: Whole grains, beans, vegetables (carrots, peas, dark leafy greens like spinach), fish, chicken, beef, milk, cheese, and eggs.

Take-home message: Choose whole-food sources of B_6 first. If your doctor prescribes a supplemental form of B_6 (along with folic acid and B_{12}) for lowering homocysteine, still include good food sources because they provide your body with additional heart-protective nutrients.

VITAMIN B_{12} (COBALAMIN)

Why it's important: Vitamin B_{12} is commonly used along with folate and vitamin B_6 to help lower homocysteine levels. Some research suggests that folic acid and vitamin B_{12} supplementation after angioplasty or coronary stenting may promote restenosis. In both instances, supplementation is not recommended. More research is needed in this area.

Although deficiency is rare (B_{12} is stored in the body for years), B_{12} absorption can become limited in the elderly or in those who have undergone gastric surgery. In addition, vegans who do not properly supplement with fortified foods can become deficient. A deficiency in B$_{12}$ results in what is called pernicious anemia. Supplementation may be necessary, and you should consult your physician.

DRI: Men and women, 2.4 milligrams a day.

Good food sources: Fish, chicken, beef, cheese, yogurt, milk, eggs, and fortified foods (e.g., soymilk).

Take-home message: Choose whole-food sources of B$_{12}$ first. If your doctor prescribes a supplemental form of B$_{12}$ (along with folic acid and B$_6$) for lowering homocysteine, still include good food sources because they provide your body with additional heart-protective nutrients. If you are vegetarian, choose foods fortified with vitamin B$_{12}$ (e.g., soymilk, tofu, tempeh, or nutritional yeast) since it is found only in animal foods.

NIACIN (VITAMIN B$_3$)

Why it's important: In supplemental form, niacin has been shown to raise the "good" HDL cholesterol more than some cholesterol-lowering drugs. What's more, supplemental niacin can lower the "bad" LDL cholesterol, although not as effectively as other cholesterol-lowering medications. Because of its ability to raise HDL cholesterol, niacin is often used in conjunction with some lipid-lowering medications, like statins. However, don't run to the nearest health food store to buy those niacin supplements just yet—an excess of this B vitamin can cause flushed skin, rashes, or even liver damage. In addition, because of its potential to raise blood sugars, niacin supplementation may be contraindicated for persons with type 2 diabetes. Always check with your physician first.

DRI: Men and women, 16–18 milligrams per day. To lower cholesterol, supplementation generally ranges from 1 to 3 grams per day (1,000–3,000 milligrams). Extended-release niacin prescriptions are available and may reduce side effects commonly experienced with some over-the-counter niacin supplements. Always talk with your physician first before you consider taking extra niacin.

Good food sources: Foods high in protein are generally good sources of niacin: poultry, fish, beef, peanut butter, and legumes. Some foods are also fortified with niacin.

Take-home message: You guessed it: choose whole foods. Few people are deficient in niacin. Supplement only when directed by your doctor.

VITAMIN C (ASCORBIC ACID)

Why it's important: As a potent antioxidant (see Q&A, page 97), vitamin C was believed to help prevent the oxidation of LDL cholesterol on arterial walls. However, a large body of evidence indicates that supplementing with vitamin C alone does not prevent heart disease.

DRI: Men, 90 milligrams a day; women, 75 milligrams a day. The upper limit is 2,000 milligrams a day.

Good food sources: Citrus fruits and their juices, berries, dark green vegetables (spinach, asparagus, green peppers, Brussels sprouts, broccoli, watercress, other greens), red and yellow peppers, tomatoes and tomato juice, pineapple, cantaloupe, mangos, papaya, and guava.

Take-home message: Evidence from large population studies links diets of whole foods high in vitamin C, such as fruits and vegetables, to a reduced risk of heart disease. Choose vitamin C–rich foods first!

VITAMIN E (ALPHA-TOCOPHEROL)

Why it's important: Like vitamin C, vitamin E is a long-revered antioxidant thought to reduce oxidation of LDL cholesterol. Vitamin E exists in eight different forms, of which alpha-tocopherol is the most active in the body. Evidence from large population studies suggested that vitamin E supplementation might be associated with reduced risk of developing cardiovascular disease. However, a series of clinical trials using vitamin E supplements failed to show any protection. In fact, some data now suggest that supplementing with vitamin E may actually do more harm than good. More research is needed in this area. As with folate, it may be that the greatest benefit is derived from adequate intake of vitamin E early in the atherosclerotic process. Again, more research is needed.

DRI: Men and women, 15 milligrams a day (22.5 International Units, or IU).

Good food sources: Vegetable oils (e.g., olive, canola, peanut), salad dressings, nuts, seeds, unrefined whole grains, wheat germ, flax seed, legumes, and dark leafy green vegetables.

Take-home message: Choose a variety of vitamin E–rich food sources and avoid supplementation unless specified by your physician for health reasons.

BETA-CAROTENE (A FORM OF VITAMIN A)

Why it's important: Beta-carotene, a member the carotenoid family, is converted to active vitamin A in the body. Just as observational data once linked diets rich in vitamin C to a lower risk of cardiovascular disease, so did some studies suggest the same was true of beta-carotene. But intervention trials—studies in which beta-carotene was added to the diet—have shown no apparent benefit. In addition, in susceptible individuals (e.g., smokers), supplementation of beta-carotene resulted in an increased risk of developing lung cancer. Supplementation is therefore highly discouraged.

DRI: No DRI has been established for beta-carotene. DRI for vitamin A: 900 micrograms a day for men; 700 micrograms a day for women.

Good food sources: Look for dark pigmented red, orange, or green fruits and vegetables like sweet potatoes, squash, carrots, red pepper, green pepper, apricots, spinach, and kale.

Take-home message: Choose brightly colored fruits and vegetables as your main defense; never exceed the DRI for vitamin A unless indicated by your physician.

Minerals

POTASSIUM

Why it's important: Adequate dietary potassium is necessary for normal blood pressure and heart muscle contraction. If you take a diuretic, you may or may not need additional potassium in your diet (some diuretics spare the loss of potassium, so always check with your physician first).

DRI: Although there is no DRI for potassium, an adequate intake level established by the Institute for Medicine is 4,700 milligrams, or 4.7 grams a day. Most health care practitioners recommend at least 3,500 milligrams each day from a variety of foods for optimal blood pressure control.

Good food sources: Dried fruits, bananas, strawberries, orange juice, apricot juice, prune juice, watermelon, cantaloupe, dark leafy greens, tomatoes, mushrooms, dried peas, beans, potatoes, chicken, beef, and fish.

Take-home message: Pills just don't cut it when it comes to blood pressure control. Remember the DASH diet described earlier in this chapter? Food sources of potassium, in addition to adequate magnesium and calcium, showed the greatest blood pressure–lowering benefit. If you are on a diuretic, check with your physician before taking any supplements.

MAGNESIUM

Why it's important: Just like potassium, adequate dietary magnesium is essential for normal blood pressure and heart rhythm.

DRI: Men, 400 milligrams a day (19–30 years), 430 milligrams a day (31+ years); women, 310 milligrams a day (19–30 years), 320 milligrams a day (31+ years).

Good food sources: Green leafy vegetables (spinach, kale), parsnips, nuts (pecans, almonds, Brazil nuts), whole grains (whole wheat bread, whole wheat pasta), dried beans and peas.

Take-home message: You've got it—food sources always first!

CALCIUM

Why it's important: Along with potassium and magnesium from whole grains, fruits, and vegetables, adequate calcium from low-fat dairy or other plant-based foods is associated with lower blood pressure.

DRI: Men and women, 1,000 milligrams a day (19–50 years), 1,200 milligrams a day (51+ years).

Good food sources: Low-fat or nonfat milk or yogurt; calcium-fortified orange juice, soymilk, or rice milk; reduced-fat cheese; salmon canned with edible bones; dark leafy green vegetables; Chinese cabbage; broccoli.

Take-home message: As part of a heart-healthy diet, increase your plant sources of calcium and consume nonfat or low-fat dairy foods. Calcium supplements may be necessary for other reasons, such as bone health. Consult with your physician.

CALCIUM Q&A

Q: I'm not really a fan of milk, but have been told that I should drink milk because it's a good source of calcium. Is it true that I need three glasses of milk each day to get the calcium I need to keep my bones strong?

A: The current dietary reference intake for calcium in adults 19 to 50 years of age is 1,000 milligrams per day, and 1,200 milligrams for those over 50. We recommend a variety of foods to get adequate calcium in your diet. If milk is your food of choice, then that is fine, as long as you choose 1% or skim. The same goes for other dairy foods; they should be reduced in fat or nonfat. But many foods in addition to milk and dairy are good sources of calcium. What's more, many of these foods, such as sardines, almonds, and kale, are also great sources of healthy fats and phytonutrients. To help reach your daily goal, incorporate the following foods in your eating plan on a regular basis.

Food	Serving Size	Calcium (in mg)
Tofu set in calcium	4 ounces	775
Calcium citrate (Citracal)	2 caplets	630
Lactaid with added calcium (for lactose intolerant)	8 ounces	550
Enriched soy yogurt	6 ounces	500
Canned sardines with bones	3.25 ounces	351
Skim or 1% milk	8 ounces	300–350
Enriched soy or rice milk	8 ounces	295–300
2% Cheddar cheese	1.5 ounces	300
Nonfat yogurt	6 ounces	260
Canned salmon with bones	3 ounces	211
Low-fat cottage cheese with added calcium	1/2 cup	200
Kale, raw	1 cup	90
Broccoli, steamed	1 cup	75
Almonds	1 ounce	70

Nutrition data derived from Food Processor for Windows, version 8.6.0, ESHA Research, Salem, Oregon.

SELENIUM

Why it's important: Like vitamins C and E, selenium is a potent antioxidant, once thought to prevent heart disease. As with the clinical trials conducted on vitamins C and E, however, intervention trials have failed to make the same association. Some people argue that selenium supplementation is necessary because the selenium content in our soil has been depleted.

DRI: Men and women, 55 micrograms per day.

Good food sources: Seafood, liver, kidney and other meats, nuts, whole grains, fruits, and vegetables.

Take-home message: High levels of supplemental selenium can be harmful, and few people have selenium deficiency. Eating a variety of fruits, vegetables, nuts, and whole grains, along with seafood, should ensure adequate intake.

ANTIOXIDANTS Q&A

Q: Why are antioxidant-rich foods so important to my heart?

A: Every cell in the body needs a constant supply of oxygen to produce energy. When these cells burn oxygen for energy, they release an oxygen by-product called a free radical. If not controlled, free radicals cause a chain reaction of damage that wreaks havoc on the body's cells, tissue, and DNA. In addition to normal body processes, environmental toxins like cigarette smoke, exhaust, and ultraviolet light can also contribute to free radical damage in your body. The destruction caused by free radicals is called oxidation, and it can lead to a variety of ailments, including cancer, aging, cataracts, arthritis, and heart disease. In heart disease, it is believed that oxidation of LDL cholesterol starts the process that forms plaque in our arteries. It would make sense then, that if we stopped oxidation of LDL from occurring in the first place we would, in effect, prevent atherosclerosis (hardening of the arteries that leads to a heart attack or stroke). Certain vitamins and minerals—including vitamins C and E, selenium, beta-carotene, lycopene, zinc, copper, and many others—are called antioxidants because they help to neutralize free radicals—basically stopping them in their tracks. What's more, these antioxidants work best together, often regenerating one another after they have neutralized the free radicals.

Unfortunately, research looking at antioxidant supplementation hasn't been as promising as once thought. Studies looking at diet patterns (such as our Healthy Eating Guidelines) rich in fruits, vegetables, whole grains, nuts, and legumes indicate that dietary forms of these potent antioxidants are probably our best choice in the fight against heart disease. What's more, phytonutrients are also powerful antioxidants that may work alongside vitamins and minerals to protect us from disease. No supplement on the market can give you nearly the power that whole foods can!

WHERE DOES SODIUM FIT IN?

Sodium is another electrolyte that plays a role in heart health. While sodium is necessary for the proper functioning of the beating heart, as a whole, Americans greatly exceed the amount necessary for this function. Excess sodium in the diet (also referred to as salt because table salt is 40 percent sodium by weight) raises the chance of developing high blood pressure; it can also cause people to retain water and has severe implications in individuals with heart failure. What's more, a diet high in sodium is likely a diet that is highly refined, filled with convenience foods, and low in fruits, vegetables, and other cardioprotective foods. You should limit your daily sodium intake to 2,300 milligrams a day, which can be achieved easily if you follow the eating guidelines in this book (current recommendations for people with heart failure generally limit sodium to 2,000 milligrams a day). We strive to keep our recipes under 600 milligrams of sodium per serving and have achieved this in almost every dish. To help keep your sodium intake in check, follow these tips and strategies.

- Look for foods labeled:
  Sodium-free: less than 5 milligrams of sodium per serving
  Very low sodium: 35 milligrams or less per serving
  Low-sodium: 140 milligrams or less per serving
  Reduced-sodium: sodium level is reduced by 25 percent
  Unsalted, no salt added, or without added salt: made without added salt, but will contain any sodium that is naturally found in the food
  Healthy: by law, foods labeled "healthy" must not exceed 360 milligrams sodium per reference amount (read: serving size). "Meal type" products (e.g., frozen entrées) must not exceed 480 mg sodium per reference amount.
- Cut back on boxed, bottled, and canned foods, which are generally higher in sodium. Choose fresh, frozen, or canned foods made without added salt.
- Avoid adding salt in recipes and use only when necessary (e.g., to control yeast in a bread dough recipe).
- Use no-salt-added or reduced-sodium beef, chicken, and vegetable broths for cooking.
- Never, ever use the salt shaker at the table. Use spices and herbs to enhance the flavor of foods instead.
- Cut down on fast foods and restaurant foods, which are high in sodium. When dining out, ask the chef not to add salt to your meal.
- Limit luncheon meats, cured meats, and most cheeses and choose reduced-sodium versions when available.
- Limit salty snacks, like chips and pretzels.
- Purchase unsalted crackers, nuts, and other snack foods.

Phytonutrients

Although they sound complicated, phytonutrients (or phytochemicals) are simply plant nutrients—*phyto* is a Greek word for plant. Although referred to as nutrients, phytonutrients are not essential for human survival like carbohydrates, fats, proteins, water, vitamins, and minerals. When it comes to optimizing the health of your heart, we strongly believe that plant compounds are an essential part of the diet. Here's why, without getting technical. Phytonutrients are chemicals that help protect plants from infestation (e.g., animals and insects), viruses, harsh weather conditions, handling, and oxygen by-products (free radicals). For example, the pungent aroma in garlic and onions protects the plant because these sulfur-containing compounds are offensive when animals or insects bite them. In addition to pungent, strong flavors, phytonutrients lend plants a rainbow range of brilliant colors—dark reds, bright yellow, deep greens and purples, navy blues, and vibrant orange. These chemicals provide us with defense against disease just as they do for plants—especially when it comes to free radical damage!

Are phytonutrients found only in brilliantly colored fruits and vegetables? The latest news is that whole grains, while not nearly as colorful as fruits and vegetables or legumes, hold phytonutrients in their cell walls, which are absorbed by bacteria in our intestines. These whole-grain phytonutrients also hold a lot of promise in prevention of heart disease and may be another reason whole grains are so closely linked to a healthier heart.

Research on phytonutrients continues to evolve, and in years to come it is likely that more of these plant compounds will be identified. Three major phytonutrient categories have been linked to heart protection.

POLYPHENOLS (FLAVONOIDS)

Polyphenolic compounds are natural components in a wide variety of plants. Flavonoids are one such polyphenolic compound with diverse chemical structures present in fruits, vegetables, nuts, and seeds. The most-studied foods within this category are tea, onions, wine, soy, and cocoa. Flavonoids have been shown to promote a healthy heart by exuding antioxidant power, reducing platelet aggregation and adhesion in the arteries, relaxing and dilating the arteries, lowering cholesterol, and reducing blood pressure.

Procyanidins in chocolate, quercetin in onions, phenolics in wine, and isoflavones in soy are just a few of the specific terms for phytonutrients in these plant foods.

CHOCOLATE Q&A

Q: Is it true that chocolate can protect my heart? I thought chocolate wasn't healthy.

A: Flavonoid phytonutrients in chocolate have been studied extensively. Research on humans has indicated that flavonoids in cocoa and dark chocolate may benefit the heart in a number of ways. They may:

- Reduce platelet activation, similar to aspirin, which prevents blood from clotting
- Relax blood vessels

- Positively affect the balance of hormonelike compounds called eicosanoids, thought to play a role in cardiovascular health
- Reduce blood pressure in a small number of individuals

Before you grab a chocolate candy bar or slice of chocolate cake, let's look at what forms of chocolate we're talking about.

- When cocoa is processed into your favorite chocolate products, it goes through several steps to moderate its naturally pungent taste (which comes from the flavonoids). The more chocolate is processed (including fermentation, alkalizing, roasting), the more flavonoids are lost. Most commercially available chocolates fit this category.
- Dark chocolate appears to retain the highest level of flavonoids. So your best bet is to choose dark chocolate over milk chocolate. Cocoa powder that has not been alkalized is another good choice.
- Some chocolate manufacturers have come up with ways to retain the highest level of flavonoids while still providing acceptable taste. Their products are generally found in chocolate bars or snack foods. Look for products that are labeled for containing/retaining these natural compounds.

The fat in chocolate, from cocoa butter, is composed of equal amounts of oleic acid (a monounsaturated fat), stearic acid, and palmitic acid. Stearic and palmitic acids are forms of saturated fat. Research indicates that stearic acid has a neutral effect on blood cholesterol, neither raising nor lowering it. Palmitic acid, on the other hand, does affect cholesterol levels but accounts for only one-third of the fat calories in chocolate. Although this is great news, it still doesn't give us license to consume as much dark chocolate as we'd like. First, be cautious about the type of dark chocolate you choose: caramel, marshmallow, or creamy fillings covered in chocolate are by no means heart-healthy food. What makes chocolate products less healthy are all of these additional ingredients. Second, the serving size of chocolate needed to reap these cardiovascular benefits has not been established. A little dark chocolate once in a while is okay, but keep in mind that 1 ounce of dark chocolate has more than 150 calories. Since most of us have a hard time limiting our serving size, keep an eye on how frequently you consume chocolate. And don't forget flavonoids aren't limited to chocolate: they also are found in apples, red wine, green and black tea, onions, and cranberries. So enjoy a variety of these foods for the greatest heart benefits.

CAROTENOIDS

Found in brightly hued yellow, red, orange, and green plants, carotenoids may promote a healthy heart through their antioxidant power. Examples of carotenoids and their sources are

- Beta-carotene (found in dark leafy green vegetables, pumpkin, and carrots)
- Lutein (found in leafy greens like turnips, kale, spinach, and collards)
- Lycopene (found in cooked tomato products like tomato sauce)

The studies that link dark leafy greens and other fruits and vegetables to a reduced risk of heart disease support the intake of carotenoids in heart protection. Remember, we are talking about a variety of carotenoid-rich foods, not supplements.

SULFUR-CONTAINING COMPOUNDS

Found in leeks, garlic, and onions, sulfur-containing compounds also provide heart-health benefits. Garlic, for example, has been shown in some studies to help lower cholesterol. Although research is still evolving, one thing is sure: these foods offer flavor to many dishes and, as an added benefit, may protect our hearts.

STEROLS

The molecular structure of sterols differs only slightly from that of cholesterol. Because of this similarity in shape, sterols compete with cholesterol for absorption in the body, thereby blocking cholesterol from entering the bloodstream. Common forms of naturally occurring sterols are sitosterol, stigmasterol, and campesterol—found in a variety of fruits, vegetables, nuts, seeds, plant oils, and legumes. Although it takes a lot of sterols, or their saturated derivative stanols, to reduce cholesterol, this is yet another reason to boost your plant food intake. In addition to whole foods sources, you may want to add sterol- and stanol-fortified foods such as orange juice and margarine spreads (discussed on page 67) to your diet.

Studies such as the Lyon Diet Heart Study link high phytochemical (phytonutrient) intakes from plant-rich diets to cardiovascular protection. Research on the role of these and many other phytonutrients will continue to evolve and likely support diets rich in whole, unprocessed plant foods as providing the greatest heart-health benefits.

Reap the Health Benefits
of Fruits and Vegetables

Here are a few tips to maximize the cardioprotective benefits of fruits and vegetables:

1. *Follow your fists.* We've taken the math out of figuring out how much you should eat. Our plating guidelines show how using your fists is a great way to portion your foods.

    Fruits: Men and women should eat at least 3 closed-fist portions of fruits each day.

    Vegetables: Men 3 to 4, women 4 closed-fist portions.

    Legumes: Men 1/2, women 1/2 closed-fist portion.

2. *Go for color.* To maximize the heart protection of fruits and vegetables, you need to eat a variety of different colored ones every day. Among your daily portions of fruits and vegetables, try to include each of these colors daily:

    Yellow—yellow peppers, acorn squash, lemons, yellow squash, corn

    Orange—oranges, sweet potatoes, orange peppers, peaches, apricots, cantaloupe, mango, papaya, pumpkin

    Red—red peppers, tomatoes, apples, red onions, strawberries, pomegranates, raspberries, blood oranges

    Dark green—spinach, asparagus, kale, bok choy, broccoli, green peppers, collard greens, kiwifruit, snap peas, zucchini, cucumber

    Purples and blues—blueberries, blackberries, purple grapes, eggplant

    Remember to eat a rainbow of color a day for optimal heart protection!

3. *Go for texture and flavor.* Add flair to your meals by including a variety of bitter, sweet, sour, crunchy, and smooth vegetables and fruits. Keep the skin on your fruits and vegetables when you can and enjoy the added fiber it will provide.

Can't I Just Take a Supplement to Get the Vitamins and Minerals My Heart Needs?

As you have seen, research analyzing the role of individual nutrients, especially as supplements, in heart disease prevention has failed to show a direct benefit. This makes sense for three good reasons. First, it's impossible to eat individual nutrients; all foods are combinations of nutrients. As part of a heart-healthy eating plan we choose a variety of foods that contain combinations of antioxidant vitamins, minerals, and phytonutrients. Each and every food we consume, especially whole, unprocessed foods like fruits, vegetables, and whole grains, provides a mixture of nutrients that, in tandem with one another, creates a risk-reduction portfolio much stronger than the sum of their individual parts.

Second, it appears that some, if not all of the nutrients or phytonutrients we've just discussed, work best when consumed together. Interactions among these antioxidants on a cellular level may be the only means by which they protect us from disease. When you factor out just one nutrient you may totally lose the benefit.

Most important, the third reason individual nutrient supplementation may not work is that researchers can't clearly link vitamins, minerals, and fiber to all of the heart-health benefits of fruits and vegetables. Enter phytonutrients. It may be that other substances not yet identified in plant foods provide the greatest protection. If we pop pills and supplements, we will never realize these benefits.

We're still unveiling the powerful protection whole foods offer our heart. Instead of falling prey to what the media and supplement manufacturers say is the next big thing in weight loss and heart protection, get back to basics and choose whole, unprocessed foods. At the end of the day, what really matters are the foods we put in our mouths.

Alcohol and Beverages— How Much Is Too Much?

CHAPTER

There is great debate surrounding the "French paradox," a term used since the early 1990s to explain why the French, with dietary practices that embrace high levels of fat and daily wine consumption, have low rates of cardiovascular disease. This theory has prompted many a position paper, magazine article, news headline, and the like to tout red wine as the cure-all for heart disease. As a result of this media-driven popularity, patients often come to us asking if wine should be a staple at their dinner tables.

Tea also has received attention for its association with low levels of heart disease. Then there are juices—pomegranate, orange, and others. Is it really true these beverages hold the key to heart disease reduction? And where does water fit in? We'll explain what the latest research tells us about the role of these beverages and others as they relate to both heart disease and weight management.

Is It True That Red Wine, Tea, Coffee, and Certain Juices Protect the Heart?

Alcohol

Large population studies have linked light to moderate alcohol consumption to a lower risk of developing cardiovascular disease in certain individuals. Contrary to the media-driven hype about red wine, this risk reduction does not differ between red or white wine, beer, and spirits (whiskey, rum, etc.). Moreover, any intake above "moderate" (one drink equivalent per day in women; two in men) offers no additional protection. So does this mean we should all start adding one to two drinks to our daily eating plan? Not so fast.

If you think this evidence sounds too good to be true—especially in light of our knowledge that alcohol consumption is implicated in more than one-third of all fatal traffic accidents and can lead to addiction, liver cirrhosis, poor judgment, sleep disturbances, and negative interactions with medications—you are right. In reality, only a small group may benefit. Research indicates that the only people who experience better cardiovascular outcomes are those who are over 60 and at highest risk of developing cardiovascular disease.

This still doesn't give us a green flag to start drinking. Persons over 60 may have a health condition, such as elevated triglycerides, that could worsen with the addition of alcohol. What's more, other health consequences need to be considered. Research indicates that death from all causes sharply increases when people drink more than the "moderate" level specified. Plus, a woman who consumes just two servings of alcohol a day increases her chances of developing breast cancer by 20 to 25 percent, especially if she consumes low levels of folic acid.

The purported cardiovascular benefits derived from drinking alcohol are thought to be due to its ability to raise heart-protective HDL cholesterol, albeit a small increase. Another theory involves alcohol's ability to reduce blood clot formation. Although alcohol can raise HDL and thin the blood, it also can increase blood triglycerides significantly, which has heart-health consequences of its own. And the blood pressure–raising effect of drinking alcohol cannot be overlooked, especially in persons already being treated for hypertension (high blood pressure).

ALCOHOL Q&A

Q: What is a "serving size" of alcohol?

A: The following amounts are considered one serving and contain the same amount of alcohol:

12 ounces beer

5 ounces wine

1.5 ounces of 80-proof distilled spirits (e.g., Scotch, whiskey, vodka, gin, rum, or brandy)

Take-home message: Should you imbibe or become a teetotaler? We've divided our recommendations based upon a person's risk:

- **If you are under age 60 and at low to moderate risk for heart attack or stroke (cardiovascular disease):** Little evidence supports adding alcohol to your daily eating plan. In fact, the risks outweigh the benefits. If you currently drink alcohol, we do not recommend increasing your intake and suggest decreasing it if you consume more than two drinks a day for men, one a day for women. If you currently abstain, we do not recommend you start drinking regularly.

- *If you are at increased risk of heart disease and over age 60:* As long as you consult with your cardiologist or primary care physician to ensure there are no interactions with medications, you do not have additional health conditions that may increase another health risk, you do not have a history of alcohol abuse or alcoholism, and you are at a healthy BMI, a two-drink equivalent for men and one for women each day may confer some heart protection. (However, the eating strategies espoused in this book can provide stronger protection.)
- *If you are trying to lose weight:* Regardless of your age or health risk, the extra calories, what we refer to as "liquid calories," contained in wine, spirits, and beer is reason enough not to drink. Downing just one glass of wine a day tacks on 105 calories. Although this doesn't seem like a lot, if not accounted for in your total daily exercise and meal plan, those "measly" 105 calories can pack on more than ten pounds in a given year! And that's for only one glass of wine, less than most people consume. In addition, if you are overweight and have insulin resistance, drinking alcohol raises the risk that your blood triglycerides will increase. Refer to the following table for a look at just how many calories some of America's favorite alcoholic drinks contain.

Caloric Content of Popular Alcoholic Beverages

Alcoholic Beverage	Serving Size	Calories
Red wine	5 ounces	105
White wine	5 ounces	100
Beer	12 ounces	140–150
Light beer	12 ounces	96–110
Vodka	1.5 ounces	100
Rum	1.5 ounces	100
Frozen margarita	5 ounces	312
Piña colada	5 ounces	273
Long Island iced tea	8 ounces	507

Nutrition data derived from Food Processor for Windows, version 8.6.0, ESHA Research, Salem, Oregon.

We strongly discourage people in the following situations from drinking:

- Individuals with a history of alcoholism or alcohol abuse
- Women who are pregnant or planning to become pregnant
- Persons taking medications that interact with alcohol, including over-the-counter medications
- People who plan to drive or engage in activities that require attention or skill
- Those under age 21
- Those under age 60 who think alcohol may reduce their risk of cardiovascular disease
- Persons trying to lose weight

So, why do those wine-drinking French have lower rates of heart disease than Americans? What's not always mentioned in the media are the other positive lifestyle attributes this culture follows, such as eating a variety of colorful vegetables (especially dark leafy greens), choosing locally grown produce (which retains the highest nutrients), eating whole grains, relaxing, and sipping red wine with meals as part of the whole dining experience. Tack on more daily physical activity than most Americans get in a week's time, and the reasons become clear.

Tea

The phytonutrients in tea also have been extensively studied for their role in health. Research on the health benefits of drinking green or black tea has included as little as two to more than five cups a day. Virtually calorie free, green and black teas have been linked to lower risk of heart disease in both clinical and large-population trials involving thousands of people across the globe. The antioxidant-rich phytonutrients in tea have been linked to reduced inflammation, LDL cholesterol, and blood clotting factors and smoother, more elastic blood vessels. This doesn't sound too different from red wine, does it?

Take-home message: Enjoying one to two cups is a great way to enjoy some additional antioxidant phytonutrients in your diet. Remember, however, that what you add to that cup of tea can put your weight and cholesterol into trouble. See page 108 to determine the caloric toll a "little" cream and sugar can have on your weight.

Coffee

Once believed to be detrimental to the heart (that is, until scientists separated the link between drinking coffee and smoking cigarettes), regular coffee consumption now appears to have no relationship to an increased risk of heart disease. What's more, the transient, albeit minimal, increase in blood pressure experienced by some people does not have any long-term effect, especially in regular coffee drinkers. Also, the link between coffee and arrhythmias (irregular heartbeats) or palpitations appears to be weak. This varies from person to person, however, and coffee should be avoided if a patient or physician feels there is a link.

There is one caveat to coffee: if you drink an unfiltered brew, such as espresso, percolator, or French press, you do raise the risk of increasing your cholesterol. Oils called terpenes appear to be the root cause of coffee's cholesterol-raising ability. However, most Americans need not worry, because paper filters effectively remove these cholesterol-raising substances. An occasional espresso or French press brew should not have any long-term effect.

Take-home message: Because the caffeine in coffee can lead to irritability, diuresis, shakiness, and sleeplessness, enjoy it in moderation (and please, not before bedtime). Two 8-ounce cups of filtered coffee each day is enough. If you think that coffee gives you the jitters, or results in palpitations or arrhythmia, avoid it. The benefit surely doesn't outweigh the risk (or annoyance).

Add-ins Can Add On Calories

Here's an example of the caloric jeopardy you place yourself in just by adding 2 ounces of nondairy creamer and 2 tablespoons of granulated sugar to two cups of tea or coffee:

16 ounces coffee or tea	negligible calories
+ 2 ounces nondairy creamer	74 calories
+ 2 heaping tablespoons or	
4 packets sugar	96 calories
total calories	170 calories

Assuming nothing else in your life changes, this can result in a weight gain of 18 pounds in one year!

Make the switch to skim milk (22.5 calories in 2 ounces) and sugar substitute (e.g., 12 calories in 2 tablespoons Splenda) and you've dropped the calories down to 35. This can still result in a weight gain of $3^1/2$ pounds in one year if nothing else changes. Make the switch to drinking two cups of plain tea or coffee, and you're virtually calorie free (about 5 calories in 16 ounces), with little to no weight gain.

CAFFEINE Q&A

Q: What is considered "moderate" caffeine intake?

A: Coffee, tea, chocolate, soda, and hundreds of medications are sources of caffeine. Moderate levels, about 250 milligrams (two cups of coffee), appear to be safe. Keep in mind that caffeine is an addictive substance and when consumed in excess can lead to a number of health problems, such as sleeplessness, anxiety, irritability, nausea, diarrhea or other gastrointestinal problems, and muscle tremors.

How do you know if you're taking in too much caffeine? For starters, if you are totally dependent on caffeine to function in the morning, the answer is clear. If you cut down or eliminate caffeine and get severe headaches or constipation, you're probably consuming too much and should gradually wean yourself. If you continue to drink coffee all day, or switch from one caffeinated beverage to another (coffee in the morning and soda all afternoon and night), it would be prudent for you to cut down as well.

Juice

Orange juice, pomegranate juice, and grape juice have been studied for their impact on cholesterol and a variety of heart disease risk factors. Like wine, tea, and coffee, there appears to be an association between the phytonutrients in the fruit juice with small improvements or reductions in certain cardiovascular markers. There is no long-term evidence linking consumption of any juice to a reduced risk of developing or dying from heart disease, so no firm conclusions can be drawn.

Take-home message: Before you start pouring yourself a daily glass of juice, there are a few things you need to keep in mind. If weight control is your concern, juice should be restricted in your diet (if not eliminated totally). Juices, like alcohol and soda, are liquid calories. These quickly add up, yet don't fill you up, which can make losing weight downright difficult. What's more, whole fruits contain the same vitamins, minerals, and phytonutrients you can find in juice, but with fewer calories and with intact dietary fiber. This fiber serves several purposes. For starters, it fills you up more quickly. Secondly, it prevents the sugar in the fruit from rapidly raising your blood sugars, which also reduces the risk your triglycerides will increase. On the other hand, drinking a glass of juice doubles your calories but leaves you feeling empty, offers no dietary fiber, and rapidly increases your blood sugars. You're left unsatisfied and soon crave more sugar. The end result: weight gain. Another problem is that not every "juice" contains 100 percent fruit juice. In fact, many are loaded with added sugars such as high-fructose corn syrup, corn syrup solids, and other sugary ingredients neither you nor a young child needs.

Q: I've heard that grapefruit juice can interact with my heart medications. Is this true? If so, why?

A: Grapefruit juice inhibits a chemical in the intestines needed to break down many drugs in the body, such as cholesterol-lowering statins and some blood pressure medications called calcium channel blockers. The absence of this drug-metabolizing chemical can lead to higher blood levels of the drug, rendering it more potent in the body. This in turn can increase the risk of a drug's serious adverse effects. Whole grapefruits, if eaten in excess, can have the same effect as the juice, but orange juice does not work in the same manner. An occasional glass of grapefruit juice or sections of fresh grapefruit should not have any serious health consequences, but we recommend you check with your physician and/or pharmacist before including grapefruit products in your diet.

Where Do Soft Drinks and Sugary Noncarbonated Drinks Fit?

Completely void of nutritional value and loaded with sucrose, high-fructose corn syrup, and other calorie-dense sweeteners, soft drinks and many noncarbonated beverages (e.g., lemonade, fruit punch, sweetened iced teas) simply don't fit into a heart- or weight-conscious eating plan. Unfortunately, not enough Americans are getting the picture. According to the latest National Health and Nutrition Examination Survey report, soft drinks have surpassed white bread as the leading source of calories in the average American diet.

Diet soft drinks, sweetened with aspartame, sucralose, or another FDA-approved sugar substitute, are fine to use as a substitute for regular soft drinks on an occasional basis. What we mean by "occasional" is no more than one 12-ounce can a day. Why only 12 ounces? Although the sugar and calories are virtually gone from diet soft drinks and other diet beverages, they still lack nutritional value, and they mean you're consuming fewer foods or beverages that have a more positive impact on your health (e.g., a glass of soy or skim milk, water, fruits, vegetables).

Take-home message: None of us needs the calories or sugar that soft drinks and sweetened noncarbonated drinks provide. Keep it simple and avoid calorie-laden beverages altogether. There are a variety of sugar and calorie-free substitutes on the market to quench your thirst on an occasional basis. Just remember that many carbonated beverages contain caffeine, so keep your daily intake to a minimum.

SOFT DRINK VS. MILK Q&A

Q: Since my child is young and growing, isn't it okay for him to drink pop every day?

A: Just as recommended for adults, soft drinks should be excluded from a child's diet—regardless of growth rate, age, activity level, or BMI. The eating patterns you model to your children are the patterns they will follow for a lifetime. Studies show that the average 12- to 19-year-old boy gets 15 teaspoons of sugar per day just from drinking soda; teenage girls consume about 10 teaspoons. The problem with soft drinks isn't just the extra calories and sugar that we all know they don't need; it's what they are pushing out of their diet that is of concern. When children or teens reach for soft drinks, they miss an opportunity to drink calcium- and vitamin D–rich milk or fortified soymilk, which can have a far-reaching impact on their bone status later in life. And when they fill up on liquid calories from soft drinks, they consume fewer nutritious fruits, vegetables, or grains. Why introduce something into your child's diet that has more health risks than benefits?

How Much Water Should I Be Drinking?

Pure and simple, with no additives, preservatives, calories, or sugar—water should be your first and most consistent beverage of choice each and every day. Every living cell in our body relies on water to function. Water regulates our temperature, is the main part of every body fluid, transports nutrients to cells, carries away waste products, moistens tissues, and helps soften stools and prevent constipation. We would not survive without water.

You may often have heard the advice, "Drink eight 8-ounce glasses of water each day for good health." But does a six-foot athlete require the same amount of fluid as a five-foot sedentary person? Recently, the Institute of Medicine (IOM) decidedly said no. The IOM stated that most healthy adults should use their thirst to guide them. Exceptions to this rule include those with a medical condition requiring fluid control (e. g., heart failure), athletes, and those engaging in prolonged physical activity or living under extreme temperature conditions. Most healthy men require around 125 ounces of fluid per day and women, 91 ounces. More or less fluid is required depending on your level of activity. If 125 and 91 ounces seem like a lot, remember that foods as well as beverages provide us with our daily fluids.

Approximately 80 percent of your fluid goal should come from beverages (about 9 cups for women, 12 1/2 cups for men). Ideally, the majority of this should come from water, either sparkling, spring, or tap, perhaps with a twist of lemon or lime. Other beverages such as tea, coffee, milk, soymilk, diet soft drinks, and juice can count toward your fluids as well. Just keep in mind the weight consequences of drinking liquid calories. The other 20 percent of your fluids should be derived from water-packed foods like fruits and vegetables. For example, a serving of watermelon contains 91 percent water by weight; broccoli, 91 percent; and yogurt, 75 percent. As you can see, it's not too difficult to get enough fluid from the foods you eat.

Don't know if you're drinking enough water? A simple test is to check your urine color. If your urine is dark or bright yellow, you're probably not drinking enough. Pale urine is a good sign that you're taking in enough fluids.

Summary

The magic key to a healthier heart and trimmer waistline will not be found in a glass of wine or juice. Any health benefits derived from these beverages are likely found in greater quantities and varieties in whole, plant-based foods. That's not to say that an occasional glass of wine or juice can't fit into a heart-healthy way of life. But we encourage you not to make these calorie-laden beverages a daily staple. Tea and up to two cups of filtered coffee appear to have no ill health effects, unless caffeine bothers you. But instead, think about sticking with cool, refreshing water to reach your fluid goals as one of many healthy lifestyle strategies. We raise our glass of sparkling water to your health!

Positive Lifestyle Strategies to Combat Stress and Smoking

CHAPTER

The recipe for a healthy heart lies not only in eating healthy and increasing physical activity but also in managing stress and avoiding harmful behaviors like smoking. When you have mastered stress and quit smoking, you will be a full participant in the heart-healthy lifestyle and experience its benefits to the max.

Managing Stress

"Life is a stressful event," we remind our patients from time to time. Stress is inescapable, it is essential to life, and not all of it is bad. Stress is an essential element of growth and development. No change, good or otherwise, occurs without stress. However, stress, whether sudden or chronic, can have an extreme impact. Chronic emotional stress can lead to hypertension, arterial damage, and atherosclerosis, with a greater chance that surges in blood pressure might break some of the plaques loose and thus increase the risk of heart attack. Heart failure, a leading cause of death among both men and women in the United States, is also affected by stress. Patients with heart failure experience a high level of depression and uncertainty, and psychological stress can affect their heart function and even cause relapse. Lower levels of stress predict higher quality of life in heart failure patients awaiting transplants.

Learning to manage stress is a key to good health. We are learning more and more about the mechanisms through which stress exerts its adverse effects. This enhanced understanding is leading to more focused and effective methods for treating stress.

Proven stress management techniques include exercise, stress-reducing medications, and increasingly popular alternative therapies such as massage, centering prayer, and acupuncture.

You can improve your ability to master stress by following a few simple guidelines.

1. Eat and drink sensibly.
2. Assert yourself in potentially stressful situations.
3. Smile and socialize. People who manage stress well tend to have two main traits—a good sense of humor and the ability to connect with other people.
4. Exercise regularly.
5. Sleep soundly, for as long as it takes you to feel rested.
6. Take responsibility for your own feelings and try to think positively and optimistically.
7. Take time to relax for at least 15 to 20 minutes a day.
8. Live by your personal values so that your life is not in conflict with your beliefs.
9. Set realistic priorities for yourself.
10. Allow yourself to be less than perfect.

When Stress Management Isn't Enough

When an individual is unable to use or respond to stress management techniques, depression is a common cause. Depression occurs in 5 to 10 percent of the general population, but it affects up to 50 percent of those who have had a heart attack. Recent evidence shows that depression after a heart attack substantially increases one's risk of an early death. Although there is no proof yet, the available research suggests that treating depression reduces this risk.

The signs and symptoms of depression that should not be ignored include:

- Depressed mood
- Loss of interest in usually pleasurable activities
- Poor motivation
- Low self-esteem
- Difficulty focusing and making decisions
- Insomnia or oversleeping
- Abnormal appetite leading to either weight loss or gain
- Mental and physical sluggishness
- Feelings of hopelessness and despair associated with suicidal thoughts

If a majority of these symptoms persist for at least two weeks without improvement, it's time to seek professional help.

Milder forms of depression often respond to help from a therapist or spiritual counselor or to proper self-administration of stress management principles. A cardiac rehabilitation program is an excellent way to access many of these services.

When depressive symptoms begin to interfere with normal function, become associated with hopelessness, and do not respond to principles of good stress management, prescription of antidepressant medication is generally the next step. This is nothing to be ashamed of or embarrassed about. Depression is a legitimate medical disorder for which antidepressant medication is a safe and effective antidote. Because these are prescription medicines, they can only be obtained from a doctor who has performed a careful medical evaluation.

Smoking

Smoking is the leading cause of preventable death in the United States. One in five deaths in the United States can be attributed to the 22 percent of Americans who smoke. What's more, it is estimated that 33 percent of all smokers in the United States experience premature death, half of which are related to a smoking-related illness.

Primary Effects of Smoking

The harmful effects of smoking are irrefutable. More than 4,000 substances are found in every cigarette, including toxins such as nicotine, tar, ammonia, arsenic, formaldehyde, hydrogen cyanide, and lead. These poisons enter all of our body's organs via the blood system, and at least 43 of these poisons cause or have been associated with cancer.

Smoking also has specific adverse effects on the heart. Smokers have two to four times the risk of developing coronary artery disease and ten times the risk of developing peripheral vascular disease compared to nonsmokers. People who smoke also have double the risk of dying from a stroke as nonsmokers.

Heart disease and stroke aside, compared to nonsmokers, smokers experience numerous other medical conditions that result in higher rates of hospitalization and missed work: periodontal disease and tooth discoloration, late-onset inflammatory bowel disease and ulcers, blood clots, hearing loss, blindness and serious eye diseases, impotence in men, infertility in women, pregnancy complications and low-birth-weight babies, osteoporosis, delayed wound healing, diabetes complications, low self-esteem, depression, and anxiety.

Benefits of Quitting

There is good news for former smokers, as well as current smokers considering stopping. The benefits of quitting smoking begin immediately and continue to accrue over time. Research has shown that, regardless of age, it is never too late to quit.

Within minutes of quitting, cardiovascular risk is reduced as heart rate, blood pressure, and body temperature return to normal. Carbon monoxide in the blood decreases, allowing oxygen to increase and facilitate nerve and tissue repair. Within a few days of quitting, improvements are noticeable in breathing and circulation. Food tastes better, and the capacity to smell is enhanced.

Quitting smoking extends longevity and improves quality of life. Smokers who quit by age 35 exceed the life expectancy of those continuing to smoke by six to nine years. Smoking cessation before the age of 50 reduces the risk of dying in the next 15 years by 50 percent compared with those who still smoke. Smokers over the age of 65 who quit exceed the life expectancy of those continuing to smoke by one to four years. This risk reduction continues over time. The risk of heart disease caused by continuing to smoke is cut in half within one year of quitting. Within 15 years of quitting, the risk of developing heart disease is the same as that of a lifelong nonsmoker. The risk of stroke is equivalent to that of a lifelong nonsmoker within 5 to 15 years of quitting. The risk of developing lung cancer is comparable to that of a lifelong nonsmoker within 10 to 30 years of abstinence. Risk of other cancers, including cancers of the mouth, esophagus, bladder, and cervix, are also cut in half within five years of quitting. With improvement in lung functioning, the risk of developing chronic obstructive pulmonary disease is substantially lower after smoking cessation. Giving up smoking also reduces cough, congestion, wheezing, and risk of respiratory infection.

Despite the benefits, many people do not quit because they already have been diagnosed with a smoking-related condition; however, such individuals also can benefit considerably from quitting smoking. These benefits include reduced risk of death from cardiovascular disease, peripheral vascular disease, cancer, and respiratory infections. Individuals diagnosed with cardiovascular disease who stop smoking reduce their risk of recurrent heart attack and heart disease–related death by 50 percent. Individuals diagnosed with cancer reduce their risk of developing a second primary cancer compared to those with a cancer diagnosis who continue to smoke. These very substantial benefits give people a very significant reason to stop smoking at any age.

Facing the Facts

"Everyone has to die from something sometime" is often the response we hear when we advise patients to stop smoking. Such a notion implies that death will be peaceful and serene, but realistically, death caused by smoking is rarely so uneventful. Long before the peacefulness of death comes a gradual deterioration of health and functioning.

Everyone has to die from something sometime, but everyone does not double their risk of heart attack, stroke, and chronic lung disease by smoking cigarettes. Everyone is not told that they may have few years or even months to live because cancer is spreading through their body. They are not forced to undergo surgery, radiation, or chemotherapy just to sustain some semblance of quality to what's left of their life. Treatments for smoking-related chronic illness also cause a number of unpleasant side effects, including fatigue, pain, memory and concentration difficulties, and changes in appearance. Unfortunately, the very treatment that is intended to improve quality of life often results in significant changes in life roles as these ill people struggle with painful feelings of dependency, inadequacy, and becoming a burden to those they love.

Effective Quit Strategies

There is no silver bullet or magic pill to quit smoking. What works best for one person may not help another. Because it is both a physical and a psychological addiction, quitting smoking and remaining smoke free is anything but easy. That said, it is not impossible! Fifty percent of all people who have ever smoked have now quit. We are confident that you or your loved one can join this ever-growing number of nonsmokers! Here are our best suggestions for kicking the habit.

- *Set realistic expectations.* This is important in maintaining your personal motivation to quit and confidence in your ability to do so. The majority of smokers who quit successfully have made repeated attempts. This persistence often pays off when individuals are able to view previous attempts to stop as opportunities to learn rather than as failures. Using this mind-set, you can objectively evaluate what went well and what changes you need to make to be more successful in the future.
- *View quitting as a process.* The idea that quitting is a onetime event that requires self-discipline and willpower is a myth. Smoking cessation is an ongoing process that evolves through education, awareness, and gradual changes in your thoughts and behaviors. Lapses become learning opportunities for reducing future slips and facilitating longer periods of abstinence.
- *Keep a record of smoking triggers.* Awareness of how your smoking behavior is associated with social, emotional, and environmental triggers that prompt you to smoke is a vital component of the process of quitting. Keeping a log or diary of smoking behavior has been shown to reduce smoking in and of itself. Just as important, self-monitoring reveals smoking frequency, patterns, and high-risk situations for smoking. Learning specific strategies for dealing with these high-risk situations and, more generally, breaking the complex associations of smoking with virtually everything you think, feel, and do is critical.

- *Challenge your faulty beliefs about smoking.* Other coping strategies are designed to address your thoughts and behaviors. The mind is a powerful tool that can work either for or against you. For example, smokers often attribute a psychological meaning to smoking that reinforces the addiction. It is important to cognitively challenge psychological meanings, such as that smoking is a best friend who will always be there or a special means for handling stress. In reality, what you perceive as a best friend is walking you to your grave and does little to help change what causes your stress. Over time, this cognitive challenging will help to change your mistaken beliefs about smoking.
- *Develop an action plan.* To quit smoking successfully, you must have a plan. Rather than deciding to quit and going cold turkey all at once, set a quit date two to three weeks away and prepare yourself. Having a well-thought-out plan is your lifeline to better health.
- *Remain watchful of triggers to smoke.* Once you've developed a plan for quitting and put it into action, remain vigilant to smoking cues. Many triggers are remote, such as the change of seasons or annual holidays and family gatherings. Subtle cues also occur in the media, such as the portrayal of smoking as glamorous, so be alert!

Comparing Smoking Cessation Strategies

Researchers have examined a multitude of smoking cessation strategies and identified those that are most effective in helping people quit.

- Behavior therapy, which focuses on changing the unhealthy behavior with principles of learning and conditioning, is proven to help people stay smoke free. Problem solving, skills training such as relaxation and exercise, and increasing social support are all elements of behavior therapy that have been found to help people kick the habit. The more intensive the behavioral treatment, the better the outcome, and the more individualized the intervention is, the higher the quit rate.
- Aversion therapy, such as rapid smoking, is another type of behavior therapy that has been shown to substantially increase quit rates. However, aversion therapy is not commonly used because it also poses significant health risks. Aversion therapy should be done only under strict medical supervision.
- Support from friends and family plays a vital role in helping someone quit smoking. If you are the support person, remember that you cannot make the change for your loved one, and no amount of prodding will convince that person to quit if he or she is not personally motivated to do so. The best type of support to give is unconditional. Regardless of whether a smoker lapses or not,

giving the individual a pat on the back for what he or she did well can help to maintain the person's motivation and confidence.

- Combining intensive behavior therapy and pharmacotherapy has achieved the highest rates of smoking cessation. Pharmacotherapy, including nicotine replacement therapy (NRT) and bupropion, has been shown to double quit rates when used appropriately. All smokers who are preparing to quit should consider the use of nicotine replacement therapy. Exceptions include adolescents, pregnant or breastfeeding women, and people smoking ten or fewer cigarettes a day. NRT also is not recommended for people with medical contraindications such as serious heart arrhythmia, angina pectoris, or accelerated hypertension or who have had a heart attack within the previous two weeks.

- Nicotine replacement therapy comes in many different forms, including the transdermal patch, gum, inhaler, nasal spray, lozenge, and sublingual (under the tongue) tablet. Research indicates that they all work equally well, but the transdermal patch is the easiest because it is applied only once a day.

- Bupropion is the only FDA-approved smoking cessation aid that does not contain nicotine. It is available by prescription only and marketed as Wellbutrin for its antidepressant effect or Zyban for its smoking cessation effect. Bupropion can be used in conjunction with nicotine replacement and behavior therapy. Many individuals are concerned about the average five-pound weight gain associated with smoking cessation. Bupropion has been shown to delay but not prevent any weight gain; however, you should consult your physician about any medical contraindications and potential side effects prior to starting bupropion.

If you are a current smoker who is ready to become a nonsmoker, congratulations on taking the first step toward achieving one of the healthiest changes you will ever make. Your next steps may be to reread this chapter and to line up additional support. Talk to your family and friends. Consult your doctor, a smoking cessation group, and community resources such as the American Cancer Society (1–877–YES–QUIT), the American Lung Association (1–866–QUIT–YES), or Internet sites such as www.clevelandclinic.org/joinjoe or www.cdc.gov/tobacco/quit/canquit.htm. Though challenging, keep in mind that smoking cessation should be your first step in protecting yourself against heart disease.

2

The Cookbook

This is a cookbook for people who want to adopt a more heart-healthy lifestyle and for those who cook for a loved one who is making that change. Ever since our first collaboration on *The Joslin Diabetes Gourmet Cookbook* fifteen years ago, we've had a reputation for writing cookbooks that bring families of people with chronic disease back to the table where everyone can enjoy the same delicious, healthy food. This cookbook will do just that. We will teach you how to cook meals so that no one feels left out or deprived. In this section you will find more than 150 recipes and variations that incorporate the magnificent flavors of good food from a variety of cuisines, with an emphasis on the cuisines of the Mediterranean—all within the eating guidelines of the Cleveland Clinic Heart and Vascular Institute. Not only is our food high in flavor, it is also low in saturated and hydrogenated fats, and therefore in cholesterol. In place of the flavor derived from fat, we've supplemented the natural flavors of the freshest of foodstuffs with herbs, spices, and unique combinations of ingredients. Often we simply let the true flavors of the food shine.

You'll find symbols indicating quick and easy recipes for a busy weeknight's meal ⏰, and for dishes children will love ☺ . There are also ideas for elegant meals for celebrations and entertaining. As busy working mothers and grand-mothers who entertain frequently, we are well versed in this style of cooking. Having heart disease ourselves, we have actually walked this walk for years.

Bonnie and Fran

Cardioprotective Pantry

Now that you have committed to following a cardioprotective lifestyle, it's time to think about restocking your pantry and refrigerator so that you have the proper foods for a heart-healthy diet—and for making the recipes in this book.

Changing your lifestyle is an opportune time to clean out and reevaluate your storage spaces, keeping like items together on shelves. Good organization makes cooking easier and less stressful. We store dried beans, pasta, and grains in glass jars with directions tucked inside so that we can see every variety we have and when we need to purchase more. Garlic and shallots are stored in cool dark places away from other produce. Onions, potatoes, and winter squashes are kept in baskets. Citrus and other fruits sit in a bowl to ripen and to remind us to eat them for snacks or use them in recipes. When they become ripe, we shift them to the refrigerator.

Following are the main ingredients that we keep on hand for our daily and weekly cooking. We have listed some brands that are easy to find at the time of publication, but brands of course change over time. Always read labels and be an informed consumer.

Baking ingredients: Unbleached all-purpose flour, whole wheat all-purpose and pastry flours, cornstarch, baking powder, baking soda, cream of tartar, cocoa powder, kosher salt, pure vanilla extract, granulated sugar substitute like Splenda or Equal, brown sugar and brown sugar substitute blend, granulated sugar, *trans*-free wafers such as Nabisco Thin Crisps for cookie crumbs
Beans and legumes: Beans (black, cannellini, chickpeas, cranberry, navy, pinto, and white beans; black, brown, green, and red lentils; black-eyed peas)
Canned and packaged goods: No-salt-added or low-salt tomato sauce, paste, and tomatoes like Del Monte or Hunt's; low-sodium ketchup like Hunt's or

Heinz; chili sauce: fat-free, reduced-sodium chicken, beef, and vegetable broths like Swanson; reduced-sodium soy sauce like Kikkoman; Thai fish sauce; oyster sauce; sugar-free jellies and preserves; dry roasted nuts; natural peanut butter; canned salmon and tuna in water; canned beans of all varieties; unsweetened dried fruits; evaporated skim milk; Worcestershire sauce; hot pepper sauce; Dijon mustard; hoisin sauce; black bean and garlic sauce; hot Asian hot chili sauce; capers; dried chiles; dried mushrooms

Cooking sprays: Aerosol and/or pump-style canola, olive, and vegetable oil; no-stick baking spray with flour; refrigerated butter-flavored cooking sprays

Dried herbs and spices: Ground allspice, basil, bay leaves, celery seed, chili powder, ground cinnamon, whole and ground cloves, ground coriander, ground cumin, curry powder, dill, fennel seed, fines herbes, garlic powder, ground ginger, nutmeg, paprika, peppercorns, crushed red pepper flakes, rosemary, Old Bay seasoning, sage, saffron, sesame seeds, thyme, turmeric

Grains: Barley; brown basmati rice; buckwheat; bulgur wheat; stoneground cornmeal, yellow and white; whole wheat couscous; flax seeds, whole and milled; kasha; rolled oats; polenta; quinoa; brown rice, both regular and instant; spelt; wild rice

Liquid fats: Extra virgin olive, canola, peanut, walnut and other nut, grapeseed, and sesame oils

Pasta: Whole wheat pastas, including angel hair, linguine, farfalle, orzo, penne, rotelle, shells, spaghetti, and ziti (three brands that pass our taste and nutrition test are Barilla Plus, Hodgson Mills, and Ronzoni Healthy Harvest); also won ton wrappers; rice sticks

Vinegars: Balsamic, herb- and fruit-infused, red and white wine, sherry, Champagne, malt, and seasoned and plain rice vinegars (also labeled rice vinegar)

Wines and liquors: dry red and white wine; sherry (Marsala); cognac; liqueurs

The basics: Garlic, onions (sweet, white, and red), shallots, potatoes (sweet and small red)

In the refrigerator:

Part-skim or low-fat cheeses: Cheddar, Swiss, feta, goat, mozzarella; hard cheese (Parmesan or pecorino Romano); low-fat and fat-free cream cheese, sour cream, ricotta

Solid fats: tub margarines like Benecol, Smart Balance, Take Control, or Promise; *trans*-free vegetable shortening for baking like Smart Balance or Crisco; light *trans*-free tub margarines for spreading; fresh ginger; fresh fruits; fruit juices; scallions, fresh herbs, and parsley; salad ingredients; fresh vegetables; dill pickles; tubes of tomato, anchovy, and herb pastes; egg substitute; whole eggs; skim milk; fat-free yogurt; fat-free half-and-half

In the freezer: Multigrain bread crumbs, puff pastry dough like Pepperidge Farm, phyllo dough like Athens, nuts, whole-grain rolls and bread, low-fat firm and extra-firm tofu like WhiteWave, silken tofu like Mori-Nu, individual turkey and chicken burgers, skinless turkey and chicken breasts, vegetables and fruits in bags, nonfat or light whipped topping

Appetizers

Appetizers can definitely be part of a heart-healthy lifestyle. True, you'll want to avoid the fat-laden hors d'oeuvres you may have enjoyed at past dinner parties, festive restaurant meals, or celebrations with friends; however, there are many healthy appetizers that fit your new way of life. In this chapter you'll be surprised by the range of tastes in our recipes, which come from all over the world.

A Few Quick Tips

Take advantage of precut or prewashed vegetables. They're more expensive, but we find the time they save worth it. Otherwise, prepare the vegetables in the morning and refrigerate them in self-sealing plastic bags atop a bowl of ice. They'll stay crisp, making crudités an easy do-ahead appetizer for parties.

- Use your freezer. You can prepare crêpes (page 333) and pot stickers (page 140) when you have time, then thaw and reheat in the oven while you await your guests. We also keep crostini (page 337) in the freezer during the year.
- Dips are the perfect easy appetizer or cocktail food because they only improve in the refrigerator as the flavors meld. Make them the night before or the morning of your party.

Cream Cheese Vegetable Dip

Nothing tastes better than a creamy dip with fresh vegetables and herbs served with toasted pita bread. This one adds tofu for smoothness, which gives it a rich taste as well as extra protein—a win-win recipe.

4 ounces low-fat cream cheese

4 ounces fat-free cream cheese

1/4 cup soft silken tofu

1 garlic clove, chopped

Freshly ground pepper

1/4 cup chopped fresh chives

1 tablespoon minced English cucumber

1 tablespoon minced red bell pepper

1 tablespoon grated carrot

Place the cream cheeses, tofu, garlic, and pepper in a food processor and pulse until combined. Add the chives, cucumber, bell pepper, and carrot and pulse for a few seconds until just combined.

DIETITIAN'S NOTE: A mixture of nonfat and low-fat cream cheese cuts the saturated fat but doesn't cut back on taste.

Makes 1 1/4 cups
(10 servings)

Per serving
(2 tablespoons):
62 calories
   (45% calories from fat)
3 g total fat
   (2 g saturated fat)
4.5 g protein
3 g carbohydrate
0 g dietary fiber
10 mg cholesterol
137 mg sodium
82 mg potassium

Fresh Herb Yogurt Dip

Makes 2 cups
(8 servings)

Per serving (¼ cup):
26 calories
  (60% calories from fat)
0 g total fat
  (0 g saturated fat)
2.5 g protein
5 g carbohydrate
0 g dietary fiber
0 mg cholesterol
34 mg sodium
2.75 mg potassium

This tasty dip is perfect not only with vegetables but also with whole wheat crackers or bread. Our dips can serve double duty as a topping for vegetables, salads, and potatoes.

2 cups Yogurt Cheese (page 335)

2 tablespoons chopped fresh tarragon

2 tablespoons chopped fresh chives

3 tablespoons chopped fresh flat-leaf parsley

2 garlic cloves, crushed

1 tablespoon sherry vinegar

Freshly ground pepper

Place the yogurt cheese in a bowl. Stir in the remaining ingredients, cover, and refrigerate for at least 2 hours or up to 24 hours. Serve with endive leaves, fennel slices, cherry tomatoes, broccoli, or your favorite vegetables cut into bite-size pieces.

DIETITIAN'S NOTE: Although the calories from fat are higher than we normally recommend, the total calories and fat grams are low, so this tasty dish can easily fit into your heart-healthy eating plan. Bon appetit!

Dips and Spreads

Dips and spreads are always popular. Ours are easy to make, delicious, and healthy to boot! Use these not only to accompany vegetables and toasted whole wheat pita but also to top greens or tomato slices, or to spread on your sandwiches—just make sure you know the calories you are adding.

The Crudité Display

We find that crudités are loved by almost everyone, from the toddler on up. They're light and delicious, healthy, inexpensive, and easy to fix.

Many vegetables served with dips benefit from a brief plunge into a pot of boiling water to make them tender but still crisp, maximize their flavor, and brighten their color. Vegetables will require differing amounts of blanching time: asparagus, 2 to 3 minutes depending on the thickness of the spears; green beans and broccoli and cauliflower florets, 2 to 3 minutes; snow or sugar snap peas, about 90 seconds. Quickly drain and immediately immerse in ice water to stop the cooking and chill the vegetables. Drain again and use as directed.

A beautiful rustic basket makes an interesting container for an array of crudités. A group of coordinated glass containers can also make a stunning display. Use the crispest and freshest vegetables you can buy and arrange them decoratively, bunching those of one kind together. Cut the larger vegetables into strips or pieces. For an attractive presentation, use a hollowed-out vegetable like a purple cabbage, red bell pepper, or a large ripe tomato to hold the dip. In go the herbs and your display is complete and lovely.

We especially like these crudité combinations:
- Cherry or grape tomatoes, red radishes, cauliflower florets, turnip slices, long celery sticks, and scallions
- Endive spears, blanched whole green beans, and carrot sticks
- Cauliflower florets, sugar snap peas, broccoli florets, and grape tomatoes
- Baby carrots, zucchini slices, and blanched asparagus spears
- Blanched green beans, carrot sticks, red bell pepper strips, and blanched asparagus spears

Eggplant Dip with Southwestern Spices

Makes about 1²/₃ cups
(13 servings)

Per serving
(2 tablespoons):
30 calories
  (60% calories from fat)
2 g total fat
  (0 g saturated fat)
1 g protein
3 g carbohydrate
1 g dietary fiber
0 mg cholesterol
5 mg sodium
88 g potassium

Serve this piquant dip with healthy dippers—blanched thin asparagus spears and blanched sugar snap peas.

2 small eggplants (about 1 pound)

2 scallions, white parts and 3 inches of the green, chopped

1 large or 2 small garlic cloves, sliced

2 tablespoons fresh lemon juice

2 teaspoons red wine vinegar

¼ cup Yogurt Cheese (page 335)

2 tablespoons extra virgin olive oil

1 teaspoon ground cumin

¼ teaspoon ground coriander

¼ cup chopped fresh cilantro

Freshly ground pepper

⅛ teaspoon kosher salt, optional

1. Preheat the oven to 450°F.

2. Place the eggplants on a baking sheet and pierce them all over with the tines of a fork. Bake, turning every 10 minutes, until the skin is blackened and the eggplants are soft, about 30 minutes.

3. Let the eggplants cool, then scoop out the eggplant flesh. Place the eggplant in a food processor. Add the remaining ingredients and process until smooth. Cover and refrigerate for at least 2 hours or up to 24 hours.

4. Transfer the dip to a small dish and serve with blanched and cooled asparagus and sugar snap peas.

DIETITIAN'S NOTE: Although the calories from fat are higher than we normally recommend, the total calories and fat grams are low, so this tasty appetizer can fit easily into your heart-healthy eating plan. Bon appétit!

Wild Guacamole

Our guacamole is a fabulous blend of tastes, textures, and colors. Avocados get three-fourths of their calories from fat, but since it is monounsaturated fat and they are low in calories, we can enjoy eating avocados while heeding our heart-healthy lifestyle. We can always add a colorful Mexican basket of low-fat tortilla chips, but sometimes we offer an arrangement of crudités.

2 medium ripe Hass avocados, halved

1 serrano, seeded and minced

2 tablespoons minced red onion

1 garlic clove, minced

1 small tomato, seeded and diced

Juice of 1½ limes

2 tablespoons minced fresh cilantro

¼ teaspoon ground cumin

⅛ teaspoon kosher salt, optional

Freshly ground pepper

1. Using a spoon, scoop the avocado pulp from the shells and place it in a bowl. Using two forks, coarsely mash the avocado, leaving some chunks. Add the chile pepper, onion, garlic, tomato, lime juice, cilantro, and cumin. Mix again with the two forks, taking care not to overmix. Add the salt, if using, and pepper to taste. Lightly mix again.

2. Transfer the guacamole to a serving dish and let stand until ready to serve at room temperature.

DIETITIAN'S NOTE: A great source of monounsaturated fat and potassium, this version beats the store-bought varieties any day!

Makes about 2 cups (8 servings)

Per serving (¼ cup):
70 calories
   (68% calories from fat)
6 g total fat
   (1.5 g saturated fat)
1 g protein
5 g carbohydrate
4 g dietary fiber
0 mg cholesterol
0 mg sodium
350 mg potassium

Edamame Hummus

Makes 1½ cups
(8 servings)

Per serving
(3 tablespoons):
70 calories
   (64% calories from fat)
5 g total fat
   (1 g saturated fat)
4 g protein
3 g carbohydrate
0 g dietary fiber
0 mg cholesterol
0 mg sodium
40 mg potassium

Edamame, or green soybeans, are available shelled or fully cooked in pods in the produce and frozen vegetable sections of supermarkets. This is a welcome variation on the usual chickpea hummus—and even healthier. Serve with toasted whole wheat pita chips or crudités.

1½ cups frozen edamame

3 garlic cloves

1 tablespoon sesame tahini

1 tablespoon extra virgin olive oil

2½ tablespoons fresh lemon juice

2 teaspoons ground cumin

½ teaspoon ground coriander

½ cup fresh flat-leaf parsley

1. Follow package directions to cook the edamame. Drain and place in a food processor. Add the garlic, tahini, oil, lemon juice, cumin, coriander, parsley, and 2 tablespoons water. Process until the hummus is smooth, adding more water if needed to make it the consistency of mayonnaise.

2. Transfer the hummus to a serving dish, cover, and refrigerate until ready to serve.

DIETITIAN'S NOTE: Although this dip contains a larger percentage of calories from total fat than we usually suggest, it is primarily in the form of monounsaturated fat. Your heart will also reap the benefit of added soy protein from the edamame.

Tuscan Bean Spread

This bean spread is perfect for either a sandwich or a party. Make it the day before and store it in an airtight container. Serve with grated carrot, radish sprouts, and chopped tomatoes on whole wheat bread for sandwiches or with a basket of interesting breads—lavosh, pappadam, and small sesame breadsticks—or crudités for a party.

6 ounces dried white beans, or two 15-ounce cans cannellini beans, drained

Olive oil cooking spray, or 1/2 teaspoon extra virgin olive oil

4 large shallots, chopped

4 garlic cloves, minced

1 1/2 tablespoons chopped fresh rosemary

1 tablespoon chopped fresh oregano

1/2 teaspoon fennel seed

3 3/4 cups fat-free, reduced-sodium chicken broth or vegetable broth

1/3 to 1/2 cup fresh lemon juice

Makes 3 cups
(16 servings)

Per serving
(3 tablespoons):
55 calories
   (0% calories from fat)
0 g total fat
   (0 g saturated fat)
3 g protein
11 g carbohydrate
3 g dietary fiber
0 mg cholesterol
116 mg sodium
245 mg potassium

1. If using dried beans, put the beans in a large pot with water to cover. Bring to a boil, remove from heat, cover, and let stand at room temperature for 1 hour. Drain the beans and set aside.

2. Lightly coat the bottom of a nonstick pot with cooking spray. Add the shallots and garlic and cook, stirring, over medium heat until the shallots are wilted, about 5 minutes. Add the rosemary, oregano, and fennel. Cook, stirring, for 1 minute more. Add the beans and broth, and bring to a boil. Reduce the heat and simmer on low heat for 30 to 40 minutes, until the beans are tender. Remove from the heat.

3. When the bean mixture is cool, transfer it to a food processor or blender. Puree, adding lemon juice as needed for the desired consistency.

Black-eyed Pea Relish with Crackers

Makes 6 cups
(24 servings)

Per serving (¼ cup):
30 calories
  (35% calories from fat)
1.5 g total fat
  (0 g saturated fat)
1 g protein
4 g carbohydrate
<1 g dietary fiber
0 mg cholesterol
4 mg sodium
100 mg potassium

On New Year's Day, black-eyed peas mean good luck. Texans call this dish caviar, but we call it a party-enhancing relish. Easy to make, you will find that it shines not only as an appetizer but also as a salad. Just add your favorite lettuce, tomatoes, and sliced cucumber. Serve this with lavosh, water crackers, or for you Texans, homemade flour tortilla chips (page 137).

½ pound frozen black-eyed peas
½ teaspoon kosher salt, optional
2 tablespoons extra virgin olive oil
3 tablespoons red wine vinegar
3 garlic cloves, minced
1 medium green bell pepper, seeded and minced
1 medium red bell pepper, seeded and minced
3 jalapeños, seeded and minced
1 medium onion, minced
3 scallions, white parts and 2 inches of the green, thinly sliced
¼ cup chopped fresh flat-leaf parsley
⅓ cup chopped fresh cilantro
1 teaspoon ground cumin
Red leaf lettuce leaves, washed, dried, and refrigerated

1. Put the peas in a saucepan, cover with water, and add salt (if using). Bring to a boil. Reduce the heat and simmer for 15 to 20 minutes, until tender. Drain and set aside.

2. Transfer 1 cup of peas to a food processor. Add the oil, vinegar, and garlic. Puree until smooth.

3. In a medium mixing bowl, combine the remaining peas, pureed peas, peppers, onion, scallions, parsley, cilantro, and cumin. Mix well. Cover and refrigerate for at least 6 hours or up to 24 hours.

4. To serve, line a serving bowl with lettuce leaves. Pile the black-eyed pea mixture in the bowl. Serve with a basket of lavosh or water crackers alongside.

NOTE: When cleaning and chopping fresh chile, wear gloves and never wipe your eyes, to avoid the burning capsaicin present in all chiles.

Spanakopitas

Traditionally these savory Greek appetizers are made with lots of butter and fresh Greek feta cheese, which is delicious but very salty—the cheese is kept fresh by covering it with a salt brine until ready to use. Here we've tweaked the recipe, using butter-flavored cooking spray to keep the fat grams down, and formed the dish into individual two-bite pieces that fit nicely in our cardioprotective way of cooking.

Olive oil cooking spray

1 small onion, minced

One 10-ounce package frozen chopped spinach

1/3 cup crumbled reduced-fat feta cheese

1/4 cup 1% cottage cheese

1/8 teaspoon ground nutmeg

1 1/2 tablespoons chopped fresh dill

Freshly ground pepper

1 tablespoon egg substitute

5 sheets frozen phyllo dough, thawed

Refrigerated butter-flavored cooking spray

Makes 20 pieces
(10 servings)

Per serving (2 pieces):
50 calories
   (22% calories from fat)
1.5 g total fat
   (0.5 g saturated fat)
3 g protein
7 g carbohydrate
0 g dietary fiber
0 mg cholesterol
180 mg sodium
60 mg potassium

1. Preheat the oven to 350°F. Coat a baking sheet with olive oil cooking spray.
2. Coat a large nonstick skillet with olive oil spray. Add the onion and spinach; sauté over medium-high heat until the spinach is thawed and the onion begins to wilt, 8 to 10 minutes. Stir frequently to break up clumps of spinach. Add the feta and cottage cheese along with the nutmeg, dill, pepper, and egg substitute; mix well. Remove from heat and cool for 5 minutes.
3. Cut the phyllo dough into 4 lengthwise strips, covering the dough you are not using with a damp tea towel so it does not dry out. Coat each strip with the butter-flavored spray. Place a tablespoon of spinach mix on top of a strip of dough and fold over once to make a triangle; continue folding over as if folding a flag. Place on the prepared baking sheet. Repeat, using all the remaining phyllo and filling. Coat each triangle with the butter-flavored spray. Bake for about 20 minutes, until browned. Serve warm.

Roasted Tomatillo Salsa with Tortilla or Jicama Chips

Makes 3 cups
(12 servings)

Per serving (¼ cup):
20 calories
  (21% calories from fat)
0.5 g total fat
  (0 g saturated fat)
1 g protein
4 g carbohydrate
1 g dietary fiber
0 mg cholesterol
50 mg sodium
180 mg potassium

In the historic Texas town of Gruene, there's a restaurant-grill in an old grist-mill on the banks of the Guadalupe River. The chef makes an excellent tomatillo salsa, but he's reluctant to part with the recipe. After many tries, Fran developed this recipe, which is a close copy.

Mexican tomatillos are related to tomatoes and in fact look like small green tomatoes with a thin parchmentlike outer husk. They add crunch and a lemony flavor to salsas.

1½ pounds tomatillos

3 serranos

3 garlic cloves, unpeeled

Leaves from 12 sprigs fresh cilantro

4 scallions, white parts and 2 inches of the green, each cut into 3 pieces

2 tablespoons fresh lime juice

¼ teaspoon kosher salt

Low-Fat Flour Tortilla Chips or Jicama Chips (recipes follow)

---

1. Preheat the broiler.

2. Remove the husks from the tomatillos and rinse with hot water to remove the stickiness. Place in a shallow baking pan along with the serranos and garlic. Broil 3 inches from the heat source, turning once, until the tomatillos are soft and slightly charred, about 7 minutes. Watch the chiles to avoid burning.

3. Peel the garlic and trim the stems from the chiles. Place in a food processor. Add the tomatillos, chiles, and garlic, cilantro, scallions, lime juice, and salt and puree until smooth. Transfer the mixture to a serving bowl, cover with plastic wrap, and refrigerate for at least 4 hours or up to 24 hours. Serve with Low-Fat Flour Tortilla Chips or Jicama Chips for dipping.

Low-Fat Flour Tortilla Chips

Eight 6½-inch low-fat whole wheat tortillas
Kosher salt, optional

Makes 64 chips
(8 servings)

Per serving (8 chips):
70 calories
  (0% calories from fat)
0 g total fat
  (0 g saturated fat)
3 g protein
20 g carbohydrate
2 g dietary fiber
0 mg cholesterol
170 mg sodium
80 mg potassium

1. Preheat the oven to 350°F. Fill a large bowl with hot water.
2. Dip the tortillas in hot water, one at a time, and shake off the excess. Stack the tortillas and, using a sharp knife, cut into 8 wedges. Arrange the wedges in a single layer on a large baking sheet.
3. Bake the chips for 4 minutes. Turn and continue to bake another 1 to 2 minutes, until the chips are crisp and lightly browned. Sprinkle with salt, if using.
4. Cool and serve with Roasted Tomatillo Salsa. If made ahead, transfer to an airtight container and store at room temperature for up to 4 days.

Jicama Chips

Jicama, also from Mexico, is a large root vegetable with a thin brown skin, crunchy texture, and sweet flavor. Peel just before using.

Makes 40 chips
(8 servings)

Per serving (5 chips):
25 calories
  (0% calories from fat)
0 g total fat
  (0 g saturated fat)
1 g protein
6 g carbohydrate
2 g dietary fiber
0 mg cholesterol
0 mg sodium
106 mg potassium

1 medium jicama, peeled and rinsed (about 1¼ pounds)

Cut the jicama in half and then into ¼-inch-thick slices with a sharp knife. Serve with salsa.

Salmon Mousse

Fresh salmon makes a delightful light mousse to pipe or spoon onto small radicchio leaves for a special party. Although the mousse needs to be prepared ahead to acquire the right consistency, don't assemble these stunning hors d'oeuvres more than an hour before your projected serving time.

Don't wait for a party to make this versatile mousse. Try stuffing a tomato with the mousse to serve as a light lunch or brunch entrée.

Makes 2 cups
(16 servings)

Per serving (2 leaves):
35 calories
  (40% calories from fat)
1.5 g total fat
  (0.5 saturated fat)
3 g protein
2 g carbohydrate
0 g dietary fiber
10 mg cholesterol
40 mg sodium
145 mg potassium

One 6-ounce skinless salmon fillet

2 teaspoons unflavored gelatin

1/2 cup light sour cream

1/4 cup 1% cottage cheese

1 1/2 tablespoons chopped fresh dill

2 teaspoons grated lemon zest

1 large plum tomato, seeded and chopped

2 teaspoons small capers, rinsed

Freshly ground pepper

1/8 teaspoon kosher salt, optional

32 small radicchio leaves (about 4 small heads)

1 bunch fresh chives, chopped

1. Place the salmon in a microwave-safe dish. Add 1/4 cup of water and cover with wax paper or plastic wrap, making sure to leave a vent for steam to escape if using plastic. Cook on High for 1 to 2 minutes, depending on the thickness of the salmon. Remove and let cool.

2. Place 2 tablespoons of water in a small bowl and sprinkle the gelatin over the top. Heat in the microwave for 30 seconds on High, or until the gelatin has dissolved. Flake the cooled salmon into a food processor. Add the gelatin, sour cream, cottage cheese, dill, and lemon zest. Process until the mixture is smooth. Transfer to a bowl and stir in the tomato, capers, pepper, and salt (if using), and refrigerate until set, about 2 hours.

3. To assemble, soften the mousse with a wooden spoon and place in a pastry bag fitted with a star tip. Pipe about 1 tablespoon of the mousse at the bottom of each radicchio leaf (or spoon the mousse into the radicchio leaf). Scatter the chives over the mousse and serve.

DIETITIAN'S NOTE: Although the percentage of calories from fat is higher than we normally recommend, the total calories and fat grams are low, so this tasty appetizer can fit easily into your heart-healthy eating plan.

Shrimp Pot Stickers

Makes 24 dumplings
(12 servings)

Per serving
(2 pot stickers):
70 calories
  (6% calories from fat)
0.5 g total fat
  (0 g saturated fat)
4 g protein
12 g carbohydrate
0.5 g dietary fiber
20 mg cholesterol
130 mg sodium
98 mg potassium

These Asian dumplings are easy to make and are a tasty appetizer or finger food. They can be filled in advance and frozen in a single layer on a cookie sheet. Once completely frozen, transfer them to a self-sealing plastic freezer bag. Later you can either steam them or simmer them in a pot of water. The latter results in softer dumplings; try both ways and decide for yourself.

1/3 pound medium shrimp, shelled, deveined, and coarsely chopped
1/8 teaspoon sugar substitute
1 tablespoon egg substitute
1/2 teaspoon cornstarch
1 teaspoon oyster sauce
1/2 teaspoon grated fresh ginger
1 tablespoon dry sherry
1/2 teaspoon sesame oil
1/4 cup sliced water chestnuts
2 scallions, white parts and 3 inches of the green, chopped
1/2 teaspoon chopped garlic
Twenty-four 3¼-inch square won ton wrappers
Dipping sauces (recipes follow)

1. Place all ingredients except the won ton wrappers and dipping sauces in a food processor or blender. Pulse until a coarse mixture forms. Transfer the mixture to a bowl; cover and refrigerate for 2 hours.

2. To make the pot stickers, cut the corners from the won ton wrappers with a sharp knife or kitchen shears to form circles. Cover the unused wrappers with a damp tea towel to keep them from drying out, removing one at a time. Place a bowl of water nearby to dip your fingers in. Place 1 teaspoon of shrimp mixture on the top half of a wrapper. With your finger, wet the rim of the wrapper. Turn the bottom of the wrapper over the shrimp mixture and seal the edges. Pleat the edges and form into a crescent with crimped edges. Place on a plate or cookie sheet with the pleated edges up.

3. To cook the pot stickers, steam them for 4 to 5 minutes over boiling water in a steamer or a large pot fitted with a rack. Or boil them in a large pot of water until they rise, 4 to 5 minutes. Transfer the cooked pot stickers to a serving plate after draining briefly on paper towels and serve immediately with dipping sauces.

Cleveland Clinic Healthy Heart Lifestyle Guide and Cookbook

VARIATION: Mushroom Pot Stickers. Instead of shrimp, use $1/2$ pound shiitake mushrooms or any combination of shiitakes, portobellos, cremini, or other supermarket mushrooms. Place in the food processor with the other filling ingredients, substituting $1/2$ red bell pepper, seeded and sliced, for the water chestnuts and adding 1 cup shredded cabbage or coleslaw mix. Follow the instructions for Shrimp Pot Stickers, making sure to drain excess liquid before you place the filling on the won ton wrappers.

Per serving
(2 pot stickers):
60 calories
  (7% calories from fat)
0.5 g total fat
  (0 g saturated fat)
2 g protein
11 g carbohydrate
0.5 g dietary fiber
0 mg cholesterol
115 mg sodium
133 mg potassium

Dipping Sauces for Pot Stickers

Dipping sauces for dumplings at Asian restaurants are often laden with sodium or extra sugar. These will satisfy your spicy, sweet, and tart tastes. You might even want to double the recipe to keep in the refrigerator for 2 weeks—these dipping sauces are excellent marinades and barbecue sauces for grilled tofu, chicken, lamb, or fish. Or add 3 tablespoons extra virgin olive oil and use as a refreshing salad dressing, especially when you add fresh fruit to your greens. Enjoy!

Lime Dipping Sauce

Makes about ½ cup
(8 servings)

Per serving
(1 tablespoon):
5 calories
  (0% calories from fat)
0 g total fat
  (0 g saturated fat)
0 g protein
1 g carbohydrate
0 g dietary fiber
0 mg cholesterol
75 mg sodium
25 mg potassium

½ cup fresh lime juice

1½ teaspoons sugar substitute

2 teaspoons reduced-sodium soy sauce

1½ teaspoons hot Asian chili sauce

1 teaspoon grated fresh ginger

1 tablespoon chopped fresh cilantro

Mix all ingredients in a bowl. Allow the flavors to meld for 10 minutes before serving. This sauce can be made the night before and refrigerated until ready to use, but add the cilantro just before serving.

Mango Dipping Sauce

Makes about ¾ cup
(12 servings)

Per serving
(1 tablespoon):
10 calories
  (0% calories from fat)
0 g total fat
  (0 g saturated fat)
0 g protein
3 g carbohydrate
0 g dietary fiber
0 mg cholesterol
15 mg sodium
28 mg potassium

1 ripe mango, diced

1 teaspoon minced fresh ginger

2 tablespoons seasoned rice vinegar

1 teaspoon hot Asian chili sauce

1 teaspoon chopped fresh mint

Place all ingredients in a food processor. Puree until smooth. Serve, or refrigerate until ready to use.

Soups

Soups can be a light appetizer appeaser before dinner or they can stand on their own as a full meal in a bowl. A soup simmering on the stove will fill your house with delicious aromas. Comforting and nourishing, soup is loved by most everyone.

It's important to us that when we call for store-bought ingredients to speed preparation, the other ingredients are the freshest and best you can afford. We want to make sure that when you taste one of our recipes—in this case, for soup—you are missing none of its potential as a great dish. It's our belief that once you've made our recipes and experience how delicious a healthy soup can be, you'll be enticed to make soup more often.

Store-bought broths, even reduced-sodium varieties, still have a significant amount of sodium. If you are on a sodium-restricted diet, cut the amount of broth and substitute either water or dry wine. Salt added to these recipes is almost always listed as optional. Therefore, it is not included in the nutritional data.

Lentil and Spelt Soup

Makes 4 servings

Per serving:
390 calories
  (11% calories from fat)
5 g total fat
  (1 g saturated fat)
22 g protein
70 g carbohydrate
12 g dietary fiber
2.5 mg cholesterol
780 mg sodium
1,019 mg potassium

Spelt, or faro, is a 9,000-year-old grain that is a member of the same family as oats and wheat. However, it is a different species and is often used by those intolerant to commercial wheat products. Its total protein content is 10 to 25 percent greater than that of common commercial wheat. In Europe, spelt flour is frequently used to make pasta and baked goods from pizza to cakes; it is becoming more common in the United States. The cooked kernels, as in this soup, are nutty, adding a southern European flavor to this one-pot meal.

---

2 teaspoons extra virgin olive oil

1 large onion, chopped

1 celery rib, chopped

2 carrots, chopped

1/8 teaspoon kosher salt, optional

Freshly ground pepper

3 garlic cloves, minced

3/4 cup spelt, rinsed and drained

2 cups seeded, chopped ripe tomatoes, or one 14 1/2-ounce can no-salt-added diced tomatoes, drained

5 cups fat-free, reduced-sodium beef broth

1 bay leaf

1/2 cup lentils, rinsed and picked over

1/2 pound spinach, stems removed, thinly sliced

1/4 cup thinly sliced fresh basil

2 tablespoons freshly grated Parmesan cheese

---

1. Heat the oil in a deep saucepan over moderate heat. Add the onion, celery, carrots, salt (if using), and pepper. Cook until the vegetables soften, about 10 minutes. Stir in the garlic, spelt, tomatoes, broth, and bay leaf. Bring to a slow boil, lower the heat, cover, and simmer for 20 minutes. Add the lentils, bring back to a simmer, cover, and cook about 50 minutes, or until the spelt and lentils are tender. (Add water if necessary.)

2. Stir in the spinach and basil. Simmer for 5 minutes. Remove the bay leaf. Serve the soup garnished with Parmesan cheese.

DIETITIAN'S NOTE: This dish is an excellent source of protein and dietary fiber. Although a little high in sodium, choosing reduced-sodium beef broth and no-salt-added tomatoes cuts the sodium content over 50 percent.

Curried Lima Bean Soup

This show-stopping soup is a gift to all of us from Diane Glass, a dear friend of Bonnie's who owned a famous catering business for years. We challenge those who decline eating these wonderful vegetables to identify them in this elegant soup, which we sometimes serve as an appetizer in a small demitasse cup before lunch or dinner or other times as a delicious meal with a salad.

Makes 4 servings

Per serving:
140 calories
   (16% calories from fat)
2 g total fat
   (0 g saturated fat)
8 g protein
24 g carbohydrate
4 g dietary fiber
0 mg cholesterol
600 mg sodium
480 mg potassium

One 10-ounce package frozen lima beans, thawed

1 tablespoon transfree margarine

1 bunch scallions, white parts and 2 inches of the green, thinly sliced

1 teaspoon curry powder

1/2 teaspoon kosher salt

Freshly ground pepper

1/2 teaspoon dried tarragon

4 sprigs fresh flat-leaf parsley

2 cups fat-free, reduced-sodium chicken broth

1/2 cup skim milk

1. Place the lima beans in a food processor. Add the margarine, scallions, curry powder, salt, pepper, tarragon, and parsley. Process until smooth.

2. Transfer the lima bean mixture to a saucepan. Add the broth and milk. Bring to a simmer, cover, and cook for 10 minutes. If the soup is too thick, add water to bring it to the consistency of a thick cream soup.

3. Ladle into 4 heated soup bowls. Serve immediately.

Sherried Tomato Broth with Crème Fraîche

Makes 4 servings

Per serving:
170 calories
  (4% calories from fat)
1 g total fat
  (0 g saturated fat)
10 g protein
33 g carbohydrate
4 g dietary fiber
0 mg cholesterol
390 mg sodium
735 mg potassium

We love this light soup, which is excellent served hot or cold, with diced peppers and cucumber floating on top. When fresh tomatoes are out of season, drain canned no-salt-added tomatoes, and proceed to tomato bliss.

---

3 cups fat-free, reduced-sodium beef broth

1/4 cup plus 1 tablespoon dry sherry

4 cups diced tomatoes (about 2 1/2 pounds)

2 shallots, quartered

6 peppercorns

1/4 cup packed chopped fresh basil, plus 4 whole leaves

1/4 cup Crème Fraîche (page 336)

---

1. Place the beef broth and 1 cup water in a saucepan. Add the 1/4 cup sherry, the tomatoes, shallots, peppercorns, and chopped basil. Bring to a simmer and cook for 15 to 18 minutes, until all vegetables are soft. Strain through a sieve, pressing the liquid from the soft vegetables. Discard solids.

2. To serve, reheat the soup and place in bowls. Place a dollop of the crème fraîche on each serving and stand a basil leaf decoratively in the crème. Drizzle each serving with one-fourth of the remaining sherry and serve.

Winter Vegetable Soup

After a morning of cross-country skiing or sledding with the kids, nothing's more warming than a bowl of hearty vegetable soup for lunch. We frequently make a double batch, freezing half for another meal. Team this soup with some crisp winter apples or pears and a serving of low-fat Cheddar cheese, and you're ready for company.

Makes 8 servings

Per serving:
130 calories
  (20% calories from fat)
3 g total fat
  (0.5 g saturated fat)
9 g protein
21 g carbohydrate
5 g dietary fiber
0 mg cholesterol
130 mg sodium
120 mg potassium

2 teaspoons extra virgin olive oil

1/2 pound leeks, trimmed, split in half lengthwise, and well rinsed

1 medium white onion, chopped

1/2 pound carrots, thinly sliced on the diagonal

2 large celery ribs, thinly sliced on the diagonal

2 tablespoons dried lentils, rinsed and picked over

2 tablespoons dried split peas, rinsed and picked over

2 tablespoons dried small white beans, rinsed and picked over

1 teaspoon dried thyme

1/2 teaspoon freshly ground pepper

2 quarts fat-free, reduced-sodium chicken or vegetable broth

One 14 1/2-ounce can no-salt-added plum tomatoes, drained and coarsely chopped

1/4 pound spinach, tough stems discarded

1. In a large soup pot, heat the oil over medium-low heat. Thinly slice the leeks and add them to the pot along with the onion. Cook, stirring, until the vegetables wilt, about 5 minutes.

2. Add the carrots, celery, lentils, peas, beans, thyme, pepper, and broth. Bring to a boil. Reduce the heat and simmer, covered, for 45 minutes, stirring occasionally.

3. Stir in the tomatoes and continue to simmer, covered, for another 15 minutes, until the white beans are tender. Stir in the spinach and simmer, uncovered, until wilted, about 3 minutes. Ladle into soup bowls and serve.

Mom's Chicken Soup

Makes 6 servings

Per serving:
250 calories
  (28% calories from fat)
7.5 g total fat
  (2 g saturated fat)
29 g protein
8 g carbohydrate
1 g dietary fiber
85 mg cholesterol
250 mg sodium
430 mg potassium

Nothing warms the soul or says family better than chicken soup. Bonnie's mother made this soup for family dinners, serving it sometimes as chicken in the pot, and other times with dumplings, brown or wild rice, or whole wheat noodles. No matter how you serve it, everyone will love it.

---

1 whole clove

1 medium onion

2½ pounds chicken breasts and thighs with legs, skin and visible fat removed

1 small sweet potato, scrubbed but not peeled

1 small turnip, peeled

1 medium carrot, peeled

2 garlic cloves

1 cup dry white wine

2 cups fat-free, reduced-sodium chicken broth

2 large sprigs fresh dill

6 peppercorns

2 bay leaves

---

1. Stick the clove into the onion and put it in a soup pot. Add the chicken, sweet potato, turnip, carrot, and garlic. Pour in the wine, broth, and 2 cups water. Bring to a simmer and add the dill, peppercorns, and bay leaves; skim the soup as needed for 10 minutes.

2. Simmer, covered, until the chicken is very tender, about 35 minutes. Strain the broth into a pot or large bowl and refrigerate so you can remove any fat that congeals as it cools. Discard the clove, onion, turnip, garlic, dill, and bay leaves. Peel the sweet potato; dice the potato and carrot. Remove the chicken and cool. Bone the chicken, cut off all fat and gristle, and dice into bite-size pieces.

3. To serve, reheat the soup to a simmer, then ladle into soup bowls. Divide the diced vegetables and chicken among the soup bowls and serve immediately.

VARIATION: Matzo Ball Soup. Use kosher for Passover dry wine and chicken broth to make the soup. To make the matzo balls, combine 1/2 cup matzo meal; 4 large egg whites, slightly beaten; 2 tablespoons canola oil; 2 tablespoons cold water; 1/4 teaspoon kosher salt; 1 tablespoon minced fresh flat-leaf parsley; and a dash of ground nutmeg. Refrigerate for at least 1 hour. To cook, bring a pot of lightly salted water to a boil. Reduce to a simmer and drop rounded teaspoons of batter into the water. (Makes 12 matzo balls.) Allow to simmer for about 15 minutes, until the dumplings rise. Drain and add to chicken soup. Garnish with parsley leaves.

Per serving:
340 calories
  (33% calories from fat)
12 g total fat
  (2.5 g saturated fat)
33 g protein
18 g carbohydrate
2 g dietary fiber
18 mg cholesterol
390 mg sodium
465 mg potassium

Tortilla Soup Texas-Style with Tortilla Stacks

Makes 6 servings

Per serving:
130 calories
  (48% calories from fat)
7 g total fat
  (2 g saturated fat)
5 g protein
13 g carbohydrate
4 g dietary fiber
5 mg cholesterol
700 mg sodium
327 mg potassium

Grady Spears, a noted Texas chef, uses this beautifully presented soup as a signature piece regardless of where he's currently cooking. The simple ingredients are quick to assemble, yet the flavor is complex.

Vegetable oil cooking spray

Four 6-inch blue- or yellow-corn tortillas, cut into very thin strips

1 medium onion, quartered

1 garlic clove, quartered

1 dried ancho chile

1/2 teaspoon dried oregano

1 small bay leaf

5 black peppercorns

2 quarts fat-free, reduced-sodium chicken broth

1 lime

1 large plum tomato, seeded and finely diced

1 large firm, ripe Hass avocado, finely diced

1/2 cup shredded reduced-fat Monterey Jack cheese

6 sprigs fresh cilantro

1. Preheat the oven to 450°F. Lightly coat a baking sheet with cooking spray.

2. Spread the tortilla strips in a single layer on the prepared baking sheet. Bake, turning once, until the strips are very crisp, about 5 minutes. Set aside to cool.

3. Put the onion, garlic, chile, oregano, bay leaf, peppercorns, and broth in a large saucepan. Bring to a boil over medium-high heat. Reduce the heat and simmer for 10 minutes. Pour the broth mixture through a fine sieve into a preheated pot. Keep hot.

4. Divide the tortilla strips among 6 shallow soup bowls, piling them in the center. Cut the lime into 6 slices, cutting off and discarding the ends. Place a lime slice and a small pile of tomato, avocado, and cheese in each bowl. Lay a cilantro sprig on top of each lime slice. Slowly ladle the broth into each bowl, taking care not to disturb the contents of the bowl. Serve the hot soup at once.

DIETITIAN'S NOTE: The majority of the fat in this delicious soup is heart-protective monounsaturated fat. This filling soup is low in calories, making it a great first course. Just watch the amount of sodium in the rest of your meal, as this soup is a bit higher in salt.

Tomato Black Bean Soup

This homey soup goes together quickly once you have chopped the vegetables. We love to make a large pot on Sunday for dinner and use it during the week for lunches. With added leftover vegetables, cooked pasta, rice, or Crostini (page 337), it becomes a new soup. The leftovers can be frozen for up to six months, but it will never be around that long. By using low-salt tomatoes, you avoid more than 100 milligrams of sodium.

2 teaspoons extra virgin olive oil

1 large onion, finely chopped

2 carrots, finely chopped

1 celery rib, finely chopped

3 garlic cloves, finely chopped

One 28-ounce can low-sodium crushed tomatoes

3 1/2 cups fat-free reduced-sodium beef broth

1/2 cup dry white wine

2 1/2 tablespoons chopped fresh mint

Freshly ground pepper

One 15-ounce can black beans, rinsed and drained

6 ounces baby spinach, roughly chopped

2 tablespoons fresh lemon juice

1. Heat the oil in a large nonstick saucepan. Add the onion, carrots, celery, and garlic. Sauté for about 5 minutes, until wilted.

2. Stir in the tomatoes, broth, wine, 1/2 cup water, mint, and pepper. Simmer for 10 minutes. Add the beans, spinach, and lemon juice. Cook just until the spinach wilts. Serve immediately in heated soup bowls.

VARIATION: South of the Border Tomato Black Bean Soup. Omit the white wine and mint. Carefully, seed, devein, and mince 1 small jalapeño and sauté it with the vegetables. Increase the broth to 4 cups and add 1/4 cup chopped fresh cilantro. Stir in 1 cup thawed frozen corn kernels with the spinach. Top each bowl with a tablespoon of grated reduced-fat Cheddar cheese, chopped scallions, and a teaspoon of fat-free sour cream.

DIETITIAN'S NOTE: Both of these tasty soups are a perfect way to reach your legume goal of 1/2 cup each day!

Makes 8 servings

Per serving:
100 calories
   (18% calories from fat)
2 g total fat
   (0 g saturated fat)
5 g protein
18 g carbohydrate
5 g dietary fiber
0 mg cholesterol
510 mg sodium
495 mg potassium

Per serving:
130 calories
   (24% calories from fat)
3.5 g total fat
   (1.5 g saturated fat)
8 g protein
23 g carbohydrate
6 g dietary fiber
5 mg cholesterol
540 mg sodium
560 mg potassium

A Simple, Delicious Onion Soup

Makes 8 servings

Per serving:
140 calories
  (10% calories from fat)
1.5 g total fat
  (0.5 g saturated fat)
7 g protein
21 g carbohydrate
2 g dietary fiber
5 mg cholesterol
640 mg sodium
142 mg potassium

The secret to a superb onion soup is to sauté the onions slowly until they take on a caramel color, then let them slowly simmer until the onions almost melt into the rich broth. The long simmering brings out the natural sweetness of the onions. If you're planning to serve this for a weeknight dinner, make the soup the night before, refrigerate it, and reheat the next day.

Refrigerated butter-flavored cooking spray

4 large yellow onions, thinly sliced into rings

2 teaspoons sugar

2 quarts fat-free, reduced-sodium beef broth

1 cup dry red wine

Kosher salt, optional

Freshly ground pepper

Eight 1/2-inch-thick slices whole wheat baguette

Olive oil cooking spray

1 garlic clove, minced

1/4 cup freshly grated Parmesan cheese

---

1. Lightly coat a Dutch oven with the butter-flavored cooking spray. Place over medium heat and add the onions. Cook, stirring, until the onions are limp, about 4 minutes. Sprinkle with sugar and continue to cook until the onions are the color of caramel, 20 to 25 minutes. Be careful not to let the onions burn. Add the broth and wine, cover, and simmer for about 2 hours, stirring occasionally, until the onions are almost dissolved into the broth. Add salt (if using) and pepper to taste.

2. Just before the soup is served, preheat the broiler. Place the bread slices on a baking sheet and lightly coat each slice with olive oil spray. Sprinkle the bread evenly with the garlic and cheese. Broil until the cheese is melted and golden brown.

3. Ladle the soup into heated soup bowls and float a cheese toast in the center of each bowl. Serve immediately.

Salads

Years ago salad meant a pale green iceberg lettuce wedge, usually partially covered with a bottled salad dressing. Today we've experienced a salad revolution. At the market, iceberg lettuce is surrounded by Belgian endive; watercress; radicchio; organic baby arugula and spinach; Asian greens such as tatsoi, mizuna, and pea shoots; spring mix (similar to mesclun); and many more options. Packages of prewashed greens and salad mixes, some complete with dressings and toppings, are nearby.

When you think about it, what can be healthier than a salad? But salads can be healthy only if the ingredients are good for you and added in appropriate amounts. Be leery of salad dressings, as they are usually full of fat and salt. This is true of the dressings in packaged salad kits as well as bottled dressings, so read the labels before consuming. Salad bars include substantial amounts of cheese, croutons, and mayonnaise-based salads such as chicken or pasta salad, all high in fat grams. Add up what's on top of the lettuce and you may have reached your calorie, fat, and salt quota for the day—or week. If you're shopping for one of our recipes and see that the ingredients listed are not at your market, feel free to substitute. Fruit is easy to change. Oranges can replace peaches, arugula can become baby spinach, and Bibb lettuce can be substituted for field greens.

A Few Quick Tips

- Herbs are available year-round and can raise your salad from a bunch of torn greens to a culinary experience. Whether you tear or cut herbs really doesn't matter. Do what you like and choose what looks good to you.
- Tomatoes are also available year-round. In the winter, we purchase vine-ripened tomatoes rather than hothouse varieties because they taste more like tomatoes in season. In the summer we patronize the farmers' markets and farm stands for heirloom varieties. Whenever they're available, grape tomatoes (baby Romas) and teardrop tomatoes (both red and yellow) are excellent for the salad bowl.
- The sweet-tart flavor of fruit adds a vibrancy to salads. Use it freely in place of croutons on green salads; sprinkle chopped fruit onto chicken or seafood salads. Try new fruits such as pomegranates or star fruit. You won't be disappointed.
- We use extra virgin olive oil in our salads (and for cooking). You may think this expensive, but remember that salad dressings should "dress" a salad, not drown it. In your new cardioprotective cooking, you'll be using teaspoons of oil in place of the tablespoons you used before. That pricey bottle of extra virgin olive oil will last a long time.

We have sprinkled salad dressing recipes throughout this book. Also, some sauce recipes can be thinned for a salad dressing. Here's where to find them: Japanese Dressing (page 204), Thousand Island Sauce (page 218), Lemon Vinaigrette (page 166), Citrus Vinaigrette (page 165), Balsamic Vinaigrette (page 169), Raspberry Vinaigrette (page 158), Dijon Balsamic Vinaigrette (with olive oil added, page 200), Mango and Lime Dipping Sauces (with added olive oil; page 142).

Making a Simple Green Salad

Nothing could be easier than making a simple green salad, but to make a superb one, you have to start with great greens that are fresh and healthy looking, with no broken or torn leaves, or signs of aging, or brown edges. For our salads we use combinations of two or three different types of greens that we have carefully selected for compatibility in flavor, color, shape, and texture. But feel free to be adventurous—try new varieties and new combinations. Also experiment with Asian greens, wild greens, and savory herbs so that you can create dozens of different combinations.

Here are some of our favorite combinations for green salads:

- Mixed baby greens with Belgian endive and pea shoots
- Baby arugula with Boston lettuce
- Fresh fennel with romaine
- Bibb lettuce with tatsoi, mizuna, mint, and opal basil
- Romaine with alfalfa or radish sprouts
- Frisée with baby spinach and Boston lettuce
- Spinach with a variety of sprouts
- Chopped or grated red and green cabbages
- Radicchio with dandelion greens and arugula
- Watercress and Belgium endive
- Spinach with arugula
- Romaine hearts with radicchio
- Frisée with Bibb lettuce and shavings of raw artichoke

Persian Chopped Salad

Makes 8 servings

Per serving:
130 calories
    (31% calories from fat)
4.5 g total fat
    (0.5 g saturated fat)
4 g protein
20 g carbohydrate
4 g dietary fiber
0 mg cholesterol
170 mg sodium
408 mg potassium

A full cup of coarsely chopped fresh mint leaves makes this a very refreshing salad when you are grilling meat, fish, or poultry. We grow mint in a large pot to keep it under control, since mint planted in the ground tends to take over the garden. Although there are more than a hundred varieties of mint, spearmint is the best to grow for everyday cooking. The leaves can be roughly chopped and frozen during the cold months, when the plant goes dormant until spring. Or you can keep a pot going on a windowsill year-round.

4 medium tomatoes, finely chopped (about 1¼ pounds)

2 small cucumbers, peeled, seeded, and finely chopped

1 medium onion, finely chopped

One 15-ounce can chickpeas, rinsed and drained

¼ cup fresh lime juice

2 tablespoons extra virgin olive oil

Kosher salt, optional

Freshly ground pepper

1 cup coarsely chopped fresh mint

Crisp lettuce leaves for lining the serving dish

1. Combine the tomatoes, cucumbers, onion, and chickpeas in a large bowl. In a small measuring cup, whisk together the lime juice and oil. Pour over the vegetables and lightly toss. Season to taste with salt, if using, and pepper. Toss with fresh mint. Cover and chill for 1 hour.

2. At least 30 minutes before serving, remove the salad from the refrigerator. Line a serving dish with lettuce leaves. Transfer the salad to the dish. Serve at room temperature.

Quinoa and Salmon Salad

Here we marry the sweetness of salmon to the nutty taste of toasted quinoa (pronounced KEEN-wah). The result is a salad that can become a dinner or lunch along with fresh fruit in the heat of the summer or one that will cheer you out of the doldrums of winter with its combination of textures and tastes. If arugula is difficult to find, substitute baby spinach with 1 teaspoon dried tarragon.

Makes 4 servings

Per serving:
285 calories
    (29% calories from fat
9 g total fat
    (1.5 g saturated fat)
19 g protein
32 g carbohydrate
3 g dietary fiber
34 mg cholesterol
278 mg sodium
718 mg potassium

1 cup quinoa

Olive oil cooking spray

¼ teaspoon kosher salt

½ pound wild salmon fillet

1½ cups chopped arugula leaves, washed and dried

1 cup cherry tomatoes, halved (6 ounces)

1 garlic clove, minced

2½ tablespoons white wine vinegar

2 teaspoons extra virgin olive oil

Freshly ground pepper

¼ cup crumbled reduced-fat feta cheese

1. Wash the quinoa in a fine sieve under cold running water. Drain well. Coat a nonstick saucepan with cooking spray. Add the quinoa and lightly toast over medium heat for 2 minutes. Add 2 cups water and the salt. Bring to a boil, lower the heat, cover, and simmer for 15 minutes, or until the liquid is absorbed. Remove from heat. Fluff with a fork and place in a bowl to cool.

2. Coat a sauté pan with cooking spray. Cook the salmon skin side up for 6 minutes over medium heat. Turn the salmon over and continue to cook until the fish is opaque and flakes easily when tested with the point of a knife. Remove from the pan and discard the skin. Cool and cut into bite-size pieces. Add to the quinoa along with the arugula and tomatoes.

3. Combine the garlic, vinegar, oil, and a generous grinding of pepper. Toss with the quinoa salad. Top with feta. Chill and serve.

DIETITIAN'S NOTE: Each serving contains 1,070 milligrams of omega-3 and is a great way to get in the recommended daily amount of this essential fat.

Spinach Salad with Oranges and Walnuts

Makes 4 servings

Per serving:
130 calories
  (48% calories from fat)
7 g total fat
  (1 g saturated fat)
4 g protein
16 g carbohydrate
4 g dietary fiber
5 mg cholesterol
160 mg sodium
164 mg potassium

The sweetness of fruit goes very well with the texture and slightly bitter taste of the spinach. Oranges are delicious in salads, but we use many other fruits as well, depending on the season—from pears and apples in the fall to a variety of berries in the spring and summer. Dried fruits processed without sugar make an excellent addition to salads when fresh fruits are expensive or not available. Toasting nuts for 4 to 5 minutes on a backing sheet in the oven is easy and makes them taste fresh.

Raspberry Vinaigrette

2 tablespoons white wine vinegar

1 tablespoon sugar-free raspberry jelly or jam

1 tablespoon extra virgin olive oil

1/4 cup fresh or thawed frozen raspberries

2 teaspoons minced shallot

1/2 teaspoon Dijon mustard

Freshly ground pepper

1/4 teaspoon sugar substitute, optional

6 ounces baby spinach

2 navel oranges, peeled and segmented (see page 159)

2 tablespoons chopped walnuts, toasted (see page 319)

1/4 cup crumbled reduced-fat feta cheese

1. In a small bowl combine all ingredients for the vinaigrette. Whisk well to combine. The fresh raspberries will fall apart and the jam will melt. Taste for seasoning and add sugar substitute if needed.

2. Place the spinach in a salad bowl. Top with the orange segments, walnuts, and cheese. Toss with the dressing and serve immediately.

NOTE: Try different fruit and nut combinations when making this salad, such as dried cherries with pecans and a bit of blue cheese, or fresh strawberries, almonds, and grated Parmesan cheese.

DIETITIAN'S NOTE: Although high in their percentage of calories from fat, these salads are a wonderful source of heart-protective monounsaturated and polyunsaturated fats (from the olive oil and nuts) as well as phytonutrients and dietary fiber.

Balsamic Vinegar

We love balsamic vinegar because it gives great depth of flavor to recipes and makes simple ingredients seem complex. We drizzle a few drops on sweet melons and berries as well as using it on our salads and in sauces. When buying balsamic vinegar, make sure that it comes from Modena, Italy. Although you can pay from a few dollars to hundreds for balsamic vinegar aged in wooden barrels for years, there are a few words to look for on the label. The word *contimento* may be on the label of more reasonably priced bottles. These are fine for most recipes. *Tradizionale* will be on the label of the more expensive vinegars and may be out of your price range for everyday cooking. We purchase authentic balsamic vinegar rather than vinegar labeled as such in the supermarket, which may be a mixture of grape juice, red wine vinegar, and caramel coloring. You can reduce it to get a more concentrated taste, but the best choice is to use less and buy a more authentic brand.

Segmenting Oranges

Using a sharp thin knife, cut thin slices from the top and bottom of the fruit so that it is steady when resting on a flat surface. Cut off the peel, pith, and outer membrane. Working over a bowl to collect any juice, remove the fruit segments by cutting next to the membrane toward the middle of the fruit on both sides of each fruit segment. Discard any seeds. Squeeze the membrane to extract any remaining juice. Discard the membrane. You're ready for your recipe.

Warm Arugula with Polenta Croutons and Mozzarella Cheese

Makes 4 servings

Michael Herschman, the executive chef of Vivo, a stylish Italian restaurant in the Gateway District of downtown Cleveland, Ohio, gave us this recipe. If you keep the croutons on hand and roast the shallots ahead of time, the salad goes together quickly.

Per serving:

460 calories
  (31% calories from fat)
16 g total fat
  (3 g saturated fat)
20 g protein
76 g carbohydrate
3 g dietary fiber
5 mg cholesterol
300 mg sodium
510 mg potassium

Polenta Croutons

Olive oil cooking spray

1 cup yellow cornmeal

1 teaspoon kosher salt

1 bunch flat-leaf parsley, chopped

Pinch of freshly ground pepper

1 teaspoon extra virgin olive oil

Juice of 1/2 lemon

Roasted Shallots

3 shallots, thickly sliced

Pinch of kosher salt, optional

Pinch of freshly ground pepper

1 teaspoon extra virgin olive oil

Balsamic Dressing

1 recipe Balsamic Vinaigrette (page 169)

1 teaspoon finely chopped fresh thyme

2 teaspoons finely chopped fresh flat-leaf parsley

1 pound baby arugula

1/2 cup shredded reduced-fat mozzarella cheese

1. Preheat the oven to 400°F. Lightly coat a baking sheet with cooking spray.

2. Combine all remaining polenta ingredients in a pot and slowly bring to a boil. When the mixture begins to thicken, after about 3 minutes, spread onto the prepared baking sheet. Cover with foil and bake for 5 minutes. Remove the foil and continue to bake until the mixture is firm and dry, about 10 minutes more. Remove from the oven and let cool. When cool, cut into 1-inch cubes. (If making the croutons in advance, store in an airtight container in the refrigerator for up to 1 week. Bring to room temperature before using.)

3. As soon as you put the polenta in the oven, prepare the shallots. Place the shallots on a piece of foil. Sprinkle with salt, if using, season with pepper, and drizzle with oil. Fold the foil over the shallots and bake alongside the polenta. Remove from the oven after 15 minutes and open the foil to cool.

4. Combine the Balsamic Vinaigrette and roasted shallots in a food processor. Add the thyme and parsley. Pulse to puree.

5. In a large stainless-steel mixing bowl, combine the arugula, mozzarella, and 8 polenta croutons. Add the balsamic dressing and place the bowl on the stove over low heat. Stir constantly with metal tongs, taking care to not bruise the arugula leaves. Continue stirring until the cheese melts and the other ingredients are warm. Remove from the stove.

6. On each of 4 large plates, place a 4-inch ring (see Note). Fill each of the rings with the warm arugula salad, pressing down to tightly fill the ring. Remove the ring. If you prefer not to use a ring mold, divide the salad among 4 plates, making a firm pile in the center.

NOTE: Although you can buy ring molds from specialty kitchenware shops and restaurant supply stores, you can simply use 4-inch pieces of 4-inch wide PVC or a tuna can with the bottom removed. Wash in hot, sudsy water and dry.

DIETITIAN'S NOTE: Although this dish is higher in calories from fat, the amount of saturated fat is low, and it is a good sources of dietary fiber and potassium.

Cold Asian Noodle Salad with Salmon

Makes 4 servings

Per serving:
410 calories
   (20% calories from fat)
9 g total fat
   (1.5 g saturated fat)
32 g protein
52 g carbohydrate
8 g dietary fiber
60 mg cholesterol
260 mg sodium
900 mg potassium

This is one of those easy recipes that will please the entire family. When making Asian dishes, have all ingredients at arm's length, prepped before you start cooking. The final assembly takes no time. You can use leftover chicken instead of the salmon for even quicker preparation. Toasted sesame seeds and chili and garlic sauces are available in the Asian foods section of your supermarket.

Garlic Sauce

2 teaspoons reduced-sodium soy sauce

3 tablespoons rice wine vinegar or dry sherry

1-inch piece fresh ginger, peeled and grated

1/8 teaspoon sugar substitute

1 to 2 tablespoons chili sauce

1 to 2 tablespoons garlic sauce

1 pound boneless, skinless wild salmon fillet

Juice of 1 lemon

8 ounces whole wheat fettuccine

1 English cucumber, halved lengthwise and sliced very thin

2 scallions, white parts and 3 inches of the green, cut diagonally into 1/4-inch slices

1/4 cup chopped fresh cilantro

1 tablespoon toasted sesame seeds

1. In a small bowl combine the soy sauce, vinegar, ginger, sugar substitute, and chili and garlic sauces to taste. Set aside.

2. Place the salmon in a microwave-safe dish. Add 1/4 cup water and the lemon juice. Microwave on High for 4 to 6 minutes. Turn the fish over; cover tightly with plastic wrap, turning one corner back to form a vent. Rotate the fish if you do not have a rotating tray. Microwave for another 4 minutes. Test with the sharp point of a knife to see if the fish flakes easily and is opaque. Cook for additional 10-second intervals if needed until cooked through. Remember that the fish will continue to cook after it is removed from the microwave so don't overcook it. It should be moist. Remove from the poaching liquid when cooked through, flake into bite-size pieces, and refrigerate until ready to assemble the salad.

3. Cook the pasta until al dente, according to package directions. Rinse with cold water, drain well, and place in a large bowl.

4. Toss the pasta with the salmon, cucumber, scallions, cilantro, and Garlic Sauce. Garnish with toasted sesame seeds and serve.

Layered Tabbouleh and Vegetable Salad

Makes 8 servings

Per serving:
240 calories
  (30% calories from fat)
8 g total fat
  (2 g saturated fat)
10 g protein
33 g carbohydrate
9 g dietary fiber
10 mg cholesterol
420 mg sodium
716 mg potassium

This is a terrific salad to take to a party because it doesn't require refrigeration. It can sit at room temperature for hours. Be sure to use your prettiest glass salad bowl (preferably one on a pedestal) to show off every layer.

6 cups Lemon and Fresh Herb Tabbouleh (page 277)

3 large jarred roasted red bell peppers, julienned (about 3 ounces)

One 15-ounce can chickpeas, rinsed and drained

One 10-ounce package frozen artichoke hearts, thawed and cut in half

1/2 English cucumber, very thinly sliced

3 ounces reduced-fat Cheddar cheese, cubed

1 large fennel bulb, trimmed

About 6 ounces mixed greens, such as mesclun

8 radishes, very thinly sliced

1 tablespoon red wine vinegar

1/2 teaspoon Dijon mustard

1 tablespoon extra virgin olive oil

1. Place the tabbouleh in the bottom of a 3-quart clear salad bowl. Place the peppers on top of the tabbouleh. Layer the chickpeas, artichoke hearts, cucumber, and cheese. Cut the fennel bulb in half from top to bottom. Cut the halves into paper-thin slices crosswise. Add the fennel to the salad and top with the greens and radishes.

2. Whisk together the vinegar, mustard, and oil. Drizzle evenly over the salad. Cover tightly with plastic wrap and refrigerate for 6 to 24 hours. When ready to serve, toss lightly to coat evenly.

DIETITIAN'S NOTE: This dish is a powerful source of potassium and dietary fiber and a great way to meet your vegetable goals!

Warm Cannellini Bean Salad with Salmon and Citrus Vinaigrette

This Italian-inspired salad is a quick workday meal for the entire family. All you need is a dessert like Caramelized Pineapple with Raspberries (page 324).

Makes 4 servings

Per serving:
320 calories
  (41% calories from fat)
14 g total fat
  (2.5 g saturated fat)
23 g protein
23 g carbohydrate
6 g dietary fiber
45 mg cholesterol
260 mg sodium
620 mg potassium

One 15-ounce can cannellini beans, rinsed and drained

Olive oil cooking spray

One 12-ounce wild salmon fillet

1 medium red onion, thinly sliced

1 garlic clove, minced

1/2 English cucumber, thinly sliced

1 red bell pepper, seeded and chopped

2 tablespoons chopped fresh mint

4 Bibb or Boston lettuce leaf cups

Citrus Vinaigrette

1/4 cup fresh orange juice

1 teaspoon grated orange zest

1 tablespoon white wine vinegar

2 tablespoons extra virgin olive oil

3/8 teaspoon kosher salt, optional

Freshly ground pepper

1. Place the beans in a salad bowl. Set aside.

2. Heat a ridged grill pan or a barbecue grill. Coat the grill or pan with cooking spray. Grill the salmon. Cook for 10 to 15 minutes, turning once, until cooked through; use a sharp knife to check for doneness. When done, cool 5 minutes and divide into 4 sections.

3. Coat a nonstick skillet with cooking spray. Sauté the onion until translucent. Add the garlic and continue to sauté for 1 minute more. Stir into the reserved beans. Add the cucumber, bell pepper, and mint. Toss the salad.

4. In a small bowl, whisk together the orange juice, zest, vinegar, oil, salt (if using), and pepper; toss with the salad. Place the lettuce cups on 4 plates. Top with salad and place the salmon alongside. Serve immediately.

DIETITIAN'S NOTE: Packed with fiber, potassium, and your daily allotment of omega-3-rich fats, this Italianate dish is a winner!

Fava Bean, Artichoke Heart, and Grape Tomato Salad

Makes 4 servings

Per serving:
190 calories
 (40% calories from fat)
9 g total fat
 (2 g saturated fat)
9 g protein
21 g carbohydrate
8 g dietary fiber
5 mg cholesterol
140 mg sodium
610 mg potassium

Fresh fava beans in the market mean that spring has arrived, in both Europe and the U.S. They have been cultivated for 5,000 years from China to Africa and the Mediterranean and are second only to soybeans in plant protein. Today this very popular vegetable is grown from Texas to California to Puget Sound. Look for these large pods with sweet beans inside, selecting bright unblemished pods without bulging beans. If you cannot find fresh fava beans, use canned favas or frozen edamame (soybeans) so you can make this revitalizing salad year-round. We frequently serve it as a light supper with artisan whole-grain bread and a refreshing granita (page 330).

Lemon Vinaigrette
3 tablespoons fresh lemon juice
2 tablespoons extra virgin olive oil
1 garlic clove, minced
1 small shallot, minced
3 tablespoons chopped fresh mint
2 tablespoons chopped fresh flat-leaf parsley
1/8 teaspoon kosher salt, optional
Freshly ground pepper

1 pound fresh fava beans, shelled, cooked, and peeled (about 1 cup; see Note)
1 cup (6 ounces) grape tomatoes
One 10-ounce package frozen artichoke hearts, thawed, drained, and dried in paper towels
6 ounces mixed greens
3 tablespoons freshly grated Parmesan cheese

1. In a small bowl, whisk the vinaigrette ingredients until well combined. Set aside to allow the flavors to meld.
2. Combine the fava beans, tomatoes, and artichokes. Stir in the vinaigrette with 2 1/2 tablespoons of water and allow to sit for at least 15 minutes. To serve, divide the greens among 4 plates and top with the bean salad. Garnish with cheese. Serve immediately.

NOTE: Preparing fava beans takes minutes. Bring a pot of water to a boil. Add the beans and cook for 1 minute. Drain. When cool enough to handle, split the skin with your fingernail and squeeze the beans into a bowl. You can also use a small sharp knife to slice the skin of the beans.

Pasta with Vegetables

Ever since Thomas Jefferson first imported a pasta machine to America in 1789, pasta has increased in popularity. Even the low-carb diet that swept the country didn't keep pasta away from its fans for long—the manufacturers simply created a "low-carb" pasta. Now heart-healthy whole wheat pasta fills our pantries. We serve it with lots of fresh vegetables for a perfect first course or a light main meal. Actually, these pasta recipes contain so many vegetables that we considered calling this chapter "Vegetables with Pasta." No matter what we call it, you're going to love our version of pastas.

A Few Quick Tips

- Some ingredients especially complement pasta: beans, especially cannellini; cheese, especially freshly grated Parmesan; chiles and bell peppers; eggplant; garlic; herbs, especially fresh basil; mushrooms; extra virgin olive oil; onions; black pepper; pesto; pine nuts; all kinds of tomatoes, especially plum; and zucchini.
- Don't skimp on the size of the pasta cooking pot or the amount of water. Use at least a 5-quart pot and a gallon of water per pound of pasta.
- Pasta should be tasted to see if it's done. Start testing fresh pasta after 30 seconds; test dried pasta after 4 minutes. When it's done, pasta should be tender but still firm with a tiny, chalky white center.
- If you want more protein than you get with whole wheat pasta, try spelt pasta. With its nutty flavor, spelt pasta has been popular in Europe for several years, and now it's available throughout America.
- When you drain cooked pasta, reserve some of the cooking liquid. You'll find it useful for thinning the sauce or reheating the pasta before it's sauced.

Penne Pasta Salad with Asparagus, Arugula, and Balsamic Vinaigrette

This room-temperature salad is perfect for a quick evening meal or for a buffet table. You can easily double the recipe. Feel free to substitute a red bell pepper for the yellow and, if you can't find pine nuts, try walnuts. This is the time to use your favorite full-bodied extra virgin olive oil and best balsamic vinegar.

Makes 4 servings

Per serving:
270 calories
  (41% calories from fat)
13 g total fat
  (1.5 g saturated fat)
8 g protein
34 g carbohydrate
6 g dietary fiber
0 mg cholesterol
35 mg sodium
530 mg potassium

4 ounces whole wheat penne

1/2 pound asparagus, tough ends removed, cut into 2-inch pieces

1 yellow bell pepper, seeded and julienned

5 ounces baby arugula or mature arugula, stems removed, torn into bite-size pieces

1 cup grape or cherry tomatoes, halved

1/4 cup fresh basil, torn

1 tablespoon toasted pine nuts

  Balsamic Vinaigrette

3 tablespoons extra virgin olive oil

3 tablespoons aged balsamic vinegar

1 garlic clove, minced

1 teaspoon minced shallot

1 teaspoon Dijon mustard

1/4 teaspoon kosher salt, optional

Freshly ground pepper

1. Cook the pasta according to package directions until al dente. Drain and let cool slightly.

2. While the pasta is cooking, simmer the asparagus until just crisp-tender, 2 to 3 minutes. Refresh under cold water, pat dry, and place in a large salad bowl. Add the bell pepper, arugula, tomatoes, and basil.

3. Make the vinaigrette by mixing the oil, vinegar, garlic, shallot, mustard, and 1 tablespoon water in a small cup. Add salt, if using, and pepper and whisk to combine well. Toss the pasta with the vegetables and dress with the vinaigrette. Serve at room temperature, garnished with pine nuts.

Roasted Italian Vegetable Pasta Salad

Makes 4 servings

Per serving:
330 calories
  (19% calories from fat)
7 g total fat
  (1 g saturated fat)
12 g protein
60 g carbohydrate
12 g dietary fiber
0 mg cholesterol
65 mg sodium
950 mg potassium

When dinner needs to be ready quickly and you want a vegetarian meal, try this roasted vegetable entrée. While you roast the chopped vegetables, cook the pasta and grate the cheese. We try to cut all vegetables about the same size so they roast in the same time frame.

1 pound cherry tomatoes, halved

1 medium zucchini, quartered and cut into 1/2-inch cubes

1 medium summer squash, quartered and cut into 1/2-inch cubes

1 shallot, minced

1 fennel bulb, cut into 1/2-inch slices and diced

1 small red bell pepper, seeded and cut into 3/4-inch cubes

1 garlic clove, quartered, plus 1 clove, minced

1 1/2 tablespoons extra virgin olive oil

1/2 teaspoon kosher salt, optional

Freshly ground pepper

8 ounces whole wheat rotini (spiral-shaped pasta)

2 tablespoons balsamic vinegar

2 tablespoons freshly grated Parmesan cheese

1/4 cup fresh basil, torn into large pieces

1. Preheat the oven to 425°F.

2. Place the tomatoes, zucchini, squash, shallot, fennel, bell pepper, and quartered garlic clove in an ovenproof nonstick skillet. Toss with the oil, salt (if using), and ground pepper. Roast for 6 minutes; turn and continue to roast for another 6 minutes. Remove from the oven.

3. While the vegetables are roasting, cook the pasta, following package directions. Drain the pasta, reserving 2 tablespoons of the cooking water, and return to the pot. Toss the pasta, roasted vegetables with their juices, reserved pasta water, vinegar, and minced garlic. To serve, plate the vegetable pasta salad and top with the cheese and basil.

DIETITIAN'S NOTE: This low-fat dish is an excellent way to meet almost half of your daily fiber needs! Low in sodium, rich in phytonutrients, and a great source of potassium—who could ask for more?

Rotini with Artichoke Hearts and Spinach in Lemon-Ricotta Sauce

Not all pasta recipes are based on the combination of tomatoes, oil, and hard Italian cheeses. This light, creamy recipe is a welcome addition to your pasta repertoire. You can substitute sautéed sliced fennel, edamame (soybeans), or fava beans for the artichoke hearts.

Makes 4 servings

Per serving:
210 calories
   (12% calories from fat)
3 g total fat
   (1 g saturated fat)
10 g protein
36 g carbohydrate
7 g dietary fiber
10 mg cholesterol
340 mg sodium
346 mg potassium

8 ounces whole wheat rotini (spiral-shaped pasta)

One 10-ounce can whole artichoke hearts, drained

1 teaspoon extra virgin olive oil

1 shallot, minced

1 garlic clove, minced

1 tablespoon chopped fresh oregano

1/4 cup dry white wine

2 tablespoons fresh lemon juice

6 ounces baby spinach

1/2 cup reduced-fat ricotta cheese

2 teaspoons grated lemon zest

Freshly ground pepper

1. Cook the pasta according to package directions, drain, and set aside.
2. While the pasta is cooking, slice the artichoke hearts into quarters and set aside. Heat the oil in a nonstick skillet. Add the shallot and garlic, and sauté over medium heat until soft, about 5 minutes. Add the oregano, wine, lemon juice, and reserved artichoke hearts. Simmer, stirring, until the artichokes are heated through. Add the spinach and continue to cook until the spinach is wilted, about 2 minutes. Remove from the heat and stir in the ricotta, lemon zest, and pepper. Add the pasta to the sauce; stir and reheat. Serve immediately.

Mac and Cheese

Makes 4 servings

Per serving:
290 calories
  (19% calories from fat)
7 g total fat
  (4 g saturated fat)
20 g protein
42 g carbohydrate
6 g dietary fiber
20 mg cholesterol
330 mg sodium
387 mg potassium

Few meals bring up fond memories of our childhoods more than this staple, which is still one of the most popular processed foods in the market. Here we present a quick and easy variety that will surely please while making sure that your family is enjoying a heart-healthy entrée. Serve this with our Roasted Vegetables (page 305).

Refrigerated butter-flavored cooking spray
6 ounces whole wheat medium shells, rotini, elbow macaroni, or other small pasta
1/2 teaspoon cornstarch
3/4 cup evaporated skim milk
6 ounces low-fat sharp Cheddar cheese, grated (about 1 1/4 cups)
2 to 3 teaspoons Dijon mustard
Freshly ground white pepper
2 medium tomatoes, seeded and diced

1. Coat an 8 × 8-inch baking dish with cooking spray and set aside. Cook the pasta according to package directions, drain, and set aside.
2. Preheat the broiler.
3. In a saucepan, stir the cornstarch into 1 tablespoon of the evaporated milk, then whisk in the remaining milk. Add the cheese, mustard to taste, and pepper. Bring to a simmer and stir until the sauce thickens a bit and the cheese is completely melted. Stir in the cooked pasta and spoon into the prepared baking dish. Sprinkle with the diced tomatoes and place under the broiler for 2 to 3 minutes, until the top browns. Remove from the oven and allow to cool for 5 minutes before serving.

DIETITIAN'S NOTE: Our mac and cheese, packed with dietary fiber and antioxidant-rich carotenoids, is a sure winner over traditional macaroni and cheese, which has 25 percent more calories and double the fat!

Linguine with Garlic, Oven-Roasted Tomatoes, and Arugula

Serve this as a first course the next time you invite your friends over for a steak barbecue. Start with some crudités and one of our savory dips (pages 127 to 136) and finish with a Summer Fruit Gratin (page 326) for dessert.

Makes 4 servings

Per serving:
280 calories
  (19% calories from fat)
6 g total fat
  (2 g saturated fat)
9 g protein
49 g carbohydrate
7 g dietary fiber
6 mg cholesterol
115 mg sodium
475 mg potassium

1/2 pound whole wheat linguine

Olive oil cooking spray

2 garlic cloves, sliced

1/2 cup finely minced fresh flat-leaf parsley

4 Roasted Plum Tomatoes (page 000), each cut into 4 horizontal slices

4 ounces arugula

2 teaspoons extra virgin olive oil

1/8 teaspoon crushed red pepper flakes

2 tablespoons Homemade Multigrain Bread Crumbs (page 334)

1 ounce Asiago cheese, shaved

1. Cook the linguine until al dente, according to package directions.
2. While the pasta is cooking, lightly coat a large nonstick skillet with cooking spray. Place over medium-low heat and add the garlic. Sauté until golden but not browned. Drain the linguine and add it to the skillet, along with the parsley, tomatoes, and arugula. Drizzle with oil and sprinkle with the pepper flakes and bread crumbs. Cook for 2 to 3 minutes, tossing to combine.
3. Divide the pasta among 4 heated pasta bowls and scatter the Asiago curls on top of each serving. Serve immediately.

Pumpkin Ravioli in a Wild Mushroom–Ginger Broth

Makes 4 servings

Per serving:
280 calories
 (5% calories from fat)
1.5 g total fat
 (0 g saturated fat)
13 g protein
55 g carbohydrate
4 g dietary fiber
10 mg cholesterol
700 mg sodium
657 mg potassium

Ravioli filled with this savory mousse will delight your family and friends. The pumpkin says that fall has arrived and luckily for us, canned pumpkin puree is always available. Use a melange of wild mushrooms in the broth. We like thinly sliced cremini, shiitakes, chanterelles, and morels. Because some of these are hard to find, we buy dried and reconstitute them. You can use other winter squashes or sweet potatoes for the filling.

Ravioli

Refrigerated butter-flavored cooking spray

1 shallot, minced

3/4 cup pumpkin puree

1/4 cup egg substitute

2 tablespoons reduced-fat ricotta cheese

2 teaspoons minced fresh sage

1/8 teaspoon ground nutmeg

Freshly ground pepper

32 won ton wrappers (3.5-inch square), defrosted if frozen

Kosher salt

Wild Mushroom–Ginger Broth

3 cups fat-free, reduced-sodium chicken broth

1 ounce dried wild mushrooms, rehydrated (see Note)

1/2 pound assorted wild mushrooms, thinly sliced

2 teaspoons grated fresh ginger

1 garlic clove, crushed

2 scallions, white parts and 3 inches of the green, thinly sliced

1. Coat a nonstick skillet with cooking spray. Sauté the shallot over medium heat until wilted, about 5 minutes. Remove from heat. In a bowl, combine the pumpkin puree, egg substitute, ricotta cheese, sage, and nutmeg. Stir in the shallot and pepper. Set aside.

2. Place 8 won tons on the counter and put 1 tablespoon of the pumpkin mousse in the middle of each. Wet the edges of the won ton and place another on top, pressing all around the edges to seal securely. Leave square or cut with a floured glass to make a circle, again making sure that each ravioli is sealed. Place on wax paper and cover with a clean kitchen towel. Place another 8 won tons on the counter and repeat the process. If not cooking immediately, transfer to a cookie sheet, cover, and refrigerate.

3. To make the broth, combine the chicken broth, rehydrated and fresh mushrooms, ginger, and garlic in a saucepan, bring to a boil, then simmer for 10 minutes. Set aside and keep warm.

4. To cook the ravioli, bring a large pot of lightly salted water to a boil. Reduce to a simmer. Slide in half of the ravioli one at a time and stir gently. Poach for 2 to 3 minutes, until the ravioli rise to the top of the pot. Remove with a slotted spoon and cook the remainder of the ravioli. While the ravioli are cooking, bring the ginger broth back to a simmer. To serve, place 4 ravioli in each of 4 shallow soup bowls. Ladle 3/4 cup broth into each soup bowl. Top with a quarter of the mushrooms and garnish with sliced scallions. Serve immediately.

NOTE: To rehydrate dried mushrooms, soak the mushrooms in boiling water to cover for about 15 minutes, or until softened. Remove the mushrooms with a slotted spoon. Strain the soaking liquid through a coffee filter to remove sediment. Use in the recipe or reserve for another use.

DIETITIAN'S NOTE: Although this dish contains about 100 milligrams more sodium than we generally recommend at a meal, it is a good source of potassium, contains dietary fiber, and is low in total fat. Just make sure you monitor the sodium content in your other meals, and serve the ravioli with a side of fresh vegetables.

Spaghetti with Fresh Tomato Sauce and Roasted Vegetables

Makes 4 servings

Per serving:
363 calories
   (10% calories from fat)
4 g total fat
   (1 g saturated fat)
15 g protein
71 g carbohydrate
15 g dietary fiber
1 mg cholesterol
160 mg sodium
825 mg potassium

Sauce only (per cup):
80 calories
   (9% calories from fat)
0 g total fat
   (0 g saturated fat)
3 g protein
18 g carbohydrate
4 g dietary fiber
0 mg cholesterol
100 mg sodium
93 mg potassium.

Homemade tomato sauce not only tastes better than store-bought, but making it yourself allows you to control the ingredients. In the summer, use fresh ripe tomatoes along with herbs from the garden. During the winter months, you can make this sauce with plum tomatoes with excellent results. You can also use canned tomatoes, but make sure you purchase a brand with no added salt. Not only are they healthier, but they taste fresh. The balsamic vinegar adds a bit of sweetness and an extra layer of flavor to a sauce that will become a staple in your refrigerator and freezer. You'll only need 2 cups of sauce for this recipe, so freeze the rest.

Tomato Sauce (makes 4 cups; 8 servings)

Olive oil cooking spray
2 garlic cloves, minced
1 small carrot, minced
1 shallot, minced
4 cups peeled, seeded, and diced ripe tomatoes, or one 28-ounce can no-salt-added
   diced tomatoes, drained
1/4 cup dry red wine
1 1/2 tablespoons balsamic vinegar
1/4 teaspoon crushed red pepper flakes, optional
1/4 cup chopped fresh basil

1/2 pound whole wheat spaghetti
3/4 pound broccoli florets and stalks, peeled and cut into bite-size pieces
2 portobello mushrooms, halved and thinly sliced
1 red, yellow, or orange bell pepper, seeded and coarsely chopped
1 1/2 tablespoons extra virgin olive oil
1 1/2 tablespoons balsamic vinegar
Freshly grated pepper
2 tablespoons freshly grated Parmesan cheese

1. Preheat the oven to 400°F. Line a rimmed baking sheet with aluminum foil.
2. To make the sauce, coat a large pot with cooking spray and sauté the garlic, carrot, and shallot over low heat until they begin to wilt, about 5 minutes. Stir in the tomatoes, wine, vinegar, and red pepper flakes, if using. Cover and simmer slowly for 30 minutes.

3. Stir in the basil; simmer for 10 minutes more. (To make a smoother sauce, cool and process in batches in either a blender or food processor.) Set aside.

4. Place the broccoli, mushrooms, and bell pepper on the prepared pan. Toss with the oil and vinegar. Roast about 10 minutes, until crisp or done to your taste. Sprinkle with pepper.

5. Cook the pasta according to package directions. Drain.

6. In a large serving bowl, toss the pasta with 2 cups tomato sauce. Top with the roasted vegetables and sprinkle with Parmesan cheese.

VARIATIONS: Feel free to substitute your favorite vegetables. Asparagus, endive, carrots, cauliflower, fennel, any type of mushroom, or summer and winter squash will work well. The sauce also dresses up plain grilled or broiled poultry or fish as well as beef, lamb, and pork.

Linguine with Spicy Broccoli and Portobello Mushrooms

Pasta and fresh vegetables go together like ham and eggs. You could substitute spinach, bell peppers, broccoli rabe, eggplant, shallots, or wild mushrooms for the broccoli and portobellos. We remove the gills of the portobello mushrooms to prevent black discoloration of the sauce. Use a spoon or a small thin knife to remove the ridges from the underside of the mushroom.

Makes 4 servings

Per serving:
360 calories
  (18% calories from fat)
8 g total fat
  (2.5 g saturated fat)
18 g protein
60 g carbohydrate
13 g dietary fiber
10 mg cholesterol
200 mg sodium
1,129 mg potassium

1/2 **pound whole wheat linguine**

1 **tablespoon extra virgin olive oil**

3 **garlic cloves, minced**

3/4 **pound broccoli florets, cut into bite-size pieces**

2 **portobello mushrooms, gills removed, halved and thinly sliced**

3 **tablespoons dry red wine**

One 28-ounce can no-salt-added diced tomatoes, well drained

1/4 **teaspoon crushed red pepper flakes**

1/4 **teaspoon kosher salt, optional**

1/2 **cup roughly chopped fresh basil**

1/2 **cup freshly grated Parmesan cheese**

1. Cook the pasta until al dente, according to package directions.

2. Meanwhile, heat the oil in a large nonstick skillet. Add the garlic, broccoli, and mushrooms. Cook over high heat for 2 minutes, stirring, until the mushrooms begin to wilt. Reduce the heat to low and add the wine, tomatoes, red pepper flakes, and salt (if using). Simmer for 2 minutes, stirring twice. Stir in the basil.

3. Drain the pasta, reserving 1/2 cup of the pasta water. Add the water to the sauce, increase the heat, and boil for 1 minute to reduce slightly.

4. Divide the pasta among 4 plates. Top with sauce and sprinkle with cheese. Serve immediately.

Cleveland Clinic Healthy Heart Lifestyle Guide and Cookbook

Vegetarian

We're not vegetarians, but like others who are concerned about their health, especially their heart health, we are eating more plant protein and less animal protein—and that means eating meatless main courses two or three times a week.

We are not talking about pretend foods—mystery meats made of ground nuts, wheat, or who knows what. You won't find recipes for that kind of food here. Nor are these recipes necessarily like those you would find in a strictly vegetarian cookbook. Not all vegetarian recipes are cardioprotective just because they don't contain animal protein. Some are very high in fat, calling for butter, cream, and large amounts of cheese and nuts. In this book we've replaced that fat with more healthful and ultimately more satisfying flavors. Without the fat, you'll begin to taste foods as nature intended. The difference between our dishes and vegetarian foods you can purchase in stores is not only a great fresh taste but a more cardioprotective meal as well.

A Few Quick Tips: Tofu 101

- We know that you will enjoy adding tofu to your diet after trying the various recipes in this chapter. There are two types of tofu, Chinese-style and Japanese-style ("silken"). Silken tofu is made from soymilk and then processed much like yogurt, which makes it smoother and creamier than Chinese-style tofu. Both types come in varying degrees of firmness, depending on the amount of water left in the tofu. We suggest extra-firm tofu for marinating and stir-frying. The softer varieties of tofu are easier to crumble or mash with other ingredients. We add soft tofu to sour cream, salad dressings, and mayonnaise for extra protein.

- Store tofu in the freezer for up to three months. If storing in the refrigerator, check the expiration date. You can store opened tofu for up to a week if you change the water daily.

- There are two ways to prepare tofu for cooking. The first is to wrap the tofu in paper towels and press it to remove all of the water. Place a weight on top of a plate placed on the wrapped tofu, changing the paper towels as they become saturated with water. The second is to freeze the tofu in its container. When ready to use, thaw the tofu and squeeze out all the liquid. Many people prefer this method because the texture becomes chewy and reminiscent of tofu in restaurants, where it is routinely prepared this way for deep-frying or stir-frying. We use this method at home for stir-frying, but try both. The tofu will be good either way.

- How can you use tofu in your heart-healthy recipes? Make mock egg salad using mashed tofu with reduced-fat mayonnaise, mustard, scallions, and fresh pepper. Add pureed silken tofu to sour cream, mayonnaise, or ricotta cheese as we do for our Tofu Manicotti (page 183). Use silken tofu mixed with chopped chives on baked potatoes instead of sour cream. Add Tex-Mex seasonings to crumbled tofu instead of beef and sauté with tomato sauce to make tacos. Use reduced-sodium barbecue sauce on sliced tofu for a delicious tofu sandwich with lettuce, tomato, and pickle slices. Use silken tofu instead of high-fat cream cheese for a creamy pie filling. Float tofu on clear soups or miso soups with thinly sliced vegetables for a Japanese-style appetizer.

Greek Tofu Salad

How fortunate we are that excellent low-fat cheeses are available to make our recipes authentic. Combining low-fat feta and tofu makes for a lighter, healthier Greek salad. Serve this salad on lettuce leaves garnished with toasted whole-grain Crostini (page 337).

Makes 6 servings

Per serving:
158 calories
   (62% calories from fat)
11 g total fat
   (3 g saturated fat)
11 g protein
7 g carbohydrate
1.5 g dietary fiber
10 mg cholesterol
500 mg sodium
278 mg potassium

3/4 cup crumbled reduced-fat feta cheese

3 scallions, white parts and 3 inches of the green, thinly sliced

12 kalamata olives, pitted and sliced

3 tablespoons fresh lemon juice

1 1/2 tablespoons extra virgin olive oil

2 teaspoons dried oregano

1 cup drained and crumbled light firm tofu

1/4 teaspoon kosher salt, optional

Freshly ground pepper

2 large ripe tomatoes, coarsely chopped

1/2 English cucumber, coarsely chopped

1/4 cup chopped fresh flat-leaf parsley

1. Combine the cheese, scallions, olives, lemon juice, oil, and oregano in a large bowl. Add the tofu and season with salt, if using, and pepper to taste. Cover and refrigerate for 30 minutes.

2. Add the tomatoes, cucumber, and parsley to the tofu mixture. Serve at once.

DIETITIAN'S NOTE: Although this dish seems high in fat, the fat is derived from healthy sources of mono- and polyunsaturated fats.

Tofu, Broccoli, Shiitake Mushroom, and Walnut Stir-Fry

Makes 4 servings

Per serving:
410 calories
  (33% calories from fat)
15 g total fat
  (1.5 g saturated fat)
20 g protein
57 g carbohydrate
7 g dietary fiber
0 mg cholesterol
420 mg sodium
580 mg potassium

This recipe comes from Parvine Latimore, an accomplished cook specializing in Mediterranean cuisine, who frequently contributes recipes to our cookbooks.

3 dried shiitake mushrooms, rehydrated (see page 175)
2 teaspoons extra virgin olive oil
1 large white onion, cut in half and then quartered
4 garlic cloves, sliced
2 carrots, thinly sliced
2 cups broccoli florets
1 cup sliced shiitake mushrooms
1 pound water-packed firm tofu, prepared for cooking (see page 180) and
  cut into 1/2-inch cubes
12 walnut halves, roughly chopped
2 tablespoons brown rice miso
Freshly ground pepper
2 cups hot cooked brown basmati rice
Fresh mint leaves, optional
Reduced-sodium soy sauce

1. Drain the soaked mushrooms, discarding the liquid, and chop roughly. Place a wok or large nonstick skillet over medium heat. When the wok is hot, swirl in the oil and add the onion and garlic. Stir-fry until the onion wilts, about 4 minutes. Add the carrots, broccoli, and fresh and rehydrated shiitake. Stir-fry for 2 minutes.

2. Add the tofu, walnuts, miso, and 1/4 cup water. Continue to stir-fry for another 1 to 2 minutes, until the tofu is hot and the vegetables are crisp-tender. Grind pepper to taste over all.

3. Press the hot rice into 1/2-cup molds. Invert onto 4 heated dinner plates, top with the stir-fry, and serve. If using mint, place the leaves on a small plate and pass them along with a bottle of soy sauce to sprinkle over each serving.

DIETITIAN'S NOTE: Although this dish may seem high in total fat, the fat is derived from heart-healthy mono- and polyunsaturated fats. In fact, because of the walnuts, each serving provides almost three-quarters of a gram of omega-3 fat.

Tofu Manicotti

Everyone needs an easy, healthy recipe that feeds the entire family or can be taken to a potluck meal. This recipe does just that. Even people who claim not to like tofu will love this dish, where the tofu is heavily disguised as cheese. Manicotti shells can be difficult to fill without tearing them. Use a spoon that is smaller than the opening, or use very clean fingers.

Makes 6 servings

Per serving:
340 calories
  (10.5% calories from fat)
4 g total fat
  (2 g saturated fat)
29 g protein
45 g carbohydrate
5 g dietary fiber
24 mg cholesterol
447 mg sodium
115 mg potassium

12 manicotti shells (8 ounces), preferably whole wheat
One 12.3-ounce container light silken tofu, drained and mashed
¼ cup egg substitute
One 15-ounce container reduced-fat ricotta cheese
One 10-ounce package frozen chopped spinach, thawed and well drained
1½ cups grated fat-free mozzarella cheese
¼ cup chopped fresh basil, or 2 tablespoons dried
3 cups Tomato Sauce (page 176)
2 tablespoons freshly grated Parmesan cheese

1. Preheat the oven to 350°F.
2. Boil the manicotti shells according to package directions. Drain and set aside to cool.
3. Combine the tofu, egg substitute, ricotta, spinach, mozzarella, and basil in a bowl. Stir until just combined. Pour 2 cups of the tomato sauce into a 13 × 9 × 2-inch baking dish. Carefully stuff the manicotti shells with the tofu mixture and arrange in the dish. Top with the remaining tomato sauce. (The shells can be made up to one day ahead, covered with aluminum foil, and refrigerated until ready to bake.)
4. Cover with aluminum foil and bake for 25 minutes. Uncover, sprinkle with Parmesan cheese, and bake for 5 minutes, or until the cheese has melted. (If refrigerated, bake, covered, for 50 minutes before sprinkling with Parmesan.) Allow the manicotti to rest for 5 minutes before serving.

NOTE: On days when you don't have the time to make fresh tomato sauce or you have used the last in your freezer, look in your market for a sauce that is low in fat (less than 3 grams of fat per serving) and salt (less than 200 milligrams per serving), with no corn syrup or sweeteners.

Vegetables, Tofu, and Soba Noodles in Sweet Ginger Sauce

Makes 4 servings

Per serving:
220 calories
  (13% calories from fat)
3.5 g total fat
  (0.5 g saturated fat)
12 g protein
40 g carbohydrate
6 g dietary fiber
0 mg cholesterol
590 mg sodium
660 mg potassium

We love to stir-fry the freshest vegetables in the market, but many recipes of this type are very high in fat and salt. The fresh ginger sauce disguises the lack of both. Make sure that you purchase soba noodles that are low in sodium. The ones we use have 15 milligrams per serving and are widely available. If you have difficulty finding them, substitute wide whole wheat noodles, which are also low in salt and are available in most supermarkets. Hoisin is a sweet sauce made from soybeans and spices that is used in many Asian dishes. Refrigerate after opening. Thai chili sauce is also available in most supermarkets and adds heat and more spices to the sauce. Like most stir-fries, this can be made in minutes if you have all the ingredients chopped and ready to go.

Sweet Ginger Sauce

1/2 cup fresh orange juice

2 tablespoons hoisin sauce

2 teaspoons reduced-sodium soy sauce

2 tablespoons minced fresh ginger

1/2 to 1 teaspoon Thai chili sauce

3 ounces buckwheat soba noodles

1 teaspoon sesame oil

1 teaspoon peanut oil

6 ounces water-packed light extra-firm tofu, frozen, prepared for cooking (see page 180) and cut into 1/2-inch cubes

4 scallions, white parts and 3 inches of the green, sliced on the diagonal into 1/2-inch slices

2 garlic cloves, thinly sliced on the diagonal

2 carrots, grated

1/4 pound snow peas, sliced lengthwise into thirds

1/2 red bell pepper, seeded and thinly sliced

6 ounces mushrooms, sliced

4 ounces baby spinach

8 ounces mung bean sprouts

1/4 cup chopped fresh cilantro

Lime wedges

1. Combine all ginger sauce ingredients in a small pan, using chili sauce to taste. Heat to a simmer and cook for 1 minute. Set aside.

2. Cook the soba noodles 1 minute less than directed on the package. Drain and set aside.

3. Heat the sesame and peanut oils in a nonstick skillet or wok over high heat until hot. Stir in the tofu, scallions, garlic, carrots, snow peas, bell pepper, and mushrooms. Stir-fry for 2 minutes. Lower the heat to medium; add the Sweet Ginger Sauce. Stir in the spinach, bean sprouts, and reserved soba noodles. Cook just until the spinach wilts, then add the cilantro. Serve immediately garnished with lime wedges.

Polenta with Eggplant Ragout

Makes 6 servings

Per serving:
230 calories
   (20% calories from fat)
6 g total fat
   (1 g saturated fat)
8 g protein
41 g carbohydrate
13 g dietary fiber
5 mg cholesterol
180 mg sodium
1,160 mg potassium

In Northern Italy polenta is a staple that is served from breakfast to dinner. Made of cornmeal, it can be soft or, as in this recipe, set aside until firm and then sliced.

Ragout

3 small eggplants

Kosher salt

1 tablespoon extra virgin olive oil

1 onion, thinly sliced

1 garlic clove, minced

1 red bell pepper, seeded and chopped

1 pound plum tomatoes, chopped

6 ounces cremini mushrooms, quartered

1½ tablespoons fresh lemon juice

1 tablespoon tomato paste

⅓ cup chopped fresh basil

⅓ cup chopped fresh flat-leaf parsley

6 pitted black brine-cured olives, quartered

1 tablespoon capers, rinsed well

Freshly ground pepper

Polenta

Olive oil cooking spray

1 cup instant polenta or stone-ground cornmeal

¼ cup freshly grated Parmesan cheese

1 teaspoon dried oregano

Freshly ground pepper

---

1. Peel the eggplants and cut into ³/4-inch slices. Place in a colander and sprinkle lightly with salt. Allow to drain for 30 minutes. Rinse, then wipe off all moisture and salt. Cut into bite-size pieces.

2. Heat the oil in a nonstick saucepan. Sauté the onion over medium heat until transparent. Stir in the garlic and sauté for 2 more minutes. Add the eggplant, bell pepper, tomatoes, and mushrooms. Cover and cook for 8 to 10 minutes over medium heat, until the vegetables begin to soften. Add the lemon juice, tomato paste, basil, and parsley. Uncover and simmer until the vegetables are cooked through. Stir in the olives and capers. Add pepper to taste and adjust the seasoning if necessary.

Cleveland Clinic Healthy Heart Lifestyle Guide and Cookbook

3. While the ragout is simmering, make the polenta. Coat a 9-inch square cake pan with cooking spray. Bring 3 cups water to a boil in a deep pot. Add the polenta and simmer, stirring frequently, for 5 minutes. Remove from heat and stir in the cheese, oregano, and pepper. Pour the polenta into the prepared pan and even out the top with a spatula. Let it sit for 10 minutes.

4. To serve, cut the polenta into 12 squares. Place 2 on each plate and spoon the ragout over the polenta.

NOTE: When you don't need a whole can of tomato paste, why not purchase it in a tube? It doesn't go bad or discolor in the refrigerator and is always ready to use.

Stuffed Eggplant

Makes 4 servings

Per serving:
100 calories
  (14% calories from fat)
1.5 g total fat
  (0 g saturated fat)
6 g protein
16 g carbohydrate
5 g dietary fiber
0 mg cholesterol
90 mg sodium
654 mg potassium

Did you know that eggplant is really a berry, which makes it a fruit? When selecting eggplants, purchase young ones without brown spots and with smooth, glossy skin. Summer is the season for fresh eggplants and you don't need to salt these just-picked vegetables. Out of season, stored eggplants can become bitter; salting for about 30 minutes and then rinsing takes away the acrid taste, and ensures that your dish will be sweet any time of year.

One 1-pound eggplant

Kosher salt for sprinkling

1 teaspoon extra virgin olive oil

1 small onion, diced

1 garlic clove, minced

$1/2$ pound cremini mushrooms, chopped

2 plum tomatoes, diced

2 teaspoons chopped fresh thyme, or $1/2$ to $3/4$ teaspoon dried

$1/8$ teaspoon kosher salt, optional

Freshly ground pepper

$1/2$ cup Homemade Multigrain Bread Crumbs (page 334)

$1/2$ cup egg substitute

1. Trim off the stem and cut the eggplant in half lengthwise. Make slits in the flesh and salt the halves. Place in a colander and allow to drain for 30 minutes. Rinse, then wipe off all salt and moisture. Leaving a $3/8$-inch shell, remove the flesh with a small paring knife or grapefruit spoon and dice.

2. Preheat the oven to 375°F.

3. Heat the oil in a nonstick skillet. Add the onion and sauté for 3 minutes. Add the diced eggplant, garlic, mushrooms, tomatoes, thyme, salt (if using), and pepper. Cook over medium-low heat, stirring frequently, until the vegetables are cooked through, about 15 minutes. When the vegetables are soft, stir in the bread crumbs and egg substitute until well incorporated and the eggs are cooked.

4. Mound the stuffing in the 2 eggplant halves. Place in a baking dish and add just enough water to cover the bottom of the dish without touching the stuffing, about a quarter way up the sides of the eggplant. Cover with aluminum foil and bake for 30 minutes. Carefully remove the foil from the baking dish and cool for 5 minutes. Slice in half with a sharp knife and serve immediately.

Asparagus, Tomato, and Shiitake Mushroom Quiche

Quiche, an egg-based savory tart, originated in the Alsace-Lorraine region of France. This light dinner entrée goes well with a simple green salad (see page 155). At various times of the year we change the vegetables to baby artichokes, broccoli, cauliflower, squashes, or fennel. Many mushrooms do well, as do oysters or even truffles for a real splurge. We wanted to share a healthier pie crust than the typical ones laden with saturated fats. The whole wheat crust takes only a few minutes to mix and roll out. Enjoy!

1 Whole Wheat Pie Crust (page 338)

Vegetable oil cooking spray

2 shallots, halved and thinly sliced

1/2 pound asparagus, tough ends discarded, sliced into 1-inch pieces

1/2 pound shiitake mushrooms, stems discarded, thinly sliced

1 cup skim milk

1/3 cup egg substitute

1/2 cup reduced-fat Swiss cheese

1 teaspoon chopped fresh thyme

1/2 teaspoon chopped fresh oregano

1 large tomato, seeded and diced

1/8 teaspoon kosher salt, optional

Freshly ground pepper

Makes 6 servings

Per serving
(quiche and crust):
280 calories
  (34% calories from fat)
11 g total fat
  (3 g saturated fat)
12 g protein
35 g carbohydrate
4 g dietary fiber
5 mg cholesterol
140 mg sodium
470 mg potassium

1. Preheat the oven to 425°F. Line a tart pan with the pie crust as directed on page 338.

2. Coat a nonstick skillet with cooking spray. Preheat over medium heat and add the shallots. Sauté, stirring, for 3 minutes, then add the asparagus and mushrooms. Cook over medium-low heat for about 8 minutes. Place the vegetables in the unbaked crust.

3. In a small bowl, whisk together the milk and egg substitute. Pour over the vegetables. Sprinkle with the cheese, thyme, and oregano. Press gently with the back of a spoon to incorporate into the egg mixture. Top with the tomato, salt (if using), and pepper. Bake for 25 to 30 minutes, until set. Remove from the oven and allow to rest for 5 minutes. Serve immediately.

DIETITIAN'S NOTE: If you compare this to a traditional quiche, which has over 500 calories and 40 grams of fat in a single slice, you'll never eat store-bought quiche again.

Vegetarian Paella

Makes 4 servings

Per serving:
190 calories
  (13% calories from fat)
3 g total fat
  (0 g saturated fat)
8 g protein
30 g carbohydrate
6 g dietary fiber
0 mg cholesterol
370 mg sodium
440 mg potassium

This Spanish favorite from Valencia will grace your table in less than 30 minutes, but tastes as if you had been cooking all day. It's versatile, too; another time use shrimp or salmon instead of the tofu. All you need is a fresh fruit dessert to finish your meal. Organic vegetable broth is lower in sodium than the others we found in the market. Chill any leftover broth and use within ten days or freeze it.

1 medium tomato, chopped, with juice

1/2 cup dry white wine

1 teaspoon extra virgin olive oil

1/2 medium onion, chopped

1 garlic clove, minced

1/2 red bell pepper, seeded and thinly sliced

1/4 pound green beans, cut into 1-inch pieces

11/4 cups instant brown rice

3/4 cup organic vegetable broth

2 sprigs fresh thyme

1 teaspoon minced fresh rosemary

1/2 teaspoon saffron threads or ground turmeric

6 ounces water-packed light extra-firm tofu, prepared for cooking (see page 180)

7 ounces canned artichoke hearts, drained and halved (half of a 14-ounce can)

1 tablespoon fresh lemon juice

4 pimento-stuffed green olives, finely minced

1 tablespoon minced fresh flat-leaf parsley

1 lemon, quartered, optional

1. Combine the tomato and its juice with the white wine in a small bowl. Set aside.

2. Place the oil in a large skillet over medium heat. Add the onion, garlic, bell pepper, and green beans. Sauté, stirring, for 5 minutes, or until the onion becomes transparent. Add the rice and continue to cook for another 2 minutes. Add the vegetable broth, 1/4 cup water, the tomato and wine, and the thyme, rosemary, and saffron and simmer for 2 minutes.

3. Cut the tofu into 1/2-inch pieces and add to the skillet, pressing the pieces into the rice. Arrange the artichoke hearts over the rice. Drizzle with lemon juice and top with the olives. Cover and cook for 10 minutes, or until the rice is cooked. Remove the thyme sprigs and sprinkle with parsley. Garnish with the lemon wedges, if using.

Italian-Style Mushroom Ratatouille in Buckwheat Crêpes

This ratatouille has no squash, but it has the great flavor we associate with a summer's day in Italy. Do try a mixture of as many different mushrooms as you can find in the market, such as portobello, shiitake, cremini, puffball, and oyster. You can always mix the more common white mushrooms with some of the exotic varieties. A combination brings more savor to the final dish.

1½ pounds mixed fresh mushrooms

Olive oil cooking spray

1 teaspoon extra virgin olive oil

1 medium onion, halved and thinly sliced

2 garlic cloves, minced

1 red bell pepper, seeded and thinly sliced

4 plum tomatoes, chopped

⅓ cup dry white wine

¼ cup chopped fresh basil

Freshly ground pepper

12 Basic Buckwheat Crêpes (page 333)

¼ cup coarsely grated Parmesan cheese

Makes 6 servings

Per serving
   (2 crêpes with filling):
120 calories
   (22% calories from fat
 3 g total fat
   (0.5 g saturated fat)
8 g protein
16 g carbohydrate
3 g dietary fiber
0 mg cholesterol
90 mg sodium
610 mg potassium

Per serving
(mushroom filling only):
70 calories (25% calories
   from fat)
2 g total fat
   (0.5 g saturated fat)
5 g protein
9 g carbohydrate
3 g dietary fiber
0 mg cholesterol
35 mg sodium
550 mg potassium

1. If using portobellos, remove the gills (see page 178), and if using shiitakes, remove the stems. Slice the mushrooms. Coat a nonstick skillet with cooking spray and add the oil. Heat the pan over medium heat. Add the onion and garlic and sauté for 4 minutes. Add the mushrooms, bell pepper, tomatoes, and wine. Simmer, uncovered, until the vegetables are cooked through, about 15 minutes. Stir in the basil and ground pepper.

2. To serve, place 2 crêpes on each of 6 large plates. Spoon some of the vegetables onto the middle of each crêpe. Fold the sides over the vegetables and turn seam side down. Top each crêpe with 1 teaspoon cheese. Serve immediately.

Crêpes with Moroccan Vegetable Curry

Makes 6 servings

Per serving
(2 crêpes and curry):
200 calories
  (16% calories from fat)
3.5 g total fat
  (0 g saturated fat)
11 g protein
36 g carbohydrate
8 g dietary fiber
0 mg cholesterol
170 mg sodium
650 mg potassium

Per serving (curry only):
150 calories
  (15% calories from fat)
2.5 g total fat
  (0 g saturated fat)
8 g protein
29 g carbohydrate
8 g dietary fiber
0 mg cholesterol
110 mg sodium
590 mg potassium

This vegetable curry is made in one pot and comes together quickly once the yogurt is drained. Italian-Style Mushroom Ratatouille (page 191) makes another good crêpe filling. Either way, round out your meal with Spinach Salad with Oranges and Walnuts (page 158) and a granita (page 330) for dessert. This curry is so delicious, you'll want other ways to serve it—try it over couscous or Brown Basmati Rice with Cilantro and Pine Nuts (page 271).

---

1 cup nonfat plain yogurt

1 medium eggplant

2 zucchini

1 summer squash

Kosher salt for sprinkling

1 teaspoon extra virgin olive oil

1 large onion, thinly sliced

2 garlic cloves, minced

1 teaspoon minced fresh ginger

1/2 tablespoon curry powder, or to taste

1/2 teaspoon ground turmeric

1 teaspoon ground cinnamon

One 3 x 1-inch piece orange zest, thinly sliced

1/8 teaspoon cayenne, optional

1/8 teaspoon kosher salt

1 red bell pepper, seeded and thinly sliced

One 15-ounce can chickpeas, rinsed and drained

2 tablespoons golden raisins

12 Basic Buckwheat Crêpes (page 333)

---

1. Place the yogurt in a sieve lined with a paper towel. Set aside to drain for 30 minutes.

2. Cut the eggplant, zucchini, and summer squash in half lengthwise. With the tip of a sharp knife, make slits in the flesh of the eggplant. Place the vegetables in a strainer and sprinkle with salt. After 30 minutes, wipe off all salt and moisture. Cut the vegetables into similarly sized thin slices. Set aside.

3. Place the oil in a large nonstick saucepan over medium heat. Add the onion and sauté, stirring, for a minute just to break up the rings. Add the garlic and ginger. Sauté for another minute. Stir in the curry, turmeric, cinnamon, orange zest, cayenne, and salt, if using.

Cleveland Clinic Healthy Heart Lifestyle Guide and Cookbook

4. Cook, stirring, for 30 seconds more. Add the eggplant, zucchini, summer squash, bell pepper, chickpeas, raisins, and 1/2 cup water. Bring to a simmer. Cover and cook for about 20 minutes, until all the vegetables are tender and cooked through.

5. To serve, place 2 crêpes on each of 6 large plates. Spoon some of the vegetables onto the middle of each crêpe. Fold the sides over the vegetables and turn the crêpes seam side down. Garnish with a dollop of yogurt.

DIETITIAN'S NOTE: This curry dish packs a nutritional punch! It's low in fat and sodium, cholesterol free, and a great source of lean protein, dietary fiber, and potassium.

Stuffed Chayote with Black Bean and Corn Salsa

Makes 4 servings

Per serving:
170 calories
  (18% calories from fat)
3.5 g total fat
  (0.5 g saturated fat)
9 g protein
33 g carbohydrate
9 g dietary fiber
0 mg cholesterol
250 mg sodium
795 mg potassium

Chayote is a member of the gourd family and is available year-round in supermarkets. Select squashes that are heavy for their size and unblemished. Store in a plastic bag in the refrigerator for up to a month.

In this recipe, chayote are baked with a piquant black bean and corn salsa. Try adding raw chayote to your slaw recipes or grating it on top of a green salad.

Four 4-ounce chayote

Olive oil cooking spray

6 scallions, white parts and 2 inches of the green, thinly sliced on the diagonal

1 garlic clove, minced

1 small jalapeño, seeded and minced

1 medium tomato, seeded and diced

One 15-ounce can black beans, rinsed and drained

1 cup fresh corn, cut from the cob (about 1 ear)

1 tablespoon fresh lime juice

2 teaspoons extra virgin olive oil

1/4 cup chopped fresh cilantro

1/8 teaspoon kosher salt, optional

1/2 cup low-fat yogurt

---

1. Preheat the oven to 350°F.

2. Slice the chayote in half lengthwise along their natural indentation. Remove the seeds and, with a melon baller, carefully remove the flesh, leaving 1/3-inch shells. Chop the flesh and set aside.

3. Coat a nonstick skillet with cooking spray. Set aside 2 tablespoons of the scallions. Add the rest of the scallions, the garlic, and the jalapeño; sauté for 1 minute over medium heat. Add the chopped chayote and tomato; cook for an additional 3 minutes. Add the black beans and corn. To finish the salsa, toss the bean mixture with the lime juice, oil, cilantro, and salt, if using.

4. Place the chayote shells in a shallow baking dish. If any are not stable, cut a very thin slice from the bottom. Mound the salsa in the shells. Put enough warm water in the baking dish to just cover the bottom of the shells. Cover the dish with aluminum foil and bake for 30 minutes. Place any remaining salsa in a small ovenproof dish, cover with foil, and bake along with the squash.

5. While the chayote is baking, drain the yogurt in a sieve lined with a paper towel.

6. To serve, place 2 chayote halves on each of 4 large plates and place a dollop of the drained yogurt on each chayote half. Sprinkle the reserved scallions over all. Pass the heated salsa separately.

DIETITIAN'S NOTE: You no longer have the "I don't know what to do with squash" excuse. Enjoy this dish as a meatless entrée to help reach your weekly legume goal.

Pizza with Arugula, Sautéed Vegetables, and Goat Cheese

Makes 5 servings

Per serving:
240 calories
    (25% calories from fat)
7 g total fat
    (2.5 g saturated fat)
11 g protein
36 g carbohydrate
5 g dietary fiber
5 mg cholesterol
440 mg sodium
310 mg potassium

Over the last few years, pizza has evolved from an unhealthy fast food featuring oily tomato sauce and cheese to a quick low-fat meal loaded with healthy toppings. When baby arugula is not available, substitute chopped fresh kale or spinach. We suggest baking the pizza on a pizza stone to ensure a crisp crust.

1 teaspoon extra virgin olive oil

1 small onion, thinly sliced

2 garlic cloves, minced

1/2 red bell pepper, seeded and thinly sliced

1/3 pound asparagus, tough ends removed, cut into 1-inch pieces (about 1 cup)

3 cremini mushrooms, very thinly sliced

2 tablespoons balsamic vinegar

3 ounces baby arugula

One 10-ounce prepared thin whole wheat pizza shell

5 ounces reduced-fat goat cheese, crumbled

Olive oil cooking spray

1. Place a pizza stone in the oven and preheat to 500°F.

2. Heat the oil in a nonstick skillet. Add the onion, garlic, bell pepper, asparagus, and mushrooms. Sauté over medium heat for 5 minutes, until the onion softens and becomes translucent and the vegetables begin to soften. Stir in the vinegar and cook over medium-high heat for another 3 minutes. Remove from heat.

3. Mound the arugula on the pizza shell, leaving a 3/4-inch border. Spread the cooked vegetables over the arugula. Drizzle with the vinegar remaining in the pan. Top with goat cheese and coat with cooking spray. Carefully place the pizza on the preheated stone. Bake for about 12 minutes, until the crust is crisp and the cheese begins to softens. Remove from the oven and allow to cool for 2 minutes. Slice into wedges and serve.

Roasted Tomato, Goat Cheese, and Arugula Sandwiches

We love all the elements of these little open-faced sandwiches—together they make a marvelous lunch. Since a sandwich like this relies on first-rate ingredients, make sure your tomato is ripe and bursting with flavor, the low-fat goat cheese is fresh, the arugula is young with a light peppery taste, and the bread was baked that morning.

2 slices whole-grain peasant bread

6 to 8 young arugula sprigs

1 ounce reduced-fat goat cheese, thinly sliced

1 roasted plum tomato, seeded and finely diced (recipe follows)

Place the 2 slices of bread on a plate. Top each with the arugula and the slices of goat cheese. Sprinkle the top with the tomato and serve immediately.

Makes 1 serving

Per serving:
180 calories
 (20% calories from fat)
4 g total fat
 (2 g saturated fat)
7 g protein
32 g carbohydrate
11 g dietary fiber
5 mg cholesterol
300 mg sodium
205 mg potassium

Roasted Plum Tomatoes

We keep roasted tomatoes in our refrigerator to use in sandwiches and salads. Plum (also called Roma) tomatoes are particularly good for roasting as there is a plentiful supply year-round.

8 plum tomatoes, cored (about 1 1/2 pounds)

Olive oil cooking spray

1. Preheat the oven to 425°F.
2. Halve each tomato lengthwise and place in a single layer on a large baking sheet. Lightly spray with cooking spray. Roast for about 30 minutes, until the edges are soft and beginning to caramelize. Remove from the oven and cool.

Makes 8 servings

Per serving
(1 roasted tomato only):
15 calories
 (0% calories from fat)
0 g total fat
 (0 g saturated fat)
1 g protein
3 g carbohydrate
0 g dietary fiber
0 mg cholesterol
5 mg sodium
138 mg potassium

Roasted Winter Vegetable Ragout

Makes 6 servings

Per serving
(vegetables only):
400 calories
  (12% calories from fat)
6 g total fat
  (1.5 g saturated fat)
12 g protein
79 g carbohydrate
19 g dietary fiber
5 mg cholesterol
260 mg sodium
2,520 mg potassium

Add some extra interest to a winter meal by exposing your family to one or more new varieties of root vegetables in this recipe—cipollini onions instead of pearl onions, whole baby turnips, celery root instead of celery, small purple Japanese eggplant, bok choy instead of white cabbage. To keep this dish visually attractive, cut the vegetables in large, uniform pieces, leaving small vegetables such as the baby turnips whole. The lemon slices will be roasted and quite delicious.

For a heartier dinner, serve the ragout over whole wheat linguine garnished with shavings of Parmesan cheese.

---

1 cup coarsely chopped bok choy or Swiss chard

4 baby turnips, trimmed

1 small celery root, peeled and cut into wedges

1/2 pound baby carrots, peeled and left whole

8 Brussels sprouts, trimmed, with an X cut in the stem end

4 cipollini onions

2 parsnips, quartered

1 small Japanese eggplant, quartered

2 heads baby cauliflower, quartered, or 1 standard cauliflower, separated into florets

4 ounces shiitake mushrooms, stems discarded

Two 28-ounce cans no-salt-added whole plum tomatoes, with juice

2 lemons, sliced thin, seeded

2 sprigs each parsley, rosemary, and thyme

Freshly ground pepper

1 tablespoon extra virgin olive oil

1/2 cup dry white wine

---

1. Preheat the oven to 475°F.

2. Arrange the fresh vegetables in an ovenproof and flameproof roasting dish. Add the tomatoes and their juice and top with lemon slices. Place in the oven and roast, uncovered, for 20 to 30 minutes, until the vegetables are nicely browned, stirring twice.

3. Transfer the pan to the top of the stove. Lay the herb sprigs on top and season with pepper. Drizzle the vegetables with the oil and pour the wine over all. Stir and cook for another 15 to 20 minutes over high heat.

4. If serving with pasta, cook the linguine until al dente following the package directions. Drain the pasta and divide among 6 shallow soup bowls. When the vegetables are tender, discard the herb sprigs and divide the vegetables among the bowls. Garnish with the shavings of cheese. Serve hot.

DIETITIAN'S NOTE: This ragout is loaded with phytonutrients, dietary fiber, and potassium. A great way to reach your daily vegetable quota!

Roasted Portobello Sandwiches with Dijon Balsamic Vinaigrette

On hectic nights we make sandwiches to eat on the go—they're good either hot or at room temperature. Instead of hamburgers we often grill or roast meaty portobello mushrooms and serve them as we would higher-cholesterol beef. To store portobellos, remove from any packaging and refrigerate in a paper bag for seven to ten days.

Makes 4 servings

Per serving:
320 calories
  (30% calories from fat)
11 g total fat
  (5 g saturated fat)
17 g protein
40 g carbohydrate
6 g dietary fiber
20 mg cholesterol
500 mg sodium
675 mg potassium

Four 4- to 5-inch portobello mushrooms, stems removed

Olive oil cooking spray

4 thin slices red onion

8 thin slices whole-grain artisanal bread

4 thin slices reduced-fat Swiss cheese (4 ounces)

2 jarred roasted red peppers, drained and sliced (about 2 ounces)

4 slices tomato

4 fresh basil leaves

 Vinaigrette

1 tablespoon balsamic vinegar

1 tablespoon Dijon mustard

3 tablespoons chopped fresh basil

1 scallion, white part and 1 inch of the green, finely chopped

1/8 teaspoon garlic powder

Freshly ground pepper

 Balsamic Mayonnaise

1 tablespoon light mayonnaise

2 teaspoons balsamic vinegar

1 teaspoon Dijon mustard

1. Preheat the oven to 450°F.
2. Coat the mushrooms with cooking spray. Mix the vinaigrette ingredients and paint the mushrooms on both sides. Marinate for 15 minutes.
3. Coat the marinated mushrooms and the onion slices with cooking spray. Roast them in the oven until cooked through, about 5 minutes. Coat the bread with the cooking spray and toast in a toaster oven. Place a slice of cheese on four of the pieces of toast. Top with a mushroom; slices of onion, red pepper, and tomato; and a basil leaf.

4. Combine the mayonnaise, vinegar, and mustard. Paint each top slice of bread with a quarter of the Balsamic Mayonnaise. Assemble the sandwiches and serve immediately.

DIETITIAN'S NOTE: A 3-ounce portobello mushroom has only 27 calories, 0 grams of fat, 1 gram of fiber, and lots of flavor! Compare that to a 3-ounce serving of ground beef (10% lean), which has 180 calories, 9 grams of fat, 4 grams of saturated fat, and 0 grams of fiber. Still want that burger?

Fish and Shellfish

Fish and shellfish are good choices for your animal protein as they can be low in calories and fat. Fish high in omega-3 fats, like mackerel, herring, and salmon, have cardioprotective attributes explained in the first part of this book.

When the menu calls for salmon, we try to buy wild rather than farm-raised salmon, because farm-raised fish have higher levels of PCBs—a potential carcinogen. Wild fish also get to eat the kinds of foods that increase their levels of omega-3 fatty acids. They have more muscle than fat mass, where PCBs are stored. There are several names of wild salmon to look for in the store, including the king, coho, Chinook, and Columbia River varieties. You'll see a difference in the wild versus farmed fish, as farmed fish tend to be larger and fatter. Our solution when cooking farm-raised salmon is to remove the fatty skin and grill or bake it using high heat to remove excess fat. The benefits of eating fish rich in omega-3 fatty acids outweigh worries over contamination for informed consumers.

A Few Quick Tips

One question we are often asked, even by experienced cooks, is, "How do I know when the fish is done?" There are a few ways to tell: the Canadian Rule of cooking 10 minutes per inch of thickness is one good guideline. A second way is to touch the fish on the thickest part of the fillet. A springy touch and an opaque color are signs that the fish is done—a mushy touch means it should be cooked longer. A third, foolproof way is to check the fish with the sharp point of a knife to see if it flakes and is cooked through.

It's late, the family is waiting, and you have fish fillets for dinner. Poaching in the microwave makes sense, especially if you have a sauce (such as Tomato Sauce, page 176) already in the refrigerator. Coat a microwave-safe dish with refrigerated butter-flavored cooking spray. Place the fillets next to each other and add liquid—white wine, skim milk, or water—a third of the way up the fish. Top with a dusting of paprika for color. Season with salt, if desired, and freshly ground pepper. Need to cook some vegetables for the dinner? Place thinly sliced zucchini, asparagus, carrots, or whatever is in the refrigerator on and around the fish. Top the fish with thin tomato, lemon, or orange slices; cover with wax paper or plastic wrap, venting one corner; and cook on High for 4 minutes. Check for doneness. If you have added lots of vegetables, this will take 6 to 7 minutes. Dinner is served.

Grilled Black Sea Bass over Summer Vegetables with Japanese Dressing

This is a perfect quick summer meal featuring fresh corn, but it's just as good in the winter with frozen. Fresh asparagus is available year-round, so make this dish any time.

Makes 4 servings

Per serving:
320 calories
  (25% calories from fat)
9 g total fat
  (1.5 g saturated fat)
33 g protein
31 g carbohydrate
5 g dietary fiber
60 mg cholesterol
170 mg sodium
1,004 mg potassium

Japanese Dressing

1¹⁄₂ tablespoons canola oil

¹⁄₂ teaspoon grated or minced fresh ginger

1 teaspoon reduced-sodium soy sauce

1 tablespoon fresh lemon juice

2 tablespoons fresh orange juice

1 shallot, minced

1 garlic clove, minced

1 tablespoon rice wine vinegar

¹⁄₄ teaspoon sesame oil

¹⁄₄ teaspoon sugar substitute

2 cups fresh or frozen corn kernels

¹⁄₂ pound asparagus, tough ends removed

Four 5-ounce black sea bass fillets, skinned and all pin bones removed

6 ounces mixed greens, washed, dried, and refrigerated until ready
  to serve (about 6 cups)

Pickled ginger, optional

1. Light the grill or preheat the broiler.
2. Combine all of the dressing ingredients with 1 tablespoon water in a blender or food processor and process until the dressing has emulsified. Set aside.
3. Bring a medium pot of water to a boil; add the corn and simmer for 2 minutes. Drain, refresh in cold water, and place in a salad bowl. Cook the asparagus in simmering water to cover until just tender, about 2 minutes for pencil-thin asparagus. Drain, refresh in cold water, and set aside.
4. Grill or broil the sea bass for about 6 minutes per side, turning once; use the tip of a sharp knife to test for doneness. The fish should be opaque in the center. Remove from heat and allow to rest while you finish preparing the dish.
5. Add the greens to the salad bowl. Whisk the dressing for a few seconds and toss with the greens and corn. Divide among 4 plates, then decorate each serving with the reserved asparagus, forming a circle around the corn and greens. Top each plate with a piece of sea bass. Garnish with a twist of pickled ginger, if using.

Slow-Roasted Arctic Char with Lemon–Mustard Seed Topping

This mild wild fish replete with omega-3 fatty acids combines the tastes of trout and salmon; it is available in the winter when wild salmon is still a month away. Slow-roasting a fish high in fat keeps it moist and flavorful. Serve with Lemon Couscous with Asparagus and Cherry Tomatoes (page 269).

Makes 4 servings

Per serving:
230 calories
  (53% calories from fat)
12 g total fat
  (2 g saturated fat)
22 g protein
2 g carbohydrate
0 g dietary fiber
25 mg cholesterol
120 mg sodium
18 mg potassium

1 teaspoon grated lemon zest

1 tablespoon extra virgin olive oil

1$\frac{1}{2}$ tablespoons Homemade Multigrain Bread Crumbs (page 334)

1 tablespoon finely chopped fresh flat-leaf parsley

$\frac{1}{4}$ teaspoon dried tarragon

2 teaspoons mustard seeds, crushed

1 tablespoon white wine vinegar

1 tablespoon fresh lemon juice

2 teaspoons Dijon mustard

$\frac{1}{8}$ teaspoon sugar substitute

Four 5-ounce Arctic char fillets, skin on

Freshly ground pepper

1. Preheat the oven to 250°F.

2. In a bowl combine the zest, olive oil, bread crumbs, parsley, tarragon, mustard seeds, vinegar, lemon juice, mustard, and sugar substitute. Line a baking pan with parchment paper and place the fish in the pan, skin side down. Sprinkle with pepper. Spread some of the lemon-herb mixture on each fillet.

3. Bake the char for 30 to 35 minutes, depending on thickness, until the fish is almost completely opaque. Allow to rest for 5 minutes before serving.

Baked Cod with Rice in Parchment, Florentine-Style

You can tell that spinach will be present in a recipe when the word Florentine is in the title. Here we present a meal in a parchment pouch that includes spinach and lots more. Any of your favorite fish fillets, herbs, and vegetables would work just as well.

Makes 4 servings

Per serving:
213 calories
   (8% calories from fat)
2 g total fat
   (0 g saturated fat)
31 g protein
19 g carbohydrate
4 g dietary fiber
62 mg cholesterol
178 mg sodium
773 mg potassium

One 10-ounce package frozen chopped spinach

1 cup cooked brown rice

2 scallions, white parts and 2 inches of the green, chopped

1 garlic clove, minced

1/4 cup fat-free, reduced-sodium chicken broth

Olive oil cooking spray

1 pound skinless cod fillet, cut into 4 pieces

2 plum tomatoes, thinly sliced

6 ounces mushrooms, thinly sliced

3 tablespoons chopped fresh chives, plus more for garnish

Juice and grated zest of 1 lemon

Freshly ground pepper

1/4 teaspoon kosher salt, optional

Chives for garnish

1. Cook the spinach in the microwave following package directions. Allow to cool, drain off all liquid, and wring out in a towel. Place in a bowl. Add the rice, scallions, garlic, and broth. Mix well and set aside.

2. Preheat the oven to 400°F.

3. Take four 12 × 16-inch sheets of parchment paper or aluminum foil and fold each one in half crosswise. Draw half a heart outline, beginning and ending at the folded edge, and cut along the outline. Repeat to make 4 packets. Open each heart and lay flat. Coat with cooking spray.

Cleveland Clinic Healthy Heart Lifestyle Guide and Cookbook

4. Place an equal portion of the rice-spinach mixture near one side of each heart at the fold line. Place a cod fillet on top. Top each piece of fish with a quarter of the tomatoes, mushrooms, chives, lemon zest and juice, pepper, and salt, if using. Fold the opposite side of the heart over the cod and, beginning at the top of each heart, make a series of tight narrow overlapping folds to seal the edges. Transfer the packets to a baking sheet. (The packages can be made 2 hours in advance and refrigerated until cooked.)

5. Bake for 20 minutes. The fish will be opaque and flake easily when done. Cut open the packet carefully as the steam will be very hot. Garnish with chives and serve immediately.

Broiled Flounder with Sweet and Sour Sauce

Makes 4 servings

Per serving:
160 calories
 (8% calories from fat)
1.5 g total fat
 (0.5 g saturated fat)
22 g protein
14 g carbohydrate
2 g dietary fiber
60 mg cholesterol
95 mg sodium
532 mg potassium

A very mild fish, flounder is wonderful when sauced with something piquant. Here we've teamed flounder with a sweet and sour sauce that complements, but does not overwhelm, the flavor of the fish. You could also use sea bass, red snapper, halibut, or whitefish instead of the flounder. You'll want to serve it with some brown rice.

Two 6-ounce flounder fillets
1/4 teaspoon kosher salt, optional
Freshly ground pepper
Olive oil cooking spray
1 teaspoon fresh lemon juice
 Sweet and Sour Sauce
1 1/2 cups diced pineapple
2 plum tomatoes, seeded and diced
1/2 cup diced sweet onion
1/3 cup diced green bell pepper
1/3 cup diced red bell pepper
2 tablespoons fresh pineapple juice
1 tablespoon finely minced fresh ginger
1 garlic clove, minced
1 teaspoon cornstarch

1. Preheat the broiler.
2. Rinse the fillets and pat dry. Cut each fillet in half crosswise. Season with salt, if using, and pepper. Set aside.
3. To make the sauce, combine the pineapple, tomatoes, onion, bell peppers, and pineapple juice in a heavy saucepan. Place over medium-high heat and bring to a boil. Reduce the heat and simmer, stirring occasionally, for 5 minutes. Stir in the ginger and garlic. Continue to simmer another 5 minutes.
4. Transfer 1/4 cup of the sauce to a small bowl and let it cool slightly. Using a fork, beat the cornstarch into the cooking liquid. Return the mixture to the saucepan. Cook, whisking constantly, until the sauce is smooth, about 2 minutes. Set aside.
5. Lightly coat the fish with the cooking spray and brush with lemon juice. Broil 4 inches from the heat source until the fish is opaque and flakes easily when tested with a knife, 4 to 5 minutes. Arrange the fish on a heated serving platter and spoon the sauce over the fish. Serve immediately.

Braised Halibut with Wild Mushrooms and Crostini

This is one of those recipes that can go from skillet to table in less than half an hour but tastes like you have been cooking for much longer. While the fish is braising, toast the crostini.

Makes 4 servings

Per serving:
370 calories
 (14% calories from fat)
6 g total fat
 (1 g saturated fat)
32 g protein
48 g carbohydrate
5 g dietary fiber
30 mg cholesterol
480 mg sodium
1,196 mg potassium

Olive oil cooking spray

1 teaspoon extra virgin olive oil

1 pound mixed wild mushrooms like shiitake, oyster, or straw

2 large shallots, minced

2 garlic cloves, minced

1 tablespoon chopped fresh tarragon leaves, or 1 teaspoon dried

3 tablespoons balsamic vinegar

Four 4-ounce halibut fillets

4 Crostini (page 337)

1/8 teaspoon kosher salt, optional

Freshly ground pepper

1. Heat a large nonstick skillet over medium-high heat. Coat with cooking spray and add the oil. Add the mushrooms and cook, stirring, until softened and any liquid has evaporated. Add the shallots, garlic, tarragon, and 2 tablespoons of the vinegar. Cook for 2 minutes, stirring.

2. Remove the vegetables from the skillet and set aside. Raise the heat to high and sear the fillets on both sides until brown, using additional cooking spray as needed to prevent sticking. Lower the heat to medium, return the reserved mushrooms, cover, and cook for about 8 minutes, until the fish flakes easily when tested with a knife. Return the vegetables to the skillet to warm.

3. To serve, place each fillet atop a crostini. Top with the mushrooms and sprinkle with the remaining tablespoon of vinegar, salt (if using), and pepper to taste. Serve immediately.

NOTE: You can substitute cultivated mushrooms for part or all of the fresh wild mushrooms if those are unavailable.

Lime-Roasted Orange Roughy Almandine

Makes 4 servings

Per serving:
210 calories
  (26% calories from fat)
6 g total fat
  (1 g saturated fat)
29 g protein
6 g carbohydrate
1 g dietary fiber
75 mg cholesterol
150 mg sodium
483 mg potassium

Orange roughy is a flat fish with a delicate flavor and a firm texture. Since it cooks quickly, making this fish for dinner is a snap. For a side dish, serve Roasted Vegetables (page 305) along with the fish. The lime sauce is so good you'll want to use it for other fish, such as flounder, cod, or halibut. For a special occasion try this recipe with Dover sole. It comes with a hefty price, but fresh sole is a meal for a king.

Lime Sauce
2 teaspoons extra virgin olive oil
1 shallot, minced
1 garlic clove, minced
1/3 cup dry white wine
1/4 cup fat-free, reduced-sodium chicken broth
Juice of 1 large lime (about 1/4 cup)
1 teaspoon cornstarch dissolved in 1 tablespoon water
1 tablespoon finely chopped fresh flat-leaf parsley

1 tablespoon unbleached all-purpose flour
Freshly ground pepper
1/8 teaspoon kosher salt, optional
1 pound orange roughy fillets
Refrigerated butter-flavored cooking spray
2 tablespoons slivered almonds, toasted (see page 270)

1. Preheat the oven to 450°F.

2. To make the sauce, heat the oil in a nonstick skillet over medium heat. Add the shallot and garlic and sauté for about 3 minutes. Add the wine, broth, and lime juice. Bring to a boil and reduce by one-third. Stir in the cornstarch and simmer until the sauce thickens. Add the parsley and set aside.

3. Combine the flour, pepper, and salt, if using. Sprinkle over the fillets and shake off any excess. Coat the fish with cooking spray and place in a baking dish. Bake until the fish is opaque and flakes easily when tested with the tip of a knife, about 8 minutes, depending on thickness.

4. Reheat the sauce. Place a quarter of the fish on each of 4 plates and surround with a quarter of the sauce. Top with the almonds. Serve immediately.

Cleveland Clinic Healthy Heart Lifestyle Guide and Cookbook

Mercury in Fish

Although fish can be a healthy part of our diets, some long-lived fish contain high levels of a mercury called methyl mercury that can harm an unborn baby's nervous system. Small fish absorb this form of mercury as they feed. The longer a fish lives, the more it absorbs. Larger fish that feed on other fish have the highest levels of mercury. In the United States, the limit for methyl mercury in commercial marine and freshwater fish is 1.0 part per million. The FDA advises that pregnant women, women who may become pregnant, nursing mothers, and young children should avoid fish high in mercury, including shark, swordfish, king mackerel, and tilefish. They also suggest that this population limit their intake of canned tuna to about 6 ounces (one can) per week.

Other fish and shellfish that sometimes contain high levels of mercury are grouper, tuna, and lobster from U.S. waters; red snapper; freshwater trout; and marine trout. Fish and shellfish with low levels of mercury are halibut, sablefish, pollock, blue crab, Dungeness crab, king crab, scallops, catfish, salmon (fresh, frozen, canned), oysters, and shrimp.

Fettuccine and Salmon Marinara

Makes 4 servings

Per serving:
370 calories
  (18% calories from fat)
7 g total fat
  (1 g saturated fat)
27 g protein
49 g carbohydrate
9 g dietary fiber
50 mg cholesterol
360 mg sodium
600 mg potassium

Whole wheat pastas come in many shapes and sizes, from spaghetti and linguine to conchiglie, fusilli, penne, and all shapes in between. We frequently make this recipe for marinara, a tomato sauce that is also delicious with shellfish like shrimp, crab, or, for a grand occasion, lobster. On other occasions substitute swordfish, fresh anchovies (which are often grilled or baked in Italy and France), or even flounder. This makes an easy dish for guests. Double or triple the recipe and use a combination of firm fish and shellfish. Serve with your favorite composed salad and fresh fruit. See the quick tips in "Sweet Endings" (page 307).

3/4 pound skinless salmon fillet

1/2 pound whole wheat fettuccine

1/4 cup chopped fresh flat-leaf parsley

  Marinara Sauce

1 teaspoon extra virgin olive oil

3 garlic cloves, minced

1 tablespoon anchovy paste

1/4 cup dry white wine

One 141/2-ounce can no-salt-added diced tomatoes, with juice

1/8 teaspoon crushed red pepper flakes, optional

2 scallions, white parts and 3 inches of the green, finely chopped

1. Cut the fish into 1-inch cubes and set aside.

2. Cook the pasta according to package directions. While the pasta is cooking, heat the oil in a large nonstick skillet. Add the garlic and anchovy paste, and sauté for 2 minutes over medium heat. Stir in the wine, tomatoes, and pepper flakes, if using. Simmer for 5 minutes. Add the scallions and fish. Cover the skillet and poach the fish for 2 minutes. Uncover and stir, making sure that the fish is cooked through.

3. Drain the pasta well and toss it with the salmon marinara. Garnish with parsley and serve immediately.

VARIATION: Baked Swordfish Marinara. We frequently oven-bake swordfish in this sauce. Preheat the oven to 400°F. Coat the top of the fish with 1/4 cup Homemade Multigrain Bread Crumbs (page 334) and place in an ovenproof dish. Surround with the sauce, cover with aluminum foil, and bake until the fish is cooked through. Timing will depend on the thickness of the fish; check after 8 minutes with the tip of a sharp knife.

Makes 4 servings

Per serving:
390 calories
   (14% calories from fat)
6 g total fat
   (1.5 g saturated fat)
31 g protein
52 g carbohydrate
9 g dietary fiber
45 mg cholesterol
390 mg sodium
490 mg potassium

Red Snapper Taco with Mango Salsa

Makes 4 servings

Per serving:
310 calories
   (11% calories from fat)
4 g total fat
   (0.5 g saturated fat)
31 g protein
48 g carbohydrate
7 g dietary fiber
40 mg cholesterol
420 mg sodium
940 mg potassium

This fish taco uses red snapper, but feel free to substitute any firm fish. The mango salsa goes well with chicken or pork, so keep it in mind for a quick meal when you are grilling.

1 pound skinless red snapper fillets, diced into 1-inch cubes

Fish stock

1 teaspoon ground cumin

1/2 teaspoon ground coriander

1/8 teaspoon cayenne

1/8 teaspoon kosher salt, optional

1 garlic clove, minced

2 tablespoons fresh orange juice

1 teaspoon extra virgin olive oil

   Mango Salsa

1 large mango, chopped

1/2 large red bell pepper, seeded and chopped

2 scallions, white parts and 2 inches of the green, chopped

1 teaspoon grated fresh ginger

1 garlic clove, minced

1/8 teaspoon crushed red pepper flakes, or to taste

2 teaspoons fresh lime juice

3 tablespoons chopped fresh cilantro

8 reduced-fat whole wheat tortillas, warmed until slightly crisp

2 cups chopped romaine lettuce

2 plum tomatoes, thinly sliced

1. To poach the fish, place in a microwave-safe dish, add fish stock or water to cover the bottom of the dish, and cover with wax paper or plastic wrap, leaving a vent. Cook on High for 1 1/2 minutes, then test for doneness. If not opaque, cook for 5 seconds at a time until done. Alternatively, place the fish in a skillet, add stock or water a third of the way up the fish, cover, and simmer until cooked through, about 3 minutes. Transfer to a plate to cool, then dice the fish and place in a bowl.

2. In a cup combine the cumin, coriander, cayenne, salt (if using), garlic, orange juice, and oil. Stir until combined and toss with the fish.

3. Combine all ingredients for the mango salsa in a small bowl.

4. Reheat the tortillas following package directions, taking care to not let them burn. Place $1/4$ cup lettuce and a slice of tomato down the middle of each tortilla. Spoon in some of the fish and top with the salsa. Fold in half and serve immediately.

Thai Swordfish in Red Curry Sauce

Makes 4 servings

Per serving:
340 calories
  (25% calories from fat)
9 g total fat
  (4 g saturated fat)
31 g protein
33 g carbohydrate
6 g dietary fiber
50 mg cholesterol
480 mg sodium
590 mg potassium

This Thai recipe can be adapted for many kinds of fresh or frozen seafood. You can use any firm fish as well as scallops, the meat of lobster tails, or shrimp. This dish easily becomes a stunning vegetarian entrée; use firm tofu instead of seafood and you'll convert any undecided guests into fans of this healthy plant protein.

Olive oil cooking spray

1 garlic clove, minced

1 shallot, minced

3/4 cup light unsweetened coconut milk

1 1/2 to 2 teaspoons red curry paste

1/8 teaspoon sugar substitute

1 teaspoon grated lime zest

1 pound swordfish, skin removed, cut into 1-inch cubes

2 teaspoons Thai fish sauce (nam pla)

1 small zucchini, cut into thin 3-inch matchsticks (about 4 ounces)

1/2 small red bell pepper, seeded and thinly sliced

10 ounces baby spinach

2 cups hot cooked brown basmati rice

2 tablespoons chopped fresh basil

1 tablespoon chopped fresh cilantro or mint

1 lime, quartered

1. Coat a large nonstick skillet with cooking spray. Add the garlic and shallot, and sauté for about 5 minutes over medium heat, until they begin to wilt. Add 1/3 cup of the coconut milk and continue to cook for 2 to 3 minutes, until it begins to thicken slightly. Add the curry paste to taste, sugar substitute, and lime zest; stir to combine.

2. Add the swordfish and cook for 1 minute, stirring constantly. Stir in the remaining coconut milk, the fish sauce, zucchini, and bell pepper. Cook, stirring, for a few minutes, until the vegetables are crisp-tender and the swordfish is cooked through. Add the spinach and cook just until it wilts. Remove from heat.

3. Lightly coat a 1/2-cup mold with cooking spray. Spoon a fourth of the hot rice into the mold and press down firmly. Unmold onto a shallow soup bowl or dinner plate. Spoon a fourth of the curried swordfish over the rice; garnish with basil and cilantro and top with lime. Repeat with the remaining servings.

Grilled Balsamic-Glazed Tuna with Tropical Fruit Salad

One of our favorite fish for the grill, tuna is best cooked rare; although you can certainly grill yours longer, overcooked tuna can be very dry and tough. When buying tuna, look for a moist, shiny pink or red flesh; avoid tuna with any hint of brown. We ask for sushi-grade tuna to make sure we are getting the best.

You'll love the mélange of tropical fruit flavors that complement the mellow taste of the tuna. Keep the salad in mind when serving other fish.

Six ¹/₂-inch tuna steaks (1¹/₂ pounds)
1 tablespoon extra virgin olive oil
2 tablespoons balsamic vinegar
¹/₄ teaspoon freshly ground pepper
   Tropical Fruit Salad
1 large ripe mango, cut into ¹/₄-inch strips
2 cups cubed papaya
2 cups cubed pineapple
³/₄ cup chopped red onion
1 small red bell pepper, seeded and diced
1 jalapeño, seeded and minced
¹/₄ cup chopped fresh cilantro
Leaves from 3 sprigs fresh basil, cut into a chiffonade
Juice and grated zest of 1 lime

1. Light a grill or preheat the broiler.
2. Rinse the tuna and pat dry with paper towels. Combine the oil, vinegar, and pepper. Brush over both sides of the tuna. Set aside.
3. To make the salad, combine all ingredients in a medium bowl. Set aside.
4. Grill the tuna for 3 minutes per side for rare, 6 to 7 minutes per side for well done. Divide the salad among 6 large plates and place the grilled tuna on top. Serve immediately.

Makes 6 servings

Per serving
(tuna and salad):
300 calories
  (30% calories from fat)
10 g total fat
  (2 g saturated fat)
35 g protein
17 g carbohydrate
3 g dietary fiber
55 mg cholesterol
60 mg sodium
670 mg potassium

Per serving (salad only):
70 calories
  (0% calories from fat)
0 g total fat
  (0 g saturated fat)
1 g protein
17 g carbohydrate
3 g dietary fiber
0 mg cholesterol
5 mg sodium
300 mg potassium

Tuna Burgers with Thousand Island Sauce

Makes 4 servings

Per serving:
430 calories
  (31% calories from fat)
15 g total fat
  (3 g saturated fat)
47 g protein
29 g carbohydrate
4 g dietary fiber
75 mg cholesterol
410 mg sodium
725 mg potassium

Nothing says "family barbecue" more than a burger. Here we do away with beef burgers and their high saturated fat, but not the great taste of the "special sauce" we remember from drive-through restaurants.

Thousand Island Sauce
1/4 cup light mayonnaise
2 tablespoons tomato-based chili sauce
2 teaspoons pickle relish
1 teaspoon fresh lemon juice
1/8 teaspoon garlic powder
1 teaspoon Worcestershire sauce
1/2 teaspoon prepared horseradish, optional

Two 6-inch whole wheat pita breads
Four 5-ounce tuna fillets
Olive oil cooking spray
Freshly ground pepper
1 large tomato, thinly sliced
1 cup shredded lettuce
4 thin slices red onion

1. Light a grill or preheat the broiler.
2. To make the sauce, combine the mayonnaise, chili sauce, relish, lemon juice, garlic powder, Worcestershire sauce, and horseradish, if using. Set aside.
3. Cut each pita bread in half to form 4 pockets. Lightly brush the inside of each pocket with the sauce. Wrap in aluminum foil and set on the outer edge of the grill to warm, or in a toaster oven on the lowest temperature.
4. Lightly coat the tuna with cooking spray. Pat with pepper and grill or broil until pink in the middle, about 3 minutes per side. Remove from heat.
5. To serve, place each tuna fillet in a warm pita pocket with slices of tomato, some shredded lettuce, and a slice of onion. Top with the remaining Thousand Island Sauce and serve immediately.

NOTE: Make sure the tuna you purchase is sushi grade, which means it is the highest quality. If not available, substitute salmon fillets or swordfish.

Cleveland Clinic Healthy Heart Lifestyle Guide and Cookbook

Tandoori Shrimp

The aroma of Indian spices cooking fills your home and naturally brings friends and family to the table. To enjoy the best of the East, pair it with Indian Vegetable Pilau (page 272). Crushed red pepper flakes are quite hot, so start with the lesser amount and taste the yogurt marinade before adding more.

Makes 4 servings

Per serving:
150 calories
   (9% calories from fat)
1.5 g total fat
   (0 g saturated fat)
27 g protein
7 g carbohydrate
<1 g dietary fiber
220 mg cholesterol
290 mg sodium
240 mg potassium

Marinade

2 garlic cloves, sliced

1/2-inch piece fresh ginger, peeled and sliced

Juice of 1 lime

1/4 teaspoon ground turmeric

2 teaspoons ground cumin

1/4 teaspoon ground cinnamon

Dash of ground nutmeg

1/4 teaspoon kosher salt, optional

1/4 to 1/2 teaspoon crushed red pepper flakes

1 cup nonfat yogurt

1 pound extra-large shrimp, shelled and deveined

Vegetable oil cooking spray

Paprika

1. In a food processor or blender, combine the garlic, ginger, lime juice, turmeric, cumin, cinnamon, nutmeg, salt (if using), red pepper to taste, and yogurt to make the marinade. Blend well and place in a glass bowl until ready to use.

2. One hour before starting to cook, add the shrimp to the yogurt marinade. If using wooden rather than metal skewers, soak them in warm water for 30 minutes to prevent burning.

3. Light a grill or preheat the broiler. Lightly coat a grill rack with cooking spray. Thread the shrimp on the skewers and sprinkle with paprika. Grill the shrimp 4 to 6 inches from the source of heat for 1 minute. Carefully turn and sprinkle again with paprika. Cook until the shrimp are cooked through, another 2 to 3 minutes. Serve immediately.

NOTE: You can substitute boneless, skinless chicken breasts or leg of lamb cubes with all fat removed for the shrimp.

American Bouillabaisse

Makes 8 servings

Per serving:
340 calories
 (15% calories from fat)
5.5 g total fat
 (1 g saturated fat)
45 g protein
26 g carbohydrate
2.5 g dietary fiber
87 mg cholesterol
585 mg sodium
872 mg potassium

In Southern France restaurants advertise authentic fish and shellfish stews made with typical Mediterranean fish that are impossible to find in the U.S. Here we bring you an all-American version that is bound to please. Make the broth early in the day, refrigerate it, and reheat just before dinner. Add the fish and shellfish and you're almost ready to eat.

Olive oil cooking spray

2 garlic cloves, minced

1 medium onion, chopped

2 leeks, white part only, washed well and thinly sliced

1/4 cup dry white wine

3 medium tomatoes, seeded and chopped (about 1 1/4 pounds)

1/2 tablespoon tomato paste

1/4 cup minced fresh flat-leaf parsley

2 sprigs fresh thyme, or 1/2 teaspoon dried

2 bay leaves

One 3-inch piece orange zest

1/4 teaspoon fennel seed

1/4 teaspoon saffron threads

1/8 teaspoon freshly ground pepper

1/8 teaspoon crushed red pepper flakes or hot pepper sauce

3 cups fish stock or bottled clam juice

Juice of 1 lemon

1 pound lobster tails, meat removed and sliced into coins, shells reserved

1/2 pound mussels, debearded and cleaned

1/2 pound cockles, cleaned

1 1/2 pounds any firm-fleshed fish, such as halibut, mahi-mahi, swordfish, grouper, and
 red snapper, cut into 1-inch strips

6 Crostini (page 337)

---

1. Coat a soup pot with cooking spray and add the garlic, onion, and leeks. Sauté over medium heat for 5 minutes, stirring occasionally, until soft. Add the wine, raise the heat, and boil until the liquid has evaporated. Lower the heat to medium and add the tomatoes, tomato paste, parsley, thyme, bay leaves, orange zest, fennel, saffron, ground pepper, and red pepper flakes. Cook for 2 minutes. Add the stock, 2 cups water, and lemon juice along with the lobster shells. Bring to a simmer and cook for 15 minutes.

2. Remove the lobster shells, thyme sprigs, and bay leaves from the broth. Remove the vegetables with a slotted spoon and puree in 4 batches with 1 cup of the broth in a blender or food processor until the soup is smooth. Return to the pot and refrigerate until you are ready for dinner.

3. Just before you are ready to serve, bring the soup to a simmer. Add the lobster and cook for 2 minutes. Stir in the mussels and cockles, cover, and simmer until they open. Add the fish and simmer, covered, until cooked through, another 3 minutes. Discard any shellfish that have not opened. Test the fish for doneness.

4. To serve, ladle the broth and seafood into shallow soup bowls. Top each serving with 2 crostini. Serve immediately.

Angel Hair Pasta with Lemon Seafood and Spinach

Makes 4 servings

Per serving:
380 calories
  (17% calories from fat)
8 g total fat
  (1 g saturated fat)
31 g protein
48 g carbohydrate
8 g dietary fiber
80 mg cholesterol
260 mg sodium
575 mg potassium

Not all pasta is drowned in tomato sauce. Here we marry seafood with lemon and dry white wine. The results make a dish you'll reinvent often with different fresh seafood combinations.

We prefer to buy scallops that are "dry packed" rather than ones swimming in liquid. Day-boat scallops mean they are brought in the day they are caught—these are worth searching for.

---

8 ounces whole wheat angel hair pasta

1 tablespoon extra virgin olive oil

1 tablespoon fresh lemon juice

2 teaspoons grated lemon zest

2 garlic cloves, minced

3 tablespoons chopped fresh flat-leaf parsley

1/4 pound medium shrimp, shelled and deveined

1/2 pound scallops, sliced into 1/3-inch coins

1/4 pound skinless salmon fillet, cut into 4 strips

1/4 cup dry white wine

4 ounces baby spinach

---

1. Cook the pasta until al dente, following package directions.

2. Meanwhile, in a small bowl, combine the oil, lemon juice and zest, garlic, and parsley. Set aside.

3. While the pasta cooks, heat a large nonstick skillet over medium-high heat. Add the shrimp, scallops, and salmon. Cook, turning once, for about 2 minutes, until the shrimp are pink and the scallops and fish are opaque and firm to the touch. Add the wine and boil over high heat for another minute. Set aside.

4. Drain the pasta and toss with the lemon-garlic mixture and spinach. Gently toss the seafood with the pasta. Serve immediately.

Cleveland Clinic Healthy Heart Lifestyle Guide and Cookbook

Poultry

Lean chicken is a boon to low-fat meals, which is why we keep boneless, skinless chicken breasts in our freezers. We prepare them so they're recipe-ready—pounded to an even 1/2-inch thickness and individually wrapped—making it easy to extract the exact number needed.

A Few Quick Tips

Boneless, skinless chicken breasts and duck breasts cook in minutes. Purchase 4- to 5-ounce breasts. If these are not available, buy larger ones and divide them into serving sizes. To add flavor before cooking, make a dry rub with 2 tablespoons dried orange zest; 1 tablespoon garlic powder; 1 tablespoon dry mustard; 2 tablespoons paprika; 1 tablespoon freshly ground pepper; 1 teaspoon kosher salt, optional; and 1 tablespoon dried tarragon. (This rub will stay in an airtight container in your refrigerator for months.) You can substitute dried thyme or ground bay leaves for the tarragon if you like. Coat the chicken or duck breast with olive oil cooking spray and pat with dry rub. Allow to marinate for 10 minutes. Coat again. Grill, broil, or sauté over medium high heat until done.

Apricot Chicken with Rosemary
in Parchment Packets

Makes 4 servings

Per serving:
200 calories
   (7% calories from fat)
1.5 g total fat
   (0 g saturated fat)
27 g protein
13 g carbohydrate
1 g dietary fiber
65 mg cholesterol,
80 mg sodium
320 mg potassium

This extremely pretty dish is also very easy to make. Baking in parchment paper makes it possible to cook without added fat. If you're opening the packets at the table, warn others that when you slit the packet you will be releasing a puff of steam. If you can't find parchment paper, aluminum foil will do. Serve with Brown Basmati Rice with Cilantro and Pine Nuts (page 271).

12 dried apricots

1/3 cup dry white wine

4 boneless, skinless chicken breast halves (about 4 ounces each)

Refrigerated butter-flavored cooking spray

2 garlic cloves, thinly sliced

1 tablespoon minced fresh rosemary, or 1 teaspoon dried

Kosher salt, optional

Freshly ground pepper

Juice and grated zest of 1 lemon

4 sprigs fresh thyme or flat-leaf parsley

1. Preheat the oven to 350°F.

2. Place the apricots and wine in a small dish and set aside to allow the apricots to plump, at least 15 minutes.

3. Remove all visible fat from the chicken. Rinse and pat dry.

4. Cut 4 circles of parchment paper 18 inches in diameter. Lightly spray one side of each circle. Place the circles, coated side up, on a large work surface. Lay a piece of chicken on half of the circle. Spread the garlic slices evenly over the chicken. Remove the apricots from the wine, reserving the wine. Cut each apricot into thin slices and distribute evenly over the chicken. Sprinkle with the rosemary. Season with salt, if using, and pepper.

5. Combine the reserved wine and lemon juice. Drizzle the mixture evenly over the chicken. Sprinkle with the zest. Lay a sprig of thyme on each chicken breast. Fold the parchment over the chicken and crimp the sides to seal. Place the packets on a baking sheet and bake for 45 minutes. Transfer the packets to dinner plates, cut open, and serve immediately.

Chicken Picadillo

Picadillo is popular in several Spanish-speaking countries and in the American South. We like it because it is easy to make. Another time serve it over cooked brown rice or creamy polenta. You can also make picadillo as a soup by adding a can of fat-free, reduced-sodium chicken broth and a can of chickpeas that have been drained and rinsed well. Here we call for serving the picadillo over shredded lettuce or cabbage, saving our calories for a fruit dessert.

Makes 6 servings

Per serving:
170 calories
  (10% calories from fat)
2 g total fat
  (0 g saturated fat)
19 g protein
19 g carbohydrate
3 g dietary fiber
45 mg cholesterol
190 mg sodium
62 mg potassium

1 pound ground white meat chicken

1 medium yellow onion, chopped

2 garlic cloves, minced

1 medium red bell pepper, seeded and chopped

1 jalapeño, seeded and minced

2 cups canned plum tomatoes, chopped, with juice from 15-ounce can

1/2 teaspoon dried oregano

1/2 teaspoon dried thyme

1/2 teaspoon ground cumin

6 green olives, pitted and chopped

1 teaspoon Worcestershire sauce

1 teaspoon paprika

1/2 cup golden raisins

6 cups shredded lettuce or cabbage

1. In a large nonstick skillet over medium heat, brown the chicken until it is no longer pink, about 10 minutes, breaking up the clumps with the back of a wooden spoon as they form. Drain off any liquid that forms. Add the onion, garlic, bell pepper, and jalapeño. Continue to cook another 10 minutes, stirring often.

2. Reduce the heat to medium-low and add the tomatoes with their juice, oregano, thyme, cumin, olives, Worcestershire sauce, paprika, and raisins. Cook another 3 to 5 minutes, until slightly thickened.

3. Arrange the shredded lettuce on a large serving plate. Spoon the picadillo over the lettuce and serve immediately.

Chipotle Chicken and Corn Tamale Pie

Makes 8 servings

Per serving:
310 calories
  (15% calories from fat)
5 g total fat
  (1.5 g saturated fat)
30 g protein
36 g carbohydrate
4 g dietary fiber
70 mg cholesterol
410 mg sodium
445 mg potassium

Culinary historians have dated the use of a cornmeal topping for tamale pie back to about 1910. In this recipe, we've updated the flavor with canned chipotle chiles, which are available on the Mexican food aisle of most supermarkets, and we use the cornmeal in a bottom crust. Dried, smoked jalapeños, called chipotles, add a smoky, sweet flavor that's popular from coast to coast and border to border. You can turn down the heat by cutting down or eliminating some of the chiles in adobo sauce.

Cornmeal Crust

Olive oil cooking spray

5¼ cups fat-free, reduced-sodium chicken broth

2¼ cups stone-ground yellow cornmeal

1 teaspoon ground cumin

½ teaspoon kosher salt, optional

¼ teaspoon cayenne

Filling

Olive oil cooking spray

1½ pounds boneless, skinless chicken breasts, trimmed of all fat and cut into 1-inch cubes

1 cup fresh or thawed frozen corn kernels

1 medium onion, chopped

2 garlic cloves, minced

1 medium tomato, seeded and chopped

2 medium tomatillos, husked and chopped

2 canned chipotle chiles in adobo sauce, chopped, plus 1 tablespoon sauce

2 tablespoons golden raisins, plumped in 2 tablespoons dry white wine or water

1 tablespoon chili powder

½ teaspoon ground cumin

1 teaspoon dried oregano

¼ cup shredded reduced-fat Monterey Jack cheese

1. Preheat the oven to 450°F. Coat a 10-inch round casserole that's at least 2 inches deep with cooking spray.

2. To make the crust, bring the broth to a boil in a large saucepan over medium-high heat. Gradually stir in the cornmeal, cumin, salt (if using), and cayenne. Reduce the heat to medium and cook, stirring constantly, until thickened, 10 to 12 minutes. Immediately spread the mixture to a depth of about ½ inch over the bottom and sides of the prepared casserole. Press firmly with the back of a spoon. Set aside.

3. To make the filling, lightly coat a large nonstick skillet with cooking spray. Place over medium-high heat. Add the chicken and sauté until brown on all sides, about 5 minutes. Add the corn, onion, garlic, tomato, tomatillos, chipotles and their sauce, raisins with their liquid, chili powder, cumin, oregano, and cheese. Stir until well blended.

4. Spoon the mixture into the prepared casserole. Bake, uncovered, for 25 to 30 minutes, until the edges of the crust are golden brown and the filling is bubbly. Remove from the oven and let stand on a wire rack for 10 minutes before cutting into wedges to serve.

Chicken Skewers, San Francisco–Style, with Asian Slaw

Makes 4 servings

Per serving:
240 calories
 (41% calories from fat)
11 g total fat
 (1 g saturated fat)
23 g protein
1,114 g carbohydrate
3 g dietary fiber
50 mg cholesterol
220 mg sodium
665 mg potassium

This recipe illustrates the influence of the Pacific Rim on San Franciscan cuisine. Here, we've marinated cubes of boneless chicken breasts in an Asian-style marinade, then threaded them onto skewers with snow peas and cherry tomatoes. After grilling, serve over our slaw, a crunchy mix of cabbage, bean sprouts, and daikon (Japanese radish).

Hoisin sauce is a sweet, spicy sauce sold in the Asian food section of most large supermarkets and Asian markets. You could substitute tomato-based chili sauce with good results.

Marinade
¼ cup hoisin sauce
¼ cup rice wine vinegar
2 tablespoons canola oil
½ tablespoon reduced-sodium soy sauce
¼ teaspoon sesame oil

¾ pound boneless, skinless chicken breasts
36 fresh snow peas (about 6 ounces)
20 cherry tomatoes (about 1¼ pounds)
Asian Slaw (recipe follows)

1. In a medium bowl, whisk together the marinade ingredients. Set aside.
2. Remove and discard any visible fat from the chicken. Rinse and pat dry. Cut into ½-inch cubes. Place in the marinade, cover, and refrigerate for at least 30 minutes or up to 2 hours. If using wooden rather than metal skewers, soak them in warm water for 30 minutes to prevent burning.
3. Light a grill or preheat the broiler.
4. Blanch the snow peas in boiling water to cover for 1 minute. Drain. Thread the chicken cubes, snow peas, and cherry tomatoes onto 4 skewers.
5. Grill over medium-high heat for 3 to 4 minutes per side. Serve hot over a bed of crunchy Asian Slaw.

Asian Slaw

1 cup shredded red cabbage

1 cup shredded green cabbage

1 cup shredded carrots

2 cups mung bean sprouts

1/2 cup shredded daikon radish

　Dressing

1 tablespoon canola oil

1 tablespoon rice wine vinegar

1 teaspoon honey

1/4 teaspoon sesame oil

1/2 teaspoon sesame seeds, toasted

Makes 4 servings

Per serving:
80 calories
　(50% calories from fat)
4.5 g total fat
　(0 g saturated fat)
3 g protein
10 g carbohydrate
3 g dietary fiber
10 mg cholesterol
39 mg sodium
265 mg potassium

In a large bowl, combine the red and green cabbage, carrots, bean sprouts, and radish. In a small bowl, whisk together the dressing ingredients. Drizzle over the slaw and lightly toss. Serve at once as a bed for the grilled chicken skewers.

Grilled Chicken Breasts with Warm Balsamic Strawberries

This savory dish rivals those found at fine restaurants. The beauty is you can make this healthy masterpiece in your own home with minimal effort. Who said following a cardioprotective diet can't get the chef a standing ovation?

Makes 4 servings

Per serving:
130 calories
  (24% calories from fat)
3.5 g total fat
  (0.5 g saturated fat)
20 g protein
4 g carbohydrate
<1 g dietary fiber
50 mg cholesterol
210 mg sodium
285 mg potassium

Four 3-ounce boneless, skinless chicken breasts, pounded thin
Juice of 1 lemon
2 teaspoons extra virgin olive oil
2 garlic cloves, minced
1½ tablespoons chopped fresh tarragon
¼ teaspoon kosher salt
Freshly ground pepper
½ cup Warm Balsamic Strawberries (recipe follows)
Minced fresh chives, optional

1. Place the chicken breasts in a shallow dish. In a small bowl, combine the lemon juice, oil, garlic, tarragon, salt, and pepper. Pour over the chicken and marinate for 30 minutes in the refrigerator.

2. When ready to cook, preheat a grooved nonstick grill pan. Remove the chicken from the marinade and pat dry with paper towels. Cook 4 to 5 minutes per side, until the juices run clear when the chicken is pierced with the tip of a knife.

3. Serve at once with 2 tablespoons of strawberries and drizzle a bit of the liquid around the edge. Decorate with chives (if using).

Warm Balsamic Strawberries

Refrigerated butter-flavored cooking spray

2 tablespoons minced red onion

2 tablespoons minced fresh chives

1 tablespoon dry red wine

2 tablespoons balsamic vinegar

Freshly ground pepper

2 cups sliced fresh strawberries

Makes about 2 cups

Per serving
(1/2 cup strawberries):
35 calories
  (0% calories from fat)
0 g total fat
  (0 g saturated fat)
1 g protein
8 g carbohydrate
2 g fiber
0 mg cholesterol
0 mg sodium
140 mg potassium

Coat a small nonstick skillet with cooking spray. Sauté the onion over medium heat until wilted. Add the chives, wine, vinegar, and pepper and simmer for 2 minutes. Add the strawberries and cook for another 3 minutes. They should keep their shape, but the flavors should blend.

NOTE: If you make the full recipe you'll have some leftover berries. Refrigerate them and serve them the next day with grilled fish or add them to a tossed green salad.

VARIATION: You could use sliced fresh peaches, plums, or nectarines in place of the strawberries.

North African Chicken with Almonds and Harissa

Makes 4 servings

Per serving
(chicken dish only):
260 calories
   (35% calories from fat)
10 g total fat
   (1.5 g saturated fat)
26 g protein
17 g carbohydrate
3 g dietary fiber
95 mg cholesterol
330 mg sodium
545 mg potassium

It's no wonder that North African food continues to grow in popularity here in the States given its foundation of fresh vegetables, healthy grains, sweet fresh and dried fruits, and tasty nuts and seeds—the very essence of a cardioprotective diet. Even the spices, herbs, and condiments are already known to us: turmeric, cinnamon, ginger, cumin, curry, and a half dozen or more other exotic flavors.

Here we've braised chicken with almonds and lemons, then spiked the dish at the end of the cooking time with a spoon or two of harissa, the fiery hot sauce of the region. Serve with whole wheat couscous.

---

4 bone-in chicken thighs (about 1 pound)

1 teaspoon extra virgin olive oil

1 large white onion, chopped

1 garlic clove, minced

1/2 teaspoon ground turmeric

2 teaspoons curry powder

1/2 teaspoon ground cinnamon

1/2 teaspoon ground cumin

1/4 teaspoon ground ginger

One 141/2-ounce can fat-free, reduced-sodium chicken broth

2 tablespoons fresh lemon juice

2 plum tomatoes, seeded and diced

1 lemon, cut crosswise into thin slices, seeds removed

4 pitted dates, quartered lengthwise

1/4 cup blanched slivered almonds

2 tablespoons Harissa (recipe follows), or to taste

---

1. Remove and discard the skin and any visible fat from the chicken thighs. Rinse and pat dry.

2. Heat the oil in a deep 12-inch skillet with a cover. Add the onion and garlic and sauté over medium heat, until the onion is golden but not browned, about 5 minutes. Push the onions to the sides of the pan and add the chicken thighs. Cook until golden on both sides, 2 to 3 minutes per side. Sprinkle on the turmeric and cook for another 2 minutes, stirring to combine.

3. Combine the curry, cinnamon, cumin, ginger, broth, and lemon juice. Pour over the chicken and onion. Sprinkle with the tomatoes. Arrange the lemon slices on top, reduce the heat, and simmer, covered, for 20 minutes. Uncover and add the dates and almonds. Continue to cook, uncovered, for another 5 to 10 minutes, until the juices run clear when the chicken is cut near the thighbone.

4. Divide the lemon slices among 4 heated dinner plates. Place a chicken thigh on top of the lemon. Stir the onions, dates, and almonds. Spoon the mixture onto each plate around the chicken. Serve immediately with the Harissa.

Harissa

Makes about 6
tablespoons

Per serving
  (1/4 teaspoon):
7 calories (92% calories
  from fat)
1 g total fat (trace
  saturated fat)
trace protein
trace carbohydrate
0 g dietary fiber
0 mg cholesterol
6 mg sodium
3 mg potassium

Although harissa is a common condiment in all North African countries, Tunisia is credited with the creation of this fiery-hot sauce. In Tunisia, harissa is the traditional accompaniment to couscous and a common ingredient in soups and a myriad of other dishes. It's also terrific with this stew. Try it.

1 ounce dried hot red chiles

1 teaspoon caraway seed

1/2 teaspoon cumin seed

1/2 teaspoon coriander seed

1/4 teaspoon kosher salt, optional

2 garlic cloves

3 tablespoons plus 2 teaspoons extra virgin olive oil

1. Wash the chiles and place in a small saucepan with water to cover. Bring to a boil, remove from the heat, and let steep covered for 1 hour. Meanwhile, using a spice mill or a mortar and pestle, grind the caraway, cumin, and coriander seeds and the salt, if using. Set aside.

2. Using tongs, remove the chiles from the saucepan; wipe dry with paper towels and chop. Reserve 2 tablespoons of the chile steeping liquid. Add the chiles and garlic to the spice mill or mortar. Grind or mash everything together. Stir in 3 tablespoons of the oil and 2 tablespoons of the reserved steeping liquid.

3. Transfer the harissa to a small serving dish for spooning sparingly into the stew at the table. Place any remaining harissa in a small glass jar. Drizzle the remaining 2 teaspoons oil over the top. Cover and refrigerate. Use within 3 months.

Chicken and Squash Stew with Wild Rice

A stew like this can warm you up on a cold night without weighing you down. Since this stew freezes well, double the recipe and freeze half to have another satisfying meal at the ready. Use within 3 months.

Makes 8 servings

Per serving:
270 calories
  (17% calories from fat)
5 g total fat
  (1 g saturated fat)
23 g protein
35 g carbohydrate
7 g dietary fiber
70 mg cholesterol
580 mg sodium
900 mg potassium

8 skinless, bone-in chicken thighs (about 2 pounds)

2 teaspoons extra virgin olive oil

4 medium carrots, cut into 1/2-inch pieces

6 celery ribs, cut into 1/2-inch pieces

3 garlic cloves, minced

1 white onion, diced

1 tablespoon dried oregano

2 teaspoons ground cumin

Kosher salt, optional

1/2 teaspoon freshly ground pepper

2 pounds butternut squash, cut into 1-inch pieces

1 cup wild rice, well washed and drained

2 quarts fat-free, reduced-sodium chicken broth

1 bunch scallions, white parts and 2 inches of the green, minced

10 sprigs fresh cilantro, finely chopped

1. Remove all visible fat from the chicken. Rinse and pat dry. Set aside.

2. In a Dutch oven, heat the oil over medium heat. Add the carrots, celery, garlic, and onion. Sauté until the vegetables soften but do not brown, 5 to 6 minutes. Add the oregano, cumin, salt (if using), and pepper. Cook another 3 to 4 minutes.

3. Add the chicken to the pot along with the squash and rice. Gently stir. Pour in the chicken broth, making sure it covers all the pieces. Bring the mixture to a boil, then reduce the heat to a simmer. Cover and simmer for about 1 hour, until the vegetables and rice are tender.

4. Meanwhile, combine the scallions and cilantro. Place in a small serving bowl.

5. Ladle the stew into 8 shallow bowls. Serve, passing the scallion/cilantro mixture to sprinkle over the stew.

6. Freeze any remaining stew.

Roasted Chicken with Root Vegetables

Makes 6 servings

Per serving (3 ounces
   chicken plus one-sixth
   of the vegetables):
280 calories
   (20% calories
   from fat)
6 g total fat
   (1.5 g saturated fat)
24 g protein
1 g carbohydrate
7 g dietary fiber
65 mg cholesterol
125 mg sodium
720 mg potassium

Roasting chickens are frequently on sale at our local supermarkets. When-ever they are, we buy two—one to roast right away and the other to put in the freezer for a future meal. Any leftovers are welcome the next day for salads or sandwiches. Here we've added a bevy of root vegetables that roast along-side. Serve with a fresh watercress and Belgian endive salad with Dijon Balsamic Vinaigrette (page 200).

One 4-pound roasting chicken
Olive oil cooking spray
Dried Italian herb seasoning
6 small Yukon Gold potatoes, quartered (about 12 ounces)
1 pound carrots
1 pound parsnips
Freshly ground pepper
Kosher salt, optional

1. Preheat the oven to 400°F.
2. Rinse the chicken, discarding the giblets, neck, and any visible fat. Pat dry with paper towels. Place the chicken on a rack in a shallow roasting pan. Lightly coat with cooking spray and sprinkle with the Italian seasoning. Roast for 30 minutes
3. Meanwhile, arrange the potatoes, carrots, and parsnips in a second shallow pan. Coat with cooking spray and sprinkle with Italian seasoning, pepper, and salt, if using. Place in the oven alongside the chicken and continue to roast for another 35 to 45 minutes, until the chicken is done and the vegetables are golden brown and tender.
4. Transfer the chicken to a carving board and the vegetables to a heated serving platter. Allow the chicken to rest for 10 minutes before carving, discarding the skin. Add the cut chicken to the platter and serve.

Asian Chicken Wraps

What can you do with leftover roast chicken? One answer is to make a fantastic second meal like this wrap, which can become a weekend lunch or light dinner. Best of all, it can be put together in less than 30 minutes. Very low fat or fat-free whole wheat tortillas are available in the bread section of your market.

Makes 4 wraps

Per serving:
325 calories
   (16% calories from fat)
6 g total fat
   (1.5 g saturated fat)
40 g protein
31 g carbohydrate
4 g dietary fiber
95 mg cholesterol
520 mg sodium
540 mg potassium

1 teaspoon sesame oil

1 cup shredded leftover white meat chicken, skin and fat removed

One 1-pound package coleslaw mix, or 5 cups shredded cabbage

3 ounces shiitake mushrooms, stems discarded, thinly sliced

5 scallions, white parts and 3 inches of the green, thinly sliced

1 tablespoon minced fresh ginger

1 garlic clove, minced

3 tablespoons hoisin sauce

1 teaspoon garlic chili sauce

Four 8-inch whole wheat tortillas

1. Heat the oil in a large nonstick skillet. Add the chicken, coleslaw mix, mushrooms, scallions, ginger, and garlic. Stir-fry over medium-high heat for 3 minutes, or until the coleslaw has wilted. Stir in the hoisin and garlic chili sauce.

2. Reheat the tortillas in the microwave following package directions. Place one-fourth of the chicken and vegetables in each wrap. Roll up and serve immediately.

NOTE: No leftover chicken in the fridge? Poach 1 pound skinless, boneless chicken breasts by placing the chicken in a covered pan with stock halfway up the sides. Bring to a simmer. Check with the point of a knife after 4 to 5 minutes. Or place the chicken in a microwave-safe dish with broth or water to cover the bottom of the dish. Cover with wax paper and cook on High for 4 minutes. Check for doneness. If not opaque throughout, microwave on High for another 1 to 2 minutes (juices should run clear when the chicken is pierced with a knife).

Spicy Chicken

Makes 4 servings

Per serving:
100 calories
  (9% calories from fat)
1 g total fat
  (0 g saturated fat)
20 g protein
2 g carbohydrate
0 g dietary fiber
50 mg cholesterol
55 mg sodium
250 mg potassium

This is a super quick way to prepare chicken that's not too hot, but spiced just right for most everyone's taste. Serve this with Maque Choux (page 291) and dessert bowls piled high with cubed fresh pineapple for a meal that's sure to please.

12 ounces boneless, skinless chicken breasts, trimmed of all fat

1 teaspoon paprika

1 garlic clove, minced

1/4 teaspoon freshly ground black pepper

1/4 teaspoon onion powder

1/4 teaspoon dried thyme

1/4 teaspoon dried oregano

1/8 teaspoon cayenne

2 tablespoons fresh lime juice

Chopped fresh flat-leaf parsley, optional

1. Cut the chicken breasts crosswise into 2-inch strips. In a small bowl, combine the paprika, garlic, black pepper, onion powder, thyme, oregano, and cayenne. Toss with the chicken strips.

2. Place the chicken in a microwave-safe covered dish. Sprinkle with lime juice. Cover and microwave on High for 4 minutes. Check for doneness. If not opaque throughout, microwave on High for another 1 to 2 minutes (juices should run clear when the chicken is pierced with a knife). Sprinkle with chopped parsley, if using, and serve.

Turkey Cutlets with Tomato and Red Pepper Sauce

This quick turkey recipe can be on the table in minutes. We like to serve it over instant brown rice alongside Persian Chopped Salad (page 156). Pounding the turkey cutlets, which are usually about 1/2 inch thick, makes them very tender, and cooking them quickly keeps them moist. If you don't have a mallet, place the cutlets between two sheets of wax paper and pound with a heavy pan or pot.

1 pound white meat turkey cutlets

1 tablespoon unbleached all-purpose flour

1 1/2 teaspoons dried Italian herb seasoning

1/8 teaspoon crushed red pepper flakes

1 teaspoon extra virgin olive oil

1/2 cup dry white wine

1/4 teaspoon chicken base

2 garlic cloves, minced

3 plum tomatoes, chopped

1/2 red bell pepper, seeded and chopped

1 1/2 tablespoons balsamic vinegar

Makes 4 servings

Per serving:
190 calories
  (11% calories from fat)
2.5 g total fat
  (0 g saturated fat)
29 g protein
7 g carbohydrate
0 g dietary fiber
45 mg cholesterol
320 mg sodium
180 mg potassium

1. Pound the turkey until it is 1/4 inch thick. Combine the flour, 1 teaspoon of the Italian seasoning, and the crushed red pepper flakes. Coat the turkey cutlets with the flour mixture, shaking off any excess. Heat the oil in a nonstick skillet over high heat until it begins to smoke. Brown the turkey on both sides, about 2 minutes per side. Transfer to a warm plate.

2. Lower the heat to medium-high and add the wine, chicken base, and 2 tablespoons water to the skillet. Reduce by a third. Add the garlic, tomatoes with any liquid, bell pepper, and remaining 1/2 teaspoon Italian seasoning. Simmer for 10 minutes. Add the turkey and reheat. Drizzle some of the balsamic vinegar over each cutlet. Serve immediately.

Moo Shu Chicken in Lettuce Leaves

Makes 4 servings

Per serving (two leaves
with moo shu):
210 calories
   (13% calories from fat)
3 g total fat
   (0.5 g saturated fat)
25 g protein
17 g carbohydrate
3 g dietary fiber
50 mg cholesterol
430 mg sodium
680 mg potassium

We all love moo shu in Chinese restaurants. Here we bring you a recipe for this tasty dish but instead of offering the pancakes that usually accompany the chicken, we serve it wrapped in lettuce leaves. Boston or butter lettuces are the preferred lettuces for the wrapping; if you can't find them, use iceberg. Making the wraps smaller can make this a wonderful appetizer or cocktail party nibble. Of course, for finger foods, all of the ingredients have to be chopped very fine. You can also serve the moo shu over brown rice or whole wheat noodles.

3/4 pound boneless, skinless chicken breast, placed in the freezer for 20 minutes

2 tablespoons vodka

2 teaspoons cornstarch

1 teaspoon peanut oil

1/2 cup egg substitute

2 garlic cloves, minced

2 teaspoons grated fresh ginger

1-ounce package dried sliced shiitake mushrooms, rehydrated (see page 175)

4 scallions, white parts and 4 inches of the green, sliced diagonally into 1/2-inch pieces

1/2 cup canned bamboo shoots, drained

1/2 pound coleslaw mix

1 head Boston or Bibb lettuce, separated into 8 large leaves

5 tablespoons plus 1 teaspoon hoisin sauce

   Sauce

1/4 cup fat-free, reduced-sodium chicken broth

1 tablespoon seasoned rice wine vinegar

2 tablespoons dry sherry

1 tablespoon reduced-sodium soy sauce

1/2 teaspoon sesame oil

1 teaspoon cornstarch

1 teaspoon Thai chili sauce

---

1. Cut the chicken into very thin slices crosswise. If the breasts are wide, slice in half lengthwise and then cut crosswise. Place in a bowl and stir in the vodka and cornstarch. Set aside.

2. Combine all of the sauce ingredients with 1/4 cup water. Stir until combined. Set aside.

3. Heat the oil in a nonstick wok or heavy skillet. Stir-fry the chicken over high heat until browned. Remove from the pan and keep warm. Add the egg substitute and stir-fry until cooked. Place in a bowl and set aside.

4. Stir-fry the garlic, ginger, and mushrooms for 2 minutes over medium heat. Add the reserved sauce and chicken, cooking for 4 minutes. Stir in the scallions, bamboo shoots, and coleslaw mix, cooking until the cabbage wilts. Stir in the cooked egg substitute to warm.

5. Place equal amounts of the moo shu on the 8 lettuce leaves. Top each with 2 teaspoons hoisin sauce. Fold each leaf into an envelope to enclose the moo shu. Serve immediately.

Cornish Hens Roasted on Dried Fruit Stuffing

Makes 8 servings

You'll find other uses for the herb and dried fruit stuffing; use it to stuff pork chops, chicken breasts, or, if you triple the recipe, a small turkey.

Per serving
(hen and stuffing):
300 calories
  (19% calories from fat)
6 g total fat
  (1.5 g saturated fat)
34 g protein
24 g carbohydrate
2 g dietary fiber
150 mg cholesterol
220 mg sodium
600 mg potassium

Per serving
(stuffing only):
110 calories
  (5% calories from fat)
0.5 g total fat
  (0 g saturated fat)
1 g protein
24 g carbohydrate
2 g dietary fiber
0 mg cholesterol
135 mg sodium
245 mg potassium

4 Rock Cornish hens (about 1 pound each)

Olive oil cooking spray

2 tablespoons minced parsley

1 garlic clove, minced

1/2 teaspoon dried rosemary

1/2 teaspoon dried thyme

Juice and grated zest of 1 lemon

Dried Fruit Stuffing

1/3 cup chopped no-sugar-added dried cranberries

8 dried apricot halves, chopped

8 dried apples, chopped

1/4 cup dried currants

1 cup chopped onion

1/2 cup finely chopped celery

1 teaspoon dried sage

1 tablespoon reduced-calorie transfree margarine, melted

1 cup Homemade Multigrain Bread Crumbs (page 334)

1/4 cup dry white wine

1/2 to 3/4 cup fat-free, reduced-sodium chicken broth

---

1. Preheat the oven to 400°F.

2. Remove and discard the skin and all visible fat from the hens. Rinse and pat dry with paper towels. Split in half lengthwise. Lightly coat the hens with cooking spray. Combine the parsley, garlic, rosemary, and thyme. Sprinkle over the hens. Set aside.

3. In a large bowl, combine the dried fruits, onion, celery, sage, and margarine. Stir in the bread crumbs. Moisten with the wine and chicken broth to desired consistency. (Makes about 2 1/2 cups stuffing.) Transfer the mixture to a large shallow casserole. Arrange the hens on top. Drizzle with lemon juice and top with lemon zest.

4. Cover with aluminum foil and roast for 30 minutes. Reduce the heat to 325°F. Uncover and continue to bake until the hens are nicely browned and a drumstick twists easily in its socket. Serve at once.

Stuffed Turkey Burgers with Apples, Onions, and Peppers

If you're making these burgers for children, you may want to serve the apples and peppers raw, on the side. Some children prefer their fruit and veggies that way.

Makes 4 servings

Per serving:
250 calories
   (12.5% calories from fat)
3.5 g total fat
   (0.5 g saturated fat)
26 g protein
34 g carbohydrate
5 g dietary fiber
35 mg cholesterol
277 mg sodium
278 mg potassium

3/4 pound ground white meat turkey

1/8 teaspoon kosher salt, optional

Freshly ground pepper

Canola cooking spray

1/2 ounce low-fat Cheddar cheese, very thinly sliced

2 large cooking apples, such as Braeburn, Granny Smith, or Macintosh, cored and cut into thin slices

1/4 cup thinly sliced red onion

1 medium red bell pepper, seeded and cut into julienne strips

4 whole wheat sandwich rolls, split and toasted

Mustard, optional

Low-sodium ketchup, optional

1. Shape the ground turkey into 4 round uniform patties. Season with salt, if using, and pepper.

2. Lightly coat 2 large nonstick skillets with cooking spray. Cook the patties over medium-high heat in one skillet for 4 minutes. Flip the burgers and top with cheese. Continue to cook another 4 minutes, or until the burgers are done or register 170° on an instant meat thermometer. Meanwhile, cook the apples, onion, and pepper in the other skillet approximately 10 minutes, until soft.

3. To serve, place a turkey burger on each roll and top with apples and vegetables. Pass the mustard and ketchup, if using.

DIETITIAN'S NOTE: Don't forget to purchase ground white meat turkey. Not all ground turkey is lean, so be choosy.

Duck Breasts with White Bean Puree

Makes 4 servings

Per serving:
330 calories
  (15% calories from fat)
6 g total fat
  (1.5 g saturated fat)
32 g protein
38 g carbohydrate
11 g dietary fiber
75 mg cholesterol
340 mg sodium
420 mg potassium

Frozen duck breasts are available in many markets with the skin and fat removed. The pureed beans are an excellent substitute for mashed potatoes with grilled or broiled entrées. Add roasted asparagus (see page 305), and you have a meal that's fancy enough for the good china and easy enough for a family dinner.

Marinade

3 tablespoons fresh orange juice

1 tablespoon Dijon mustard

1 garlic clove, minced

One 1/2-inch piece fresh ginger, peeled and minced

White Bean Puree

1 teaspoon extra virgin olive oil

1 onion, chopped

2 garlic cloves, minced

Two 15-ounce cans cannellini beans, rinsed and drained

1 teaspoon chopped fresh sage

2 teaspoons balsamic vinegar

1/2 teaspoon kosher salt, optional

Freshly ground pepper

2 large plum tomatoes, seeded and finely chopped

Olive oil cooking spray

Four 4-ounce boneless, skinless duck breasts, all fat removed

Olive oil cooking spray

Freshly ground pepper

1. Combine the marinade ingredients on a plate. Score the breasts and place them on the plate, turning to cover both sides. Let stand for 30 minutes.

2. Preheat the broiler.

3. Meanwhile, make the bean puree. Heat the oil in a nonstick skillet; add the onion and cook, stirring, over medium heat until the onion wilts, about 5 minutes. Add the garlic and continue to cook for another minute.

4. Place the beans in a food processor. Add the cooked onion and garlic, sage, vinegar, salt (if using), and pepper. Process until smooth. Place in a saucepan with the tomatoes, cover, and heat at the lowest setting.

5. Remove the duck from the marinade and wipe dry with paper towels. Coat the breasts with cooking spray and sprinkle with fresh pepper. Broil the duck 7 to 8 minutes for medium rare, turning once after 4 minutes.

6. Transfer the duck to a carving board and allow to rest for 5 minutes. Slice thin. To serve, divide the warm pureed beans among 4 plates and top with the sliced duck breasts. Serve immediately.

Supreme Turkey Loaf

The hidden veggies in this meat loaf not only add taste but also guarantee a moist loaf that tastes even better the next day.

Makes 8 servings

Per serving:
240 calories
  (36% calories from fat)
10 g total fat
  (2.5 g saturated fat)
27 g protein
11 g carbohydrate
2 g dietary fiber
75 mg cholesterol
310 mg sodium
238 mg potassium

Olive oil cooking spray
1 medium onion, minced
1 small carrot, grated
1 medium zucchini, grated and squeezed dry
1/2 red bell pepper, seeded and minced
2 garlic cloves, minced
2 pounds ground white meat turkey
1/2 cup egg substitute
1 1/2 teaspoons dried sage
1 1/2 teaspoons dried thyme
1/2 teaspoon dried marjoram
1 tablespoon Dijon mustard
2 tablespoons tomato paste
2 tablespoons Worcestershire sauce
3/4 cup rolled oats
Freshly ground pepper
1 tablespoon low-sodium ketchup
2 large bay leaves
6 slices very lean turkey bacon

1. Preheat the oven to 350°F. Line a baking dish with aluminum foil and coat with cooking spray.

2. Coat a nonstick skillet with cooking spray. Add the onion, carrot, zucchini, bell pepper, and garlic. Cover and cook over medium heat until the vegetables are tender, about 10 minutes, stirring twice.

3. In a large bowl, combine the turkey, cooked vegetables, egg substitute, sage, thyme, marjoram, mustard, tomato paste, Worcestershire sauce, rolled oats, and pepper. Form the turkey mixture into a loaf and place it in the prepared baking dish. Top with the ketchup, bay leaves, and bacon. Bake for about 1 hour, or until the center of the loaf springs back to the touch. Remove from the oven; cool for 10 minutes before discarding the bacon and slicing the loaf. Serve immediately, or chill and serve cold.

Lean Meats

Meat can be part of a cardioprotective lifestyle if you buy
the leaner cuts, cut back on serving sizes, and eat meat sparingly—ideally no more than once a week and in small servings.
Our recipes will maximize your eating pleasure with some of
the most mouthwatering meat dishes you've ever had. You'll
learn what cuts of meat to buy and how to cook them to
ensure tenderness.

A Few Quick Tips

Lean meats especially benefit from a dry rub, which fires up their flavor. Coat the meat with a cooking spray and pat the meat with the dry rub of your choice. Loosely cover the meat with plastic wrap and refrigerate from 15 minutes to 24 hours. You're ready to cook the meat as you like. Here are two of our favorite dry rubs.

- Asian Blend: Combine 3 tablespoons five-spice powder, 3 tablespoons hot paprika (or 1 teaspoon crushed red pepper flakes), 1 teaspoon ground ginger, 1 teaspoon freshly ground pepper, and 1/4 teaspoon ground allspice.
- Mojo Dry Spice Rub: When cooking Cuban and Latin American food, use a spice rub of 1 tablespoon each cumin seeds and coriander seeds, ground to a fine powder in a spice mill and mixed with black pepper, sugar, and a dash of salt.

Liquid marinades are also easy to make and will act as a meat tenderizer. Combine an acid like citrus juice, wine, or vinegar with herbs and spices from the style of food you are preparing and 1 to 2 tablespoons extra virgin olive oil. To this add freshly ground pepper and 1/2 teaspoon kosher salt, if desired. Make the marinade in a heavy-duty self-sealing plastic bag that's large enough to hold the meat flat. Then add the meat and seal. Turn the bag several times to coat the meat evenly, place on a small tray, and refrigerate for the time specified in the recipe, turning the meat several times. Here are some terrific additions to a basic marinade.

- For the taste of Mexico, the Pacific Rim, or the Middle East, add varieties of seeded, diced chiles, oregano, cumin, and garlic.
- To bring a taste of the Orient, add freshly grated or minced ginger, star anise, sesame seeds, lime zest, fish sauce, hot pepper sauce, a drop or two of sesame oil, and some chopped fresh cilantro or mint.
- For a curry marinade, add fresh ginger, cloves, turmeric, cinnamon, cumin, garlic, and cayenne to nonfat yogurt and red wine vinegar.
- For a Continental flavor, you can depend on balsamic vinegar and garlic with fresh basil, tarragon, or thyme, or chopped shallots.
- To make a red or white wine marinade, include one part wine, two parts broth, tarragon, thyme, bay leaves, garlic, onion, and tomato paste.

Beef Chili with Butternut Squash

With a perfect flavor balance between the sweetness of the squash and the heat of the chili, this one-pot meal will please adults and children alike. To peel the butternut squash quickly and easily, use a sharp paring knife or a vegetable peeler.

1 pound ground sirloin

1 medium onion, chopped

1 red bell pepper, seeded and chopped

One 14 1/2-ounce can no-salt-added diced tomatoes with juice

1 small butternut squash chopped into 1/2-inch dice (about 3 1/2 cups)

1 1/2 tablespoons tomato paste

2 teaspoons dried oregano

1 tablespoon ground cumin

1 tablespoon chili powder

Two 15-ounce cans black beans, rinsed and drained

3 garlic cloves, minced

1/2 jalapeño, seeded and minced, optional

1/2 cup chopped fresh cilantro, plus 6 sprigs for serving

3 scallions, white parts and 3 inches of the green, thinly sliced

1/3 cup light sour cream

1/2 cup shredded low-fat Cheddar cheese

1. Sauté the beef, onion, bell pepper, and tomatoes in a large Dutch oven over medium-high heat, stirring to break up the meat.

2. Drain the meat and vegetables in a colander and return to the pot. Add the squash, 2 cups water, the tomato paste, oregano, cumin, chili powder, beans, and garlic. Bring to a simmer. Continue to cook for about 20 minutes, stirring occasionally, until the squash is tender. Add the jalapeño, if using, and the cilantro; simmer for 10 minutes. Add more water if needed.

3. Ladle the chili into soup bowls. Garnish each bowl with a cilantro sprig. Pass the scallions, sour cream, and cheese.

VARIATION: The chili is equally good made with white meat turkey, chicken, or buffalo.

Makes 6 servings

Per serving:
300 calories
    (18% calories from fat)
 6 g total fat
    (2.5 g saturated fat)
26 g protein
44 g carbohydrate
14 g dietary fiber
46 mg cholesterol
518 mg sodium
996 mg potassium

Grilled Steak with Chimichurri Sauce

Makes 6 servings

Per serving
(steak and sauce):
200 calories
 (45% calories from fat)
10 g total fat
 (2.5 g saturated fat)
23 g protein
5 g carbohydrate
0 g dietary fiber
50 mg cholesterol
55 mg sodium
360 mg potassium

Per serving
(Chimichurri Sauce only):
50 calories
 (90% calories from fat)
5 g total fat
 (0.5 g saturated fat)
0 g protein
3 g carbohydrate
0 g dietary fiber
0 mg cholesterol
0 mg sodium
75 mg potassium

Chimichurri sauce is as popular in Argentina as ketchup is here in the States. A sauce that's full of fresh chiles, herbs, and onions, chimichurri will liven up most everything that you grill. Serve the steak with Spinach Salad with Oranges and Walnuts (page 158) and finish the meal with Pear Tart with Chocolate Shavings (page 317).

Chimichurri Sauce

1 cup loosely packed chopped fresh cilantro leaves and tender stems

1/3 cup chopped fresh flat-leaf parsley

1/4 cup chopped fresh oregano

4 garlic cloves, minced

2 serranos, finely minced

1/4 cup sherry vinegar

2 tablespoons extra virgin olive oil

Marinated Steak

1 pound top sirloin steak

2 tablespoons balsamic vinegar

1 teaspoon extra virgin olive oil

1/4 teaspoon hot pepper sauce

1 garlic clove, minced

1. Combine all of the sauce ingredients in a bowl. Cover and set aside.

2. Trim all visible fat from the steak. Rinse the beef and pat dry. Place in a shallow dish. Combine the vinegar, oil, hot pepper sauce, and garlic in a glass measuring cup. Whisk together with a fork. Pour over the steak, turning to coat both sides. Let stand for 15 minutes.

3. Meanwhile, light a grill. When the grill is hot, place the steak on the grill and sear for a minute on each side. Continue to grill for 4 to 5 minutes more, turning once, for medium rare. Cook for 1 to 2 minutes more per side for medium-well. Transfer the steak to a heated platter and keep warm.

4. Place the sauce mixture in a small sauté pan. Cut the steak on the diagonal into 6 portions and set on heated plates. Pour the meat juices from the platter into the sauté pan. Quickly bring the sauce to a boil. Ladle the sauce over the steaks and serve.

NOTE: Chimichurri Sauce is also wonderful as a dipping sauce for your cooked seafood.

Choosing Lean Meats

Anyone who will be grocery shopping for this cardioprotective program needs to know what cuts of meat to buy. Since meat is included in How Often Should I Eat Red Meat and Other Proteins? guidelines (page 81) only once a week, it should be the very best you can afford. Remember that the total fat and saturated fat grams, cholesterol milligrams, and calories vary with the type, grade, and cut of meat.

Here's a general guideline to the leanest cuts of meat:

- Beef—round, rump, sirloin, tenderloin, and dried beef
- Pork—loin, center-cut roasts or chops, lean ham, center-cut ham, and Canadian bacon
- Lamb—sirloin, leg, cutlets, and sirloin chops

Thai Grilled Steak Salad with Rice Noodles

Makes 4 servings

Per serving:
240 calories
   (12.5% calories from fat)
6 g total fat
   (2 g saturated fat)
21 g protein
23 g carbohydrate
2 g dietary fiber
30 mg cholesterol
637 mg sodium
607 mg potassium

Thai restaurants have opened all over the country, bringing new flavors and sauces to our meals. Here we bring you the best of Thai with little fat and less sodium than you'd find in a restaurant. You could substitute chicken breasts or tofu for the flank steak.

Marinade
3 garlic cloves, minced
1¹/₂ tablespoons Thai fish sauce (nam pla)
1 packet sugar substitute
Salad
³/₄ pound flank steak
3 ounces rice stick noodles
¹/₂ cucumber, halved lengthwise and thinly sliced (about 4 ounces)
4 cups mixed greens
¹/₄ cup chopped fresh mint
¹/₂ cup chopped fresh basil
1 tablespoon chopped dry-roasted peanuts
Sauce
3 garlic cloves, minced
1 tablespoon Thai fish sauce (nam pla)
2 tablespoons fresh lime juice
¹/₂ teaspoon sugar substitute
¹/₈ teaspoon crushed red pepper flakes, or to taste

1. Combine the ingredients for the marinade in a shallow bowl. Add the flank steak, cover, and marinate in the refrigerator for 4 hours or up to 24 hours, turning once.

2. Light the grill or preheat the broiler. Lightly coat the grill rack with cooking spray.

3. To make the sauce, place ¹/₄ cup water, the garlic, fish sauce, lime juice, sugar substitute, and red pepper flakes in a food processor or blender. Pulse until well combined; set aside.

4. Place the noodles in a deep bowl. Cover with warm water and let soak for 10 minutes. While the noodles are soaking, bring a pot of water to a boil. Drain the noodles and then place in boiling water for 2 to 4 minutes, until cooked through. Drain, rinse under cold running water, and drain again. Set aside.

5. Remove the steak from the marinade. Score the meat in a cross-hatched pattern and grill until done, about 8 minutes per side for medium. Transfer the steak to a carving board and let rest for 10 minutes before cutting diagonally into very thin slices.

6. To assemble the salads, divide the cucumber, greens, mint, and basil among 4 dinner plates. Mound the noodles in the center of each plate and top with an equal portion of the steak slices. Toss with the sauce. Garnish with peanuts.

Cuban Flank Steak with Citrus Mojo

Makes 8 servings

Per serving:
140 calories
  (39% calories from fat)
6 g total fat
  (2.5 g saturated fat)
18 g protein
2 g carbohydrate
0 g dietary fiber
30 mg cholesterol
45 mg sodium
315 mg potassium

Flank steak, a lean and thrifty choice for the grill, needs to marinate to bring the steak to its succulent, tender best. The marinade we've chosen for this recipe is based on a Cuban mojo, the signature marinade of Cuba and piquant condiment served with meals at Latino restaurants for dipping meat, poultry, and fish. Our version uses a minimum of oil to keep the fat grams low, and a combination of orange, lemon, and lime for the traditional sour orange, which is very hard to find in the United States.

1½ pounds flank steak

1 tablespoon Mojo Dry Spice Rub (page 248)

1 teaspoon dried thyme

2 garlic cloves, minced

1 tablespoon minced fresh cilantro

Vegetable oil cooking spray

Citrus Mojo Marinade

3 garlic cloves, minced

1 teaspoon whole peppercorns

1 habañero, seeded, optional

1 tablespoon dried oregano

¾ cup fresh orange juice

⅓ cup fresh lemon juice

⅓ cup fresh lime juice

1. Trim all visible fat from the flank steak. Combine the spice rub with the thyme, garlic, and cilantro. Rub both sides of the steak with the mixture. Place the steak in a large self-sealing heavy-duty plastic bag. Set aside.

2. Place the marinade ingredients, including the chile, if using, in a food processor and pulse until smooth. Pour the marinade over the steak in the bag, and seal it tight. Refrigerate for at least 1 hour or up to 1 day, turning the bag over occasionally.

3. Preheat the grill to high. Lightly coat a grill rack with cooking spray.

4. Lift the steak from the marinade and pour the marinade into a small saucepan. Place the steak on the grill and grill for 4 to 5 minutes per side for medium-rare, turning once. Transfer the steak to a carving board and let stand for 5 minutes.

5. While the steak is cooking, bring the marinade to a rapid boil for 2 minutes. Pour the marinade into small bowls to share as dipping sauce.

6. Carve the steak diagonally across the grain into very thin slices. Serve immediately. Offer the marinade as a dipping sauce for the steak.

Shepherd's Pie

This is one of those family meals that re-create our childhoods. If it is true that we are a meat-and-potato country, then this recipe will fill the bill of "what's for dinner?" any weeknight and taste great as leftovers. Here we used ground sirloin, but feel free to substitute ground white meat turkey or even buffalo.

Makes 6 servings

Per serving:
240 calories
  (16% calories from fat)
4.5 g total fat
  (1.5 g saturated fat)
23 g protein
29 g carbohydrate
3 g dietary fiber
50 mg cholesterol
210 mg sodium
466 mg potassium

Refrigerated butter-flavored cooking spray

1 small onion, chopped

1¼ pounds ground sirloin

½ cup fat-free, reduced-sodium beef broth

1 tablespoon Worcestershire sauce

1 tablespoon tomato paste

Freshly ground pepper

2 russet potatoes, peeled and cut into uniform-size pieces (about 1½ pounds)

3 garlic cloves, cut in half

¼ cup skim milk

2 tablespoons egg substitute

¼ teaspoon kosher salt, optional

1 cup frozen baby peas, thawed

Ground paprika

1. Preheat the oven to 425°F. Coat a casserole with cooking spray.

2. Coat a nonstick skillet with cooking spray. Add the onion and sauté over medium heat until wilted, about 5 minutes. Add the meat and cook, breaking it up with a wooden spoon, until browned. Strain the meat mixture in a colander to drain all fat and liquid. Return to the skillet. Add the broth, Worcestershire sauce, tomato paste, and pepper. Simmer for 10 minutes.

3. Meanwhile, boil the potatoes with the garlic in lightly salted water until done. Drain the potatoes and remove the garlic. Mash the potatoes with the milk and egg substitute. Season with salt, if using, and pepper.

4. Place the meat mixture in the prepared casserole and top with the peas. Spread the mashed potatoes over the top. Coat with cooking spray and sprinkle with paprika. Bake for 25 to 30 minutes, until heated through and nicely browned. Serve immediately.

Herbed Roasted Beef Tenderloin

Makes 10 servings

Per serving:
250 calories
  (40% calories from fat)
10 g total fat
  (4 g saturated fat)
35 g protein
1 g carbohydrate
0 g dietary fiber
95 mg cholesterol
80 mg sodium
460 mg potassium

When guests or family come for a festive meal, tenderloin of beef may be the answer. We buy ours from a butcher who will remove every bit of fat and the silver skin, which curls during roasting if not cut away. After marinating, we roast the meat quickly, searing in the deep flavors of the herbs and wine. Serve with Lemon Couscous with Asparagus and Cherry Tomatoes (page 269), using the freshest vegetables you can find.

---

2 tablespoons minced fresh tarragon

2½ tablespoons minced fresh thyme

3 garlic cloves, quartered

1 large shallot, quartered

1 tablespoon grated lemon zest

1 teaspoon freshly ground pepper

1 tablespoon Dijon mustard

2 tablespoons dry full-bodied red wine, such as Cabernet Sauvignon

1 tablespoon brandy

1 tablespoon extra virgin olive oil

One 3-pound fillet of beef cut from the thick end of the loin, all fat and silver skin removed, tied every 2 inches

Olive oil cooking spray

---

1. Place the tarragon, thyme, garlic, shallot, zest, pepper, and mustard in a food processor. With the motor running, slowly pour in the wine, brandy, and oil. Process until well combined, 1 to 2 minutes. Place the meat on a large sheet of plastic wrap. Pat the marinade over the fillet, making a thin layer over the entire roast. Wrap in the plastic and refrigerate at least 6 hours and up to 24 hours.

2. When almost ready to roast the beef, preheat the oven to 450°F. Place a rack in a large roasting pan.

3. Unwrap the fillet and coat it with cooking spray. Roast until a meat thermometer registers 125°F in the center of the meat for rare, 30 to 35 minutes. Allow the roast to rest for 10 minutes before slicing. It will continue to cook as it rests. Serve immediately.

NOTE: If you have guests who prefer their meat well done, cut off steaks of meat from the thin end of the roast. They will roast quicker while the remainder of fillet is roasting and be ready after the rare meat has rested.

Substitutions for Alcohol in Recipes

We call for alcohol in some of our recipes; it adds authentic taste. If you are concerned about the amount of actual alcohol that remains in the final product, review the following information.

Cooking Time	Percentage of Alcohol Remaining
15 minutes	40%
30 minutes	35%
45 minutes	30%
1 hour	25%
$1^1/_2$ hours	20%
2 hours	10%
$2^1/_2$ hours	5%

The following are substitutes for alcohol if your physician suggests that you avoid any amount:

- An equal amount of nonalcoholic wine
- $7/_8$ cup fat-free, reduced-sodium broth of your choice or $1/_8$ cup lemon juice with $1/_2$ cup water
- $1/_2$ the alcohol amount of water with flavored extracts such as rum or brandy extract
- Frozen orange concentrate for orange liqueur in desserts
- $7/_8$ cup water with $1/_8$ cup red or white wine vinegar or fruit-flavored vinegar

Internal Temperature for Doneness of Meats

Beef and Lamb

Rare	140°F
Medium	160°F
Well done	170°F

Ground Meats

Beef, lamb, pork	160°F
Chicken, turkey	165°F

Pork

Chops, roast	160°–165°F

Poultry

Bone-in turkey	180°F
Boneless turkey	170°F
Chicken and duck	175°–189°F

3-Bean Beef Stew

To bump up the fiber in our favorite beef stew, we added two cans of fiber-rich beans to the pot ten minutes before the end of the cooking time. Leftovers are welcome as the stew tastes even better the next day.

Makes 12 servings

Per serving:
311 calories
   (31% calories from fat)
7 g total fat
   (3 g saturated fat)
27 g protein
24 g carbohydrate
8 g dietary fiber
50 mg cholesterol
393 mg sodium
770 mg potassium

Olive oil cooking spray

1 teaspoon extra virgin olive oil

2 pounds rump or top sirloin, all fat removed, cut into 1-inch pieces

2 medium onions, coarsely chopped

3/4 pound cremini mushrooms, quartered

12 ounces baby carrots with 1/2-inch greens

3 garlic cloves, coarsely chopped

1 1/2 cups dry full-bodied red wine

2 cups fat-free, reduced sodium beef broth

4 sprigs fresh thyme

1/4 teaspoon kosher salt, optional

1/2 teaspoon freshly ground pepper, or to taste

One 14 1/2-ounce can no-salt-added diced tomatoes with juice

2 tablespoons tomato paste

3 bay leaves

1 red bell pepper, seeded and cut into strips

1 pound green beans, ends snipped, sliced on the diagonal into 1-inch pieces

One 15-ounce can kidney beans, drained and rinsed

One 15-ounce can cannellini beans, drained and rinsed

1. Coat a Dutch oven with cooking spray, add the oil, and heat over medium-high heat. Dry the meat on paper towels. Add to the pot and brown on all sides. Remove to a bowl. Lower heat to medium. Add the onions, mushrooms, carrots, and garlic. Cook, stirring occasionally, for 5 minutes. Return the beef to the pot and add the wine and beef broth. Add the thyme, salt (if using) pepper, tomatoes with juice, tomato paste, and bay leaves. Bring to a boil; lower heat, cover, and simmer for 1 to 1 1/2 hours, until the beef is tender, adding water as needed.

2. Add the red bell pepper, green beans, kidney beans, and cannellini beans. Continue to cook for 10 minutes. If the stew is too thick, add up to 1/2 cup additional wine or water to obtain desired consistency. Just before serving discard the bay leaves and thyme sprigs. Ladle into bowls and serve hot.

Creole Beef and Vegetables with Cheese Grits

Bell peppers, onions, and celery are usually the flavor base of a Creole dish. This particular recipe was inspired by the Creole casserole dish called grillade, which is traditionally served with grits. We cook our dish on top of the stove and serve it with grits flavored with cheese to take the place of the usual melting butter.

Makes 6 servings

Per serving (beef only):
270 calories
  (20% calories from fat)
6 g total fat
  (2 g saturated fat)
36 g protein
17 g carbohydrate
5 g dietary fiber
80 mg cholesterol
410 mg sodium
787 mg potassium

1½ pounds top round steak

Garlic powder

Olive oil cooking spray

1 teaspoon extra virgin olive oil

1 medium onion, coarsely chopped

1 medium red bell pepper, seeded and chopped

3 celery ribs, finely chopped

One 28-ounce can whole tomatoes with juice

Kosher salt, optional

Freshly ground pepper

½ teaspoon dried thyme

1 bay leaf

½ cup dry red wine

1 tablespoon Worcestershire sauce

¼ teaspoon hot pepper sauce

One 10-ounce package frozen artichoke hearts, thawed

Cheese Grits (recipe follows)

1. Trim all visible fat from the beef. Wipe the beef with a damp paper towel and dry. Cut the beef into ½-inch cubes. Lightly sprinkle with garlic powder and pound ¼ inch thick.

2. Lightly coat a Dutch oven with cooking spray. Add the oil and place the pan over medium-high heat. Working in batches, brown the beef about 2 minutes, turning once. Transfer the meat to a dish and set aside. Repeat until all the beef is browned.

3. Add the onion, bell pepper, and celery to the Dutch oven and sauté until the vegetables are limp, about 5 minutes. Cut the tomatoes crosswise into 1-inch slices. Add the reserved meat to the pot, along with the juice and ½ cup water. Season with salt, if using, and add the pepper, thyme, bay leaf, wine, Worcestershire sauce, and hot pepper sauce. Reduce the heat to low and stir to combine. Simmer, covered, for about 45 minutes, adding more water if necessary.

4. Arrange the artichoke hearts on top of the beef and cook covered for 15 minutes longer, until the meat is very tender. Uncover, raise the heat, and cook rapidly for 4 to 5 minutes to reduce the sauce to the desired thickness. Serve in a shallow bowl alongside a serving of the grits.

Cheese Grits

¼ teaspoon kosher salt, optional
1 cup quick grits
½ cup shredded low-fat sharp Cheddar cheese

Bring 4 cups of water to a boil in a large pot. Stir in the salt, if using. Slowly add the grits to the pot, whisking constantly. Lower the heat to a simmer and continue to cook, whisking constantly, until the mixture is thick and smooth, 3 to 5 minutes. Remove from heat and stir in the cheese. Keep warm until ready to serve.

Makes 6 servings

Per serving:
110 calories
   (8% calories from fat)
1 g total fat
   (0 g saturated fat)
5 g protein
21 g carbohydrate
0 g dietary fiber
10 mg cholesterol
60 mg sodium
42 mg potassium

Spinach-Stuffed Roast Leg of Lamb

Makes 8 servings

Per serving:
270 calories
  (40% calories from fat)
12 g total fat
  (4 g saturated fat)
35 g protein
5 g carbohydrate
2 g dietary fiber
105 mg cholesterol
150 mg sodium
550 mg potassium

Holidays and celebrations are a perfect time to serve lamb. We had our favorite butcher bone half of a leg for us so that we had a 2¼-pound roast. We asked him to remove all fat and to roll and tie the roast. All of the hard work was done, and all we had to do was to make the stuffing and insert it carefully into the tied roast. We served the leg of lamb with Great Northern Beans with Tomatoes and Herbs (page 281), white beans being a traditional French accompaniment to leg of lamb.

Stuffing
One 10-ounce package frozen chopped spinach, thawed
1 teaspoon extra virgin olive oil
1 small onion, minced
3 garlic cloves, minced
2 tablespoons pine nuts
2 tablespoons currants
1 tablespoon chopped fresh thyme
1 tablespoon Dijon mustard

One 2¼-pound boned leg of lamb, all visible fat removed, tied at 1½-inch intervals
Olive oil cooking spray
¼ teaspoon kosher salt, optional
Freshly ground pepper
2 sprigs fresh rosemary

1. Preheat the oven to 425°F.
2. Place the thawed spinach in double-ply paper towels or a clean tea towel and wring out all liquid. Set aside.
3. Heat the oil in a nonstick skillet. Add the onion and sauté for 5 minutes over medium heat, until it wilts. Add the garlic and pine nuts. Continue to cook for another 3 minutes, making sure the garlic does not burn. Stir in the spinach, currants, thyme, and mustard; combine well, remove from heat, and let cool.

4. Stuff the leg of lamb using your fingers to carefully press spinach stuffing into the center of the roast. Tuck in the ends of the meat and tie lengthwise with kitchen twine. Coat with cooking spray and season with salt (if using) and pepper. Insert a sprig of rosemary under the butcher's twine on both the bottom and top of the roast. Place on a rack in a roasting pan. Roast for 1 hour, or until a meat thermometer registers 140°F for rare (160°F for medium).

5. Remove from the oven and discard the rosemary. Allow the roast to rest for 10 minutes. Carve into thin slices of lamb and stuffing, removing the twine as you proceed.

Cold Soba Noodles with Pork

Makes 4 servings

Per serving:
310 calories
  (32% calories from fat)
11 g total fat
  (2.5 g saturated fat)
28 g protein
30 g carbohydrate
3 g dietary fiber
55 mg cholesterol
420 mg sodium
620 mg potassium

Pork tenderloins are often packaged in pairs, so we roast one following a recipe or package directions and have one left over for another meal, such as our Honey-Orange Grilled Pork Tenderloin with Chipotle Chiles (page 265). Soba noodles are Japanese noodles made from buckwheat and wheat flour. We can buy them at our supermarket, but you may find them only in an Asian market, so feel free to substitute whole wheat fettuccine.

Dressing
1/4 cup rice wine vinegar
1 tablespoon reduced-sodium soy sauce
1 1/2 teaspoons minced fresh ginger
1 1/2 tablespoons sesame oil
1/8 teaspoon crushed red pepper flakes, or to taste

4 ounces soba noodles or whole wheat fettuccine
2 cups chopped roasted pork tenderloin
1 medium red bell pepper, seeded and thinly sliced crosswise
3/4 pound mung bean sprouts, rinsed and drained
3 scallions, white parts and 2 inches of the green, thinly sliced
1/4 cup chopped fresh cilantro, plus additional leaves for garnish
2 tablespoons chopped unsalted, dry-roasted peanuts
Lime wedges

1. Prepare the dressing by whisking the ingredients in a small bowl. Set aside.
2. Cook the soba noodles according to package directions. Drain, then refresh in cold water. Drain again and place in a large bowl. Combine with the pork, bell pepper, bean sprouts, scallions, and chopped cilantro and chill at least 1 hour.
3. Just before serving, toss the noodle mixture with the dressing. Divide among 4 shallow pasta bowls. Garnish each serving with the reserved cilantro leaves, peanuts, and a wedge of lime.

Honey-Orange Grilled Pork Tenderloin
with Chipotle Chiles

The savory, sweet coating for this roast, with the kick of chipotle chiles, adds a rich flavor to the already succulent grilled pork. Add a side dish of Sweet Potato Mousse (page 299), and dinner's ready.

Canola oil for brushing the grill

3 canned chipotle chiles in adobo sauce plus 1 tablespoon sauce

3 tablespoons orange blossom honey

3 tablespoons fresh orange juice

1 tablespoon Dijon mustard

2 garlic cloves, peeled

1 pork tenderloin, all fat removed (1 to 1¼ pounds)

Freshly ground pepper

4 orange wedges, optional

1. Preheat the grill to high. Lightly brush the grill rack with oil.

2. Put the chiles and sauce, honey, orange juice, mustard, and garlic in a food processor or blender and process until smooth. Sprinkle the pork with pepper to taste and brush the chile-honey mixture over all sides.

3. Place the tenderloin on the grill and cook for 20 to 25 minutes, until an instant meat thermometer inserted in the center reaches 150°F. Transfer the pork to a carving board and let rest for 5 minutes. Cut the pork on the diagonal into thin slices. If desired, serve with orange wedges to squeeze over the meat.

Makes 4 servings

Per serving:
200 calories
  (18% calories from fat)
4 g total fat
  (1.5 g saturated fat)
24 g protein
16 g carbohydrate
0 g dietary fiber
75 mg cholesterol
135 mg sodium
475 mg potassium

Per serving (¼ cup of sauce/marinade only):
60 calories
  (0% calories from fat)
0 g total fat
  (0 g saturated fat)
0 g protein
16 g carbohydrate
0 g dietary fiber
0 mg cholesterol
80 mg sodium
60 mg potassium

Pork Chops with Dried Cherry Balsamic Sauce

Makes 6 servings

Per serving:
150 calories
  (30% calories from fat)
5 g total fat
  (2 g saturated fat)
18 g protein
7 g carbohydrate
0 g dietary fiber
50 mg cholesterol
95 mg sodium
234 mg potassium

These pork chops cook quickly and will soon become a family favorite. You can vary the fruit—cranberries, diced dried apricots, or golden raisins can be used instead of cherries. We use our best aged vinegar because this recipe warrants breaking out the good stuff.

1/4 cup dried cherries

1 1/2 tablespoons Dijon mustard

6 center-cut loin pork chops, 3/4 inch thick (approximately 1 1/4 pounds)

Kosher salt, optional

Freshly ground pepper

Refrigerated butter-flavored cooking spray

3 tablespoons aged balsamic vinegar

1. Mix the cherries and mustard in a small bowl. Set aside.

2. Trim all visible fat from the chops. Season with salt, if using, and pepper. Use cooking spray to lightly coat a nonstick skillet just large enough to hold the chops comfortably. Place over medium-high heat and sear the chops for 2 to 3 minutes per side, until nicely browned, turning once. Spoon the cherry and mustard mixture over the chops.

3. Cover, reduce the heat to low, and simmer for 15 to 20 minutes, until the chops are done. Transfer to a platter and keep warm.

4. Add the balsamic vinegar to the skillet and increase the heat to medium. Bring the juices to a boil and stir, scraping up the bits. When the mixture reduces to make a sauce, pour it over the chops and serve immediately.

Grains, Beans, and Legumes

A staple of the Mediterranean diet, this category of food has been praised by food experts as being very healthy, but our children, grandchildren, and friends really don't care. They and others among our taste testers simply like to eat these dishes.

A Few Quick Tips

Following are cooking times for some of the most popular and easy-to-find grains, plus some ideas on what to add to the cooking pot. Note that size plays a role, and some of these grains are available in grades from coarse to fine. We use the most popular grades and sizes available in our markets. We also suggest that you use whole grains rather than refined ones. Just reading the nutritional data on the label will convince you of the merit of this decision.

Grain (1 cup dry)	Liquid	Cooking Time
Barley, pearled	3 cups	20 to 25 minutes
Buckwheat groats	2 cups	15 minutes
Bulgur wheat	2 cups	15 minutes
Cornmeal (polenta, firm)	3 cups	15 minutes
Cornmeal (polenta, soft)	4 cups	15 minutes
Whole wheat couscous	1 cup	1 minute + 5 minutes standing
Quinoa	2 cups	15 minutes
Brown long-grain rice	2 1/2 cups	45 minutes
Brown basmati rice	2 1/2 cups	35 minutes
Wild rice	3 cups	50 minutes or when grains puff open
Spelt	3 1/2 cups	45 minutes

Try these ways to brighten the flavor of the grains.

- Add lemon zest and juice or orange zest to the grains along with chopped fresh or dried fruits that have been rehydrated in dry sherry, Marsala, or fruit juice.
- Add toasted almonds, walnuts, or pine nuts to the cooked grain.
- Use spices from the Mediterranean, where many of these grains are popular. We suggest cumin, cilantro, mint, and fresh ginger.
- For a more European flair, add sautéed aromatic vegetables, including mushrooms, onions, shallots, leeks, and carrots, along with other vegetables such as asparagus, broccoli, and spinach.
- For a Northern African taste, stir Harissa (page 235) into your couscous and other foods.
- In summer add fresh chopped vegetables with Lemon Vinaigrette (page 166) and herbs to celebrate the meal.

Lemon Couscous with Asparagus and Cherry Tomatoes

Couscous sparkles with the addition of lemon. Here we add asparagus and a hint of nutty flax seeds to boost the fiber. All you need to make a lunch or light dinner are a salad and a fresh fruit dessert. This meal will help you reach your goal of nine fruits and vegetables per day.

1 teaspoon extra virgin olive oil

3 scallions, white parts and 2 inches of the green, thinly sliced

1 garlic clove, minced

$1/2$ pound asparagus, tough ends removed, sliced into 1-inch pieces

1 cup whole wheat couscous

1 cup fat-free, reduced-sodium chicken broth

3 tablespoons fresh lemon juice

2 teaspoons grated lemon zest

2 cups cherry tomatoes, halved (about 18, or $2/3$ pound)

$1/4$ cup shredded fresh basil

1 tablespoon lightly toasted flax seeds, coarsely ground

1. Heat the oil in a deep nonstick skillet. Add the scallions, garlic, and asparagus. Cook, stirring, until the asparagus is crisp-tender. Add the couscous, broth, lemon juice, and zest. Bring to a boil, lower the heat, cover, and simmer for 5 minutes.
2. Remove from heat and fold in the tomatoes, basil, and flax seeds. Cover for 5 minutes and fluff with a fork.

NOTE: Flax seeds are high in fat and therefore should be stored in the refrigerator or freezer, where they will keep for up to 6 months.

Makes 4 servings

Per serving:
160 calories
  (14% calories from fat)
2.5 g total fat
  (0 g saturated fat)
7 g protein
31 g carbohydrate
7 g dietary fiber
0 mg cholesterol
120 mg sodium
370 mg potassium

Mango Quinoa

Makes 6 servings

Per serving:
190 calories
  (22% calories from fat)
5 g total fat
  (0 g saturated fat)
6 g protein
32 g carbohydrate
4 g dietary fiber
0 mg cholesterol
110 mg sodium
320 mg potassium

Quinoa (KEEN-wah) is the seed of a plant that is a distant relative of spinach, but it tastes and looks like a grain and has more complete protein than other grains. It can be substituted for any other grain in recipes, is easy and quick to prepare, and has a pleasing light and fluffy quality.

1 cup quinoa

3 tablespoons slivered almonds

1½ teaspoons extra virgin olive oil

1 small onion, minced

2 teaspoons ground cumin

¼ teaspoon ground turmeric

½ teaspoon ground cinnamon

1 cup fat-free, reduced-sodium chicken broth

One 14½-ounce can no-salt-added diced tomatoes, well drained

1 mango, diced

1. Preheat the oven to 350°F.

2. In a fine sieve, thoroughly rinse the quinoa under cold running water. Drain well and set aside.

3. Place the almonds in a small baking pan and toast in the oven until browned, for about 8 minutes, watching carefully that they do not burn. Set aside.

4. Heat the oil in a saucepan over medium heat. Add the onion and sauté until it begins to wilt. Add the cumin, turmeric, and cinnamon, stirring for 30 seconds. Add the quinoa and cook for another minute, stirring frequently. Stir in the broth, ⅔ cup water, and the tomatoes. Bring to a simmer, cover, and simmer for 15 minutes, or until the liquid is absorbed. Remove from heat, stir in the mango, and re-cover. Allow to sit for 5 minutes. Fluff with a fork and fold in the almonds.

VARIATIONS: Substitute fresh grapes, sliced peaches, or apricots for the fresh mango. Add leftover poultry or fish to quinoa for a light lunch or dinner.

DIETITIAN'S NOTE: Incorporating quinoa into a meatless meal is a great way to reap the benefits of a plant food that is a complete protein.

Brown Basmati Rice with Cilantro and Pine Nuts

Brown basmati rice may take longer to cook than white rice, but its nutty texture and added fiber are worth the wait. Always refrigerate rice, whole wheat flour, and other whole grains for extended shelf life. This prevents their oils from becoming rancid.

Olive oil cooking spray

1 cup brown basmati rice

2 tablespoons pine nuts, toasted

1 teaspoon grated fresh ginger

1 garlic clove, minced

2^1/$_2$ cups packed fresh cilantro

^{1}/$_4$ teaspoon kosher salt, optional

Coat a nonstick pot with cooking spray. Sauté the rice, pine nuts, ginger, and garlic for 2 minutes over medium-high heat. Add 1^1/$_2$ cups water and 2 cups of the cilantro. Bring to a boil, lower the heat, cover, and simmer for 20 minutes. Stir in the salt, if using, and remaining cilantro. Cover and let sit for 15 minutes. Serve immediately.

Makes 4 servings

Per serving:
190 calories
   (20% calories from fat)
4.5 g total fat
   (0.5 g saturated fat)
5 g protein
36 g carbohydrate
3 g dietary fiber
0 mg cholesterol
10 mg sodium
83 mg potassium

Indian Vegetable Pilau

Makes 4 servings

Per serving:
270 calories
  (15% calories from fat)
4.5 g total fat
  (0.5 g saturated fat)
7 g protein
51 g carbohydrate
7 g dietary fiber
0 mg cholesterol
32 mg sodium
597 mg potassium

Taking a break from heavy meals does not mean you have to feel deprived. Here we share a recipe that may become a favorite comfort food once you experience the aroma and taste of this rice. Serve with Cucumber Raita (page 274).

1 teaspoon canola oil

1 tablespoon grated fresh ginger

1/2 teaspoon ground turmeric

1 small cauliflower, trimmed and cut into 11/2-inch florets (about 3/4 pound)

1 cup brown basmati rice

Vegetable oil cooking spray

1 medium onion, finely chopped

1 bay leaf

1/2 teaspoon ground cloves

1/2 teaspoon ground cinnamon

1 teaspoon curry powder

1/2 cup frozen green peas

One 3-ounce summer squash, chopped

3 tablespoons golden raisins

2 tablespoons slivered almonds, toasted

1. In a large nonstick skillet, heat the oil and stir in the ginger and turmeric. Cook for 30 seconds. Add the cauliflower and cook, stirring, until the edges begin to brown, about 3 minutes. (The cauliflower should remain firm.) Set aside.

2. Rinse the rice in cold water; set aside.

3. Coat a large saucepan with cooking spray and add the onion and bay leaf. Cook over medium heat until the onion begins to color. Add the cloves, cinnamon, and curry powder and stir over medium heat for 1 minute.

4. Add the cauliflower, peas, squash, and rice. Stir for 3 to 4 minutes to combine seasonings. Add 2 cups water, bring to a simmer, cover, and cook until all of the liquid has been absorbed, 20 to 25 minutes. Remove the bay leaf. Stir in the raisins and almonds. Serve immediately.

Cleveland Clinic Healthy Heart Lifestyle Guide and Cookbook

Crunchy Bistro Lentil Salad

Lentils are chock-full of dietary fiber and protein. The addition of crunchy walnuts (a healthy fat) makes a delectable whole-meal salad. If arugula is not available, substitute red or green leaf lettuce.

Makes 10 servings

Per serving:
260 calories
   (29% calories from fat)
8.5 g total fat
   (1 g saturated fat)
16 g protein
33 g carbohydrate
16 g dietary fiber
0 mg cholesterol
32 mg sodium
660 mg potassium

2½ cups dried lentils, picked over, rinsed, and drained

6 cups fat-free, reduced-sodium chicken broth

1 bay leaf

3 tablespoons fresh thyme, or 1 tablespoon dried

3 garlic cloves, minced

2 carrots, cut into ½-inch dice

½ medium green bell pepper, seeded and cut into ½-inch dice

½ medium red bell pepper, seeded and cut into ½-inch dice

3 tablespoons white wine vinegar

3 tablespoons walnut oil

1 teaspoon grated orange zest

Kosher salt, optional

Freshly ground pepper

1 cup thinly sliced scallions, white parts and 1 inch of the green

½ cup coarsely chopped walnuts

½ cup chopped fresh flat-leaf parsley

2 large bunches baby arugula

---

1. Place the lentils in a large pot and add the broth, bay leaf, thyme, and garlic. Set over moderate heat and bring to a boil. Reduce the heat and skim any foam that may appear. Cover and simmer for 25 minutes, or until the lentils are tender but still hold their shape. Drain and set aside to cool.

2. Combine the carrots and bell peppers in a large bowl. In a glass measuring cup, whisk together the vinegar, oil, and orange zest. Pour over the vegetables and toss to coat evenly. Add the lentils and toss again. Season to taste with salt, if using, and pepper. Just before serving, stir in the scallions, walnuts, and parsley. Line a serving bowl with arugula. Pile the salad into the bowl and serve at once.

Curried Lentils and Cauliflower
with Cucumber Raita

Makes 6 servings

Per serving:
200 calories
  (11% calories from fat)
2.5 g total fat
  (0 g saturated fat)
14 g protein
34 g carbohydrate
14 g dietary fiber
0 mg cholesterol
80 mg sodium
653 mg potassium

Per serving
(1/4 cup raita only):
20 calories
  (0% calories from fat)
0 g total fat
  (0 g saturated fat)
2 g protein
4 g carbohydrate
0 g dietary fiber
0 mg cholesterol
25 mg sodium
55 mg potassium

This curried lentil dish is frequently on the menu at Indian restaurants. If you like very spicy Indian food, use Madras curry powder as called for in the recipe. If you prefer a mild curry, use regular curry powder or decrease the amount. Madras curry can be found in Indian stores and upscale supermarkets. Spicy or not, the dish will benefit from a chilled raita—a yogurt-based condiment often served with spicy Indian food to provide a cooling counterbalance.

Cucumber Raita (makes about 2 cups)

1 cup nonfat yogurt

1 garlic clove, minced

1/2 English cucumber, peeled and finely minced

2 scallions, white parts and 2 inches of the green, finely minced

1/3 cup loosely packed cilantro leaves, chopped

Kosher salt, optional

Freshly ground pepper

1/4 teaspoon cumin seed

Curried Lentils

1 cup dried brown lentils, picked over, rinsed, and drained

2 teaspoons extra virgin olive oil

1 medium onion, finely chopped

2 garlic cloves, minced

1 jalapeño, seeded and minced, optional

2 tablespoons Madras curry powder (see headnote), or to taste

1 pound small cauliflower florets

One 28-ounce can no-salt-added diced tomatoes with juice

1. Combine all of the raita ingredients in a small bowl. Cover and refrigerate for at least 1 hour before serving.

2. Place the lentils and 3 cups water in a pot and bring to a boil over medium-high heat. Lower the heat, cover, and simmer for 25 to 30 minutes, until the lentils are tender but still hold their shape.

Cleveland Clinic Healthy Heart Lifestyle Guide and Cookbook

3. While the lentils are cooking, heat the oil in a nonstick Dutch oven over medium heat. When hot, add the onion, garlic, and chile, if using. Sauté until the vegetables are limp, about 5 minutes. Stir in the curry powder, cauliflower, and tomatoes with their juice. Cover and simmer until the cauliflower is tender, 15 to 20 minutes.

4. Drain the lentils and gently stir into the cauliflower mixture. Transfer to a serving bowl and offer the raita to spoon on each serving as desired.

Spicy Black Bean Cakes with Cilantro Yogurt

Makes 4 servings

Per serving:
160 calories
  (14% calories from fat)
2.5 g total fat
  (0 g saturated fat)
9 g protein
35 g carbohydrate
8 g dietary fiber
0 mg cholesterol
630 mg sodium
453 mg potassium

As we include more plant protein in our own daily diets, we find ourselves reaching more and more for a can of black beans to use as a starch, add to a salsa, puree for a quick soup, or turn into these tasty bean cakes.

1 teaspoon extra virgin olive oil

1/3 cup finely minced red onion

2 garlic cloves, minced

1 jalapeño, seeded and minced

2 tablespoons minced red bell pepper

One 15-ounce can black beans, rinsed and drained

Kosher salt, optional

Freshly ground pepper

1/4 cup minced fresh cilantro

1 teaspoon ground cumin

1/2 teaspoon hot pepper sauce

1 small sweet potato, peeled and coarsely shredded

1/4 cup egg substitute

1/4 cup Homemade Multigrain Bread Crumbs (page 334)

  Cilantro Yogurt

1 cup nonfat yogurt

1/4 cup minced fresh cilantro

2 tablespoons fresh lime juice

1 teaspoon ground cumin

1. Preheat the broiler.

2. Set a medium nonstick skillet over medium heat. Add the oil, onion, and garlic. Sauté, stirring occasionally, until the onion is limp, about 5 minutes. Add the chile and bell pepper; cook for another 2 to 3 minutes, stirring often.

3. While the vegetables are cooking, combine the Cilantro Yogurt ingredients in a small bowl.

4. Put the onion mixture in a large bowl. Add the black beans and mash with a fork or potato masher, leaving about one-fourth of the beans whole. Season with salt, if using, and pepper. Stir in the cilantro, cumin, hot pepper sauce, sweet potato, and egg substitute. Form into 4 patties. Place bread crumbs on a plate. Lightly press patties one at a time into crumbs, coating both sides.

5. Broil for 5 to 6 minutes, until brown and slightly crisp. Carefully turn and continue to broil for another 3 to 4 minutes. Serve with the Cilantro Yogurt.

Lemon and Fresh Herb Tabbouleh

We've been making tabbouleh for years, but when Fran's Iranian friend Parvine Latimore made it for a special party, we both changed our recipes. Parvine used extra lemon juice and more fresh herbs than we were used to. The result was incredible—a delicious taste of lemon with every bite of grain and a burst of freshness from the blend of fresh herbs with every mouthful.

Makes 8 servings

Per serving:
80 calories
  (45% calories from fat)
4 g total fat
  (0.5 g saturated fat)
2 g protein
12 g carbohydrate
3 g dietary fiber
0 mg cholesterol
15 mg sodium
237 mg potassium

1/2 cup medium- or fine-grain bulgur

2 tablespoons extra virgin olive oil

2 garlic cloves, minced

2 cups finely chopped fresh flat-leaf parsley (about 3 bunches)

3/4 cup diced red onion

2 medium tomatoes, seeded and diced

1/3 cup finely chopped fresh mint

1/4 cup finely chopped fresh basil

3 tablespoons finely chopped fresh dill

3 tablespoons finely chopped fresh cilantro

1/3 cup fresh lemon juice

1. Bring a kettle of water to a boil. Stir together the bulgur and 1 tablespoon of the oil in a heatproof bowl. Add boiling water to cover. Cover the bowl tightly with plastic wrap and let stand for 15 minutes. Drain in a sieve, pressing on the bulgur to remove any excess liquid.

2. Transfer the bulgur to a large bowl and toss with the remaining 1 tablespoon oil and the rest of the ingredients until everything is well mixed. Cover and refrigerate for at least 3 hours. Serve cold.

DIETITIAN'S NOTE: Although high in the percentage of calories from fat, this salad is low in total calories and a good source of dietary fiber and monounsaturated fat.

Mexican Barley Risotto

Makes 6 servings

Per serving:
200 calories
  (9% calories from fat)
2 g total fat
  (0 g saturated fat)
6 g protein
40 g carbohydrate
8 g dietary fiber
0 mg cholesterol
210 mg sodium
510 mg potassium

Barley risottos have become very popular in restaurants. Here we marry Mexican ingredients with this healthy grain. We prepare our risotto to be served al dente, that is, with a bit of a bite.

One 14¹/2-ounce can no-salt-added or low-sodium whole tomatoes with juice

3 garlic cloves

2¹/2 cups fat-free, reduced-sodium chicken broth

1 teaspoon extra virgin olive oil

1 onion, chopped

1 poblano, seeded and chopped

1 red bell pepper, seeded and chopped

1 cup pearled medium barley

¹/2 teaspoon dried thyme

¹/2 teaspoon dried oregano

¹/2 cup dry white wine

1 cup fresh or thawed frozen corn kernels

¹/4 cup chopped fresh cilantro

1. Puree the tomatoes with their juice and the garlic in a blender or food processor. Pour the puree into a large pot and add the broth and 1¹/2 cups water. Heat to just below a simmer and keep warm.

2. Meanwhile, heat the oil in a large nonstick pot and stir in the onion, chile, and bell pepper. Cook for 2 minutes over medium heat, stirring frequently. Add the barley and cook for another 3 minutes, continuing to stir. Add the thyme, oregano, and wine and cook, stirring, until the wine is absorbed.

3. Begin adding the tomato-broth mixture, ³/4 cup at a time, waiting until the liquid is nearly absorbed before adding more. Continue to add the broth until the barley is al dente, stirring frequently. Stir in the corn and cilantro when the risotto is a minute or two from being done. Serve immediately.

DIETITIAN'S NOTE: Here's an all-natural way to cut your cholesterol! Include barley and other foods rich in soluble fiber on a daily basis.

Brown Rice and Kasha Pilaf with Dried Porcini Mushrooms

This Eastern European–style dish makes a tasty side dish. Because the grains contain protein, it can also be a main course when served with a salad of mixed baby greens, Belgian endive, and pea shoots with Balsamic Vinaigrette (page 169). Dried porcini mushrooms are available in most supermarkets in the fresh mushroom section. They take only a few minutes to rehydrate. Use 1 cup of the soaking liquid to cook the brown rice for a wonderful flavor.

Makes 8 servings

Per serving:
160 calories
  (13% calories from fat)
2.5 g total fat
  (0 g saturated fat)
5 g protein
30 g carbohydrate
3 g dietary fiber
0 mg cholesterol
70 mg sodium
147 mg potassium

Caramelized Onions
1½ teaspoons transfree margarine
1 large onion, quartered and thinly sliced
¼ teaspoon sugar substitute

1 ounce dried sliced porcini mushrooms, rehydrated (see page 175)
1 cup instant brown rice
½ cup kasha
2 tablespoons egg substitute
1 cup fat-free, reduced-sodium beef broth
3 tablespoons chopped fresh flat-leaf parsley
2 tablespoons slivered almonds, toasted (page 320)

---

1. Melt the margarine in a skillet with a lid. Add the onion and sugar substitute. Cover and sauté over medium-low heat for 25 minutes, stirring every 5 minutes, until the onion is browned and soft.

2. Drain the rehydrated mushrooms, reserving 1 cup of the liquid, strained through a coffee filter to remove any grit. Bring the mushroom liquid to a boil in a small saucepan. Coarsely chop the mushrooms and set aside.

3. Simmer the brown rice in the reserved mushroom liquid for 5 minutes. Remove from heat and set aside, covered, for another 5 minutes.

4. Combine the kasha with the egg substitute in a large nonstick pot, stirring well to coat each grain. Toast the kasha over medium heat for a few minutes, until the grains separate. Add the beef broth, cover, and simmer until the broth is absorbed, 7 to 10 minutes. Combine with the brown rice, mushrooms, and onions.

5. When ready to serve, reheat and toss with the parsley and almonds.

Wild Rice and Orzo Salad

Makes 8 servings

Per serving:
170 calories
  (26% calories from fat)
5 g total fat
  (0.5 g saturated fat)
5 g protein
27 g carbohydrate
2 g dietary fiber
0 mg cholesterol
75 mg sodium
97 mg potassium

We are always looking for an easy crowd-pleaser and this recipe is just that. This salad is good year-round, but seems most appropriate as part of a casual buffet during the long, hot summer. The recipe can be doubled for even larger groups, plus the salad can be made the day before. That's our kind of perfect party recipe. You may be able to find whole wheat orzo in the bulk section of your local health food store.

1/2 cup wild rice

2 tablespoons extra virgin olive oil

1 1/2 cups orzo, preferably whole wheat

2 tablespoons fresh lemon juice

2 scallions, white parts and 2 inches of the green, chopped

1/4 teaspoon kosher salt

Freshly ground pepper

2 tablespoons chopped walnuts, toasted (page 319)

1/3 cup no-sugar-added dried cherries

2 tablespoons chopped fresh mint

1. In a saucepan, combine the rice with 1 1/2 cups water and simmer, covered, for 40 to 45 minutes, until the water is absorbed and the rice is al dente. Toss with 1 tablespoon of the oil and set aside.

2. Cook the orzo according to package directions. Drain and add to the rice. Stir in the remaining tablespoon of oil with the lemon juice and scallions.

3. Just before serving, season with salt and pepper and toss in the walnuts, cherries, and mint. Stir until just combined. Serve at room temperature.

Great Northern Beans with Tomatoes and Herbs

We all know that beans and their fiber are an important part of healthy meals. To take the work out of preparing them, we use canned beans. They're perfect for a quick and easy side dish or vegetarian main course. Rinse them well under running water and be careful not to overcook these table-ready gems.

Makes 8 servings

Per serving:
160 calories
  (3% calories from fat)
0.5 g total fat
  (0 g saturated fat)
10 g protein
29 g carbohydrate
7 g dietary fiber
0 mg cholesterol
15 mg sodium
578 mg potassium

Two 15.5-ounce cans Great Northern beans
Olive oil cooking spray
1 small onion, finely chopped
1 carrot, finely chopped
2 garlic cloves, minced
5 large plum tomatoes, chopped
1/3 cup dry red wine
1 sprig fresh rosemary
4 fresh sage leaves, chopped
Freshly ground pepper

1. Place the beans in a colander and rinse well under cold water. Set aside.
2. Coat a nonstick pot with cooking spray. Add the onion and carrot. Sauté for 5 minutes over medium heat, until the onion wilts. Add the garlic and tomatoes. Continue to sauté for another 5 minutes, until the tomatoes soften.
3. Stir in the red wine, rosemary, and sage with the drained beans. Simmer, uncovered, stirring occasionally, for 10 minutes, or until the sauce is reduced by a quarter and the flavors have blended. Discard the rosemary and season with pepper. Serve immediately.

Quick Soaking Method for Beans

You can soak beans overnight, but if you forget, use this shortcut. Put the beans in a pot with water to cover by 2 inches. Bring to a boil over medium-high heat and cook for 2 minutes. Remove from the heat, cover, and allow to stand for 1 hour. Drain the beans and rinse well under cold water twice. The beans are now ready for your recipe.

A Texas Pot of Pintos

Makes 8 servings

Per serving:
250 calories
  (5% calories from fat)
5 g total fat
  (0 g saturated fat)
14 g protein
47 g carbohydrate
12 g dietary fiber
0 mg cholesterol
310 mg sodium
1,066 mg potassium

When Fran's niece, Karen Stickney, moved from Seattle, Washington, to El Paso, Texas, she soon learned that "pot luck" invariably meant "a pot of pintos"—sometimes a long-treasured family recipe that had been cooked for hours and other times a pot of beans hastily made by opening several cans of beans and adding a secret blend of spices.

Karen prefers to use dried beans, and after several attempts to adapt her recipe for baked beans, she came up with this recipe for pinto beans.

---

1 pound dried pinto beans

3 large yellow onions, finely chopped

2 tablespoons chili powder, or to taste

1 teaspoon ground cumin

1 teaspoon ground coriander

Kosher salt, optional

1/3 cup chopped cilantro leaves and tender stems

Two 10-ounce cans whole tomatoes with green chiles

1 large red bell pepper, seeded and diced

1 large green bell pepper, seeded and diced

---

1. Sort and wash the beans, removing any debris. Use the Quick Soaking Method for Beans (page 281).

2. Return the beans to the Dutch oven and add 5 cups cold water, along with the onions, chili powder, cumin, coriander, salt (if using), cilantro, tomatoes, and bell peppers. Bring to a boil over medium heat, then reduce the heat, cover, and simmer until the beans are tender, about 2 1/2 hours. Add water if needed. Near the end of the cooking time, the liquid should be almost absorbed.

Vegetables

Vegetables are defined as any part of a plant that can be eaten, and we love to prepare and serve many parts of plants, from roots (carrots and beets) and stems (asparagus), to flower stems (broccoli), leaves (lettuce), and fruit like tomatoes, squash, peppers, and eggplants, to name a few. We know that these vitamin-, mineral-, and fiber-rich foods help keep us healthy with phytonutrients (see page 98). We also know that vegetables are very low in calories and that they sate appetites. How can we not love this class of food? We can't think of a vegetable that we don't like. Today we cook vegetables in new and inventive ways. No more overcooked, boiled green beans or carrots for us.

A Few Quick Tips

Vegetables are a staple in our diets, but there are nights when we just don't have time to do much cooking. This is when we turn to our microwaves. It cooks vegetables quickly and retains their color, flavor, and nutrients. If you wash your vegetables, you don't need to add cooking liquid. If you wish, however, you can add a tablespoon or two of liquid such as citrus juice, fat-free, reduced-sodium broth, or reduced-sodium soy sauce.

Stir-Fried Sesame Asparagus with Pickled Ginger

Makes 6 servings

Per serving:
60 calories
   (29% calories from fat)
2 g total fat
   (0 g saturated fat)
3 g protein
8 g carbohydrate
3 g dietary fiber
0 mg cholesterol
150 mg sodium
395 mg potassium

Asparagus means spring even though imported ones are available year-round. Select firm, straight stalks with tightly closed tips, whether you like pencil-thin or thick stalks. Many people peel thick stalks (as we do), but do not peel thinner ones. Choose stalks of uniform size for even cooking. This recipe has an Asian taste that marries sweet and sour flavors.

1 teaspoon sesame oil

1 shallot, sliced into thin rings

1 pound asparagus, tough ends removed, sliced diagonally into 1-inch pieces

1/2 pound shiitake mushrooms, stems discarded, thinly sliced

1/8 teaspoon crushed red pepper flakes

3 tablespoons chopped fresh cilantro

2 teaspoons hoisin sauce

2 tablespoons finely minced pickled ginger

2 tablespoons sesame seeds, toasted

1. Heat the oil in a nonstick skillet or wok. Add the shallot and stir-fry over medium-high heat for 1 minute. Add the asparagus and mushrooms and continue to cook, tossing the vegetables constantly, until crisp-tender, about 3 minutes. Lower the heat to medium. Add the red pepper flakes, cilantro, and hoisin sauce. Stir to mix well.

2. Place in a serving bowl. Top with ginger and sesame seeds. Serve immediately.

Roasted Beets with Oranges

Roasted beets are easy to prepare and handy to have on hand in the refrigerator to slice for salads or serve as a side dish, embellished with a few simple ingredients.

8 small beets (about 1 pound when trimmed)

1/2 cup fresh orange juice

2 tablespoons raspberry vinegar

1 large navel orange, peeled and segmented (see page 159)

Kosher salt, optional

Freshly ground pepper

1. Preheat the oven to 400°F.

2. If greens are still attached to the beets, trim to within 1 inch and reserve the greens for another use. Trim off the root. Scrub the beets, but do not peel. Wrap each beet in a square piece of aluminum foil. Put in a baking dish and bake until the beets are tender, 30 to 40 minutes. Remove from the oven. Cool the beets slightly, until you can gently slip off the skins. Cut the beets in halves or quarters, depending on the size.

3. Combine the orange juice and vinegar in a saucepan. Add the beets and reheat over medium heat. Stir in the orange sections. Sprinkle with salt, if using, and pepper. Transfer the beets to a serving dish. Serve warm.

DIETITIAN'S NOTE: This easy dish is an excellent way to reach the 4,700 milligrams of potassium you should be getting through foods each day. Plus in only 100 calories, you're 20 percent closer to your daily minimum fiber goal!

Makes 4 servings

Per serving:
100 calories
 (0% calories from fat)
0 g total fat
 (0 g saturated fat)
3 g protein
23 g carbohydrate
5 g dietary fiber
0 mg cholesterol
130 mg sodium
653 mg potassium

Brussels Sprouts with Shallots, Lemon, and Walnuts

Makes 6 servings

Per serving:
130 calories
  (35% calories from fat)
5 g total fat
  (0 g saturated fat)
7 g protein
18 g carbohydrate
5 g dietary fiber
0 mg cholesterol
45 mg sodium
615 mg potassium

A special dinner at our homes during the cold months usually includes a bowl of fresh Brussels sprouts, but more and more we find ourselves including them for weeknight suppers. The stalks of fresh sprouts in our markets are simply too good to pass up. Sprouts are excellent just simmered, but here we cook them ahead and then give them a quick sauté with shallots. A splash of lemon juice and a few walnuts make this dish special.

1½ **pounds fresh Brussels sprouts, trimmed**

2 **teaspoons transfree margarine**

3 **shallots, thinly sliced**

1 **garlic clove, minced**

Kosher salt to taste, optional

Freshly ground pepper

1½ **teaspoons fresh lemon juice**

¹⁄₃ **cup coarsely chopped walnuts, toasted (page 319)**

1. Cut an X in the stem end of each Brussels sprout. Put the sprouts in a pot with cold water to cover by 1 inch. Bring to a boil, reduce the heat, and simmer until the sprouts are tender, about 15 minutes. Drain and set aside until almost ready to serve.

2. Place a large nonstick skillet over medium-high heat. Add the margarine, shallots, and garlic. Sauté until the shallots are translucent, about 5 minutes. Add the Brussels sprouts and cook for another 5 minutes, tossing the sprouts occasionally. Season with salt, if desired, and pepper. Toss again with lemon juice and walnuts. Serve hot.

Cabbage Walnut Strudel

This savory strudel will make cabbage a favorite at mealtime. We used packaged shredded coleslaw mix, but feel free to shred your own cabbage and save the remainder for another recipe. The sweetness of the filling ensures that the cabbage is never bitter. No time to bake the strudel? Serve the filling as is with grilled fish or chicken and expect raves. Try other vegetables such as leeks and spinach, or bell pepper, for a strudel of your own. (You can omit the sweetener.)

Makes 6 servings

Per serving:
90 calories
  (31% calories from fat)
3 g total fat
  (0 g saturated fat)
2 g protein
14 g carbohydrate
2 g dietary fiber
0 mg cholesterol
120 mg sodium
168 mg potassium

Filling

1 teaspoon canola oil

1 leek, white part only, well washed, sliced lengthwise, and thinly sliced crosswise

1/2 pound coleslaw mix or 1/2 green cabbage, shredded (about 2 1/2 cups)

1/8 teaspoon kosher salt

1 tablespoon sugar substitute

2 tablespoons currants

4 sheets phyllo dough, thawed

Refrigerated butter-flavored cooking spray

2 tablespoons finely chopped walnuts

---

1. Preheat the oven to 375°F.

2. To make the filling, heat the oil in a large nonstick skillet. Add the leek, coleslaw mix, salt, sugar substitute, and currants. Sauté over medium-high heat until the cabbage and leeks are wilted and just tender, about 3 minutes. Remove from the heat and allow to cool.

3. Place one sheet of phyllo dough on a baking sheet. Coat with cooking spray and one-third of the chopped walnuts. Repeat two more times and top with a sheet of phyllo. Spoon the cabbage filling about 2 inches from the bottom of the phyllo layers and roll the dough from the long end into a log, leaving the seam on the bottom. Coat the top of the log with cooking spray and tuck in the ends.

4. Bake for about 30 minutes, until the phyllo is browned and crisp. Let cool for 5 minutes. Slice and serve warm.

Thai Green Beans

Makes 4 servings

Per serving:
80 calories
(37% calories from fat)
3.5 g total fat
(0.5 g saturated fat)
3 g protein
11 g carbohydrate
4 g dietary fiber
0 mg cholesterol
50 mg sodium
285 mg potassium

We love Thai food with its sweet and hot sauces and flavors of cilantro or Thai basil. Here we add the tastes of Thailand to our favorite green beans to make a side dish that pleases people of all ages. We also use this sauce over grilled white fish and chicken.

1 pound green beans
1 teaspoon sesame oil
1 tablespoon rice wine vinegar
1 teaspoon reduced-sodium soy sauce
1/4 teaspoon sugar substitute
1/8 to 1/4 teaspoon crushed red pepper flakes, optional
1 garlic clove, minced
Juice of 1 lime
2 tablespoons chopped fresh cilantro or Thai basil
2 tablespoons crushed or chopped unsalted dry roasted peanuts

1. Cook the green beans in boiling water to cover until just crisp. Drain and return to the pot.
2. Combine the oil, rice vinegar, soy sauce, sugar substitute, red pepper flakes, garlic, and lime juice. Toss with the green beans. Just before serving, stir in the cilantro and top with the peanuts.

Chinese-Style Broccoli

Broccoli is available year-round, but be sure to look for stalks that are bright green with crisp stems and tiny closed buds. Yellowing, limp stalks should be left at the market. Don't discard the stalks; you can include them in your recipes after you peel them and remove the leaves. Here we re-create a basic Chinese restaurant dish with less fat and salt. Get out your chopsticks and enjoy.

Makes 4 servings

Per serving:
100 calories
   (15% calories from fat)
2 g total fat
   (0 g saturated fat)
8 g protein
18 g carbohydrate
7 g dietary fiber
0 mg cholesterol
370 mg sodium
830 mg potassium

1 teaspoon peanut oil

2 pounds broccoli, florets cut into 1-inch pieces, stems peeled and sliced

1/4 pound shiitake mushrooms, stems discarded, thinly sliced

2 garlic cloves, minced

2 tablespoons fat-free, reduced-sodium chicken broth

1/4 teaspoon crushed red pepper flakes

1 tablespoon oyster sauce

1 teaspoon reduced-sodium soy sauce

2 scallions, white parts and 3 inches of the green, sliced diagonally into 1-inch pieces

1. Heat the oil in a wok or heavy nonstick skillet. When hot, add the broccoli and stir-fry for 4 minutes.

2. Add the mushrooms, garlic, and chicken broth and stir-fry for another 3 minutes, adding a bit of water if all the liquid evaporates. Stir in the red pepper flakes, oyster sauce, soy sauce, and scallions. Serve immediately.

NOTE: This recipe can be used for asparagus, fresh spinach, and green beans. If you can't find shiitakes, use any fresh mushrooms you like. And for more nutrients, add grated carrots.

DIETITIAN'S NOTE: A great dish that packs almost one-third of a day's quota of dietary fiber in only 100 calories.

Spicy Broccoli Rabe

Makes 4 servings

Per serving:
100 calories
  (43% calories from fat)
4 g total fat
  (0 g saturated fat)
5 g protein
8 g carbohydrate
<1 g dietary fiber
0 mg cholesterol
35 mg sodium
100 mg potassium

Broccoli rabe is a cousin to broccoli. Although it is available year-round, its peak season is from late fall to early spring. As with its larger cousin, look for bright green, firm stems and compact closed flowers.

1 pound broccoli rabe, stems peeled and 1 inch trimmed from each stalk

1 teaspoon extra virgin olive oil

2 garlic cloves, minced

1/2 cup halved cherry tomatoes

1/4 teaspoon crushed red pepper flakes, or to taste

1/8 teaspoon kosher salt, optional

2 tablespoons pine nuts, toasted

1. Cook the broccoli rabe in 2 tablespoons water over high heat until crisp-tender, about 3 minutes. Drain well.

2. Heat the oil in a skillet and sauté the garlic for a few minutes, making sure it doesn't burn. Add the broccoli rabe and sauté, stirring, for 3 minutes over medium heat. Add the tomatoes and 2 tablespoons water and continue to sauté for about 10 minutes, until the vegetables are cooked through. Add red pepper flakes to taste and salt, if using. Place in a serving bowl and garnish with pine nuts.

DIETITIAN'S NOTE: This spicy side dish packs more than 180 percent of the DRI for antioxidant-rich vitamin C.

Maque Choux

When the Acadians came to Louisiana they encountered Native Americans, who introduced them to corn. The lore about Maque Choux that makes the most sense is that the newcomers used an Indian word to describe a Cajun adaptation of the local indigenous corn. Many versions of this dish exist, but we prefer this one given to us by Chesley Sanders, a sixth-generation Texan and third-generation Fort Worth fireman.

Serve Maque Choux piled on a large round serving platter, surrounded by strips of Spicy Chicken (page 238) for a quick and easy supper.

Makes 4 servings

Per serving:
110 calories
  (8% calories from fat)
1 g total fat
  (0 g saturated fat)
4 g protein
25 g carbohydrate
4 g dietary fiber
0 mg cholesterol
245 mg sodium
350 mg potassium

Olive oil cooking spray
1 medium onion, chopped
1 medium red bell pepper, seeded and chopped
2 garlic cloves, minced
4 large dry-packed sun-dried tomatoes, soaked in warm water
    to cover for 10 minutes and drained
Pinch of cayenne
Kosher salt, optional
Freshly ground black pepper plus 3 whole peppercorns
2 cups fresh or frozen corn kernels
1 cup fat-free, reduced-sodium chicken broth
1 bay leaf
1 whole clove
1/2 teaspoon dried thyme

1. Lightly coat a large saucepan with cooking spray. Add the onion, bell pepper, and garlic. Sauté over low heat, stirring often, for 2 minutes. Chop the sun-dried tomatoes and add to the pot along with the cayenne, salt (if using), black pepper, and corn. Continue to cook for another 3 minutes, stirring often.

2. Stir in the chicken broth, bay leaf, clove, thyme, and peppercorns. Cover and simmer until most of the liquid has evaporated, about 15 minutes. Discard the bay leaf, clove, and peppercorns. Transfer to a serving dish and serve immediately.

A Pot of Down-Home Greens

Makes 6 servings

Per serving:
170 calories
  (19% calories from fat)
3.5 g total fat
  (0 g saturated fat)
10 g protein
32 g carbohydrate
10 g dietary fiber
0 mg cholesterol
250 mg sodium
1,130 mg potassium

Traditionally, boiled greens are cooked with a country ham bone, a ham hock, or several rashers of smoked bacon and finished with a splash of cider vinegar. Since we cook to protect our hearts, we refashioned the recipe by relying more on the flavor of the greens themselves. We then added some chopped root vegetables and garlic to the pot for extra flavor and marinated a handful of tiny hot peppers in vinegar to pass at the table.

Peppers in Vinegar

2 ounces mixed tiny red and green dried pequín chiles

3/4 cup cider vinegar

Greens

4 pounds greens, such as collard, turnip, or beet greens or kale, in any combination

2 teaspoons canola oil

1 medium carrot, finely chopped

1 medium celery rib, finely chopped

1 medium onion, finely chopped

3 garlic cloves, minced

1 3/4 cups fat-free, reduced-sodium chicken broth

1/4 teaspoon freshly ground pepper

1. At least 12 hours before using, rehydrate the peppers in warm water for 15 minutes. Drain. Place in a small saucepan and cover with the vinegar. Bring to a boil over high heat. Remove from the stove and let the peppers steep in the vinegar for at least 12 hours.

2. Working in batches, thoroughly wash the greens in a large sink of lukewarm water, agitating the leaves to remove any grit. Carefully remove the greens from the water and drain. Discard the tough stems and coarsely chop the greens and tender stems. Set aside.

3. Heat the oil in a large Dutch oven over medium heat. When hot, add the carrot, celery, onion, and garlic. Cook, stirring occasionally, until the vegetables begin to wilt, about 5 minutes. Add the broth and ground pepper to the pot along with the greens. Bring to a boil, then reduce the heat to a simmer. Cook, covered, stirring occasionally, until the greens are very tender, about 1 1/4 hours. With a slotted spoon, transfer the greens to a heated serving bowl. Transfer the vinegar and peppers to a small serving dish. Pass separately to spoon over the cooked greens.

DIETITIAN'S NOTE: Much lower in saturated fat and sodium than traditional greens, but with the same Southern flair! Enjoy this potassium-boosting dish, rich in folic acid, antioxidants, and monounsaturated fats.

Roasted Eggplant with Mint Yogurt Sauce

Makes 4 servings

Per serving:
60 calories
  (0% calories from fat)
0 g total fat
  (0 g saturated fat)
4 g protein
14 g carbohydrate
4 g dietary fiber
0 mg cholesterol
40 mg sodium
275 mg potassium

Roasting eggplant slices is a quick and easy way to prepare this essential Mediterranean dish. It is not necessary to peel the eggplant if you think it is very fresh. One way to tell is by the number of seeds in the eggplant; the more seeds, the older the fruit. The yogurt sauce is excellent with many vegetables, as a dip with crudités, or as a marinade or sauce for chicken.

Mint Yogurt Sauce
1 cup nonfat yogurt
2 tablespoons chopped fresh mint
2 teaspoons grated lemon zest
1 teaspoon grated fresh ginger
2 teaspoons fresh lemon juice

One 1-pound eggplant, cut into 1/3-inch slices
Kosher salt for sprinkling the eggplant
Olive oil cooking spray
Freshly ground pepper
2 tablespoons balsamic vinegar

1. To make the sauce, drain the yogurt in a paper-towel-lined colander for 30 minutes, discarding the liquid. Place the drained yogurt in a bowl. Stir in the remaining sauce ingredients and set aside to allow the flavors to blend.

2. Place the eggplant slices in a strainer and sprinkle with salt. Allow to drain for 30 minutes. While the eggplant finishes draining, preheat the oven to 400°F.

3. Rinse and wipe off all salt and liquid, and place the eggplant on a nonstick baking sheet. Coat both sides of the slices with cooking spray and sprinkle with pepper. Bake for 5 minutes, turn, and bake another 5 minutes. Place the eggplant on a serving dish and drizzle with vinegar. Serve immediately with the yogurt sauce.

Baked Fennel with Tomatoes and Yukon Gold Potatoes

Fennel is grown throughout the Mediterranean and the United States. It is a fragrant bulb with feathery stems, both of which are often found in salads. When cooked, fennel becomes very mild and delicate, different from its anise flavor when raw. Here we marry fennel with other vegetables, but it is also good baked by itself with just a hint of garlic and lemon. In fact, you could top this with some white fish fillets for the last 10 to 15 minutes of cooking.

Makes 4 servings

Per serving:
150 calories
 (9% calories from fat)
1.5 g total fat
 (0 g saturated fat)
5 g protein
32 g carbohydrate
6 g dietary fiber
0 mg cholesterol
70 mg sodium
655 mg potassium

Refrigerated butter-flavored cooking spray

2 fennel bulbs

4 plum tomatoes, thinly sliced

1 garlic clove, minced

1 pound small Yukon Gold potatoes, scrubbed clean and thinly sliced

1 teaspoon extra virgin olive oil

1 tablespoon fresh lemon juice

1/8 teaspoon kosher salt, optional

Freshly ground pepper

3 tablespoons chopped fresh flat-leaf parsley

1. Preheat the oven to 400°F. Coat a baking dish with cooking spray.

2. Slice the fennel bulbs in half lengthwise. Remove the stems and any discolored outer leaves. Remove the hard base of the fennel and cut the bulb into very thin slices. Place in the baking dish. Top with the tomato slices, garlic, and potatoes. Drizzle with oil, lemon juice, salt (if using), and pepper. Cover with aluminum foil and bake for 30 minutes. Uncover and stir in the parsley. Continue to bake, uncovered, stirring twice, until the vegetables are tender and cooked through and the potatoes begin to brown. Serve immediately.

Peruvian Potato Salad

Makes 8 servings

Per serving:
220 calories
  (31% from fat)
7 g total fat
  (1.5 g saturated fat)
7 g protein
31 g carbohydrate
2 g dietary fiber
5 mg cholesterol
95 mg sodium
109 mg potassium

Peru has been cultivating potatoes for more than 6,000 years in the high Andean slopes near Lake Titicaca. A walk through the public markets reveals a startling number of sizes, shapes, and colors—including the famous Peruvian blue potatoes with their purplish-blue skin and flesh. It's fun to use these blue potatoes, but if your market doesn't carry them or you prefer other potatoes, you can always use a small red or white potato.

Kosher salt

1¼ pounds small Peruvian blue potatoes

¼ cup minced red onions

1 red bell pepper, seeded and diced

1 yellow bell pepper, seeded and diced

1 large tomato, seeded and chopped

1 jalapeño, seeded and minced

3 tablespoons red wine vinegar

3 tablespoons extra virgin olive oil

1 teaspoon sugar substitute

2 hard-boiled egg whites, chopped

2 tablespoons chopped fresh oregano

½ cup crumbled reduced-fat feta cheese

2 tablespoons sliced black olives, optional

1. Bring a pot of lightly salted water to a boil. Simmer the potatoes until cooked through, 15 to 20 minutes, depending on size. Drain and cool. Quarter or slice into bite-size pieces and place in a bowl.

2. Combine the potatoes with the onion, bell peppers, tomato, jalapeño, vinegar, oil, ¼ teaspoon salt (if using), sugar substitute, egg whites, oregano, and cheese. Refrigerate until ready to serve. Garnish with olives, if using.

Potato Latkes

These traditional pancakes served during Hanukkah portend gifts for the children and the retelling of the brave Maccabees' story over the festival meal. Here we have removed much of the fat; the resulting potatoes no doubt will become a family weekend tradition as well as healthful holiday fare.

5 medium russet potatoes, peeled and shredded (about 3 pounds)

1 large onion, grated

1/2 cup egg substitute, or 2 egg whites

1/4 cup unbleached all-purpose flour

1/8 teaspoon kosher salt, optional

Freshly ground pepper

Olive oil cooking spray

1 1/2 cups natural applesauce, no sugar added

1/2 cup light sour cream

1. Preheat the oven to 350°F.

2. Place the shredded potatoes in a large strainer and press down to extract liquid. Place the drained potatoes in a clean kitchen towel and wring out any remaining moisture. In a large bowl, combine the potatoes with the onion. Add the egg substitute, flour, salt (if using), and pepper. Mix well.

3. Lightly spray a nonstick cookie sheet with cooking spray. Pat the potatoes onto the sheet in a rectangle about 8 × 12 inches. Spray the top with cooking spray. Bake for 45 minutes, until nicely browned and crisp. Cut into twenty-four 2-inch squares.

4. To serve, place the latkes on a heated serving platter; garnish each square with 1 tablespoon applesauce and 1 teaspoon sour cream. Serve at once.

Makes 24 pieces
(12 servings)

Per serving (2 latkes):
150 calories
  (3% calories from fat)
0.5 g total fat
  (0 g saturated fat)
4 g protein
31 g carbohydrate
3 g dietary fiber
0 mg cholesterol
25 mg sodium
690 mg potassium

Ginger Sweet Potato Pancakes

Makes 18 pancakes
(6 servings)

Per serving:
110 calories
   (0% calories from fat)
0 g total fat
   (0 g saturated fat)
3 g protein
25 g carbohydrate
4 g dietary fiber
0 mg cholesterol
65 mg sodium
330 mg potassium

Sweet potatoes are tubers that are members of the morning glory family. Don't refrigerate them; rather, keep them in a cool dark place and use within a week. They are a good source of dietary fiber and vitamins A and C. A fixture at holiday time, their usual preparation requires an abundance of sugar and butter. By contrast, these light pancakes are a perfect accompaniment to chicken breasts year-round.

One 1-pound sweet potato, peeled
1 medium sweet onion like Vidalia, Maui, or Walla Walla
2 teaspoons grated fresh ginger
1/4 cup egg substitute
1/4 cup whole wheat pastry flour
1/4 teaspoon baking powder
1/4 teaspoon kosher salt, optional
Freshly ground pepper
Vegetable oil cooking spray

---

1. In a food processor fitted with the grating blade, or with a handheld grater, grate the potato and onion. Place in a bowl. Stir in the ginger, egg substitute, flour, baking powder, salt (if using), and pepper.

2. Coat a nonstick skillet with cooking spray and preheat over medium-low heat. Drop 1/4 cup of the potato mixture at a time onto the skillet, pressing each pancake down with the back of a spatula. Cook for 6 to 8 minutes per side, turning once when browned on the bottom. Spritz the other side with cooking spray as you turn the pancake. Remove from the pan when they are browned and slightly crusty on both sides.

3. Serve immediately, or reheat as needed in a microwave.

Sweet Potato Mousse

A mousse can be sweet or savory, like this lighter-than-air side dish. It makes a lovely accompaniment to simple meals but will also become a tradition at holiday festivities. It can be made ahead of time and reheated in the microwave at 50 percent power for a minute or two. Here we use sweet potatoes and bake them in 6-ounce soufflé cups, but you can use a gratin or casserole and bake for about 30 minutes. Well-drained cooked shredded zucchini, spinach, or any combination of leftover cooked vegetables you have in the refrigerator will make a mousse that makes simple grilled chicken an occasion.

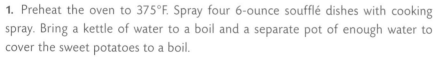

Refrigerated butter-flavored cooking spray

One 8-ounce sweet potato, peeled and quartered

1 shallot, minced

1/2 teaspoon grated fresh ginger

1/4 cup egg substitute, plus 1 egg white

3/4 cup evaporated skim milk

Freshly ground pepper

1/4 teaspoon freshly grated nutmeg

1. Preheat the oven to 375°F. Spray four 6-ounce soufflé dishes with cooking spray. Bring a kettle of water to a boil and a separate pot of enough water to cover the sweet potatoes to a boil.

2. Cook the sweet potato in boiling water until very tender, 15 to 20 minutes. Drain. Place in a blender or food processor.

3. While the potato is cooking, coat a nonstick skillet with cooking spray. Add the shallot and ginger and sauté over medium heat until the shallot is very soft, 10 to 12 minutes. Place in the food processor with the potato. Add the remaining ingredients and process until smooth.

4. Pour the sweet potato mixture into the soufflé cups and set inside a larger baking pan positioned on the center rack of the oven; pour boiling water halfway up the sides. Bake for about 20 minutes, until a knife inserted in the center comes out clean. Remove from the water bath and allow to rest for 10 minutes. Serve warm.

Makes 4 servings

Per serving:
110 calories
(7% calories from fat)
1 g total fat
(0 g saturated fat)
6 g protein
18 g carbohydrate
1 g dietary fiber
0 mg cholesterol
125 mg sodium
401 mg potassium

Grilled Radicchio

Makes 4 servings

Per serving:
100 calories
  (72% calories from fat)
8 g total fat
  (2 g saturated fat)
3 g protein
6 g carbohydrate
1 g dietary fiber
5 mg cholesterol
100 mg sodium
218 mg potassium

Radicchio is a favorite for salads, but it rises to sublime when it's grilled and served as a vegetable. Although you could use the Verona variety (round, loose leaf head), we suggest you try Treviso radicchio for this recipe. It's narrow with pointed, more tapered heads with prominent ribs, and holds together better on the grill.

Olive oil cooking spray

4 large heads radicchio, preferably Treviso

1/4 cup freshly grated Asiago or Parmesan cheese

1 1/2 tablespoons extra virgin olive oil

2 1/2 tablespoons balsamic vinegar

1. Light a grill. Lightly coat the grill rack with cooking spray.

2. Remove the loose outer leaves of the radicchio and trim the bases, leaving the inner heads intact. Cut the heads into quarters lengthwise. Lightly spray the cut surface with cooking spray. Grill the radicchio until the outer leaves are browned and the heart tender, 8 to 10 minutes, turning frequently.

3. About 2 minutes before the radicchio is done, sprinkle the cheese evenly over the cut sides. Continue to grill without turning until the cheese melts, about 2 minutes.

4. Transfer the radicchio to a heated serving platter and sprinkle evenly with oil and balsamic vinegar. Serve warm.

DIETITIAN'S NOTE: Although the calories from fat are higher than we normally recommend, the total calories are low, so this tasty dish can easily fit into your heart-healthy eating plan. Bon appetit!

Scalloped Heirloom Tomatoes with Herbs

Heirloom tomatoes are becoming easier to find at farm stands and farmers' markets. If none are to be found, use any local summer tomatoes. This recipe is a perfect example of how just a few snippets of fresh herbs can enhance flavor exponentially. When you cook with herbs, there's no need for salt.

Makes 6 servings

Per serving:
90 calories
   (35% calories from fat)
3.5 g total fat
   (0 g saturated fat)
3 g protein
15 g carbohydrate
3 g dietary fiber
0 mg cholesterol
60 mg sodium
411 mg potassium

Olive oil cooking spray
6 medium ripe tomatoes, thickly sliced
1 tablespoon balsamic vinegar
1 tablespoon chopped fresh basil
1 tablespoon chopped fresh flat-leaf parsley
1 teaspoon chopped fresh rosemary
1 teaspoon chopped fresh thyme
1/4 teaspoon freshly ground pepper
1 cup soft whole wheat bread crumbs (see Note)
1 tablespoon extra virgin olive oil

1. Preheat the oven to 425°F. Lightly coat a shallow 2-quart baking dish with cooking spray.

2. Arrange the tomato slices slightly overlapping in the prepared dish. Sprinkle with vinegar. Mix the basil, parsley, rosemary, thyme, and pepper in a bowl. Sprinkle half of the herb mixture over the tomatoes. Set aside the second half. Sprinkle the crumbs over the tomatoes and drizzle with the oil.

3. Bake for 35 minutes or until the tomatoes are tender and the bread crumbs are crisp and golden. Sprinkle with the remaining herb mixture. Serve hot.

NOTE: To make soft bread crumbs, place whole wheat bread in a food processor and pulse until the crumbs are the size of small peas.

Squash Gratin

Makes 4 servings

Per serving:
80 calories
  (24% calories from fat)
2 g total fat
  (0.5 g saturated fat)
3 g protein
13 g carbohydrate
3 g dietary fiber
0 mg cholesterol
125 mg sodium
485 mg potassium

When buying zucchini, look for small, unblemished, brightly colored vegetables—these should be tender and have fewer seeds and thin skin. The same is true for summer squash. These varieties of squash should be refrigerated and used within four or five days of purchase.

This gratin is the perfect accompaniment to grilled chicken or fish, bringing flavor to a weekday meal. You could substitute or add a thinly sliced Japanese eggplant to make a roasted ratatouille.

---

1 teaspoon extra virgin olive oil

2 medium yellow onions, halved and thinly sliced

1 tablespoon balsamic vinegar

1/8 teaspoon kosher salt

Freshly ground pepper

2 garlic cloves, minced

2 small zucchini, thinly sliced

1/4 cup chopped fresh basil

2 small summer squashes, thinly sliced

2 plum tomatoes, thinly sliced

2 tablespoons freshly grated Parmesan cheese

Olive oil cooking spray

---

1. Preheat the oven to 375°F.

2. Heat the oil in a nonstick skillet with a lid. Add the onions, vinegar, salt, and pepper; cover and cook over medium heat for 20 minutes, stirring two to three times. Add the garlic. Cook, uncovered, for another 5 minutes over low heat. The onions will have halved in volume and caramelized.

3. Layer the zucchini on the bottom of a 10- to 11-inch gratin dish. Cover with half the onions and half the basil. Layer with summer squash. Top with the remaining onions and basil. Cover with tomato slices and more pepper. Sprinkle with the cheese. Cover with aluminum foil and bake for 40 minutes. Uncover, coat with cooking spray, and bake for another 10 minutes, until the cheese begins to brown. Allow to sit for 10 minutes before serving.

Tomato Tidbits

As long as they are kept at room temperature, tomatoes will continue to ripen and develop their flavor. We keep our tomatoes in a shallow bowl on the countertop, inspecting them daily to see if they are ready to use. *Don't refrigerate them.* When tomatoes are chilled below 55°F, the ripening comes to a halt and the flavor never develops.

To speed up the process, keep tomatoes in a brown paper bag; this traps the ethylene gas that helps them ripen. Adding an ethylene-emitting apple or pear to the bag can also hasten ripening.

Once they are fully ripe, tomatoes can be held at room temperature for several days.

To peel: Drop a tomato into a pan of boiling water for 30 seconds. Drain and cool. Remove the stem ends and slip off the skins.

To seed: Cut tomatoes in half crosswise. Gently squeeze each half, using your fingers to remove the seeds. Reserve the juice and use in dressings, sauces, or soups.

Mashed Turnips with Apples

Makes 6 servings

Per serving:
49 calories
  (14% calories from fat)
1.6 g total fat
  (3.8 g saturated fat)
1 g protein
9 g carbohydrate
2 g dietary fiber
0 mg cholesterol
206 mg sodium
151 mg potassium

Turnips are often maligned for their flavor, which can be bitter if the turnip is too large. Here, we cook very small, young turnips with sweet apples for an especially appetizing side dish that goes well with any roasted meat, chicken, or fish. There's no need to peel the very young white turnips—just give them a good scrub. If the turnips are julienned, they cook very quickly.

8 small white turnips, scrubbed and julienned (about 1 pound)

2 medium Granny Smith apples, peeled and cut into thin julienne

1 tablespoon *trans*-free margarine

1 tablespoon fresh lemon juice

Kosher salt, optional

Freshly ground pepper

1/8 teaspoon ground cinnamon

Dash of ground nutmeg

1. Bring a pot of water to a boil. Add the turnips, reduce the heat to a simmer, and cook for 5 to 6 minutes, until the turnips are very tender. Drain and place in a food processor with the remaining ingredients. Pulse until smooth.
2. Transfer the turnip mixture to a heated serving dish and serve.

Roasted Vegetables

Roasting brings out the sweetness of vegetables as they caramelize. It is a quick and easy way to prepare everything from asparagus to zucchini. After roasting, toss with balsamic or sherry vinegar, grated citrus zest or juice, roasted garlic, chopped fresh herbs, or freshly ground pepper to taste. For this recipe, we used a quarter-pound each of asparagus, red peppers, zucchini, and onions, but the nutritional information won't vary significantly if you substitute other similar vegetables.

Olive oil cooking spray
1 pound fresh vegetables, cut into large pieces
1 teaspoon extra virgin olive oil

Preheat the oven to 400°F. Coat a large rimmed baking sheet with cooking spray. Place the vegetables on the baking sheet. Drizzle with oil and roll to coat. Roast for 5 to 20 minutes, depending on the size and consistency of the vegetables. Test frequently with the tip of a sharp knife. Refer to the headnote for optional seasonings. Serve immediately.

Makes 4 servings

Per serving:
40 calories
  (27% calories from fat)
1.5 g total fat
  (0 g saturated fat)
2 g protein
7 g carbohydrate
2 g dietary fiber
0 mg cholesterol
0 mg sodium
290 mg potassium

Sweet Endings

What's for dessert? Without a doubt, dessert is still extremely important to people trying to lose weight or live with chronic diseases. One in three of the e-mails sent to our Web site is a request for a dessert recipe, and not always diet-friendly requests! We too live with chronic diseases and admit to checking the dessert section before we buy a new cookbook. In reality, however, we don't make dessert unless company's coming. Instead, dessert is a piece of fresh fruit or a handful of fresh berries or grapes.

To save calories, we use granulated sugar substitute that has been developed to bake and cook like sugar. Some of our recipes call for a brown sugar blend, a fairly new product that combines regular brown sugar with sugar substitute. However, when a recipe requires granulated sugar to meet our standards, we use it. We also use whole wheat pastry flour to increase fiber and protein content whenever possible.

A Few Quick Tips

Nothing is easier for dessert than fresh fruit. Here are some ideas for dessert fruit salads and fruit desserts that demand no cooking.

- Fresh fruit is wonderful sprinkled with balsamic vinegar. Slice fresh peaches, nectarines, plums, strawberries, pineapple, or melon. Grate fresh pepper on top and sprinkle with your very best balsamic vinegar.
- Make frozen fruit bites by slicing fresh bananas, melon, grapes, peaches, nectarines, mangoes, and so forth. Dredge them in finely chopped walnuts. Place on a tray and freeze. When frozen, transfer to plastic freezer bags. Remove from the freezer a few minutes before serving. Pile into stemmed glasses or small dessert dishes.
- For company, make a platter or basket of fresh fruit and low-fat cheeses. Decorate with fresh grape leaves.
- For a fruit salad for six people, cube 2 cups each seedless watermelon, honeydew, and cantaloupe. Toss with 1 tablespoon grated lemon zest and top with 2 tablespoons toasted pecans.
- For a tropical fruit salad for six, cube a mango, a papaya, and half a pineapple. Toss with lime juice and sprinkle with 2 tablespoons unsweetened shredded coconut.

Elegant Citrus-Filled Cake

Makes 16 servings

Per serving:
170 calories
  (37% calories from fat)
7 g total fat
  (2 g saturated fat)
4 g protein
23 g carbohydrate
0 g dietary fiber
40 mg cholesterol
200 mg sodium
70 mg potassium

When people realize they have to cut back on calories, many wonder if they'll ever get to enjoy a holiday or birthday cake again. The emphatic answer is yes. Just remember, this is a dessert for special occasions and not for a daily meal.

Cake

No-stick baking spray with flour

2 cups sifted cake flour

1/4 cup sugar

1/4 cup sugar substitute

1 tablespoon baking powder

1/2 teaspoon kosher salt

1/3 cup canola oil

2 large egg yolks (whites reserved)

1/2 cup egg substitute

1 1/2 teaspoons pure vanilla extract

Grated zest of 3 lemons or 2 oranges, or a combination of both,
    1 tablespoon reserved for garnish

1 cup egg whites (2 reserved whites plus 6 or 7 more), at room temperature

1/2 teaspoon cream of tartar

1 1/2 cups frozen light whipped topping, thawed

Citrus Filling

1/4 cup sugar

2 tablespoons sugar substitute

2 tablespoons unbleached all-purpose flour

1/4 cup fresh lemon juice

2 tablespoons grated lemon zest

1/4 cup fresh orange juice

1 egg, slightly beaten

3/4 cup frozen light whipped topping, thawed

---

1. Preheat the oven to 325°F. Lightly coat two 9-inch nonstick round cake pans with baking spray.

2. In a large bowl, sift together the flour, sugar, sugar substitute, baking powder, and salt.

3. Using an electric mixer, combine the oil, egg yolks, egg substitute, 1/2 cup water, the vanilla, and fruit zest. Add the flour mixture and beat until well blended. In a separate large mixing bowl, beat the egg whites until frothy. Add the cream of tartar and beat to form stiff peaks. Fold about 1/2 cup of the egg whites into the cake batter to lighten it. Gently fold in the remaining whites.

4. Divide the batter between the two prepared pans and bake for 25 to 30 minutes, until the cake layers are golden and start to pull away from the sides of the pans. Do not open the oven while baking as the cakes may fall.

5. Run a small knife or spatula around the edge of each cake pan and turn out on a rack to cool completely.

6. While the cakes are cooling, prepare the filling. In a saucepan combine the sugar, sugar substitute, flour, lemon juice and zest, orange juice, 1 tablespoon water, and the egg. Cook over low heat, stirring, until the mixture thickens. Remove from heat. The custard will continue to thicken as it cools. When cool, fold in the whipped topping, blending carefully so as not to deflate the filling.

7. To assemble the cake, place one layer top (rounded) side down on a serving plate. Cover with the citrus filling. Gently place the second layer on the cake, top side up. Cover the top with whipped topping in a decorative manner. Sprinkle the outside edge of the cake with the reserved zest. Refrigerate until ready to serve.

Zesting Citrus

In this cookbook we often use the outer rind of citrus fruit to add flavor to our recipes. There are easy ways to remove this colored part of the rind with its aromatic oils without the white bitter pith layer underneath. You can either purchase a zester from your local kitchen supply store or use your grater. If you use a zester, you'll get long, thin strips of zest, which you may have to chop later. If you use your grater, guard your knuckles, use the size grate needed, and be sure to remove only the colored zest and not the bitter white pith beneath.

Carrot Cake

Makes 16 servings

Per serving:
120 calories
  (33% calories from fat)
4.5 g total fat
  (0 g saturated fat)
3 g protein
17 g carbohydrate
1 g dietary fiber
15 mg cholesterol
180 mg sodium
125 mg potassium

The entire family will love this cake. It has just the right texture, like a slightly sweetened, lighter corn bread. We like it just as it comes from the oven; however, you may want to add a dollop of frozen whipped topping or nonfat ice cream.

No-stick baking spray with flour
1 cup unbleached all-purpose flour
1/2 cup whole wheat flour
1/2 cup granulated sugar substitute
1/4 cup packed light brown sugar
1/4 cup nonfat dry milk
1 1/4 teaspoons baking soda
1 1/2 teaspoons baking powder
1 teaspoon ground cinnamon
1/4 teaspoon ground cloves
1/2 teaspoon ground nutmeg
1/2 teaspoon ground allspice
1/4 cup canola oil
1 large egg
3/4 cup egg substitute
1 1/2 cups finely grated carrots
2 tablespoons finely chopped walnuts
2 tablespoons golden raisins
One 6-ounce can unsweetened crushed pineapple, drained
2 tablespoons confectioners' sugar, optional

1. Preheat the oven to 350°F. Coat a 10-inch springform pan with baking spray.
2. Sift the white and whole wheat flours into a large bowl. Add the sugar substitute, brown sugar, dry milk, baking soda, baking powder, and spices. Stir to mix well. Using the medium setting of an electric mixer, beat in the oil, egg, and egg substitute until the batter is smooth. Fold in the carrots, walnuts, raisins, and pineapple.

3. Spread the batter into the prepared pan and bake for 30 minutes, until a toothpick inserted in the center of the cake comes out clean. Cool in the pan. Remove the outer ring of the pan and sift confectioners' sugar over the top, if desired. Serve at room temperature.

DIETITIAN'S NOTE: Never has carrot cake tasted so good, and been so guiltless! When compared to traditional carrot cake with icing, you save 180 calories, 12 grams of fat, and 4 grams of saturated fat!

Orange Upside-Down Cake

Makes 8 servings

Per serving:
150 calories
  (18% calories from fat)
3 g total fat
  (0.5 g saturated fat)
4 g protein
26 g carbohydrate
1 g dietary fiber
55 mg cholesterol
60 mg sodium
130 mg potassium

We like to bake this luscious cake in a cast-iron skillet, but you could use a 10-inch ovenproof skillet. Stone-ground yellow cornmeal replaces the traditional wheat flour for an interesting change in texture and flavor.

Orange Layer

1 large thin-skinned orange, such as Valencia

¼ cup sugar

Polenta Cake Layer

2 tablespoons skim milk

⅓ cup sugar

½-ounce package active dry yeast

2 large eggs, separated, plus 2 additional large egg whites

2 tablespoons *trans*-free margarine

2 teaspoons finely grated orange zest

2 teaspoons pure vanilla extract

⅔ cup stone-ground yellow cornmeal

---

1. Preheat the oven to 350°F.

2. Wash the orange. Cut off and discard the ends. Cut the orange crosswise into slices about ¼ inch thick. Remove any seeds. Put in the skillet, add ¼ cup water, and sprinkle with sugar. Bring the mixture to a boil over high heat, gently stirring to keep the fruit from sticking. Cook until the liquid is almost gone and the orange slices are caramelized. With a fork, move the orange slices into an attractive pattern in the bottom of the skillet.

3. In a small saucepan, heat the milk until warm but not hot. Remove from heat and add 1 teaspoon of the sugar and the yeast. Stir until the yeast is dissolved. Set aside.

4. In a large bowl, beat together the 2 egg yolks, the remaining sugar, and the margarine until pale yellow and thick. Add the orange zest and vanilla; mix well. Sift the cornmeal into the egg mixture, stirring constantly. Stir in the yeast mixture, which should now be frothy.

5. In a clean bowl, beat all 4 egg whites until they form stiff peaks. Stir a third of the beaten whites into the cornmeal mixture. Carefully fold in the remaining whites. Spoon the batter in dollops over the orange slices in the skillet. Smooth the top.

Cleveland Clinic Healthy Heart Lifestyle Guide and Cookbook

6. Bake for 25 to 30 minutes, until a cake tester inserted in the middle comes out clean. Run a knife between the sides of the skillet and the cake. Cool on a rack for 10 minutes. Hold a flat serving plate over the skillet and invert the cake. Serve while still warm.

NOTE: If you can't find a Valencia orange in your market, substitute a navel orange and peel it before slicing.

DIETITIAN'S NOTE: By using the fewest egg yolks possible—without compromising taste—we've kept the saturated fat and cholesterol in this decadent dessert to a minimum.

Luscious New York–Style Cheesecake

Makes 14 servings

Per serving:
190 calories
   (38% calories from fat)
8 g total fat
   (4.5 g saturated fat)
14 g protein
14 g carbohydrate
0 g dietary fiber
45 mg cholesterol
420 mg sodium
85 mg potassium

Think creamy New York–style cheesecake can't fit into a heart-healthy diet? Think again. This one is delicious, yet keeps the fat grams and sugar under control. Serve with fresh berries or diced pineapple.

4 cups low-fat cottage cheese
1 teaspoon transfree margarine
1/4 cup graham cracker crumbs
1/4 cup sugar
11/4 cups sugar substitute
1/4 cup unbleached all-purpose flour
1 tablespoon grated lemon or orange zest, or a combination of both
Two 8-ounce packages low-fat cream cheese, at room temperature
1/4 cup nonfat sour cream
1 large egg
1 cup egg substitute
1 tablespoon pure vanilla extract

1. Drain the cottage cheese in a sieve or colander over a bowl for 30 minutes.

2. Preheat the oven to 325°F. Grease a 10-inch springform pan with the margarine. Place the graham cracker crumbs in the pan and pat into the bottom and sides.

3. Place the drained cottage cheese in a food processor. Add the sugar, sugar substitute, flour, and zest. Process for at least 2 minutes, until smooth and light in texture. Transfer to a large mixing bowl.

4. Place the cream cheese, sour cream, egg, egg substitute, and vanilla in the processor. Process until smooth. Add to the cottage cheese mixture and stir until just combined so that air bubbles don't form. Pour into the prepared pan.

5. Bake in the bottom third of the oven for 11/2 hours. Turn off the oven and allow the cake to cool in the oven for 1 hour. Remove from the oven, run a sharp knife around the outside edge, and bring to room temperature. Release the spring and remove the sides of the pan, leaving the cheesecake on the removable bottom. Chill for 4 to 8 hours before serving.

Rustic Fresh Blueberry Tart

Frozen puff pastry comes to the rescue for a quickly assembled dessert that can be adapted as various seasonal fruits arrive at the market.

Makes 12 servings

Per serving:
140 calories
   (36% calories from fat)
 6 g total fat
   (1.5 g saturated fat)
2 g protein
20 g carbohydrate
3 g dietary fiber
0 mg cholesterol
70 mg sodium
40 mg potassium

Refrigerated butter-flavored cooking spray
1 quart fresh blueberries
2 tablespoons cornstarch
1 tablespoon grated lemon zest
1/3 cup sugar substitute
Unbleached all-purpose flour, for dusting
1 sheet frozen puff pastry (1/2 of a 17.3-ounce package), thawed
1 tablespoon fresh lemon juice
Frozen light whipped topping, thawed, optional

1. Preheat the oven to 400°F. Coat a nonstick baking sheet with cooking spray.

2. Place the berries in a bowl. Stir in the cornstarch, lemon zest, and sugar substitute, making sure that all berries are well coated.

3. On a lightly floured board, roll the puff pastry to a 12 3 14-inch rectangle. Place on the prepared baking sheet.

4. Mound the berries on the pastry, leaving a 11/2-inch border. Fold in the four corners. Using wet fingers, bring the border of the dough over the edge the berries, pleating as you go to form a rustic free-form oval or rectangle. Sprinkle the berries with lemon juice. Generously coat the top of the tart with cooking spray and bake for 40 to 45 minutes, until the berries are cooked and the pastry is golden.

5. Serve warm or at room temperature with a dollop of light whipped topping, if desired.

VARIATION: Apple Currant Tart. Substitute 3 large peeled, thinly sliced Granny Smith apples for the berries. Add 1/4 cup dried currants that have been macerated in 2 tablespoons dry sherry. Reduce the sugar substitute to 2 tablespoons. Add 1/2 teaspoon ground cinnamon. Bake according to the master recipe.

Per serving:
130 calories
   (36% calories from fat)
6 g total fat
   (1.5 g saturated fat)
2 g protein
20 g carbohydrate
2 g dietary fiber
0 mg cholesterol
70 mg sodium
65 mg potassium

Key Lime Mousse Pie

Makes 8 servings

Per serving:
80 calories
  (15% calories from fat)
1.5 g total fat
  (0.5 g saturated fat)
8 g protein
9 g carbohydrate
0 g dietary fiber
5 mg cholesterol
160 mg sodium
60 mg potassium

This pie is light yet rich tasting and can be made ahead—a great dessert for any party. We use bottled Key lime juice since it can be difficult to find fresh Key limes. Buying cookies with no trans fats is becoming easier and easier. We readily found these chocolate wafer crisps, so there is no excuse for buying cookies high in any fat. To protect from salmonella you can use pasteurized packaged egg whites, available with the egg substitutes in your market.

2 packets thin crisp chocolate wafers
Refrigerated butter-flavored cooking spray
1 packet unflavored gelatin
4 ounces fat-free cream cheese
1/2 cup reduced-fat ricotta cheese
1/4 cup Key lime juice
1/2 cup sugar substitute
Grated zest of 1 lime
1/2 cup plus 1 tablespoon pasteurized egg whites
1/8 teaspoon cream of tartar

1. Process the wafers in a food processor until you have a uniform fine crumb. Set 1 tablespoon aside for garnish. Generously coat a 9-inch pie pan with cooking spray. Sprinkle the crumbs over the pan, rotating the pan until the sides and bottom are covered, and press gently into a crust with your fingers if necessary.
2. In a small saucepan, sprinkle the gelatin over 1/4 cup cold water and let stand for 1 minute. Stir over low heat until dissolved, about 5 minutes. Set aside.
3. Place the cream cheese, ricotta, lime juice, sugar substitute, and half of the zest in a food processor. Process until well blended. Add the gelatin and process for a few seconds to incorporate.
4. In a medium bowl, beat the egg whites with the cream of tartar until they form stiff peaks. Gently fold the lime and cheese mixture into the egg whites. Pour into the prepared pie pan, swirling the top in a decorative manner. Refrigerate for about 2 hours, until cold and set. Garnish the rim of the pie with the reserved zest and chocolate crumbs.

Pear Tart with Chocolate Shavings

Fruit tarts are easy to make and can vary as the seasons change. Use pears that are still semifirm to ensure they keep their shape when thinly sliced. You'll find shaved semisweet chocolate on the aisle with other baking chocolates in your market. If you don't want to use chocolate, melt 1/2 cup sugar-free jam or preserves with 1 tablespoon fresh lemon juice and 2 tablespoons sugar substitute. Simmer until the mixture begins to thicken and brush over the fruit to add shine and great taste. The whole wheat crust adds a crunchy texture and extra fiber to any fruit tart.

Makes 8 servings

Per serving:
160 calories
  (39% calories from fat)
7 g total fat
  (2 g saturated fat)
3 g protein
21 g carbohydrate
3 g dietary fiber
5 mg cholesterol
30 mg sodium
114 mg potassium

1 Whole Wheat Pie Crust (page 338)

2 ounces low-fat cream cheese

2 ounces fat-free cream cheese

1 teaspoon grated lemon zest

3 1/2 tablespoons fresh lemon juice

1 tablespoon sugar substitute

1/4 cup egg substitute

3 small or 2 large Anjou or Bartlett pears

1/2 teaspoon sugar

2 tablespoons shaved or grated semisweet chocolate

1. Preheat the oven to 400°F.

2. Roll out the dough as instructed in the recipe and place in a 10-inch tart pan with a removable bottom, pressing into the fluted rim. Trim any excess, then set in the freezer while you prepare the filling.

3. In a food processor, puree the cream cheese, lemon zest, 1 tablespoon of the lemon juice, the sugar substitute, and egg substitute until smooth. Spread evenly over the prepared tart shell.

4. Add 2 tablespoons of the lemon juice to a bowl of water. Peel and core the pears, placing the peeled fruit in the water to prevent browning. Thinly slice the pears. Form two concentric circles of the pear slices, overlapping slightly, on top of the cream cheese mixture. Sprinkle with the sugar and remaining 1/2 tablespoon lemon juice. Bake for 20 to 25 minutes, until the crust browns, the filling is set, and the pear slices are tender. Cool, and just before serving top with shaved chocolate. Serve chilled or at room temperature.

Palmiers

From her childhood Bonnie remembers palmiers, cookies made from puff pastry with caramelized sugar and cinnamon between thin layers of flaky dough. Today we can enjoy this chocolate-raspberry variety at home using frozen puff pastry from the supermarket.

Makes 42 cookies
(42 servings)

Per serving (1 cookie):
35 calories
  (45% calories from fat)
2 g total fat
  (0.5 g saturated fat)
1 g protein
5 g carbohydrate
0 g dietary fiber
0 mg cholesterol
20 mg sodium
2 mg potassium

Refrigerated butter-flavored cooking spray
1 sheet frozen puff pastry (1/2 of a 17.3-ounce package), thawed
Unbleached all-purpose flour, for dusting
1/4 cup sugar-free raspberry preserves
2 ounces semisweet chocolate, grated
1 tablespoon unsweetened cocoa
1 tablespoon sugar substitute
1 teaspoon sugar

1. Preheat the oven to 400°F. Coat a nonstick baking sheet with cooking spray.
2. Roll the sheet of pastry into a 10 × 14-inch rectangle on a lightly floured board.
3. Place the preserves in a microwave-safe container and microwave on High for 20 seconds, until melted. Combine the chocolate, cocoa, and sugar substitute in a small bowl. Sprinkle one 5 × 14-inch side of the pastry with half of the chocolate mixture, pressing it into the dough. Brush the other half with the preserves. Carefully fold each of the longer sides into the midline of the dough. You'll have two 14-inch jellyroll shapes meeting at the midline.
4. Slice the dough into 1/3-inch slices. Place on the prepared pan and bake for 10 minutes. Turn the cookies over, sprinkle with sugar, and bake another 4 to 5 minutes, or until browned and crisp. Cool on a rack. Store in an airtight container.

Per serving (1 cookie):
30 calories
  (48% calories from fat)
1.5 g total fat
  (0 g saturated fat)
0 g protein
4 g carbohydrate
0 g dietary fiber
0 mg cholesterol
20 mg sodium
1 mg potassium

VARIATION: Cinnamon Palmiers. In a small bowl combine 2 tablespoons sugar substitute, 1 teaspoon ground cinnamon, and 1 tablespoon finely ground walnuts. Roll the dough as in the main recipe and press the mixture onto the dough. Fold in the long sides as in the master recipe. Bake as directed, sprinkling with 1 teaspoon sugar after turning the palmiers.

DIETITIAN'S NOTE: Although the percentage of calories from fat is high, these decadent palmiers are relatively low in calories. Enjoy these delicious cookies as part of your heart-healthy eating plan in moderation.

Cleveland Clinic Healthy Heart Lifestyle Guide and Cookbook

Raspberry-Filled Hazelnut Meringue Cookies

These old-fashioned European-style cookies are very easy to make and will bring raves of approval when offered by themselves or included in an array of holiday cookies. Since they are meringue cookies, don't attempt to make them on a hot or humid day. Wait until the weather is cool and dry.

5 large egg whites, at room temperature

1/4 teaspoon cream of tartar

1 cup superfine sugar

1 1/2 cups (about 8 ounces) ground roasted hazelnuts (see Note)

3 tablespoons sugar-free raspberry jam

1. Preheat the oven to 200°F. Line 2 baking sheets with parchment paper.
2. With an electric mixer set on medium speed, whip the egg whites and the cream of tartar until the egg whites form soft peaks. Increase the speed to high and continue to whip the egg whites, gradually adding the sugar, 1 tablespoon at a time, until stiff, shiny peaks form, about 3 minutes. Carefully fold in the ground hazelnuts.
3. Place the meringue mixture in a pastry bag fitted with a star tip. Pipe rounded 3/4-inch S-shaped cookies onto the parchment, making 24 cookies on each prepared baking sheet. Since the cookies are delicate, pipe a few extra on each sheet to allow for breakage.
4. Bake until the meringues start to color, about 15 minutes, rotating the baking sheets after 8 minutes. Turn the oven off, but leave the meringues in the oven to dry for at least 4 hours or as long as 8 hours.
5. To fill the sandwiches, loosen the meringues from the parchment. Turn half the meringues over and spread about 1/2 teaspoon jam on each flat side. Top with a second meringue. Store in an airtight container and use within 2 to 3 days.

NOTE: Toasting hazelnuts and removing their skins is easy. Place on a baking sheet in a preheated 350°F oven for 10 to 15 minutes, until the skins begin to flake off. Shake the pan once to prevent burning. Place in a tea towel a handful at a time and rub the nuts together or roll on the kitchen counter. Not all of the skins will come off but most will. You can then continue with your recipe.

Makes 2 dozen sandwich cookies (8 servings)

Per serving (3 cookies):
200 calories
  (41% calories from fat)
9 g total fat
  (0 g saturated fat)
4 g protein
28 g carbohydrate
1 g dietary fiber
0 mg cholesterol
35 mg sodium
145 mg potassium

Classic Orange-Almond Biscotti

Makes about 3 dozen biscotti (36 servings)

Per biscotti:
50 calories
  (21% calories from fat)
1.5 g total fat
  (0 g saturated fat)
2 g protein
9 g carbohydrate
0 g dietary fiber
5 mg cholesterol
40 mg sodium
25 mg potassium

When it comes to a sweet treat, these crispy Italian cookies will please. Store them in an airtight container for up to a month, but never fear, they won't last that long.

3/4 **cup slivered almonds**

1 large egg

1/2 **cup egg substitute**

1/2 **cup sugar**

1/2 **cup sugar substitute**

1/2 **teaspoon pure vanilla extract**

1/4 **teaspoon almond extract**

2 1/4 **cups unbleached all-purpose flour, plus more for handling the dough**

1/2 **teaspoon baking powder**

1/4 **teaspoon baking soda**

1/4 **teaspoon kosher salt**

2 tablespoons grated orange zest (from 1 large orange)

---

1. Preheat the oven to 350°F. Line a large baking sheet with parchment paper.

2. Place the almonds in a small pan and toast for 3 to 5 minutes, shaking the pan occasionally, until nicely browned. Set aside.

3. Using an electric mixer, beat the egg, egg substitute, sugar, sugar substitute, vanilla, and almond extract until the mixture lightens and begins to thicken, about 5 minutes. Sift the flour, baking powder, baking soda, and salt over the egg mixture. Add the almonds and orange zest. Fold to incorporate until just combined. The dough should be somewhat sticky.

4. Drop the batter onto the prepared baking sheet by large spoonfuls, forming two rows. Using floured hands, form each row into a log 10 3 2 inches long with a slightly rounded top.

5. Bake for 30 to 35 minutes, turning the baking sheet once, until the tops begin to crack and the logs feel solid. Remove the logs from the pan and cool for 10 minutes on a rack. (Leave the oven on.)

6. Place the logs on a cutting board and slice on the diagonal into 1/2-inch cookies. Place on the baking sheets and bake for 15 minutes to ensure crispness. Transfer to a cooling rack. Store in an airtight container.

VARIATION: Spiced Biscotti. Follow the recipe for Orange-Almond Biscotti. Macerate 1/2 cup currants in 2 tablespoons brandy for 1 hour. Omit the almonds, orange zest, and almond extract. Add 1/2 teaspoon ground cinnamon, 1/4 teaspoon ground ginger, and 1/2 teaspoon ground cloves. Fold in the currants and 2 teaspoons of the brandy.

DIETITIAN'S NOTE: Our Classic Orange-Almond Biscotti have 41 percent fewer calories and 30 percent less fat than traditional almond biscotti.

Per biscotti:
50 calories
  (21% calories from fat)
1.5 g total fat
  (0 g saturated fat)
2 g protein
9 g carbohydrate
0 g dietary fiber
5 mg cholesterol
40 mg sodium
25 mg potassium

Chocolate-Walnut Biscotti

Makes 3 dozen biscotti
(36 servings)

Per biscotti:
60 calories
  (37% calories from fat)
3 g total fat
  (1 g saturated fat)
2 g protein
9 g carbohydrate
0 g dietary fiber
0 mg cholesterol
45 mg sodium
30 mg potassium

This version of biscotti should satisfy any chocolate lover.

3 tablespoons transfree vegetable shortening

1/2 cup sugar

1/2 cup sugar substitute

3 ounces unsweetened baking chocolate

3/4 cup egg substitute

2 cups all-purpose unbleached flour, plus more for handling the dough

2 teaspoons baking powder

1/8 teaspoon kosher salt

2 teaspoons ground cinnamon

1/4 cup chopped walnuts

1/4 cup semisweet mini chocolate chips

1. Preheat the oven to 350°F. Line a large baking sheet with parchment paper.

2. Using an electric mixer, combine the shortening, sugar, and sugar substitute. The shortening will not cream as other fats do. Rather, the mixture will resemble tiny ball bearings. Melt the chocolate either in a double boiler or in the microwave according to package directions. Stir to make sure all chocolate is melted. Pour the hot chocolate into the sugar mixture to melt the shortening, and beat for 2 minutes. Add the egg substitute and beat at high speed for 4 minutes.

3. Sift the flour, baking powder, salt, and cinnamon together and then beat into the egg mixture for about 3 minutes, starting at a low speed until incorporated. Continue to mix at medium speed until a stiff dough forms. Add the walnuts and chocolate chips; stir to combine. Using lightly floured hands or a large spoon, form two 10 × 2-inch logs with slightly rounded tops.

4. Bake for 40 to 45 minutes, until the tops crack and the logs feel solid. Remove from the pan and cool for 10 minutes on a rack. (Leave the oven on.) Place on a cutting board and slice on the diagonal into 1/2-inch cookies. Place on the baking sheets and bake for 15 minutes. Cool and store in an airtight container.

Oatmeal Nugget Cookies

Nothing says home better than oatmeal cookies. This dough can be mixed in one bowl. Lightly toast oats until fragrant in a 350° oven, about 5 minutes. You can add your favorite dried fruits or chopped nuts, or change the spice to ginger or cinnamon.

Makes 2½ dozen cookies (15 servings)

Per serving (2 cookies):
60 calories
   (15% calories from fat)
1 g total fat
   (0 g saturated fat)
1 g protein
10 g carbohydrate
0 g dietary fiber
0 mg cholesterol
95 mg sodium
25 mg potassium

¼ **cup whole wheat pastry flour**

⅓ **cup unbleached all-purpose flour**

½ **cup quick rolled oats, lightly toasted (see headnote)**

⅓ **cup packed brown sugar blend (see page 306)**

¼ **cup egg substitute**

½ **teaspoon pure vanilla extract**

¼ **teaspoon baking soda**

½ **teaspoon baking powder**

¼ **teaspoon kosher salt**

1 **teaspoon pumpkin pie spice**

2 **tablespoons transfree margarine**

1. Preheat the oven to 375°F. Line a baking sheet with parchment paper or a Silpat liner or coat a nonstick sheet with cooking spray.

2. Combine all ingredients in a bowl along with 2 tablespoons water and blend with a fork until incorporated. The dough will be stiff.

3. Using a teaspoon measure, place rounded nuggets of dough on the prepared baking sheet. Bake for 15 minutes, or until the bottoms are browned and the nuggets are set. Cool on a wire rack. Store in an airtight container.

DIETITIAN'S NOTE: Compared to a traditional homemade oatmeal cookie recipe, you save 70 calories and 4 grams of fat!

Caramelized Pineapple with Raspberries

Makes 6 servings

Per serving:
118 calories
  (25% calories from fat)
3 g total fat
  (1 g saturated fat)
0.1 g protein
22 g carbohydrate
2 g dietary fiber
0 mg cholesterol
0 mg sodium
122 mg potassium

This is a last-minute dessert that can be made while you brew the coffee and finish clearing the table. Have everything ready beforehand; just be sure to turn the pineapple once and give the skillet a couple of shakes. Serve this lovely dessert on your finest dessert plates.

---

¹/₄ **cup sugar**

¹/₄ **cup sugar substitute**

1 pineapple, peeled, cored, and sliced into 6 wedges lengthwise

Refrigerated butter-flavored cooking spray

1 tablespoon *trans*-free margarine

2 tablespoons Cognac or fresh orange juice

1 cup fresh raspberries

---

1. Combine the sugar and sugar substitute. Sprinkle half of the mixture over one side of the pineapple. Turn and sprinkle the rest on the other side.

2. Lightly coat a large nonstick skillet with cooking spray. Add the margarine and place over high heat. Place the pineapple in the skillet and cook, turning once and shaking the pan often, until it turns golden brown, 10 to 15 minutes. (The pineapple can be prepared to this point and held for 1 hour.) Transfer the pineapple wedges to 6 dessert dishes, leaving the sauce that has formed in the pan.

3. Stir the Cognac into the pan to thin the sauce. Heat briefly. Drizzle the sauce over the pineapple and sprinkle with equal portions of the raspberries. Serve warm.

Grilling Fresh Fruit

Grilling or broiling fresh fruit is easy, and the caramelization of the fruit adds another layer of sweetness. The easiest way to grill fruit is to coat the slices with a refrigerated butter-flavored cooking spray. Then sprinkle the fruit with grated lime or lemon zest. Just before removing from the heat, baste with a sugar-free jelly or jam that you have melted in the microwave with a tablespoon of your favorite brandy or fresh lemon, orange, or lime juice. The fruit looks best with grill marks, but only needs to be warm throughout, so this is a quick fix. The grilling time will vary by the type of fruit. Use a large flat spatula for turning the fruit on the grill.

If you don't want to grill slices of fruit, cut it into chunks and place on skewers. If using wooden skewers, first soak them in water for 30 minutes to prevent them from burning. You can grill pineapple, apples, pears, peaches, nectarines, kiwis, bananas, and mangoes. Another yummy option is to sprinkle your grilled fruit with a combination of sugar substitute, cinnamon, and nutmeg halfway through cooking. Serve with fat-free or low-fat ice cream, yogurt, or frozen whipped topping. Top with melted semisweet chocolate.

Makes 4 servings

Per serving:
240 calories
  (23% calories from fat)
6 g total fat
  (1 g saturated fat)
3 g protein
39 g carbohydrate
7 g dietary fiber
0 mg cholesterol
55 mg sodium
275 mg potassium

Winter Fruit Gratin

This quick dessert will be welcomed by both family and friends at the end of a substantial meal—just a bite of sweet, cooked fruit with a crunchy topping. If you have calories to spare, top the hot fruit with a scoop of fat-free or low-fat ice cream or frozen yogurt. We use half of the usual amount of sugar called for in most recipes, so you save extra calories.

Refrigerated butter-flavored cooking spray
2 Bartlett pears, peeled and cut into bite-size pieces (about 2 cups)
2 Gala apples, peeled and cut into bite-size pieces (about 2 cups)
1 cup frozen cranberries
2 tablespoons brown sugar blend (see page 306)
3 tablespoons Grand Marnier or other orange liqueur
  Topping
1/3 cup rolled oats
1/4 cup sliced almonds
2 tablespoons brown sugar blend
2 tablespoons whole wheat flour
1/4 teaspoon ground cinnamon
2 tablespoons transfree margarine, cut into small pieces

1. Preheat the oven to 400°F. Lightly coat an 8-inch casserole with cooking spray.
2. Toss the pears, apples, and frozen cranberries with the sugar blend and Grand Marnier in the prepared casserole.
3. In a small bowl, combine the oats, almonds, sugar blend, flour, and cinnamon. With your fingers, work in the margarine to make a crumbly topping. Sprinkle over the fruit and bake for 18 to 20 minutes, until the top is browned and the fruit bubbling. Let cool for 5 minutes before serving in dessert bowls.

VARIATION: Summer Fruit Gratin. Substitute 4 cups of cut-up stone fruit—peaches, plums, or nectarines—for the apples and pears. Substitute 1 cup fresh or unsweetened frozen blueberries, blackberries, or raspberries for the cranberries. Toss with the sugar blend and Grand Marnier. Sprinkle with the topping and bake as directed.

Decadent Chocolate Soufflé

Makes 4 servings

Per serving:
130 calories
  (17% calories from fat)
2.5 g total fat
  (0.5 g saturated fat)
5 g protein
24 g carbohydrate
3 g dietary fiber
0 mg cholesterol
70 mg sodium
260 mg potassium

Soufflés sound intimidating, but in reality they are easy to prepare, and, wonder of wonders, you can have everything ready to put together before the guests arrive. From that point, the soufflés will be on the table in 15 minutes. If you don't want to use Cognac, substitute 1/2 teaspoon vanilla extract. Either way, you have an haute cuisine dessert that can be made with ease.

1½ teaspoons transfree margarine

¼ cup plus 1 teaspoon sugar

1 tablespoon ground toasted almonds (see page 320)

3 tablespoons plus 1 teaspoon good-quality cocoa

4 large egg whites, at room temperature

1 tablespoon Cognac

½ teaspoon ground cinnamon

1 teaspoon confectioners' sugar

12 strawberries, thinly sliced and fanned

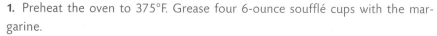

1. Preheat the oven to 375°F. Grease four 6-ounce soufflé cups with the margarine.

2. Mix 1 teaspoon of the sugar with the almonds and 1 teaspoon of the cocoa. Coat the insides and bottom of the soufflé cups, tapping the sides to make sure they are coated.

3. Heat 2 tablespoons water with the remaining sugar in a nonstick small pot. Bring to a simmer and cook until the mixture becomes thick, about 3 minutes. Do not allow the syrup to color. Brush down the sugar crystals on the sides of the pot with a wet pastry brush as the syrup thickens. It will be quite hot, so be careful.

4. While the sugar and water are simmering, beat the egg whites until stiff in the bowl of an electric mixer. While continuing to beat, slowly and carefully pour the hot sugar syrup into the egg whites. Add the 3 tablespoons cocoa, the Cognac, and cinnamon.

5. Spoon the mixture into the soufflé cups, tapping each cup to make sure there are no bubbles. Bake for 10 minutes, or until the soufflés are puffed and set. Immediately place the soufflés on dessert plates. Sift the confectioners' sugar over the tops and decorate each plate with 3 strawberries. Serve immediately.

Frozen Mexican Fruit Pops

Makes twelve 2-ounce
pops (12 servings)

Per serving:
50 calories
  (0% calories from fat)
0 g total fat
  (0 g saturated fat)
0 g protein
14 g carbohydrate
1 g dietary fiber
0 mg cholesterol
0 mg sodium
145 mg potassium

Whenever we visit Mexico, whether just crossing the border for a day of shopping or going deeper into the interior for a few days' visit, we keep our eyes peeled for the inevitable display of pastel-colored pops. Actually little more than a frozen puree of tropical fruit, these pops never fail to satisfy our sweet tooth and quench our thirst.

Although several kinds of molds are available, the pops can also be made in muffin tins or 3-ounce paper cups. Remove the paper cups (you can peel them off) or molds just before serving.

1 cup pureed mango (about 2 medium)
1 cup pureed papaya (about 1 medium)
1 cup pureed pineapple (about 1 small)
3 tablespoons superfine sugar
3 tablespoons fresh lime juice
12 wooden Popsicle sticks

1. Put the fruit purees in separate bowls. To each bowl, add 3/4 cup water, 1 tablespoon sugar, and 1 tablespoon lime juice. Mix well. Divide each puree among 4 molds, muffin cups, or paper cups. (Steady the paper cups by setting them in a small square metal pan.)
2. If using molds, set the lids in place and insert the sticks in the slots. Freeze until firm, at least 3 hours. If using the muffin tin or paper cups, partially freeze for about 1 hour before setting the sticks in the center of each cup. Freeze until firm, at least 3 hours; unmold and let soften at room temperature for 3 to 4 minutes before enjoying.

Sorbet and Granita

In France, it's called sorbet, *while Italians take pride in their "ices," called* granita. *We keep our freezer stocked with one or another for a refreshing ending to any meal. Although you can purchase sorbet and granita at the store, we prefer our versions, which are made without any (or much less) sugar.*

Start with the master recipe. Experiment with other fruit combinations—your flavor choices are limited only by your imagination and the fresh fruit available at the market.

Makes 4 servings

Per serving:
80 calories
  (0% calories from fat)
0 g total fat
  (0 g saturated fat)
1 g protein
19 g carbohydrate
4 g dietary fiber
0 mg cholesterol
0 mg sodium
200 mg potassium

Fresh Fruit Sorbet

1 ripe banana, sliced

1¹/₂ cups raspberries or sliced strawberries

1 cup fresh orange juice or other fruit juice

1. Place all ingredients in a food processor or blender and process until smooth. Transfer the mixture to a freezer container and freeze until firm.

2. To serve, let the sorbet rest at room temperature for 10 minutes before scooping into 4 dessert dishes.

VARIATION: Mango-Banana Sorbet. Use 1 mango, peeled and chopped, instead of the berries. Proceed with the recipe as directed. Makes 4 servings.

Per serving:
90 calories
  (0% calories from fat)
0 g total fat
  (0 g saturated fat)
1 g protein
22 g carbohydrate
2 g dietary fiber
0 mg cholesterol
0 mg sodium
310 mg potassium

Per serving:

45 calories

  (0% calories from fat)

0 g total fat

  (0 g saturated fat)

1 g protein

11 g carbohydrate

3 g dietary fiber

0 mg cholesterol

0 mg sodium

105 mg potassium

VARIATION: Blackberry Sorbet. Combine $1^1/2$ cups fresh or frozen blackberries in a blender or food processor with $1/4$ cup fresh lemon juice, $3/4$ cup sugar substitute, and $1/2$ cup water. Process until smooth. Freeze as directed. Makes 4 servings.

Pineapple Granita

Nothing could be simpler for a year-round dessert that will satisfy your sweet tooth.

Makes 4 servings

Per serving:

60 calories

  (0% calories from fat)

0 g total fat

  (0 g saturated fat)

1 g protein

16 g carbohydrate

2 g dietary fiber

0 mg cholesterol

150 mg potassium

1 small pineapple, peeled and cored

2 tablespoons sugar substitute

2 tablespoons fresh lemon juice

1. Cut the pineapple into chunks. Place in a food processor or blender. Add the sugar substitute and lemon juice. Process until smooth. Pour into an ice cube tray and freeze for 1 hour. Pop the cubes into a bowl. Break up the crystals with a wooden spoon. Using a handheld electric mixer, beat the mixture until smooth.
2. Transfer the granita to a covered container. Return to the freezer for at least 5 hours. Spoon into small dessert dishes. Granita will keep in the freezer for up to 1 week.

VARIATION: Very Berry Granita. Substitute 3 cups fresh or frozen raspberries, blackberries, or blueberries for the pineapple. Add the sugar substitute and lemon juice; process and freeze as directed. Makes 4 servings.

Per serving:
50 calories
  (0% calories from fat)
0 g total fat
  (0 g saturated fat)
1 g protein
12 g carbohydrate
6 g dietary fiber
0 mg cholesterol
0 mg sodium
150 mg potassium

VARIATION: Tangy Cherry Granita. Substitute 3 cups fresh or frozen pitted sour cherries for the pineapple. Add sugar substitute to taste and 2 tablespoons fresh lime juice instead of lemon juice. Process and freeze as directed. Makes 4 servings.

Per serving:
60 calories
  (0% calories from fat)
0 g total fat
  (0 g saturated fat)
1 g protein
16 g carbohydrate
4 g dietary fiber
0 mg cholesterol
0 mg sodium
210 mg potassium

Basics

This chapter holds the master recipes and techniques that you will turn to again and again as you make many of the dishes in this cookbook. Feel free to experiment and enjoy.

Basic Buckwheat Crêpes

Crêpes are easy to make and can be frozen to have on hand when you need to dress up a quick dinner (see pages 191 and 192) or make an elegant dessert. They can also do wonders for leftovers. For this recipe we use buckwheat, which makes blini, a crêpe with a Russian accent.

1 tablespoon *trans*-free margarine, melted

1 cup skim milk

1 large egg

1/2 cup egg substitute

2/3 cup unbleached all-purpose flour

1/3 cup buckwheat flour

1/4 teaspoon sugar substitute

1/8 teaspoon kosher salt, optional

Refrigerated butter-flavored cooking spray

1. Place the margarine, milk, 1/2 cup water, the egg, and egg substitute in a food processor or blender. Process for 10 seconds. Add the flours, sugar substitute, and salt, if using. Process until smooth, stopping occasionally to scrape down the sides. Allow the batter to rest for 30 minutes.

2. Coat an 8-inch nonstick skillet or crêpe pan with cooking spray and place over high heat. When hot, add 1/4 cup of the batter and tilt the pan so the batter spreads evenly over the bottom. Cook the crêpe until the surface seems dry and the edges begin to curl, about 1 minute. Carefully turn the crêpe using your fingers and a wooden spoon and cook until lightly browned, about 30 seconds. Turn the crêpes out in a single layer onto wax paper or clean tea towels. Continue making crêpes until all the batter is used.

NOTE: To freeze crêpes, stack them with a small square of wax paper between each crêpe. Wrap the stack with plastic, then slip the stack into a self-sealing plastic freezer bag. The frozen crêpes will easily separate, so you can remove exactly the number that you need. Let the crêpes thaw before using in a recipe. The crêpes should be used within 3 months.

Makes 28 crêpes

Per serving (2 crêpes):
50 calories
   (20% calories from fat)
1 g total fat
   (0 g saturated fat)
3 g protein
7 g carbohydrate
0 g dietary fiber
15 mg cholesterol
35 mg sodium
60 mg potassium

Homemade Multigrain Bread Crumbs

Makes 4 cups

Per serving
(1 tablespoon):
10 calories
  (0% calories from fat)
0 g total fat
  (0 g saturated fat)
0 g protein
2 g carbohydrate
0 g dietary fiber
0 mg cholesterol
20 mg sodium
0 mg potassium

Supermarkets and bakeries are now filled with a variety of whole-grain breads. By making your own homemade bread crumbs, you can control the excess salt and other seasonings often found in store-bought crumbs. You can also control the texture of the crumbs and store some in your freezer for last-minute needs.

One 8-ounce multigrain or whole wheat baguette

1. Preheat the oven to 325°F. Line a baking pan with aluminum foil.
2. Break the bread into small pieces and place half of it in a food processor. Process until you have a coarse crumb. Place in the baking pan. Process the remaining bread and add to the baking pan. Smooth the crumbs to cover the entire pan evenly.
3. Bake for 10 to 15 minutes, turning the crumbs after 8 minutes so they are browned and dry throughout. Allow to cool. Place in a freezer bag and freeze. Use as needed.

Yogurt Cheese

If you haven't made yogurt cheese, you'll wonder why it took you so long to become acquainted with this centuries-old Middle Eastern staple. When a recipe calls for sour cream, cream cheese, or mayonnaise, use this to cut down on calories, fat, and saturated fat. The yogurt takes a while to drain, but it needs no attention while it's draining. Traditionally, yogurt cheese is made in a cheesecloth bag or a colander lined with a double layer of cheesecloth; we find it easier to use a coffee filter.

2 cups nonfat yogurt

Line a sieve with a coffee filter or double thickness of cheesecloth. Suspend the sieve over a deep bowl. Spoon the yogurt into the filter, cover with plastic wrap, and allow the whey to drip out. When the yogurt has the consistency of soft, velvety, spreadable cheese, about 6 hours, scrape it into a plastic or glass container. Discard the liquid in the bowl. Refrigerate and use within 1 week, discarding any accumulated liquid before using.

Makes 1 cup
(16 servings)

Per serving
(1 tablespoon):
10 calories
  (0% calories from fat)
0 g total fat
  (0 g saturated fat)
1 g protein
2 g carbohydrate
0 g dietary fiber
0 mg cholesterol
15 mg sodium
0 mg potassium

Crème Fraîche

Makes about 2 cups

Per serving (¼ cup):
35 calories
  (22% calories from fat)
1 g total fat
  (0.5 g saturated fat)
3 g protein
4 g carbohydrate
0 g dietary fiber
5 mg cholesterol
45 mg sodium
133 mg potassium

This thick, tangy cream is a staple in our refrigerators, ready to top desserts and fresh fruits, mix with flavored vinegars for a salad dressing, or use as a recipe ingredient. Gourmet markets sell crème fraîche, but it's usually made with whipping cream. Our easy-to-make version cuts the fat grams by using low-fat yogurt.

2 tablespoons 1% cultured buttermilk
2 cups low-fat yogurt

In a heavy saucepan, combine the buttermilk and yogurt. Heat until just lukewarm (do not overheat). Remove from heat and transfer to a covered container. Let stand at room temperature for 24 hours. Refrigerate until needed. Use within 1 week.

DIETITIAN'S NOTE: When compared to full-fat crème fraîche, our ¼-cup portion saves you 140 calories, 18 grams of fat, and 11.5 grams of saturated fat. Just one serving of the full-fat version has 67 percent of your daily saturated fat allowance!

Crostini

Crostini are easy to make and can be used with spreads, dips, and salsas and as a snack with low-fat cheeses or roasted vegetables.

Olive oil cooking spray

One 12-ounce whole wheat baguette

2 garlic cloves, sliced

1. Preheat the oven to 350°F. Coat a baking sheet with cooking spray.

2. Slice the baguette diagonally into 1/3-inch slices, discarding the ends. Arrange on the baking sheet and coat the tops of the slices with cooking spray. Bake until lightly browned, 10 to 15 minutes, turning once. Remove from the oven and immediately rub each slice with cut garlic. Set aside to cool.

3. Store in an airtight container for up to 3 days.

Makes 20 servings

Per serving (1 slice):
45 calories
   (9% calories from fat)
0 g total fat
   (0 g saturated fat)
2 g protein
9 g carbohydrate
1 g dietary fiber
0 mg cholesterol
95 mg sodium
1 mg potassium

Whole Wheat Pie Crust

Makes 6 servings
(one 9-inch pie crust or
10-inch tart shell)

Per serving (crust only):
170 calories
  (53% calories from fat)
10 g total fat
  (2.5 g saturated fat)
3 g protein
18 g carbohydrate
2 g dietary fiber
0 mg cholesterol
50 mg sodium
40 mg potassium

We wanted a healthier pie crust than the ones we are used to, which are laden with saturated fats. The crust takes only a few minutes to mix together and roll out.

3/4 cup unbleached all-purpose flour, plus more for dusting

1/2 cup whole wheat pastry flour

1/8 teaspoon salt

5 tablespoons transfree vegetable shortening

---

1. In a mixing bowl, combine the white and whole wheat flours and the salt. Add the shortening and with a pastry blender cut the fat into the flour. You can also quickly use your fingers to break up the shortening and form a coarse meal. Sprinkle with ice water, 1 tablespoon at a time, and mix with a fork until a moist dough forms. You'll use 5 to 6 tablespoons water.

2. For a filled crust: Roll the dough into an 1/8-inch-thick round on a floured piece of wax paper or a pastry cloth. Roll the dough onto a rolling pin and then unroll it onto the pie pan. Cut off the excess, leaving an inch to fold under. Crimp the edge with the tines of a fork. Freeze for 10 minutes before baking.

3. For a baked crust: Prepare the dough as for a filled crust. Prick the sides and bottom with a fork and bake in a 450°F oven for 10 to 12 minutes, or until lightly browned.

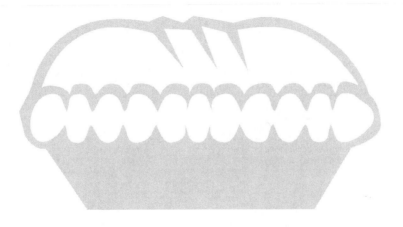

Meal Plans

1,600-Calorie One-Week Meal Plan

This meal plan is appropriate for inactive women who wish to lose some excess body weight.

	DAY 1	DAY 2	DAY 3
Breakfast	• 1 cup cooked cracked wheat cereal topped with 1 teaspoon brown sugar, dash of vanilla extract, and 1 cup fresh or frozen unsweetened blueberries • 8 ounces skim milk • 8 ounces black coffee	• 1 cup cooked oat bran topped with 2 tablespoons crushed walnuts, 1/8 teaspoon ground cinnamon, and 1 medium pear, diced • 8 ounces skim milk	• 2 frozen whole wheat waffles topped with 2 tablespoons light maple syrup • One 2-ounce light turkey sausage link • 1 cup mixed fresh berries • 8 ounces green tea
Snack	• 1 medium pear • 8 ounces water	• 1 medium apple • 8 ounces water	• 1 small mandarin orange • 16 ounces water
Lunch	• 1 1/2 servings Fava Bean, Artichoke Heart, and Grape Tomato Salad with Lemon Vinaigrette (page 166) • 6 trans-free whole wheat crackers • 16 ounces sparkling water with wedge of lime	• 1 serving Polenta with Eggplant Ragout (page 186) • 1 cup fresh baby carrots • 16 ounces sugar-free, caffeine-free sparkling beverage	• 1 serving Roasted Portobello Sandwich with Dijon Balsamic Vinaigrette (page 200) • 1 cup mixed greens salad with carrots, onions, and cucumber, topped with 2 tablespoons light vinaigrette • 8 ounces skim milk
Snack	• 8 ounces unsweetened soymilk • 1 trans-free crunchy granola bar	• 1/2 cup 1% cottage cheese topped with 12 whole raw almonds • 8 ounces herbal tea	• 1 medium apple • 8 ounces water
Dinner	• 1 serving Grilled Chicken Breasts with Warm Balsamic Strawberries (page 230) • 2 cups steamed broccoli florets • 1 cup cooked wild rice (page 268) • 1 cup fresh raspberries topped with 2 tablespoons light chocolate syrup and 2 tablespoons light whipped topping • 16 ounces water	• 1 serving Tuna Burgers with Thousand Island Sauce (page 218) • 1 cup corn and bean salad with fresh cilantro • 1 ounce dark chocolate • 8 ounces water	• 1 serving Honey-Orange Grilled Pork Tenderloin with Chipotle Chiles (page 265) • 1 serving Lemon Couscous with Asparagus and Cherry Tomatoes (page 269) • 1 cup tossed vegetable salad topped with 1 tablespoon rice wine vinegar and 2 tablespoons roasted unsalted soy nuts • 8 ounces herbal tea
	• 1,560 calories (23% calories from fat) • 45 g total fat: 7 g saturated fat • 81 g protein • 246 g carbohydrate • 56 g dietary fiber • 65 mg cholesterol • 1,160 mg sodium • 3,278 mg potassium	• 1,600 calories (23% calories from fat) • 42 g total fat: 88 g saturated fat • 100 g protein • 227 g carbohydrate • 48 g dietary fiber • 100 mg cholesterol • 1,400 mg sodium • 3,591 mg potassium	• 1,690 calories (23% calories from fat) • 43 g total fat: 11 g saturated fat • 85 g protein • 234 g carbohydrate • 33 g dietary fiber • 165 mg cholesterol • 1,670 mg sodium • 2,845 mg potassium

DAY 4	DAY 5	DAY 6	DAY 7
• ½ cup egg substitute omelet filled with 2 slices fresh avocado and 1 tablespoon chopped fresh cilantro • ½ multigrain bagel topped with 2 teaspoons light trans-free margarine • 1 cup diced papaya • 8 ounces black coffee	• 8 ounces nonfat yogurt topped with ½ cup high-fiber bran cereal and ¾ cup fresh or frozen unsweetened blueberries • 1 slice whole rye bread, toasted and topped with 2 teaspoons natural peanut butter • 8 ounces green tea	• 1 cup cooked old-fashioned oatmeal topped with 1 teaspoon brown sugar, dash of vanilla extract, 2 tablespoons ground flax seed, and 1 small banana, sliced • 8 ounces unsweetened calcium-fortified soymilk • 8 ounces black tea	• 1 slice homemade frittata made with egg substitute and filled with asparagus, tomato, and shiitake mushrooms • 1 slice 100% whole wheat bread, toasted and topped with 2 teaspoons light trans-free margarine • 1 small banana • 8 ounces black coffee
• 8 ounces skim milk • 2 whole wheat graham crackers	• 1 medium apple • 8 ounces water	• ½ cup 1% cottage cheese topped with 12 raw almonds • 8 ounces water	
• 1 serving Greek Tofu Salad (page 180) over 2 cups chopped romaine lettuce • 1 slice whole-grain bread • 16 ounces sparkling water with wedge of lime	• 1 serving Roasted Tomato, Goat Cheese, and Arugula Sandwiches (page 197) • 1 ounce trans-free taro chips • 1 cup reduced-sodium vegetable soup • 16 ounces sparkling water	• 1 serving Asparagus, Tomato, and Shiitake Mushroom Quiche (page 189) • 2 cups mixed greens topped with 2 tablespoons light ranch salad dressing • 16 ounces sparkling water with wedge of lemon	• 1 small sprouted-grain tortilla spread with 1 tablespoon natural peanut butter and 1 tablespoon no-sugar-added fruit preserves • 1 ounce whole wheat hard pretzels • 2 cups fresh cut vegetables: carrots, peppers, celery, cucumber • 16 ounces water
• 1 cup diced apple and orange wedges topped with ⅛ teaspoon cinnamon, 2 tablespoons slivered almonds, and 2 tablespoons nonfat plain yogurt • 8 ounces water	• 2 unsulfured dried figs • 8 ounces sugar-free hot chocolate	• ¾ cup sliced mango • 8 ounces water	• ¼ cup Yogurt Cheese (page 335) spread over 1 small whole wheat pita • 8 ounces sparkling water
• Slow-Roasted Arctic Char with Lemon–Mustard Seed Topping (page 205) • 2 cups steamed broccoli drizzled with 1 teaspoon extra virgin olive oil • 1 small baked sweet potato topped with 1 tablespoon brown sugar substitute • 8 ounces water	• 1 serving Penne Pasta Salad with Asparagus, Arugula, and Balsamic Vinaigrette (page 169) • 1 cup mixed greens salad topped with 1 tablespoon red wine vinegar • 1 serving low-fat, reduced-sugar ice cream • 8 ounces herbal tea	• 1 serving Turkey Cutlets with Tomato and Red Pepper Sauce (page 239) • 1 cup cooked whole wheat couscous • 2 cups steamed asparagus drizzled with 1 teaspoon extra-virgin olive oil • 8 ounces herbal tea	• 1 serving Stuffed Eggplant (page 188) • 1 cup cooked whole wheat pasta shells drizzled with 2 teaspoons olive oil and 1 ounce crumbled reduced-fat feta cheese • 1 cup tossed vegetable salad topped with 1 tablespoon red wine vinegar • 8 ounces low-fat yogurt topped with 2 tablespoons crushed pecans • 8 ounces herbal tea
• 1,590 calories (28% calories from fat) • 55 g total fat: 9 g saturated fat • 93 g protein • 228 g carbohydrate • 38 g dietary fiber • 35 mg cholesterol • 1,720 mg sodium • 3,419 mg potassium	• 1,560 calories (27% calories from fat) • 50 g total fat: 8 g saturated fat • 53 g protein • 254 g carbohydrate • 56 g dietary fiber • 20 mg cholesterol • 1,320 mg sodium • 2,985 mg potassium	• 1,580 calories (24% calories from fat) • 44 g total fat: 6 g saturated fat • 96 g protein • 215 g carbohydrate • 40 g dietary fiber • 75 mg cholesterol • 1,400 mg sodium • 2,431 mg potassium	• 1,660 calories (30% calories from fat) • 57 g total fat: 9 g saturated fat • 58 g protein • 240 g carbohydrate • 33 g dietary fiber • 15 mg cholesterol • 1,370 mg sodium • 2,900 mg potassium

2,000-Calorie One-Week Meal Plan

This meal plan is appropriate for active women who wish to maintain their body weight or inactive men who wish to lose excess body weight.

	DAY 1	DAY 2	DAY 3
Breakfast	• 1 cup cooked cracked wheat cereal topped with 1 teaspoon brown sugar, dash of vanilla extract, and 1 cup fresh or frozen unsweetened blueberries • One 100% whole wheat English muffin spread with 1 tablespoon natural peanut butter • 8 ounces skim milk • 8 ounces black coffee	• 1½ cups cooked oat bran topped with 2 tablespoons crushed walnuts, ⅛ teaspoon ground cinnamon, and 1 medium pear, diced • 1 slice oatmeal bread, toasted and topped with 1 tablespoon light trans-free margarine • 8 ounces skim milk	• 3 frozen whole wheat waffles topped with 2 tablespoons light maple syrup • Two 2-ounce light turkey sausage links • 1 cup mixed fresh berries • 8 ounces green tea
Snack	• 1 medium pear • 8 ounces water	• 1 medium apple • 8 ounces water	• 1 serving Edamame Hummus (page 132) with 1 cup snap peas and baby carrots • 16 ounces water
Lunch	• 2 servings Fava Bean, Artichoke Heart, and Grape Tomato Salad with Lemon Vinaigrette (page 166) • 6 trans-free whole wheat crackers • 16 ounces sparkling water with wedge of lime	• 1 serving Polenta with Eggplant Ragout (page 186) • 1 cup fresh baby carrots • 16 ounces sugar-free, caffeine-free sparkling beverage	• 1 serving Roasted Portobello Sandwich with Dijon Balsamic Vinaigrette (page 200) • 1 cup mixed greens salad with carrots, onion, and cucumber, topped with 2 tablespoons light vinaigrette • 8 ounces skim milk
Snack	• 8 ounces unsweetened soymilk • 1 crunchy trans-free granola bar	• 1 cup 1% cottage cheese topped with 12 whole raw almonds • 8 ounces herbal tea	• 1 medium apple • 8 ounces water
Dinner	• 1½ servings Grilled Chicken Breasts with Warm Balsamic Strawberries (page 230) • 2 cups steamed broccoli florets • ½ cup cooked wild rice (page 268) • 1½ cups fresh raspberries topped with 2 tablespoons light chocolate syrup and 2 tablespoons light whipped topping • 16 ounces water	• 1 serving Tuna Burgers with Thousand Island Sauce (page 218) • 1½ cups corn and bean salad with fresh cilantro • 1 ounce trans-free baked tortilla chips • 1 ounce dark chocolate • 8 ounces water	• 1½ servings Honey-Orange Grilled Pork Tenderloin with Chipotle Chiles (page 265) • 1 serving Lemon Couscous with Asparagus and Cherry Tomatoes (page 269) • 1 cup tossed vegetable salad topped with 1 tablespoon rice wine vinegar and ½ ounce roasted unsalted soy nuts • 1 ounce dark chocolate • 8 ounces herbal tea
	• 1,960 calories (24% calories from fat) • 60 g total fat: 10 g saturated fat • 104 g protein • 289 g carbohydrate • 66 g dietary fiber • 90 mg cholesterol • 1,810 mg sodium • 3,865 mg potassium	• 2,100 calories (24% calories from fat) • 57 g total fat: 11 g saturated fat • 125 g protein • 300 g carbohydrate • 57 g dietary fiber • 110 mg cholesterol • 2,540 mg sodium • 3,981 mg potassium	• 2,050 calories (26% calories from fat) • 62 g total fat: 19 g saturated fat • 112 g protein • 281 g carbohydrate • 39 g dietary fiber • 235 mg cholesterol • 2,080 mg sodium • 3,200 mg potassium

DAY 4	DAY 5	DAY 6	DAY 7
• 1/2 cup egg substitute omelet filled with 2 slices fresh avocado and 1 tablespoon chopped fresh cilantro • 1 multigrain bagel topped with 2 teaspoons light trans-free margarine • 1 cup diced papaya • 8 ounces black coffee	• 8 ounces nonfat yogurt topped with 1/2 cup high-fiber bran cereal and 3/4 cup fresh or frozen unsweetened blueberries • 2 slices whole rye bread, toasted and topped with 1 tablespoon natural peanut butter • 8 ounces green tea	• 1 cup cooked old-fashioned oatmeal topped with 1 teaspoon brown sugar, dash of vanilla extract, 2 tablespoons ground flax seed, and 1 small banana, sliced • 8 ounces unsweetened calcium-fortified soymilk • 8 ounces black tea	• 1 1/2 slices homemade frittata made with egg substitute and filled with asparagus, tomato, and shiitake mushrooms • 1 slice 100% whole wheat bread, toasted and topped with 2 teaspoons light trans-free margarine • 1 small banana • 8 ounces black coffee
• 8 ounces skim milk • 2 whole wheat graham crackers	• 1 medium apple • 8 ounces water	• 1 cup 1% cottage cheese topped with 12 raw almonds • 8 ounces water	
• 2 servings Greek Tofu Salad (page 181) over 2 cups chopped romaine lettuce • 1 slice whole-grain bread • 16 ounces sparkling water with wedge of lime	• 1 serving Roasted Tomato, Goat Cheese, and Arugula Sandwiches (page 197) • 1 ounce trans-free taro chips • 1 cup reduced-sodium vegetable soup • 16 ounces sparkling water	• 1 serving Asparagus, Tomato, and Shiitake Mushroom Quiche (page 189) • 2 cups mixed greens topped with 2 tablespoons light ranch salad dressing • 16 ounces sparkling water with wedge of lemon	• 1 large sprouted-grain tortilla spread with 2 tablespoons natural peanut butter and 2 tablespoons no-sugar-added fruit preserves • 1 ounce whole wheat hard pretzels • 2 cups fresh cut vegetables: carrots, peppers, celery, cucumber • 16 ounces water
• 1 cup diced apple and orange wedges topped with 1/8 teaspoon cinnamon, 2 tablespoons slivered almonds, and 2 tablespoons nonfat yogurt • 8 ounces water	• 2 unsulfured dried figs • 1 tablespoon raw almonds • 8 ounces sugar-free hot chocolate	• 3/4 cup sliced mango mixed with 6 ounces nonfat fruited yogurt • 8 ounces water	• 1/4 cup Yogurt Cheese (page 335) spread over 1 small whole wheat pita • 8 ounces sparkling water
• 1 1/2 servings Slow-Roasted Arctic Char with Lemon–Mustard Seed Topping (page 205) • 2 cups steamed broccoli drizzled with 1 teaspoon extra virgin olive oil • 1 medium baked sweet potato topped with 1 tablespoon brown sugar substitute • 8 ounces water	• 1 1/2 servings Penne Pasta Salad with Asparagus, Arugula, and Balsamic Vinaigrette (page 169) • 1 cup mixed greens salad topped with 1 tablespoon red wine vinegar • 1 serving low-fat, reduced sugar ice cream • 8 ounces herbal tea	• 1 1/2 servings Turkey Cutlets with Tomato and Red Pepper Sauce (page 239) • 1 1/2 cups cooked whole wheat couscous • 2 cups steamed asparagus drizzled with 2 teaspoons extra virgin olive oil • 8 ounces herbal tea	• 1 serving Stuffed Eggplant (page 188) • 1 1/2 cups cooked whole wheat pasta shells drizzled with 2 teaspoons olive oil and 1 ounce crumbled reduced-fat feta cheese • 1 cup tossed vegetable salad topped with 1 tablespoon red wine vinegar • 8 ounces low-fat yogurt topped with 2 tablespoons crushed pecans • 8 ounces herbal tea
• 2,030 calories (29% calories from fat) • 74 g total fat: 13 g saturated fat • 115 g protein • 277 g carbohydrate • 45 g dietary fiber • 40 mg cholesterol • 2,310 mg sodium • 3,455 mg potassium	• 1,970 calories (28% calories from fat) • 64 g total fat: 11 g saturated fat • 70 g protein • 308 g carbohydrate • 62 g dietary fiber • 40 mg cholesterol • 1,800 mg sodium • 3,200 mg potassium	• 2,050 calories (26% calories from fat) • 60 g total fat: 8 g saturated fat • 133 g protein • 258 g carbohydrate • 44 g dietary fiber • 100 mg cholesterol • 2,300 mg sodium • 3,323 mg potassium	• 2,032 calories (32% calories from fat) • 73 g total fat: 12 g saturated fat • 70 g protein • 289 g carbohydrate • 41 g dietary fiber • 15 mg cholesterol • 1,520 mg sodium • 3,050 mg potassium

2,400-Calorie One-Week Meal Plan

This meal plan is appropriate for active men who wish to maintain their body weight.

	DAY 1	DAY 2	DAY 3
Breakfast	• 1 cup cooked cracked wheat cereal topped with 1 teaspoon brown sugar, dash of vanilla extract, and 1 cup fresh or frozen unsweetened blueberries • One 100% whole wheat bagel spread with 2 tablespoons natural peanut butter • 8 ounces skim milk • 8 ounces black coffee	• 2 cups cooked oat bran topped with 2 tablespoons crushed walnuts, $\frac{1}{4}$ teaspoon ground cinnamon, and 1 medium pear, diced • 2 slices oatmeal bread, toasted and topped with 1 tablespoon light trans-free margarine • 8 ounces skim milk	• 3 frozen whole wheat waffles topped with 2 tablespoons light maple syrup • Two 2-ounce meatless sausage links • 1 cup mixed fresh berries • 8 ounces green tea
Snack	• 1 medium pear • 1 ounce reduced-fat Cheddar cheese • 8 ounces water	• 1 medium apple • 8 ounces water	• 1 serving Edamane Hummus (page 132) with 2 cups snap peas and baby carrots • 16 ounces water
Lunch	• 2 servings Fava Bean, Artichoke Heart, and Grape Tomato Salad with Lemon Vinaigrette (page 166) • 6 trans-free whole wheat crackers • 16 ounces sparkling water with wedge of lime	• 1$\frac{1}{2}$ servings Polenta with Eggplant Ragout (page 186) • 1 cup fresh baby carrots • 16 ounces sugar-free, caffeine-free sparkling beverage	• 1 serving Roasted Portobello Sandwich with Dijon Balsamic Vinaigrette (page 200) • 1 cup mixed greens salad with carrots, onion, and cucumber, topped with 2 tablespoons light vinaigrette dressing • 8 ounces skim milk
Snack	• 8 ounces unsweetened soymilk • 1 crunchy trans-free granola bar	• 1 cup 1% cottage cheese topped with 22 whole raw almonds • 8 ounces herbal tea	• 1 medium orange • 8 ounces water
Dinner	• 2 servings Grilled Chicken Breasts with Warm Balsamic Strawberries (page 230) • 2 cups steamed broccoli florets • 1 cup cooked wild rice (page 268) • 1$\frac{1}{2}$ cups fresh raspberries topped with 2 tablespoons light chocolate syrup and $\frac{1}{4}$ cup light whipped topping • 16 ounces water	• 1 serving Tuna Burgers with Thousand Island Sauce (page 218) • 1$\frac{1}{2}$ cups corn and bean salad with fresh cilantro • 1 ounce trans-free baked tortilla chips • 1 ounce dark chocolate • 8 ounces water	• 1$\frac{1}{2}$ servings Honey-Orange Grilled Pork Tenderloin with Chipotle Chiles (page 265) • 1 serving Lemon Couscous with Asparagus and Cherry Tomatoes (page 269) • 1 cup tossed vegetable salad topped with 1 tablespoon rice wine vinegar and 2 tablespoons roasted unsalted soy nuts • 2 ounces dark chocolate • 8 ounces herbal tea
	• 2,410 calories (27% calories from fat) • 76 g total fat: 15 g saturated fat • 133 g protein • 337 g carbohydrate • 76 g dietary fiber • 130 mg cholesterol • 2,250 mg sodium • 4,066 mg potassium	• 2,380 calories (24% calories from fat) • 68 g total fat: 12 g saturated fat • 134 g protein • 340 g carbohydrate • 63 g dietary fiber • 110 mg cholesterol • 2,700 mg sodium • 4,300 mg potassium	• 2,410 calories (32% calories from fat) • 88 g total fat: 23 g saturated fat • 123 g protein • 304 g carbohydrate • 43 g dietary fiber • 175 mg cholesterol • 2,220 mg sodium • 3,090 mg potassium

DAY 4	DAY 5	DAY 6	DAY 7
• $^3/_4$ cup egg substitute omelet filled with 3 slices fresh avocado and 1 tablespoon chopped fresh cilantro • 1 multigrain bagel topped with 2 tablespoons natural peanut butter • $1^1/_2$ cups diced papaya • 8 ounces black coffee	• One 100% whole wheat English muffin filled with one 2-ounce light turkey sausage patty, 1 slice melted soy cheese, 2 tablespoons tomato salsa • $^1/_2$ cup leftover baked sweet potato, thinly sliced and sautéed in olive oil with $^1/_2$ cup chopped onion, 1 tablespoon reduced-sodium ketchup • $1^1/_2$ cups mixed fresh berries, mango, and papaya • 8 ounces green tea	• $1^1/_2$ cups cooked old-fashioned oatmeal topped with 1 teaspoon brown sugar, dash of vanilla extract, 2 tablespoons ground flax seed, and 1 small banana, sliced • 8 ounces unsweetened calcium-fortified soymilk • 8 ounces black tea	• 1 slice homemade frittata made with egg substitute and filled with asparagus, tomato, and shiitake mushrooms • 1 slice 100% whole wheat bread, toasted and topped with 2 teaspoons light trans-free margarine • 1 small banana • 8 ounces black coffee
• 8 ounces skim milk • 2 whole wheat graham crackers	• 1 medium apple • 1 reduced-fat mozzarella string cheese • 8 ounces water	• 1 cup 1% cottage cheese topped with 1 ounce chopped pecans • 8 ounces water	• 6 ounces low-fat fruited yogurt topped with $^1/_2$ ounce slivered almonds and $^1/_2$ cup fresh blueberries
• 2 servings Greek Tofu Salad (page 181) over 2 cups chopped romaine lettuce • 1 slice whole-grain bread • 1 medium banana • 16 ounces sparkling water with wedge of lime	• 2 servings Roasted Tomato, Goat Cheese, and Arugula Sandwiches (page 197) • 1 ounce trans-free taro chips • 2 cups reduced-sodium vegetable soup • 16 ounces sparkling water	• 2 servings Asparagus, Tomato, and Shiitake Mushroom Quiche (page 189) • 2 cups tossed salad greens topped with 2 tablespoons light ranch salad dressing • 16 ounces sparkling water with wedge of lemon	• 1 serving Roasted Vegetables (page 305) • 2 slices whole-grain bread with 2 teaspoons commercial pesto • 1 ounce whole wheat pretzel sticks • 2 cups fresh cut vegetables: carrots, peppers, celery, cucumber • 16 ounces water
• 1 cup nonfat yogurt topped with 1 cup diced apple and orange wedges, $^1/_8$ teaspoon cinnamon, and 2 tablespoons slivered almonds • 8 ounces water	• 2 unsulfured dried figs • 1 tablespoon raw almonds • 8 ounces sugar-free hot chocolate	• $^3/_4$ cup sliced mango mixed with 6 ounces nonfat fruited yogurt • 8 ounces water	• $^1/_2$ cup Yogurt Cheese (page 335) spread over 8 trans-free whole-grain crackers • 8 ounces sparkling water
• $1^1/_4$ servings Slow-Roasted Arctic Char with Lemon–Mustard Seed Topping (page 205) • 2 cups steamed broccoli drizzled with 1 teaspoon extra virgin olive oil • 1 medium baked sweet potato topped with 1 tablespoon brown sugar substitute • 8 ounces water	• 2 servings Penne Pasta Salad with Asparagus, Arugula, and Balsamic Vinaigrette (page 169) • 1 cup mixed greens salad topped with 1 tablespoon red wine vinegar • 1 cup low-fat, reduced-sugar ice cream • 8 ounces herbal tea	• 2 servings Turkey Cutlets with Tomato and Red Pepper Sauce (page 239) • $1^1/_2$ cups cooked whole wheat couscous • 2 cups steamed asparagus drizzled with 2 teaspoons extra virgin olive oil • 2 whole wheat fig cookies • 8 ounces sugar-free hot chocolate made with water	• 1 serving Stuffed Eggplant (page 188) • $1^1/_2$ cups cooked whole wheat pasta shells drizzled with 2 teaspoons olive oil and 1 ounce crumbled reduced-fat feta cheese • 1 cup tossed vegetable salad topped with 1 tablespoon vinegar • 8 ounces low-fat yogurt topped with 2 tablespoons crushed pecans • 8 ounces herbal tea
• 2,420 calories (29% calories from fat) • 87 g total fat: 13 g saturated fat • 132 g protein • 337 g carbohydrate • 52 g dietary fiber • 40 mg cholesterol • 2,490 mg sodium • 4,035 mg potassium	• 2,370 calories (25% calories from fat) • 66 g total fat: 16 g saturated fat • 77 g protein • 382 g carbohydrate • 76 g dietary fiber • 50 mg cholesterol • 1,960 mg sodium • 4,908 mg potassium	• 2,420 calories (26% calories from fat) • 72 g total fat: 11 g saturated fat • 156 g protein • 296 g carbohydrate • 48 g dietary fiber • 125 mg cholesterol • 3,270 mg sodium • 3,700 mg potassium	• 2,390 calories (28% calories from fat) • 76 g total fat: 15 g saturated fat • 87 g protein • 357 g carbohydrate • 50 g dietary fiber • 45 mg cholesterol • 1,940 mg sodium • 4,132 mg potassium

Food Diary

Day/Date: _____

Meal or Snack	Time of Meal	Foods and Beverages Consumed	Amount	Preparation Method	Feelings
Example: Breakfast	6:30 A.M.	Rolled oats Skim milk Fresh blueberries Green tea	½ c. raw 8 oz. ½ c. 8 oz.	Microwave Plain	Hungry and tired

Index

Asian Slaw, 229
    Chicken Skewers, San Francisco–
        Style with, 228
asparagus
    Asparagus, Tomato, and Shiitake
        Mushroom Quiche, 189
    Grilled Black Sea Bass over Summer
        Vegetables with Japanese
        Dressing, 204
    Lemon Couscous with Asparagus
        and Cherry Tomatoes, 269
    Penne Pasta Salad with Asparagus,
        Arugula, and Balsamic
        Vinaigrette, 169
    Pizza with Arugula, Sautéed
        Vegetables, and Goat Cheese,
        196
    Stir-Fried Sesame Asparagus with
        Pickled Ginger, 284
aspartame, 44–45
atherosclerosis, new treatments,
    xix
avocados, 69, 77, 78
    Tortilla Soup Texas-Style with
        Tortilla Stacks, 150
    Wild Guacamole, 131

bad cholesterol. See LDL cholesterol
Baked Cod with Rice in Parchment,
    Florentine-Style, 206–7
baked goods, 58, 65
    See also bread(s); crackers; desserts
balsamic vinegar, 159
    Balsamic Vinaigrette: Penne Pasta
        Salad with Asparagus,
        Arugula, and, 169; Warm
        Arugula with Polenta
        Croutons and Mozzarella
        Cheese, 160–61
    Dijon Balsamic Vinaigrette, Roasted
        Portobello Sandwiches with,
        200–201
    Dried Cherry Balsamic Sauce, Pork
        Chops with, 266
    fresh fruit with, 307
    Grilled Balsamic-Glazed Tuna with
        Tropical Fruit Salad, 217
    Warm Balsamic Strawberries, 231;
        Grilled Chicken Breasts with,
        230
bananas
    Fresh Fruit Sorbet, 329
    Mango-Banana sorbet (variation),
        329

barley, 52, 54, 268
    Mexican Barley Risotto, 278
basic recipes, 333–38
beans, 281
    Beef Chili with Butternut Squash,
        249
    Black Bean and Corn Salsa, Stuffed
        Chayote with, 194–95
    Curried Lima Bean Soup, 145
    White Bean Puree, Duck Breasts
        with, 244–45
    Fava Bean, Artichoke Heart, and
        Grape Tomato Salad, 166–67
    Great Northern Beans with
        Tomatoes and Herbs, 281
    green: Thai Green Beans, 288;
        3-Bean Beef Stew, 259;
        Vegetarian Paella, 190
    Spicy Black Bean Cakes with
        Cilantro Yogurt, 276
    Texas Pot of Pintos, 282
    3-Bean Beef Stew, 259
    Tomato Black Bean Soup, 151
    Tuscan Bean Spread, 133
    Warm Cannellini Bean Salad with
        Salmon and Citrus
        Vinaigrette, 165
    Winter Vegetable Soup, 147
bean sprouts
    Asian Slaw, 229
    Cold Soba Noodles with Pork, 264
    Vegetables, Tofu, and Soba
        Noodles in Sweet Ginger
        Sauce, 184–85
beef, 249–61
    about, 251; internal temperatures
        for doneness, 258; saturated
        fats, 59, 61; trans fats, 62
    Beef Chili with Butternut Squash,
        249
    Creole Beef and Vegetables with
        Cheese Grits, 260–61
    Cuban Flank Steak with Citrus
        Mojo, 254
    Grilled Steak with Chimichurri
        Sauce, 250–51
    Herbed Roasted Beef Tenderloin,
        256
    Shepherd's Pie, 255
    Thai Grilled Steak Salad with Rice
        Noodles, 252–53
    3-Bean Beef Stew, 259
beet greens
    Pot of Down-Home Greens,
        292–93

Beets, Roasted, with Oranges, 285
bell peppers
    Black-eyed Pea Relish with
        Crackers, 134
    Broiled Flounder with Sweet and
        Sour Sauce, 208
    Chicken Picadillo, 225
    Creole Beef and Vegetables with
        Cheese Grits, 260–61
    Crunchy Bistro Lentil Salad, 273
    Grilled Balsamic-Glazed Tuna with
        Tropical Fruit Salad, 217
    Italian-Style Mushroom Ratatouille
        in Buckwheat Crêpes, 191
    Layered Tabbouleh and Vegetable
        Salad, 164
    Maque Choux, 291
    Penne Pasta Salad with Asparagus,
        Arugula, and Balsamic
        Vinaigrette, 169
    Peruvian Potato Salad, 296
    Pizza with Arugula, Sautéed
        Vegetables, and Goat Cheese,
        196
    Roasted Italian Vegetable Pasta
        Salad, 170
    Spaghetti with Fresh Tomato Sauce
        and Roasted Vegetables,
        176–77
    Stuffed Turkey Burgers with Apples,
        Onions, and Peppers, 243
    Texas Pot of Pintos, 282
    Tomato and Red Pepper Sauce,
        Turkey Cutlets with, 239
    Vegetables, Tofu, and Soba
        Noodles in Sweet Ginger
        Sauce, 184–85
berries
    Summer Fruit Gratin (variation),
        326
    Very Berry Granita (variation), 331
    See also specific berries
beta-carotene, 93–94, 101
beverages, 104–12
    alcohol, 104–7
    avoiding liquid calories, 18, 106,
        108, 109, 110, 112
    coffee, 107–9, 112
    fiber intake and, 90
    fruit juices, 109, 110
    juices, 109–10
    milk, 95, 111
    soft drinks and sweet
        noncarbonated drinks, 18, 46,
        110–11